D1096739

Top, left to right: Bill and Tom
Second row: Merrill, Rosana, and Danny
Bottom row: Janet and Steve.

HE
Gave Me a
Song

A Back Country Saga of a Family
in Search of a Dream

Rose Marie Saleen Rebillet

Historical Memoirs with Roots in Idaho

ISBN 0-89288-271-9
Library of Congress Catalog Card Number: 97-76584

Printed by
Maverick Publications • P.O. Box 5007 • Bend, Oregon 97708

Prologue

As a young girl, she had an unusually isolated childhood, growing up in the remote Idaho wilderness, where her family struggled to make a living. She, through necessity, took on woman's work while yet a child to aid the family in their plight for the bare necessities of life.

Innocent and vulnerable, Rose ventured to the outside world unprepared to handle the situations she encountered there. She soon found herself in an abusive marriage. She gave birth to seven babies in ten years which weakened her physically, but gave her strength in her weakness, and she found the LORD.

Her faith as a testimony, she gently guided her husband to a new life in Christ. His life changed miraculously to a man who loved and lived his love for others. He only enjoyed his new life in Christ for a short time and the Lord took him home.

The family, devastated and frightened, could not understand why God had done this to them. The responsibility of raising her children to be God-fearing adults as a 29-year-old widow seemed unimaginable. The emotional impact took its toll, until Rose nearing a complete breakdown, poured herself into church work and struggled to help her grieving children, ultimately found her way.

Becoming uncomfortably involved in a church dispute threatened her new faith, but eventually strengthened her walk with the Lord. She, believing the answers were in the scriptures, was miraculously guided by God's hand to find the scriptures necessary to present God's doctrinal plan for the church, to the board. Eventually every member examined himself. The congregational structure was then rebuilt according to the scriptures.

This experience proved to be a blessing to her, which helped to equip her for launching out into a new work where the Bible had not yet been opened.

The new work was accompanied by a complete change in lifestyle. The children were happy beyond measure.

The tranquil and peaceful setting was the very thing that kept Rose from the inevitable breakdown the doctor feared would be her destiny.

The challenge of an antiquated lifestyle most certainly was appointed by God and became a beautiful memory etched on the minds and hearts of each family member.

"HE Gave Me A Song"

Many have encouraged me to write a book telling of my unique and exciting challenges in life.

You will not find the eloquence of a refined and polished author, but to capture the mood for the story, I found it gratifying to use the talent God gifted me with to write the story He gave me.

Preface

May God be glorified for the testimony in this book. He chose us before the creation of the world—He predestined us to be adopted as His sons—in Him we were also chosen having been predestined according to His plan.

Eph 1:4-5, 11 (in part)

Dedication

————————

I dedicate this book to my children for the great role they have played in my life. For their love and support through the hard times and for being my playmates and best friends through good times for all of my life.

Galatians 4:19 "My Dear Children, for whom I am again in the pains of childbirth until Christ is formed in you all."

I PRAY DEAR LORD THAT YOU WILL GUIDE MY MIND AND MY HAND WITH INSPIRATION THAT THIS STORY WILL BE A BLESSING TO ALL WHO READ IT AND BRING THEM TO A CLOSER WALK WITH YOU. THAT THE UNSAVED MAY COME TO KNOW YOU AND ACCEPT YOU AS THEIR SAVIOR.

IN JESUS NAME, AMEN

Contents

Roy, Rose and Ed McCracken.

Chapter 1

"The Great Depression"

1936

It was dark and cold as I sat beside my mother and tiny baby sister, Donna. She was wrapped with blankets to keep the terrible cold from her. My mother cried. I didn't know why. I felt it had something to do with my stepfather who remained inside the small two-room, tar-papered shack where we lived.

I was so frightened for my mother. I wanted to help her but I didn't know what to do. I just sat quietly beside her with tears streaming down my face while Donna slept. I knew Mom was unhappy with my stepfather whom she had been married to about a year. I knew because she never talked but cried when he wasn't around.

My mother grieved after my own father left her five years ago, taking my two brothers at the ages of four and six. He left without a trace during the Great Depression in 1931. I was two years old.

We had no place to live when we returned home from Orofino, Idaho, where Mom had been in the hospital. We were left with nothing. The winter ahead would typically be long and cold with possibly 6-8 feet of snow.

My father had brought our family to Pierce when I was just a baby. He worked in the timber industry. We moved from Troy, Idaho, where my mother's family lived. Pierce was a small town of not more than 800 people at that time. One grocery store, a hotel, cafe, and a pool hall, which was the liveliest place in town. I remember walking through town and seeing terrible blood-letting fights out in the street. All the loggers came to town from headquarters logging camp in the evening to get drunk.

It had always been a wild town from what we were told. This was where the first gold was discovered in Idaho in 1860. There were still some

11

Rose McCracken.

Little Donna in Pierce.

die-hards left when we were there but I don't think anyone got rich. The Chinese could go behind other miners and find gold after everyone else left. They were more diligent in their mining techniques. They washed every rock and stacked it in a neat pile, and it paid off for them. They were the last ones to leave an area.

There was a ranger station located just outside of town. They were in charge of the Civilian Conservation Corp. (CCC's) that were sent up there in the early thirties. We seldom saw any of them as they were out in work camps. They did a lot of work, in fact a great service for the country. Blister Rust had spread over much of the forest and was spreading to all the trees in the area. They brought in hundreds of CCC's and got it under control. They had to clean out complete forests to eradicate the problem and it was quite a large project.

Mother eventually found a place to live in an old house that had been used as a Chinese laundry. It was a cold, dark and dreary old building. The walls and floor were made from rough lumber, darkened by age. With big cracks in the walls and floor, weather came in uninvited, spreading streaks of snow across the floor.

The tubs, benches, washboards, and buckets were there in the house. I remember Mom saying the Chinese were probably killed or run out of town which was a common thing in those days. A big barrel stove was in the front room and a big cook range in the kitchen. Mom was in business. She went to the school and talked to the teachers. She got all the laundry jobs she could possibly take care of.

The work was very hard. She worked day and night. She carried water, cut and carried wood, heated water on the stove and moved it to a bench where she scrubbed on the board using homemade soap. She rinsed in two waters, dried the clothes on lines in the house, and she ironed with flat irons heated on the stove. Her work was no less than perfect, the teachers were delighted. The pay was little but we could eat and had a place to lay our heads. Mom was thankful but always hoping to make enough money to find her boys and bring them home to live with us.

Mom worked until she collapsed one day in a heap on the floor. She had been in constant pain from a prolapsed uterus; she frequently took hot sitz baths to relieve the pain, but it did very little to help. She was so exhausted from the heavy lifting and long hard hours. She was taken to the hospital in Orofino. I stayed with friends in Pierce, Lucille and Antone Floor. They were wonderful to me and I loved them. I should have been content but I was lonesome without my mother and was afraid she would never return as my father had done.

My mother was gone for several weeks. I later learned she suffered a breakdown and also had surgery to suspend her uterus.

When she returned, we moved to an old house uptown (Pierce) and Mom cooked at a local cafe. It was there she met and married my stepfather, Fred Erickson. We moved into the cabin he had built by the creek on the outskirts of town.

There was a strike in the lumber industry and the unions sent in truck loads of men carrying rifles, which were laid across the top of the rack, ready to shoot anyone who attempted to cross the picket lines. People were afraid to go outside of their homes. There was a lot of violence, killings, fighting, and men hiding in fear of their lives. Their families were without food and fathers were desperate to work. If they could get out to headquarters to work, there would be guards there to keep the union out. My stepfather drove a vehicle which transported men back and forth. The old truck was hidden in our backyard. Men would slip through the bushes in the dark and load up. My stepfather would travel back roads without

Ed, Roy and cousin in Oregon.

lights, taking the men back and forth. It was very dangerous and he could have been shot if he were discovered. When the strike was settled, he was looking for other work.

My little sister arrived shortly. She was the highlight of my life, the only doll I ever played with. I took her everywhere with me, when she was older. I sat her in the sand and built sand mountains with a match stick lookout on top with roads going around and around the mountain clear to the top. We had no toys but we found ways to play and things to play with.

One day my mother took the two of us and went to town to meet the bus. Two brothers, Ed and Roy, got off the bus and came into my life. After five years, I didn't know them and I didn't know what to think of them. Two ragged little boys with shaggy hair. Their clothes were dirty and their shoes were hardly more than soles tied to their feet. I held baby Donna and stood back watching as my mother gathered them in her arms and cried. We took them home where Mom began feeding and cleaning them.

Two bunks were set up on the screened porch where they slept winter and summer. When it got miserably cold, Mom piled on more quilts. They rushed into the nice warm house in the mornings to get dressed.

I guess I was a little jealous of all the attention they were getting and they certainly didn't care for me. We spent a lot of time staring at each other. Occasionally we had a dispute. I remember Ed one day bragging to me that no matter what I did to him I could not hurt him. I didn't answer him but I began to plot, I soon had it figured out what I was going to do and I just waited for the opportunity. He was sitting in a chair near the stove putting on his boots. I picked up a book and slipped up behind him and with the corner aimed at the top of his head, with both hands I lifted the book up as high as I could reach and brought it down on his head. He began to squeal and yell and to this day I remember how I felt. I thought maybe it wouldn't hurt him, I was quite surprised when he cried. Mom gave me a good scolding, I never did that again. I found out he wasn't as tough as he thought he was.

Many times they conned me into washing and drying their share of the dishes and they would take me hunting with them. I hurried and finished and ran out the door and got shot at with their B B guns. They hid behind the trees up on the hill behind our house. I turned and went back into the house. I didn't know if I liked them very well.

We gradually became friends and to this day I adore my brothers. We have had some great times together.

Mother kept busy sewing, cooking, and keeping house. She seemed happy at times but there was still a lot of stress and tension in the air. Something was wrong, I felt it but I didn't understand. I didn't find out until I was grown that Mom didn't tell my stepfather she had two sons until after they were married. Mom was a very honest person but I can only imagine a mother doing anything to ensure a means of caring for her children. Mom never told me this but it was passed down on the grapevine. Through the years there were several things to verify this. She probably thought that he wouldn't marry her with three children. It was impossible for a woman to earn enough money to keep herself, let alone a family. After I was grown, I also learned she had another boy that was taken by his father and she never saw him again. That was very likely the reason for her obsession to work and her depression. She never mentioned it to any of us. She was a very private person and did not discuss her past, as was the case with all her family.

She paid dearly for not telling Fred, she paid for the rest of her life. We all did. He never forgave her for that. He treated us all as if we didn't exist, like we were shadows, never acknowledged or spoken to. Never talking to us, never looking at us. We were just there and tried to stay out of his way. He loved his own daughter, Donna. The only time he ever smiled is when he talked to her. He never held her but he was kind to her. He was a bitter man, there must have been more tragedy in his life, we thought sure he had a past. The only thing we ever knew about him was that he was in World War I. He saw a lot of action and was gassed with mustard gas. The lining of his throat was burned badly and his lungs were also damaged which entitled him to a disability and an $18 a month pension. We also knew that he had lived in Montana, but he never spoke of his life there and we never asked. In later years he told me that he had a ranch named the "Box Elder" in Montana. He had been married, no children that we knew of. We knew he hated pistols so we assumed his mysterious past had to do with a pistol. (We kids had a big imagination and we worked on that story.) He never spoke of a family or mother or childhood. He drank occasionally when neighbors would drop in on a holiday but he didn't drink to excess. After a few drinks, he brought out his mouth harp and played beautiful melodies which brought smiles to his solemn features. Mom played the German accordion and played songs like "Carolina Moon" or "Night Time in Nevada." They knew all the old songs which were popular at that time. She and her sisters had sung together since they were little children. When they came to visit throughout the years, they always sang and their brother (Uncle Tom) played with them on the piano accordion. There was dancing and laughing among children and adults. It was wonderful to see happy smiling faces. Sometimes it would last until the wee hours of the morning. I would hope it would never end.

My brother Roy won favor with my stepdad. He just seemed to wiggle his way into a soft spot in his heart, so he was occasionally addressed in conversation at meal times and if anything had to be said, it was said to him. It wasn't much but it was more than Ed and I got. But our attitude was different, we gradually grew as independent and indifferent to him as he was to us. We completely ignored him. He didn't seem to care.

Being a "scab" so to speak, my stepdad never worked in the timber industry again. He got a job with the Forest Service. We moved into an old trading post at Muscleshell outside of Pierce, near a forest camp. It was a wonderful summer. My stepdad was gone most of the time. So, as a family we really got acquainted, laughed, worked and played together. We became a happy family for the first time. We got a cow and we seemed to have plenty of food. Mom was a trouper when it came to food. It was often said about her she could make a meal out of empty cupboards. My stepdad was never very generous with his money, he seldom gave Mom anything to buy groceries. I remember one time when Mom got pretty desperate, we were out of flour and other staples. We got into the old Model A Ford and began our trip to find the camp he was staying in. The car broke down out in the forest on a deserted road (all roads were deserted then) and we sat there all night in the car. At daybreak Mom sent the boys to find someone to help us. They brought back a man driving a Forest Service truck. Mom was very hesitant to tell him what we needed but she had to.

He drove us to the camp and Mom found Fred in a bunk house reading, it was on a Sunday. We stayed outside and we heard some yelling, pretty soon Mom came out crying. The man came out and drove us home. The car was left where it broke down and Fred got it started and drove it home later. Mom didn't get any money. I didn't know why he even came back or why he lived with us. He must have enjoyed making us suffer for what Mom did, not telling him she had the boys. He must have been heartless to not understand that.

My mother was raised in a very strict Lutheran home. Her mother was religious to the point of fanaticism, which is typical of old-country Christianity. There was never any forgiveness for sins. You carried them for the rest of your life. Mom lived with a lot of guilt for what she had done, and I believe she felt like she deserved any treatment she got. She was never able to forgive herself until she became a Christian many years later.

My mother's mother came from Nomadahl, Norway in about 1885. She was then married to her first husband from Hollingdohl, Norway (name unknown) and they had three children. Thora was two years old when they arrived in America. Anna and Gina were born here. Their father died in a mental institution soon after arriving when they were very young.

Grandmother Julia became housekeeper for Tossen Hagen, worked for him for seven years and then became his wife. Tom, Martha, Tom, Gina, Oscar, Clara, and Bertha were all born to the Hagen marriage in Norma Lake County, Brooten, Minnesota.

Gina from first marriage, and Tom and Martha from the Hagen marriage died in a influenza epidemic 1897. Julia was left childless as Thora and Anna were married and gone from home. The other Tom was born in 1898, Gina in 1900, Oscar in 1901 (stillborn), Clara in 1903, and Bertha in 1905. Tossen Hagen was 72 and Julia was 42 when Bertha was born. Tossen died in Minnesota when Bertha was three months old. Much later in life Grandmother Julia married Carl Thyr in Deary, Idaho, where Julia had moved with her family. No children were born to this marriage. Julia died in 1938 at the age of 75. Carl died in 1941.

Bertha Hagen married Frederick Gunner Nelson, July 1, 1919 at the age of 14. Alvin Valermor Nelson was born to this marriage Oct. 24, 1921. Bertha married Archie McCracken in Coeur d'Alene in 1923. Edward Thomas was born in 1925, LeRoy Archie was born in 1927, and Rose Marie was born in 1929. Bertha married Fred Erickson in 1935. Donna was born in 1936. Bertha married Clyde Umbra Osborn in 1945.

Mom seldom spoke of anything to do with religion. She spoke of God but like that was something she didn't want to get into. She said many times that religious fanatics were terrible. It seemed to me that anyone who practiced their own faith was in that category according to her. I was never satisfied with that, even as she spoke, I could see my Grandmother sitting in front of the window in her rocking chair, reading her Bible. I didn't consider her a fanatic. I carried that picture in my mind of my Grandmother in her rocking chair. When I saw a church I thought of her and I had a deep longing to go there and know more about the Bible. I wanted to know God. I felt like He wanted to know me but I didn't know how to respond. There

Aunt Gina, friend, and Bertha (Mom).

Grandma Hagen.

18

was a longing inside me. I believe Grandma prayed for us kids, three of us came to know the Lord before our mother did. God had chosen me from before the foundations of the earth, just as He does every other Christian. He then leaves it up to us to accept or reject Him.

I only remember seeing two churches in my childhood. I had a feeling of wanting to belong. Something drew me when ever I saw the church. There was a Catholic church in Pierce and a Christian church in Kooskia, where it still stands facing the bridge over the Clearwater.

Muscleshell was beautiful, it was unspoiled by civilization, we could actually see what life was like when it was a trading post and stage stop. Muscleshell Creek ran through the middle of a lush green valley, surrounded by timber on all sides. The road went through the valley and over the Lolo Pass into Montana. The old Oregon Trail crossed the valley on the upper end. I was so intrigued with the history that was so evident wherever you looked. The remains of old wagons and buckboards were scattered around the barn. The trading post was an overnight stop for the stage coach as well as an Indian trading post.

There were several cabins with built-in bunks lining the walls. Straw was still in the bunks, which served as a mattress. The Post itself was a large log building. In the kitchen the old cookstove still sat in the corner. There was an old hand pump on the back porch. The post house was filthy, with dust and dirt, mouse and rat droppings like any old house that has been empty for years. It didn't take Mom long to clean it

Roy, Ed, and Jeff. Home at last.

up after we arrived. The logs were cleaned and the floors were scrubbed and bleached; the kitchen stove shone like new where she fried sourdough hotcakes. As usual, she had a tablecloth on the table and doilies on everything that had a flat top.

We worked and played all day until dusk and then we'd gather around the fire in the backyard sitting on blocks of wood and listened to Mom play the accordion and sing. I loved to hear her sing. Her voice seemed to drift up over the tree tops and peace settled over the valley.

One day about sundown, some wagons rolled in and stopped by the creek. Old Indian men and women, young Indians and many, many Indian children came from the wagons and began to unload the wagons.

We watched curiously and didn't know what to think. We had never seen that many Indians except in books. We did know there was a reservation down on the Clearwater somewhere.

It wasn't long until we were looking at an Indian village. Smoke from camp fires soon began to circle up around the tepees. We knew they should be peaceful, but way back up here where there was no law enforcement we weren't very sure what they might do. We were not sure if we should be afraid. They didn't acknowledge us at all. Little by little we ventured closer. They didn't chase us away and the mere fact that they were Indians, we were sure they knew we were there. Our older brother, Ed, saw all he wanted to see and went back to the house. Roy and I were not satisfied until one of them spoke to us. We saw one man by his fire, he didn't look very mean so we walked up to him and spoke to him. I should say Roy spoke to him. I stood back and watched. Roy said in as manly a voice as he could muster up, "Hello."

The Indian said, "Hello." but didn't turn his head to look at us, nor did any other Indians look at us. They just went on with their duties in silence, speaking an occasional word to each other in Indian.

My brother said, "You gonna live here now?"

The Indian then looked over at him and said, "Uh huh."

Roy couldn't think of anything else to say except, "Guess we better go now." The Indian did not respond.

As time went on we got braver and came closer, but we never did get much conversation out of them.

We went swimming with the kids and played some, but every day they took the kids out to dig camas root and pick huckleberries. They were there several weeks. We continued to be fascinated with them and we were not far away during the time they were there. It was quite an adventure living by the Indian village. I was always in hopes they would teach me some of their ways that I heard about. I was walking one day with an Indian girl about my age, and I said to her, "I know Indians can run much farther than white people. Can you teach me how to do that?"

She responded, "Sure, just keep your mouth shut when you run." I ran with flared nostrils for a long time trying to do that, but I could never make it work. I thought us whites must be in terrible shape.

They did show us where the good huckleberries were but not by word of mouth—we followed them. We went back after they left and found the despicable way they picked. The women and kids sat on a blanket and the men broke off branches, and took them to the women. They would shake the berries off the branch over the blanket, then toss the branches in a pile.

We groaned about the way they destroyed these lovely bushes. Then we figured it out, since they came back to the same spot every year and the berries were more abundant and much larger than any others we had seen, the pruning was what they needed. They left enough for us. We picked and canned 100 quarts that year. We were all so sick of picking huckleberries, we didn't care if we ever saw another huckleberry.

We loved playing in the big barn and with the old wagons. One day we pushed and pulled a wagon until we got it on the hill going down to the creek. The tongue should have held it back, we thought, but we gained speed as we rolled down the hill. We were lucky to be able to hang on. Big brother Ed sat in the drivers seat. Roy and I jumped on, the hill was pretty steep and the wagon kept rolling. It rolled over the spot where the Indians camped and splat, right over the bank and into the creek. We were not planning on it going so far. We came out of the water wondering how in the world we were going to get this thing out of the creek and back up the hill and into the barn.

We had some friends from Weippe who came to see us one Saturday. We told them how much fun we had and sure enough they helped us get the wagon back up the hill. Kids hung all over that wagon, down the hill they went and flew into the creek, just like we did, except it was a lot more fun for us when they did it. We laughed and laughed. They didn't want another ride so we pushed the wagon back up the hill and into the barn where it belonged and didn't take it out again.

One day we went to visit the Bee Man. As far as we knew he was the only resident within miles. He lived there year-round and raised honey bees.

After the honey was harvested, someone from Pierce came to pick it up. They brought a year's supply of groceries and traded it for the honey. The old man never left the place. He was a kind old gent with a white beard hanging down on his chest. His white hair hung down his back in waves. His beautiful white clean hair impressed me. I was also very curious about how he could handle the bees and never get stung.

Since I was the only one who showed any interest in the bees, he offered to take me out to the hives. He said if I did everything he said, I wouldn't be stung either. I was a bit dubious, but he said I could not be afraid. He emphasized that I could not be afraid. The bees would sense that and know I was a stranger. So I found all the courage I ever had and walked out there with the bee man. Bees came out to meet us, they were all over us. It was so hard not to be afraid, not to swat at them, but I was more afraid of being afraid, than I was afraid of the bees. I did just as he said and neither of us got stung. I felt so victorious that I had so much self control. I have always remembered what he taught me. I have not since been stung unless I sat on, or stepped on a bee with bare feet.

There were a lot of coyotes around Muscleshell which were howling most of the time. I began mocking their howling. I practiced by the hour and finally got them to answer me. This was great, I spent a lot of time talking with them. There was something wonderful and exciting about communicating with a wild animal. I could hear their calls as they circled me, they came in quite close. The longer I called, the closer they came until they were all around me. I could hear them from every direction. I didn't want them to get too close, so I ran home. They followed me but not close enough for me to see. This is just one of the ways I entertained myself way back when, I was never bored when I could be in the outdoors. I remember a telephone we rigged up with two tin cans and a string between them. We could actually hear the other person talking. We had a lot of fun with that.

Muscleshell was a wonderful summer for all of us. We needed to heal and become a family. We needed to talk, laugh and play. All too soon it came to a close. When work was over in the fall, my stepfather came home. There was no rejoicing, not even a happy hello. Everyone was silent as to greetings. There was another long winter of silence with a sullen man.

We spent the winter in a little house in the community called Dawson City outside of Weippe only a few miles from Pierce. We were very poor but Mom always seemed to have food laid by. Where she got fruit and vegetables to can I didn't know. There was always canned venison and meatballs and steaks put down in lard in big crocks. Fruit of all kinds in the jars.

During the dead of winter there came a knock at the door. Aunt Clara, Uncle Fred, and their eight kids came to live with us. They came from Oregon where they had lived for several years, but like so many, these days they had no work, no home, no money or food. All they had was an old sedan and what clothes and blankets could be stuffed in around the kids.

I hadn't seen them for a long time, they were strangers to us kids. Mom hadn't seen them for several years, but the doors were open to them to share what we had.

Our house was a bit more lively, but the kids did learn some manners, in short order. I watched my stepdad and was amazed at how he treated them. He liked Aunt Clara, everyone liked Aunt Clara, she was fun. She was not one to worry about anything. She wasn't very ambitious, she wasn't pretty and she didn't try to be. That was the least of her worries. Surprising to me our stepdad hid a lot of his bad disposition, but he didn't like Uncle Fred, he was a German and Dad had fought a bitter war with the Germans. Uncle Fred didn't stay long, I didn't know where he went. I never knew where the oldest daughter was, why she didn't come with them. There was a lot we didn't know then because the adults could talk in Norwegian. We were taught never to ask questions. If someone wanted us to know something, they would tell us.

Sleeping was tough. I gave Aunt Clara my bed and there were kids rolled up in blankets all over the house. Some of the older kids slept up in the attic, climbing a ladder from the outside of the house. It was cold. The wind and snow blew in through the cracks. I'm sure they weren't very warm up there.

Those kids were hungry and it was hard for Mom to do but she rationed food for every meal. We had all we needed. We weren't hungry but just the idea of knowing, "this is all you can have" had a certain effect on everyone.

Our store house of food did last through the winter and in the spring Aunt Clara moved to Weippe, where she got "relief" from the county. After they all left, Mom went out to the cellar to take inventory. She found a lot of empty jars pushed back against the wall. There were spoons hid behind jars. The poor kids were more hungry than we realized.

On "relief" they ate better than we did. We had never eaten an orange until Aunt Clara gave us one. We thought Mom ought to get on "relief" so we could have oranges. She said we didn't need oranges. Mom would never dream of asking for or accepting relief. She didn't want us to eat the oranges. I couldn't figure all this out.

In search of a place to raise a garden, we went to Kooskia country where the climate was more conducive to growing food. We traveled down the Greer grade and south up the Clearwater River. It probably wasn't over 60 miles but it was a whole different country. We found a place that had been deserted up in the hills where we could plant potatoes. Herb Weston, a family friend, came with us and helped plant. We were there only until the potatoes were planted. We stayed in the old farmhouse.

We were on our way home when we found another deserted place we could rent for the summer to grow food. There was a one-room cabin with porches and an attic. We made out fine with that. This place was on Clear Creek. It was an old deserted farm. There was about everything there to grow a living from: an orchard, pasture, barn, a wonderful garden spot, all the water we could use, a place for chickens. The house sat down in a little draw by a small creek. The banks were quite steep, on one side there was a dirt road, on the other side was the barn and orchard. There were many wild berries and fruit along the roads, it was a rich area. I can't imagine anyone leaving there at a time like this, when work was so scarce and food was a premium. Of course we had to work for it but it was there for anyone who was willing to work.

Mom was so pleased to have such a wonderful garden spot. The soil was loamy and right beside the creek, where very little irrigation was needed and if it was, the water was diverted by a ditch from the creek. The amount of food that was put up this year was phenomenal. I worked in the garden with Mom and canned with her. I didn't mind doing anything with her, but I sure resented it when she sat me on the porch with a wash tub of green beans to snap, or maybe peas to shell, jars to wash, all by myself. I didn't like doing it alone. It took so much longer.

The boys worked with Fred (Dad) in the orchard and in the fields growing hay. The orchards up on the hill by the barn was a mass of blooms when we got there. They were all in jars when we left.

When fall came we moved up to Big Cedar where there was a school for us kids. We rented the Klutz place. Of course we had plenty of food the first winter but we were on a dry land farm up there and we had to hustle for everything we got from that place. We were there two years. It didn't get any easier to farm that place, even the garden was hard to grow. We drew water up out of a well a bucket at a time to water the garden. The soil was like clay, it would harden as soon as the sun hit the water. Miracle of miracles Mom got 1000 quarts of food in the cellar, plus crock after crock of dill pickles, crabapple pickles, sauerkraut, and meat of all kinds. Dad brought in venison whenever he went out. He only took one cartridge and always brought back meat. The boys asked him why he only took one. He said "I never waste a bullet, I wait until I get a good shot, I take a better aim, and more careful to get the game I shoot. I don't want to lose a wounded animal and I don't want to walk home for another bullet."

The only money we had for ammunition and other staples that couldn't be grown was his $18 a month. That bought coffee, sugar, flour, and salt. Mom made all of our clothes and knitted all our socks. Aunt Gina brought up clothes given to her from friends for Mom to make over, she was good at it and I always felt well dressed except for shoes and they were pretty scarce. Aunt Gina brought us kids shoes for Christmas. We weren't hurting and we sure weren't hungry. We never wasted anything. If we put it on our plate, we ate it.

We somehow acquired some livestock, probably through bartering. We brought our cow from Weippe. We had some pigs, chickens, turkeys, sheep, goats, and two renegade Forest Service horses. We used the horses for field work and saddle horses. We had a lot of run-a-ways and rodeos. Old Red and Bucko. Red didn't like to be ridden. They could saddle him, tie him and go to the house and just as soon as they came out of the house Old Red knew, and he would buck and carry on until they came up along side of him and he'd stop until they got on. Sometimes he would crow-hop a little but most of the time he wouldn't do anything. You never knew what he was going to do though. He tried to scare someone and if that didn't work, he'd settle down. Bucko was a follow the leader with Red.

We fed them well and handled them gently and they became much easier to handle. Dad was a good horseman. Later in the summer he bought Donna a horse, Dolly, or maybe she was given to him. She was so skinny it was doubtful she would ever live. With good care she had a few more years, she was great for the girls to ride. Ed and Roy rode Red and Bucko but I sure didn't.

We had a battery radio. Dad was the only one to turn it on. We got the news for 15 minutes every day and the "Grande Ole Opry" on Saturday night. We learned all the new songs from the Opry. The news was dominated by war news, about the Germans invading Norway which upset Mom considerably.

Our home life never changed, it was always the same. Dad was the same, silent, sulking person all his life except when we had company. As we got older it got worse, it wasn't so easy to stay out of his way now. The boys especially, they worked with him outside.

Mom had a way of looking at us that would freeze us in our tracks, so as not to disturb him. We spent as little time in the house as possible when he was there. The boys, especially Ed, began to resent him more and more. There was a lot of tension and Mom was afraid of what might happen if Ed and Fred clashed.

At meal time he sat down and ate as if there was no one else in the house. He never spoke at the table. He had beautiful table manners and we were expected to have the same. If he ever saw us violate those manners, he would speak so sharp it would scare us to death, "Set straight or leave the table." Which was good for us to know. He was very much a gentleman according to his speech, his conduct and his carriage. At least as gentlemen were rated in those days. He was very sophisticated and cold, like an old army general. He always carried a pair of soft leather gloves in his hand unless he was wearing them. He was also a very handsome man.

Ed was 14 years old and just at the age of young men when they want their independence. He became resentful of Fred telling him what to do. Ed was so dependable and could be trusted with any task he was given to do. I think Ed felt like he should have a little respect and independence from everyone. He deserved to be treated like a man when he carried the responsibility of a man. Ed was unusually proud for a young man his age. He was dignified and proper. I always admired him for being the kind of person he was.

I remember one time when Roy was teasing me (again) and I had seen someone do this in school, so I too thumbed my nose at Roy. Ed saw me and came at me like he was going to bop me. With a terrible scowl on his face he said, "Rose, do you know what that means?"

I began backing away, he had never spoke to me like that.

Very timid I answered, "No."

So angrily he said, "Go ask Mom, I can't tell you."

Oh man! I did not want to ask Mom if it was that bad. I didn't ask her and I didn't find out for a long time.

Ed and Roy delivered some hay to a neighbor one day. They took the horses and wagon. They were visiting and were gone a little longer than Fred thought they ought to be. On the way home they met Fred walking down the road looking for them. They knew they were in trouble. Fred grabbed the reins and pulled the horses to a stop. He stepped up on the wagon, stepped over to Ed, looked him in the face and with his gloves in his hand, he slapped Ed across the face. Ed fell to his knees, stood up, stepped off the wagon and walked home. Not a word was spoken. Fred picked up the reins and drove the horses to the barn.

Ed knew how strict Fred was and he shouldn't have stayed. He came to the house and told Mom. Mom was very frightened because she knew how violent he could be. She told Ed he had better leave, she was afraid for him. Ed was devastated. He went upstairs when Fred came in and avoided him. He put some clothes together and left early the next morning. I knew Ed must be afraid, I would have been. We were all afraid for him. Was there more to be afraid of from Fred or going out alone like that? What may happen to him? Is he going to sleep out in the bushes somewhere?

My heart was breaking but I couldn't say anything to him. I just stood back and watched him leave. I ran after him until I couldn't see him anymore. I'll never forget the pain I felt, seeing him leave alone.

I don't think Ed ever really forgave Mom for telling him to go, but I felt like that was her way of protecting him from Fred. She was constantly in fear of Fred for all of us.

A few days later Mom received a call from a lady who lived on a farm about 10 miles from us. She told Mom Ed was fine. He was going to stay there and work for room and board until school started and they would take him to town. He got a job at a grocery store and would live with the owners. His first year of high school was not the happy event it should have been.

When we were all so poor during the depression, it was not uncommon for kids to be sent out on their own to work for their living if the folks couldn't feed them. That was not the case with Ed, however. Fourteen years old seemed much older than it does now. A young boy that age was a man.

After the traumatic experience Ed and Roy had when our Father took them to Oregon, this must have been devastating for him.

He took them to live with Uncle Ed. They were soon asked to leave, probably because our dad didn't have a job and Uncle Ed couldn't afford to keep them. Our dad got a job then at a box factory. He got some lumber and built a tent frame, and put a tent over it, for them to live in down by the railroad tracks. He came home after work, fixed supper and went to town. The boys were lonely and found friendship with the bums that hung out there by the tracks. They fed them once in a while and were good to the boys. They were so pitiful themselves, dirty, hungry and only a blanket to keep warm at night by the fire.

Roy the younger of the two, couldn't go to sleep unless Ed laid beside him and told him stories. He was so afraid down there alone. They had to stay there. They didn't know where they were or where to go.

The authorities finally got after our Dad and made him get a house and a housekeeper so the boys would be taken care of. He rented a parsonage beside a church and got a housekeeper. He left then and never came back. They were then taken to another Aunt but she didn't want them either. She lived on a farm and they helped hoe corn and whatever they could do for her, but she couldn't feed them.

Uncle Ed came down one day and asked them if they would like to go see their mother. They were so happy, the first hope they had in over five years.

Those two little boys lived a lonely existence for five years. No one wanted them and even when they went to play with other kids they were run off. They didn't want them around. I suppose they were unkempt and it's hard to say what people thought of them.

After Uncle Ed contacted Mom and she found out where the boys were, she began to make plans to get them back. She got married to Fred Erickson and got a home where they could live.

My father never once made contact with us. Uncle Ed contacted brother Ed in 1954 that our Dad had died. I was a little saddened at first because I guess I had always hoped he would come back to find us. After thinking about it for awhile I decided I was better off not having ever seen him since I probably would not have had any respect for him or worse. I have no memory of him at all, being only two years old when he left.

You may think that those little boys would have some far reaching effects from all this but they are wonderfully adjusted, successful, happy, people. And as I have said before, they have very strong characters and it would take a lot more than that to defeat them. I adore both of my brothers.

During the depression many children were abandoned, mostly from parents who were destitute. Parents often felt that the children would have a better life without them. If there was a chance that they would be fed and cared for, the parents suffered the loss.

I remember the stories of the orphan trains traveling through the country with thousands of children, stopping at every station to see if anyone would take a child or two. The ones that were old enough to work had a better chance of being taken. There were so many terrible tragedies resulting from the depression.

A typical father's reaction to not being able to take care of his family and leaving them or giving the children up, was the same as it would be today. Considering himself a complete failure, it took many men down the road of depression and self destruction. They lost every bit of self respect, and without it there is no man.

The depression ended when WWII began. When the US started building ships, guns, tanks, trucks, in mass production and all of the other needed equipment, every civilian went back to work, every able bodied man under 45 went to war.

The greatest tragedy of all was when mothers left their homes and families and went out into the workplace, made big money and became independent. The "Dear John" letters went flying over the sea and found a lonely soldier there to light on. The beginning of the fall of the American family. Our country has never been the same.

———————

Fred (Dad) would change so dramatically when someone came to visit. A drink or two was all it took for him to be the greatest guy around. No one ever knew what he was to his family. Aunt Clara and her new husband, Kirk, with all their children (nine by then) came often. It was loads of fun. Mom was busy cooking but she didn't mind. She was always certain that her homemade bread, deserts and other delectable dishes that came from her pantry were very much appreciated. The kids loved Aunt Bertha's meals.

Aunt Gina and Uncle Johnnie came at Christmas time with the only gifts we got. Fred took the horses and sled down to the school to meet them. They could drive their car that far, but the roads were not kept open any further. Old Red and Bucko proudly strutted with their heads high and a nice smooth trot. I'll never forget watching by the window to get the first glimpse of them coming around the bend above the barn. The road circled around out of my sight and then into the barn yard, through the gate and to the house. This is one of my favorite memories of my childhood, it is imprinted indelibly on my heart.

The three of them sat on the seat, Aunt Gina was in the middle, dressed in her fur coat and hat, looking as pretty as a picture, with a big smile as they drove up into the yard.

They pulled the blankets off from around them and climbed down from the sled and came into the house to get warm. Greetings and hugs were exchanged, it was always such a happy time. I was so anxious to see what was under the tarp on the back of the sled.

When the time finally came and the men went out to take the tarp off, I was at my spot by the window. The boys helped carry things in. They kept filing through the kitchen with beautifully wrapped gifts and laid them under the tree in the front room. With each gift that was laid down, I became more excited. I wanted so much to go look at the tags but Mom gave me one of those looks so I stood a good distance from the tree.

I loved Aunt Gina. She made me feel so special by noticing me and giving me a hug, just every so often. She always brought me shoes and a doll for Christmas. The happiness she brought was the greatest gift of all. She did fill our home with joy and happy memories. Uncle Johnnie was very special to me also. He was such a kind gentle man.

———————

Being isolated as we were then, it was difficult to keep up with the outside world. We never saw a newspaper. Without electricity, radio was a luxury we could not often enjoy. Mail service was slow and seldom used; many people couldn't afford a stamp.

We had a telephone for the first time at Big Cedar. Each person on the line had a different ring. Our ring was 4 longs. If we needed operator assistance to call out of our area, we rang one long, the operator answered, "Middle."

Telephones were left in the house when you moved. The line was maintained by the people using the telephones. A pastime for some people was to listen to all of the calls.

The telephone was an oblong box on the wall. A crank on the right side of the box was used to ring the number you wanted to reach. The receiver, on the left side of the box, was to be hung on the hook before the telephone could ring out. After the ring, you picked up the receiver to listen and talked into the mouthpiece, which was a horn-shaped instrument on the front of the telephone.

―――――――

Our dear friends, the Floors from Pierce, moved into a deserted old place down the hill about two miles from us. I loved staying with them. Lucille took care of me when Mom was gone. She had one son Robert, who was like a brother to me. We had spent most of our lives together. They didn't own a car (in fact I don't think either of them could drive). Fred took our old Ford truck and moved them from Pierce to Kooskia.

The place where they lived had been sitting there for at least 20 years. There were no windows, only two doorways or openings to the house; one on each end of the house. Animals had come in at will and left their droppings there. Rat signs were everywhere. They did not complain. They were happy to have found a place. Both of them were hard workers and they were immaculate people. Glad to be where they could raise some food.

One of the first things they did was get their garden ready to plant. Another priority was splitting cedar shakes to put on the house and construct other buildings. They cleaned until it shone. There was a complete transformation of the place in no time. For two very small people they accomplished wonders. Antone found a spring coming out of the hill and piped water, with gravity flow, into the house. They built a barn with poles and shakes, they found where an old root cellar had been. They dug it out and braced it up again. Just a few steps from the house, they had the coolest little place to keep their milk, cream, strawberries and all their canned fruit and vegetables.

It didn't take long for them to have this place in full production. Antone took berries, eggs, and other produce to the mail shed for the mail man to pick up. He took the produce to town and returned with an order of coffee, sugar, nails or whatever was needed. I don't remember them ever going to town after they moved there.

They lived right there the rest of their lives. Robert went to grade school with us at the Big Cedar school and then after we left, he went to

Mom, Donna, and Fred at Big Cedar.

high school in Kooskia. I believe he boarded out. Robert met a pretty little girl by the name of Betty and married her. They lived in Kooskia and bought a shake mill. They operated that and sold shakes all over the northwest.

I went back to visit the Floors after I had grown. That really took me back in time. Everything in their house was the same as it was 30 years before. An example of how far back, Lucille was so excited when she told me she was looking through the catalog one day and she saw some aprons that were made of plastic. She read up on that and found out what plastic was,

"Wouldn't it be wonderful if you didn't have to wash and iron aprons? I thought about all the other things you could make out of plastic fabric. Why your work would be cut in half." I didn't tell her we had been using plastic aprons for years and plastic curtains and table cloths etc. Bless her heart, she thought she had really found a gold mine.

They were raising some white leghorn chickens down in the barn yard. White leghorns are pretty flighty anyway, but these guys were very scared when they saw strange people. When we walked down toward the barn, you would have thought a pack of coyotes was bearing down on them. They saw us and they all started squawking and running and flying off into the timber. They were completely out of sight in about a minute. I had never seen chickens act like that. I asked Antone what was the matter with them and he said, "They don't see many people and they are afraid I guess." I asked if they would come back. He laughed and said, "Eventually, when everyone is gone. They are used to us but I don't think they have ever seen anyone else."

I loved going down to see Lucille and Antone when I was a girl. They were such gentle, kind people. They had a way of making everyone feel so important and cherished with their exceptional hospitality. They always had cold milk, fresh bread, homemade butter and strawberry jam. We had the same thing at home, but it was always so special there. I hated moving away from them.

Home at Big Cedar.

Ray (on center horse, leaning over), Mary Ann Leavitt and Rose (at left), 1937.

4th of July family gathering.

Chapter 2

"Those Lonely Hills"

1940

We were aware the place where we lived at Big Cedar was for sale, but we didn't think it would ever sell. Money was so hard to come by, but Klutz gave us notice that they had a buyer, and we moved with much remorse. After we got the place all fixed up and producing well, it was hard to leave it. Especially the animals, we had to sell all of them.

Our stepdad was interested in mining and wanted to pursue that field. Little did we know what that would bring us to, but of course we didn't have a choice. He sent some letters of inquiry out.

In the meantime we moved to Kooskia, which was a very small town. To us it was big. We rented a nice big old home on the hill overlooking the river and the community. It was a lovely house. It stood so stately up on the hill, with rock steps leading up the trail through the trees and shrubbery. A big porch spanned across the front of the house, a perfect place for a swing, we had an old bench there and a rocking chair. I loved sitting on the porch watching the activities down below.

One day the folks were gone and I didn't feel too well, I thought I should stay home. When I stepped out to call the dog to feed him, I found the porch, the rain and the view were too much for me to resist. I got a heavy quilt, wrapped up and spent the day in the rocking chair, on that wonderful porch.

Since we lived near the tracks, we had many "bums" coming to the back door for food. After Mom got over being so afraid of them, she fed them. Then we heard about the husband of a neighbor lady being killed, with a big butcher knife, by a "bum". The husband was supposedly butchering a pig, when this "bum" attacked him. We locked our doors to all "bums" and we ran like crazy for home when we saw one. You can take the kid out of the country, but when you haven't seen very many people, you could be afraid of your own shadow.

Later we heard the bum had been visiting the wife when the husband was gone. An outraged husband was laying for him, but he wasn't fast enough. The bum was sentenced to 50 years. After he was incarcerated, Mom felt free to feed the "bums" again; but she never felt too comfortable. She opened the door a crack, handed the plate out, and shut the door quickly. They ate and left their plate on the chopping block.

We rented out the upstairs to a family by the name of Jackson. We certainly couldn't use all of this big house. The boys kept their sleeping room up there, it was out of the way of the renters. I thought one of their boys was especially nice, Jimmy was his name. I don't remember the rest of the family.

We lived next to an Indian family, the Parsons, they were great people. Mr. Parson had a guide service for hunters. They were hard working people, yet they followed their traditional way of life. They tanned all their hides and made all kinds of clothes and beaded jewelry. Their two daughters worked with the parents doing bead work, sewing and tanning etc. I had some things they made for me that I cherished but through the years they disappeared.

When we moved to Kooskia, Ed came back home to live with us. Roy, Ed and I went to school there. Ed was a freshman and Roy and I were in the 6th grade. Ed continued to work in the store. I saw a big change in him. I believe he found some of the independence he had been seeking. He was grown up and a real gentleman by now, he wore nice clothes and was so neat. He no longer did fun things with Roy so I became Roy's buddy. Living in a big city like Kooskia was quite a treat for us. We especially enjoyed the railroad station. We had never seen a depot or a train for that matter except from a distance. We watched the trains come in and people getting off and on. We spent a lot of time there the first month.

We sold old gunny sacks to the station master. I believe he paid us one cent a sack. We looked all over the country for them and found quite a few. Roy rigged up a harness and made a little cart for Spot, our little dog. She pulled it while we scouted the country for gunny sacks, then hauled them back to the railroad station. The guys working around there looked forward to seeing the little dog pulling the little cart full of gunny sacks.

Tom Nevitt.

One day our folks told us we were moving to Snowshoe mine as soon as school was out. Our stepdad had received a letter back from Tom Nevitt, the mine owner. Mr. Nevitt lived in Lewiston and was a professor at Lewis and Clark College. Dad had a job in the mine and Mom had a cook job. We had no idea where Snowshoe Mine was but it sounded exciting.

As soon as school was out, we were on our way. All of our belongings were loaded into our 1929 Ford truck. Mom and Donna were sitting in the truck with Dad, Ed was in the car with Herb Weston, the potato planter who also needed work, and was helping us move. The folks felt so very fortunate to get work. Jobs were hard to find at that time.

Roy and I stood in the back of the truck leaning against the side boards. We were so excited, we were heading for adventure. The wind was blowing in our faces, it felt so good. We must have been traveling about 25 miles an hour. That was fast. I had never traveled more than 50 miles since I could remember. By the time we got to Grangeville, the excitement had worn off. We were wondering when we were going to get there.

Roy and I gave up the watch and found a place to lay down. I wasn't feeling well. We drove until midnight and arrived at the Yellow Pine camp ground on Johnson Creek just out of Yellow Pine. I had slept most of the way and was trying to keep warm. I had missed seeing so much but I didn't care.

When we were unloading and getting our camp set up, I climbed out of the truck shivering and Mom asked me, "What is the matter, are you sick?" I told her I was, she quickly made a diagnosis of mumps. I was to sleep in the cab of the truck, it would be warmer. I froze all night and was cramped up with no pillow. I was miserable. By morning I was really sick and the last thing I wanted to do was travel. Little did I know what was ahead of us. The load had all been moved around so I had to hunt for a good warm sleeping spot. I found it, and just when I started getting warm, Roy wanted me to look at something. It wasn't much fun for him when there was no one to share it with.

The road was terrible from Yellow Pine to Big Creek store, rough, crooked, steep, and narrow. I wasn't sure if it was the road or the mumps that made me sick. It took us all day to go 25 miles. We spent the night camped out again. It wasn't much fun for me. I couldn't eat the camp cooking, which I loved, it was hard to drink water. Oh, for a nice warm bed.

Early the next morning we started on the last leg of the trip from Big Creek to Snowshoe. We only had 18 miles to go so it shouldn't take long. The road from Yellow Pine to Big Creek was a boulevard compared to this road. It looked like someone had taken a cat and made one swipe through there with the blade.

Big rocks were sticking up in the road, I mean so big they couldn't be moved. When the truck crawled over them I thought sure it was going to tip the truck over into Big Creek about 50 giant steps below.

We went around a steep switchback above Big Ramie. That was one I will never forget. I couldn't lay down there, I had to look. It was a switch back but it was the sharpest one, it was more like a V on the downhill side. It was so narrow, so steep, so sharp, we had to back up and inch forward, back up again and inch forward turning just a fraction each time. We finally got around the corner only to find more rocks, more holes and places where the road had slid down the mountain. The brakes were hot, if they gave out, that would have been the end of us. We had to dig above the road making our own road inch by inch. In places the road was built on shale rock slides. The first one was treacherous. We slowly inched our way into the slide. The shale began to move, but after we started we were committed, we couldn't go back. Don't stop, don't even hesitate—just go. As the wheels pushed through the rock, I could feel the truck sliding downhill. The front wheels were moving but the weight was in the back and it was pulling us back down the hill. When at last the front wheels hit solid ground, Dad just kept pulling steady but slowly until the whole truck was on solid ground.

Standing in the back of the truck and getting such a first hand look at what was going on, it took all the courage I had to keep from jumping out of the truck. That was the worst slide. There were others but not as treacherous. In some places there was no road, just a big washout and a creek running through it. It wasn't so bad in the truck but we watched to see that the car didn't get washed away. It took us another day to get to Snowshoe. A horse could travel faster on this road than a motor vehicle.

I have never been so terrified in my life. Another place on the road that was bad for me was up above Ramie Hole. The road went higher and higher straight up, until it came to a point. The car would go up to the point, the driver could not see any road on the other side, only blue sky. We crawled over the top and finally the car tipped forward and the road was there to take us on. It takes real faith to go on over the top when you are not sure if the road is there and I wasn't. I don't think the drivers were sure either. I left my stomach on the top of the hill. No one seemed to worry but me.

We finally arrived at the camp. Dad got out and inquired as to where we were to stay. Looking around at the dinky desolate camp didn't help my spirit any. Needless to say none of us were very happy. He came back and drove to a cabin on the upper side of camp. The camp consisted of four one room cabins, a bunkhouse, a woodshed, and a cookhouse. A road went through the camp and turned up between two cabins and up the hill to the assay office and on up to the mine operations.

There was no grass or anything growing except by the cookhouse where a spring coming down the draw, kept the trees and shrubs growing there. There were vines growing on the front of the cookhouse. Beautiful cottonwood trees outlined the cookhouse and green bushes were abundant where the water was. The spring ran down by the bunkhouse, so there was also some greenery there. This was the only place in the camp that was attractive, the rest was rocks and dirt.

They pulled logs into the camp and sawed them up as they needed them for wood. It was very unsightly, with chips and sawdust laying around in the center of the camp. With trash, rocks and mess around it wasn't a pretty sight. The ground was so rocky nothing would have grown there if it did have water. It was a depressing place at first sight.

Our belongings were unloaded into the cabin on the floor and Mom found bedding to make me a bed. I crawled in and covered up my head. I didn't leave that bed for four days.

Mom went to the cookhouse and the temporary cook said "How do you do. It's all yours," and walked out, Mom was quite disturbed, but she cooked a meal for 25 men and had it on the table on time for supper.

There was not much room for anything but beds in our cabin. A large bed for the folks and Donna. I had a cot. Ed and Roy slept in the bunkhouse with the men. There was a small table, two chairs and a small cookstove for heat.

Mom went to work early the next morning and Fred went to the mine. Mom worked long hours, sometimes 16 hours a day. There was no place to go or nothing to do but work so I guess they got a lot of hours out of the employees that way. When I was over the mumps, I helped Mom in the kitchen.

The miners were delighted to have a good cook. She seemed to enjoy her job. It was getting her away from the hectic and stressful life she had

Bertha (Mom) and Rose.
Donna in the background.

40

before. We seldom saw Fred, he worked, he ate and went to the cabin and read.

The camp sat down in a hole dug out of a rocky hillside. There were steep mountains all around us. Very little timber could be seen from the camp. There were some trees at the top. Snow slides on those steep mountains had brought down anything that dared to grow on the side hills above camp. Going down by the mill and on up Crooked Creek were some wooded areas of nice scenery. It was a relaxing change to go for hikes up there. Crooked Creek came down a canyon and by the mill. The Jensen brothers, the original owners of the mine, had dug a ditch around the mountain side, for at least a mile to get a head of water for an overshot waterwheel. The waterwheel was about 12 feet in diameter and was made up of hand-hewed lagging. The boards were about two inches thick. This wheel fitted together beautifully and it was doweled. There wasn't a nail in it any place. This big wheel had a small bull wheel on it and a flat belt that drove the bull wheel and a one stamp mill. Both bull wheels were also hand-made out of lagging and doweled together. This was a very symmetrical and beautiful work. It was a mystery where the one stamp mill had come from. The only metal in the whole thing was the battery, the stamp, and of course the shoes, the dies, camshaft and an amalgamating plate.

Fred Bachich met the brothers Jake and Eric on the Big Creek trail hauling supplies into the mine. He later told this story about the operation and the brothers. He recalled that the Jensens sold the mine sometime prior to 1924. Eric was the ingenious one as a mechanic. He could design and build anything. Jake was more of a cultured, refined, gentleman, who played the violin beautifully.

According to Fred they spent the whole winter chloriding the ore, getting a few pounds here and a few pounds there of the richest stuff and stockpiling the rest. In the spring they would open up the ditch and turn the water in and get this waterwheel to spinning and the mill pounding. All they ever salvaged was what they could amalgamate on the amalgamating plate. Any of the gold that was in the sulfides was pretty much free gold, (very few sulfides as most of the ore they were getting was right near the surface and the sulfides were leached out.)

They amalgamated the gold from the ore that they had gathered all winter. They made about $1,200 to $2,000 during the summer which was all the money they needed to carry them over through the winter.

41

Jake Jensen and Rose at Snowshoe Mine.

This was an ingenious setup, and it should have been preserved in the Smithsonian Institute because we will never see anything like that again.

The Jensens worked during the early days of the Thunder Mountain boom near the turn of the century. They made enough money to get their mine opened up on Crooked Creek which they had discovered a few years earlier.

The following story was told by J.J. Oberbillig. Eric Jensen was quite a gambling man, poker was his game. Eric gambled while Jake played the violin wandering through the miners playing the soulful music. He got a lot of requests and a lot of tips also.

If there was a stiff hand and a pretty big pot, Jake made his way around the table. He took a quick peek at the opponents hand and signaled Eric with the music. They had this worked out to perfection and no one ever caught on. They made enough money to set up the mill and build their houses.

I had a picture taken holding a large ball of gold in a pan. It was about the size of a grapefruit, it was very heavy, I could barely hold it up long enough to get the picture. I wonder what it would be worth today. I believe gold was $35 an ounce then compared to about $350 now.

There were two other women in camp. Helen Court, her husband was a miner and Annabelle Riksem, whose husband was a mine foreman. The Riksems had a little girl about a year old which was entertainment for Donna and me. We liked little Annette.

Roy and I hiked around exploring and just checking things out. We got acquainted with Jake and Eric Jensen. I believe they still owned some shares in the mine because they stayed in there and lived in the cabin down on Crooked Creek. They were nice old Swedish gents. They wore flannel shirts and ties with a big nugget tie pin. Eric spent all his time in bed and I assumed he couldn't walk. I never knew what was wrong with him but Jake took care of him. He was in bed all of the time. Eric had rigged up his bed with battery-operated levers to raise and lower the bed. They lived there all winter when we first went in but later they went out in the winter and stayed in the Idanha Hotel in Boise. Jake came back one spring and Eric was not with him. He didn't make it through the winter. Jake continued to come in for short summers after Eric had passed away. Jake was lonely after his lifelong partner was gone. He didn't have much enthusiasm for life. After a time he no longer came at all.

They had their cabin fixed up very nice, it was always as neat as a pin. The cabin sat by Crooked Creek, so they had irrigation for their yard. They kept everything green and pretty.

We were surprised to see Uncle Tom walk into camp with a big pack on his back. I ran to meet him and gave him a big hug. Mom ran out of the cookhouse to greet him. She was so happy to see him. They walked to the cookhouse arm in arm. He and Mom sat down at the table with a cup of coffee and visited for awhile. She had a lunch fixed for him before he had his coffee finished. He told us the mill closed down in Oregon where he was working. He took off for Idaho as soon as he heard, hoping to get work.

We all loved Uncle Tom, he was a good guy and lots of fun. Tight with his money but that's fine he had a reason to be, it was hard to find. When we lived in Pierce, before my Dad left, Mom wrote to Tom and told him we didn't have anything to eat. He was working in Yakima Valley harvesting fruit. He bought four boxes of apples and jumped on a freight car. He had a terrible time trying to hang onto those apples with a car load of hungry people. He didn't dare go to sleep or they would have stolen all of them. He protected those apples with his life and he got them to us. Those apples got us through the winter. We were forever grateful to Uncle Tom.

Uncle Tom got a job at Snowshoe. He said he couldn't go to work until he checked out all the fishing holes around there. Mom seemed to be so happy now. She was changing, I saw something in her that I had never seen before. She laughed, she visited with everyone, there were no more tears. The different atmosphere, less stress, and she was good at the work she was doing. She was around other people. She was praised and complimented constantly. She felt good about herself and she was earning money. How long had it been since she had even seen money. She had her family together again. The depression was over for her.

The only time Dad was around was for meals and once in a while for pinochle. There was a card party once or twice a week in the cookhouse. I was anxious to learn and since there was not much else to do here, I began watching and picked up quite a bit about the game. I played with Dad as my partner, I wasn't too happy about that because he was just as rigid in his card playing as he was in life. He taught me how to play, however I didn't play with his fool-proof strategy after I learned for myself. It was more fun my way. He left nothing to chance.

Ed and Roy went down on Big Creek to cut wood for camp. They took a batching outfit and a tent and old Spot. They camped on the other side of Miners Hill, down by the bridge. They drove the Model A down there. Mom and I went down to see them once or twice. It looked to me like they were having a lot of fun, but they assured me they were not. This was hard work. They had a lot of wood cut and stacked there.

They came home on weekends to get caught up on good home cooking. One weekend when they went back, a bear had been in their camp and tore everything to bits; ripped open all the food and scattered it around. The tent was torn to shreds. Their bedding was also scattered all over and ripped up. I was so glad the boys were not there when that bear came around. Mom said no more of that. They didn't go back.

Tom Nevitt, the mine owner, hired a school teacher. Her husband worked as a medic and in the assay office. Johnnie and Bernice Chiarello. They were very nice people and added some sparkle to the camp. A little log cabin was renovated and became our school house. The first and only school that was ever back there. The Chiarellos lived upstairs, they took their meals at the cookhouse. Desks, blackboards, books and everything that was needed was brought in. The house was cleaned and the logs were varnished and it literally shone. It was a beautiful little school house. There were only three of us in school. Donna was five but she took the first grade and Roy and I were in the seventh grade. Ed went back to Orofino to go to high school.

Tom Nevitt, being a teacher himself was always good to get anything we needed and kept a curious eye on how we did. I think it was his pet project.

The school house was located up Crooked Creek, about a quarter of a mile from camp. The trail going by was a busy one. All the hunters, packers and travelers came down that trail, it was quite a short cut off the trail from lower Big Creek to upper Big Creek. This trail cut off several miles. So we were in the right place to see the action.

School was over for the day when a pack string came down the trail and stopped at the corrals out front. We couldn't concentrate on what we were doing so the teacher said, "Go ahead, there isn't much recreation here so I won't keep you from this."

Donna, Bernice
(the school teacher), and Mom.

Sometimes they were delayed there for awhile, waiting for another packstring to meet them and exchange the string, taking new hunters back to the hunting camps. The hunters and their elk would go on out. This was exciting for us.

I met Clark Cox there the first time. He was a good natured little guy. I think he would have been quite a bit taller if his legs were straighter. He must have spent a lot of time on a horse by the looks of things. He always had a chew in his cheek and was an expert spitter. I followed him around talking to him about the horses. One day he said, "Do you want to ride one?"

I didn't think he would ever ask, but I didn't want to show too much enthusiasm, I nodded my head and said a meek little, "Yes."

Clark said "What's wrong, can't you ride?"

Not being what I considered a horse woman, I had to say, "Not very well."

Clark picked out a gentle horse and I stretched up to reach the stirrup and he boosted me on up. When I got situated in the saddle, my feet in the stirrups and took hold of the reins, I nudged the horse with my knees and started back up the trail. Clark yelled at me, "Don't you lie to me anymore, You could ride any horse I've got." He laughed and said, "Go on get out of here."

I took off on a trot and everything was fine until the horse decided he didn't want to go anywhere without the other horses. We had a little tiff there and I slapped him a couple times across the neck and he did a little crow hopping and then cut loose. He dumped me so quick I didn't know what happened. I landed across an old dead log. He couldn't have picked a better place, it was a soft landing. I jumped up for fear someone would see me, and I couldn't let that horse walk in to camp without me. Clark thought I was a pretty good rider. The horse went down the trail just a ways and stopped, bless his heart. He waited for me. I really didn't want to get back on, but it may be okay if he is headed down the trail. I was trembling a little. Thinking about the alternative, I had to get back on, I wasn't going to be the object of the joke. The horse and I did fine the rest of the way, but I thought Clark was a better judge of horsemanship than that, and he probably was. Oh well he made me feel good.

Lafe Cox, Clark's son and his bride, Emma, came riding down the trail from Mile High Ranch one afternoon. Roy and I were out there to meet them. We took them up to the cookhouse to say hello to Mom. They were invited to stay for dinner. Everyone enjoyed their company, Lafe is quite a storyteller, he kept them entertained all evening. They spent the night, it was good to have company. Everyone came to the cookhouse to visit.

They were on their way to Cox's Dude Ranch in Yellow Pine to spend the winter. Guests were able to get into Yellow Pine much later than at Mile High. They helped the folks and by then I'm sure they needed it. They were a working family. They had more than their share with all the guests and keeping up the two ranches, all the stock, and everything that goes with guest ranching. Their hospitality was known all over the country.

When the power line was put into Stibnite in about 1941 the workers stayed at Cox's. They got room and board there. When it came time to leave, they all grieved. They really enjoyed that hospitality and good food. They had road workers, engineers, and anyone who needed a place to stay. They seemed to work in everyone who needed to stay and not give up their own guests. They were pretty busy for a couple of summers. They were the people who could handle it.

In the winter they made furniture and painted and varnished the lodge inside and out every year. The place was kept beautifully all the time.

Jim Carpenter stayed at the Mile High ranch for the winter. Lafe and Emma were there to take care of guests during summer fishing and fall hunting. Big Creek was well known for the good fishing even back then.

The following summer I worked for Clark and Beulah at the Dude Ranch. I was there about two months. I helped in the kitchen, serving and cleaning rooms. Lafe and Emma were still there as they didn't have guests yet at Mile High. They teased me mercilessly about a young wrangler who was working there. I couldn't look at the guy, I was so embarrassed, I knew if I even went near him or looked in his direction, someone was watching and when everyone left, it was, "Rose I saw you looking at him today. Are you liking him now." I got so sick of the guy, I couldn't stand him, and he hadn't done a thing. But the Coxes had a lot of fun out of that. I've laughed about it a lot since.

I did have a great time there. They had a jukebox, first I had ever seen. I could trip it to play without putting money in so I had it playing all the time. All the new songs, "Leaning on the Old Top Rail," and "Always." Well, they were new to me. I learned those songs that summer and I sang them forever after. I was in heaven at the ranch. Everything was so beautiful. I loved sitting on the front porch just looking at the green meadow where their new colts were kept. Everywhere I looked there was something beautiful to see. I didn't get to ride much unless the wrangler was out on the trail, then usually all the horses were gone. The Coxes were very good to me, I will never forget my summer with them.

I didn't want to leave, it would be terrible going back to that old dingy mine. Then I thought of school and the packstrings and the cowboys. Standing on the fence watching them pack and unpack and change loads. I thought about walking down the trail to see Jake and Eric Jensen. I was ready to go back.

Winter came on with a fury. Down in a deep canyon whatever comes stays until spring. It just keeps piling up. Frost froze the top of the snow, and it got harder each time it got below freezing and I don't think it got above freezing all winter. Very little sun all winter. All in all the place was the most depressing place I had ever been. The days were short and nights were very long. It was so dark down in that hole. Didn't seem to bother the adults but I hated every day of the winter. Mom was the only woman to stay in, the others went out.

Fred Erickson at Snowshoe Mine.

School took up some of our time but as dark as it was, in the school house we seldom got to spend the whole day.

After dinner one evening the mine foreman asked, "Would anyone like to go up to the big dam for ice skating tomorrow." I think everyone put up their hands, they were probably getting cabin fever too. There were plenty of snowshoes and ice skates. Most everyone went even if they didn't want to ice skate. Mom fixed sandwiches and hot coffee in the thermos. We started out in the morning dressed for the occasion. Everyone on snowshoes, we had a lot of laughs the first few miles as it was the first time some of us had been on them. I kept stepping on the other shoe and falling down and it is mighty hard to get up with those big things on.

We must have been quite a sight. A long line of people trudging along in slow motion. We were dressed like Eskimos. At one point someone up front passed back a message and quietly it went back all the way without a sound from anyone.

49

Mom in dog sled. At left, Jake, Al Riksem, Mike and Howard Elkins.
Rose in the background.

"Look at the cougar sitting back there watching us." He must have been a curious cougar to stay that long or else we didn't look very threatening to him.

When we got to the dam, Al Riksem was the first one on the ice, clearing it off. We all were amazed at his skill in skating. Growing up in Norway he said that was a way of life.

Many of us went out but we were down as much as we were up. It was a great day though. Everyone laughed until they hurt, we were still laughing when we got to camp. It felt so good to laugh. It was good knowing there was still something to laugh about.

There was a party line telephone in the cookhouse. One morning at breakfast the emergency ring came through. It was one continuous ring for about 30 seconds and when everyone around the country got on the line, it was announced. "The Japanese have bombed Pearl Harbor and President Roosevelt has declared war."

Mom answered the phone. Everyone sat looking at her with a terrible fear of what they were going to hear showing in their faces. Mom listened for a few moments and hung up the phone. She turned to everyone and gave the devastating news. An "Oh no" came simultaneously from everyone in the room. All the men got up and went out the door to go to their bunk where they had a radio to get the details. Everyone was stunned thinking about our country being in war.

Uncle Tom sat with our family with everyone in shock. I wasn't feeling the impact of this news. I had heard of wars all over the world, from adults talking, and in school but other than that, I just knew it was bad. Before the day was over when different ones came in with details of what happened at Pearl Harbor, I thought of my two brothers having to go to war. That frightened me, and I felt the terror of war for the first time in my life. Everyone went their own way to do their thinking. I didn't ask any questions for fear it would be worse than I wanted to hear.

The men didn't go to work at all that day and they didn't feel much like eating, so Mom just put out lunches with fruit and cookies.

One morning after breakfast Uncle Tom stayed to have a cup of coffee with Mom. With a very somber expression he announced,

"Well Bert, I'm going out to sign up. I want to do my share."

Mom replied in shock, "Tom, you are too old."

Tom said, "No, I'm 42 and if I wait till my next birthday, I will be too old, so I'm going now."

"How Tom, how will you get out?"

"I will snowshoe."

There was no talking him out of it, we knew that. The next day he put a few things together, Mom fixed him a big lunch, and he left early the next morning. He had a 43 mile walk to Yellow Pine. With some luck he would catch the mail man who came to Yellow Pine with a dog team from Cascade. Mom checked by phone all the way to Big Creek, there were no phones from there on. Mom was worried about the trip out, anything could happen out there. He was her only brother and they were very close. He was my only uncle, a very special uncle. I was sad to see him go.

Uncle Tom spent most of his time in Iran. He was in the Engineer Corp. He spent four years serving his country. After he returned home from the war, he told us quite a story about his trip out on snowshoes. He said he was going up Profile and stopped to roll a cigarette while sitting beside the road on the bank. He heard a rumble like thunder, very distant at first but gradually it got louder. He jumped up and looked all around as the roar became louder. Then he looked back of him and he could see it coming. A snow slide. It was taking everything in its path; bushes, trees, and rocks. The farther down it came the more momentum it picked up. He couldn't take off his snow shoes, the snow was too deep, he wouldn't turn his back for a moment. He began backing up little by little. Big trees were going end over end, the deafening sound grew louder and louder, he continued to go backward on his snowshoes, to where he hoped to be safe. As it came closer he stepped back further. It finally crossed the road in front of him and hit the bottom of the gully. It began to pile up. Before it stopped moving, a mountain of debris and snow slid slowly to a stop. Uncle Tom stood there looking and gave thanks. If he had gone on and not stopped, he couldn't have got out of the way. We would never have known what happened to him. No one would have ever had an occasion to look under that pile of trees and rocks when the snow disappeared. That was one time a cigarette saved a man's life.

Our days were getting a little longer and we saw the sun for a few moments each day. The snow began to melt, I could finally see some bare ground under a tree on the north slope. I looked at that, longing to put my feet on some dirt. The hill was steep and the snow was deep, I asked myself if I wanted to touch the dirt that bad. It wasn't long till I had an answer. I climbed the hill and was so tired when I got up there I laid down, I could have kissed the ground. It felt so good and smelled so good.

I was terribly lonely there and I felt like a caged lion, Donna couldn't get out in the snow, it was too deep for her to walk in and it was too cold. Mom was working all the time, it was wearing her down and she was getting depressed. I am sure that winter was hard on her, she worked hard to compensate for the solitude.

School was my salvation. It was only five or six hours a day but with only three students, we got all the help we needed and could get the work done easily. After school, I helped Mom get supper which was the big meal of the day. That still wasn't enough to keep me busy, so I contracted with the men to do their laundry. There was a gas washer which wasn't my favorite thing to use but if I got it started, I was able to get the job done. I washed shirts and underclothes one day and towels and sheets another day and those big heavy pants another day. After each washing, I hung the clothes to dry in the bunk house and had to have them dry and down before the men came home. I was frantic thinking about being there when they came in or not having the clothes dry. I poked wood in that old barrel stove all day to keep it good and warm in there. I ironed all the shirts, oh, what a job. That only lasted about a month. Guess I didn't want to be that busy.

One day Mom collapsed in the kitchen. She couldn't breathe. I ran up to the assay office to get Johnnie. He ran down, examined her there, and got help to take her to our cabin. She was still struggling to breathe. I thought she was dying, she tossed and pulled at her clothes. She moaned, "I can't breathe, help me, please help me."

I put my arms around Donna and held her in front of me as we watched Mom. Silent tears running down Donna's face, I was trying to be brave for her sake, but my heart was breaking. Johnnie gave her a shot of adrenaline. It seemed to help, she began to settle down.

The mine foreman went to the mine and got Fred. When he came down, Johnnie told him she had to go out, he thought it was her heart. We called Howard Elkins at Little Ramie, which was about eight miles from Snowshoe. Howard was there in no time it seemed. He loaded Mom and Donna in a small dog sled pulled by a horse. They were covered with warm quilts and were on their way.

When I saw them leaving, I panicked. They were going down the hill by the mill and to the main road, I ran to a place where I might get another glimpse of them. I was standing in a clump of willows when I saw them go by. I didn't call to them, I just watched until they were out of sight. I sat down with my arms across my knees and with my head on my arms, I cried and cried.

I was crying for all the hurts I had and was not able to cry for before. I hated this place, I couldn't stand it here without Mom and Donna. What if she died, would I ever see her again. I couldn't stop crying, I wanted to run away but there was no place to go. The snow was too wet for snowshoes. I had the most helpless feeling in my life. I sat there and cried, I didn't know how long. I heard men calling my name, I didn't answer. My brother found me and asked "What the hell is wrong with you?" I wouldn't respond, he said, "You had better get yourself up there, you are the only woman to cook. The foreman is looking for you." He grabbed my arm and with a jerk I was on my feet. I went to the cookhouse, I looked around, I have never felt so alone in my life. I missed Mom being there, I was afraid, I didn't want to cook. The emotions, the pain I had at that time is indescribable.

I felt like I didn't have a choice, I had to do this. I tucked my feelings down in my shirt and got busy. I finished what Mom had started for supper, set the table, went out and rang the dinner bell. Then there were dishes to clean and lunches to prepare.

I didn't get through until after midnight.

The next morning at five o'clock I went down to the cookhouse. The fire was going, coffee was made and there was Mike Marrinoff sitting at the table. He said, "Get a cup of coffee and sit down. I'll help you with breakfast." It was all I could do to say thank you, I was so close to tears. Did I ever appreciate him.

Mike was a little dark fellow about 50 years old, he came from Bulgaria. He had quite an accent, I didn't have a problem understanding him, but many of the men did. He helped me all the time he wasn't in the mine. He cut meat off the quarters hanging frozen in the meat house. Mom brought in a quarter at a time and let it thaw just a little and cut it up and cooked it while it was still fresh. I didn't get that organized, but I made out fine with Mike's help. I baked bread every day for lunches and meals. I was so thankful I had helped Mom as much as I did. I would never have been able to do this if I hadn't. At 12 years old that was quite a responsibility. God Bless Mike. He saved me from disgrace. The men were pleased or at least they said they were. I worked hard to please them and I soon forgot about feeling sorry for myself.

School was put on hold for a while, but Bernice brought my work up and helped me with it so I wouldn't get too far behind.

The foreman sent a letter out to Mr. Nevitt at Lewiston to send in a cook. She arrived about six weeks later. I was so glad to see her, I was anxious to get out of the kitchen, but I helped her for a few days. I felt as free as the breeze. What a wonderful feeling! The snow was about gone in camp and it looked good after being cooped up for so long. While I worked there I seldom saw the light of day. I wanted to go somewhere, but there was still no place to go.

We never heard much from Mom. We knew she was in Orofino with Aunt Gina and she was better but she couldn't go back to work.

Fred our stepfather quit as soon as he could get his truck out of there. He went to Logan Creek to work his claim. He found an old shack and set up housekeeping there.

———

Roy came up to the cabin one night, "You know, I'm getting pretty tired of this place. What do you want to do?"

I said, "I guess I'm supposed to stay here until Mom gets back. Fred didn't say anything when he left."

"Yes I know, I don't think he wants us up there. But I'm not going to worry about it, lets get around and see the country, what do you say?"

I replied, "Anything to get out of here."

"How would you like to go to Mile High?"

I perked up at that, "I'd love it, lets go."

Roy quit his job on the crusher, and we were free.

Roy decided he wanted to paint his Model A before we left so it would be dry when we came back. He worked all winter on the car and had got it all fixed up. He ordered paint from the catalog, it was called Powder Puff paint. We painted the car, we painted everything on the car. The license plates were all rusty so we painted them too. Everything was a tannish color, and I'll admit it did look funny, but it looked bad before. We left it to dry and took off for Mile High to see Jim Carpenter.

We had no idea how far it was or where to go. Roy said, "Don't worry about it we'll just follow the trail." We followed the trails as long as we could see them. We kept going toward Big Creek as we knew Mile High was on Big Creek. When we left Snowshoe, the snow was frozen on top and we made good time, walking fast. We were enjoying just being free, we were happy kids. We walked until we could hardly take another step, we were really getting tired.

It was late evening when we came up over a little rise and before us laid the most beautiful green meadow. We knew we were close, we walked out into the meadow and looked around. We saw the buildings about a half mile away. As we got closer, Jim spotted us. Of course he didn't know we were coming but we got a royal welcome. Jim looked at me and said, "Girl, you look tired, I am going to fix you something to eat and you go to bed in Lafe and Emma's room." I felt like a princess in that lovely room. The decor was dark, matching the dark log walls. The drapes were colorful and bright, hanging in luxurious folds like a gown, over the windows. Beautiful velvet pillows and spread to match the drapes adorning the huge bed. Emma was a beautiful lady and she left beauty everywhere she went.

Jim Carpenter stayed at the ranch as a ranch hand. He took care of the stock and helped with the haying. He also helped Lafe in the hunting camps in the fall and with fishing parties in the summer. He was a good old fellow. He had a reputation of being a rough character when he was drinking but he was certainly a perfect gentleman when we were there and any other time I was around him.

I slept until I heard Jim's call that breakfast was ready. I could smell bacon and coffee, that's what I needed to get me out of bed. What a feast; sourdough pancakes, fried potatoes and eggs and bacon, with coffee. We ate until we couldn't hold another bite, but he wouldn't let us leave the table until we ate another pancake.

After breakfast, I went outside to look around. I was standing on the front porch waiting for Jim and Roy to come out.

I feasted my eyes on the view from the front. The lush green meadow was on a gentle slope, the house stood at the top of the slope facing the creek. Big Creek ran crystal clear down the canyon, rumbling down over the rocks more like a river than a creek. The meadow was surrounding the house and out buildings on all sides. Above the meadow, in the back of the house the great Yellow Pines stood tall and noble where they had never been disturbed by a woodcutter. As far as you could see, the great trees embellished the land. I had never seen such a breath-taking scene.

The open hillside got a lot of sun and therefore stayed green most of the time. Snow was not a problem with that much sun. The deer and elk fed most of the year in the meadow. A windsock hung at one end of the field, I assumed there was a landing strip.

Jim showed us his smoke house full of meat. That was one of his winter jobs to keep the smoke house going all the time as the meat they got in the fall would not keep long with the mild winters. Jim walked us by the wood shed to show us the puppies. They really got my attention, those furry little fellers in there with their mother. Of course I had to stop and play with them and love them a little.

Jim caught the old wrangling mare that was in a small pasture close to the house. He put a halter on her and boosted me up on her. He said, "You have a long way to walk home so we will let you ride here." He and Roy walked ahead and Jim led the horse. I felt like a little child. They were talking up a storm about everything under the sun. We followed a trail through the pasture and went down into a draw where a little stream was running. We went by the barns and down toward Big Creek. We could see around the bend in the creek from there, which was more spectacular scenery. We went from one end of the place to the other—it was all beautiful. We saw some deer grazing down along the creek, they didn't bother to even look up.

Everything, wherever you looked was kept up so beautifully. It all looked like it was freshly manicured. Spring came to this country much sooner than it did to Snowshoe because of the high mountains and the narrow valleys. This was all open country and lower altitude.

It was so warm and pleasant there. We came back to that beautiful house and sat on the front porch, still wanting to feast our eyes on the green meadow and dry ground. Jim brought a lunch out to us. We all sat out there and visited while we ate sandwiches and cold milk, while we listened to Jim's stories. We were not bored in the least.

Jim was a tall, slender man, probably in his mid-sixties. He leaned forward somewhat when he walked. He may have had an accident but it must not have been a problem to him as he worked like a man in his thirties. He was limber and not in the least handicapped.

We sat and listened to stories until late in the day when the sun went down. It began to get chilly and we went inside. Jim had put on a pot of beans that morning so we had our supper ready whenever we were ready to eat. He brought out fresh bread that he had baked, with fresh butter and strawberry jam. It was a wonderful desert after a bowl of beans. When we finished eating, Roy and Jim were leaning back on their chairs. Jim was smoking a cigarette, they were spinning more yarns so I got up to do the dishes. Jim said "No, my guests do not do dishes." He was so adamant I didn't argue. He and Roy were still telling stories and I began to get sleepy so I excused myself and went to bed. I loved laying in bed and looking around that lovely room, especially in the lamp light. Who would ever dream of seeing such elegance as this, way back here in cowboy country.

Jim's call for an early breakfast of bacon and eggs roused me again from a sound sleep. I jumped up and dressed quickly in anticipation of another meal cooked by an old cowboy. Roy was already up drinking coffee with Jim. After our good mornings, Roy said to me, "Jim said we could have a couple pups. What do you think?"

My mind went back to the mine and their restrictions about having dogs. I missed having a dog, since poor Spot died of salmon poison, down on Big Creek, I was lost without her. I knew we probably wouldn't be at Snowshoe very long. "What kind of dogs are they Jim?"

"Australian Shepherd and Border Collie." Jim responded, "That is the best all around breed of dog there is."

Roy added "Yep, it's the best."

After breakfast, we went out to look at the pups, I had first choice. I looked at the pups carefully looking for the characteristics I liked in a dog. I liked a gentle, submissive dog, very sensitive and quiet, non-aggressive but proud and brave.

The puppies were excited, the black pup jumped on the grey pup, knocking him down. He recovered himself quickly and sat down, wagging his tail and looking at us, from one to the other.

I walked up closer looking at him. I had his exclusive attention. He continued to wag his tail and look straight at me, not seeming to feel intimidated at all. He didn't back up or look away. The black pup lost the attention of his audience, jumped on him again. The grey pup angered, growled and snapped. The black pup backed off. The grey pup again came back to where I stood, he sat down, wagged his tail and looked at me. I liked those eyes. I believed he sensed my admiration for him and he responded to me. Jim and Roy could see this was going to take awhile and they wandered off talking about the deer grazing down in the meadow.

I picked up the gray pup and walked over to the guys and said, "I'll take this one. His name is Jim."

Jim had a big hearty laugh and said, "Thank you girl, that's a compliment."

Roy took the black pup. We picked up our packs, thanked Jim and started off across the meadow. We stopped before we were out of sight of the house and looked back. Jim was standing on the porch watching us. We waved and called to him once more, "Good-bye Jim and thank you."

We were a little sad as we walked away, not saying anything until Roy stopped and turned to me to get my attention and pointed out some deer grazing, many more than we had seen before.

They looked up and saw us, lifted their heads, ran off a few steps and stopped. They watched until we were out of sight.

We put the pups down to walk but their curiosity was slowing us down. We were constantly calling them back to us, so we decided we should carry them to make better time. We were thinking about the long walk ahead.

We walked for an hour or so, the needles were soft under our feet, the sun was shining down though the sparse stand of Jack Pines. It was quiet and peaceful, the birds were singing and squirrels were scolding. It was spring here and oh so beautiful.

Roy stopped abruptly putting his hand up to motion me to stop and listen. There was first a vibration, then the sound that echoed in the little valley. It got louder, was it thunder? We stood turning our ear to the sound one way and then the other. What could it be? We instinctively ran toward a stand of trees, the biggest ones in the little valley. We listened, it was coming closer. Roy said, "Can you climb that tree?"

I became very anxious, "With this pup?"

Roy shouted, "If you want that pup, you'd better take him up with you." The tree was a little small to climb, but I reached over and pulled another small tree with a few more branches and pulled it over to me. I wrapped my leg around it and pulled for everything I was worth to climb that tree with one arm and the other holding the pup. I looked around for Roy, I didn't see him, but I knew I just had to hold on and climb. I looked down, I had to go higher, I was barely off the ground. The sound was coming closer, so close, I was afraid to look. I tried to climb higher, I pulled with my legs and my one arm, I was only moving inches upward. Jim was scared and holding on to me for dear life, his little nails digging into my arm. I stiffened and held my breath looking straight ahead. They were beneath me. I had to look. Elk by the dozen were stampeding down through the draw. There must have been more than a hundred. They paid no attention to us but ran on at top speed out of sight.

I couldn't move but I called softly, "Roy."

From around the other side of the clump of trees came a "Yeah, are you alright?"

I assured him I was fine, but I didn't know if I could get down, I was shaking so bad. He climbed down and came over and took Jim and my pack, and steadied me as I got down. I asked him, "Were you scared?"

He looked at me and yelled, "You're damned right I was scared! Who wouldn't be."

He was rearranging his pack and he pulled his rifle from the side of his pack and said, "If I hadn't shot all those shells up there at Jim's, I could have turned that herd with one shot, but I knew I didn't have any shells." He jerked back the hammer and a bullet flew out. We just looked at one another and gathered up our packs and took off again.

We walked until noon making good time. We were approaching a shaded area in the draw where the snow was deep. The day we came up the crust was hard and we walked on top. The couple days we were up there it was pretty warm, so we should have expected this. But we didn't give a thought to the crust softening. We took a few steps sinking into our ankles, then to our knees, we were not making very good time this way. We walked on stepping easy, but it didn't matter, we were soon to our waist, then our armpits. The snow was wet and mushy. We had to let the pups go so we could crawl out of the snow. They thought it was great running up, licking us in the face and playing with our hair, and pulling off our hats. This was a real problem. We began to wonder why we brought these dogs. We had to crawl out of the snow and pull our bodies along the top of the snow to keep from falling back in and at the same time push the dogs back. We became so exhausted but we had to keep on crawling. It was getting later and colder. The crust would begin to firm up soon but we continued to crawl. We could go a little faster as it got colder. We finally got into the deeper canyon of Crooked Creek where the sun spent very little time. We got to our feet, picked up the dogs and took off at a trot, wanting to get home before it got too dark and cold.

Since we had no family there at camp, no one had missed us. If they did they may have thought we went to Logan Creek. The camp was dark when we arrived home. We didn't make it until long after dark. We quietly slipped in and went to bed. Roy went up in the loft and I went to my cot. Our dogs went with us, Jim must have been as tired as I was. I put him at the foot of my bed and he didn't move until I woke up at 8 o'clock. I was famished so I went to the cookhouse, got some scraps for the dogs, then began to fill my hollow spot. Roy soon came around and we talked about the trip over breakfast.

While we were finishing up breakfast, a call came in from Big Creek telling us that Faye Kissinger would be coming in with supplies and mail. The roads were never kept open in the winter so only when weather permitted, we got delivery in the winter. It took about two days for Faye to come the 18 miles with a cat and sled. There were several places he delivered to on the way in, so he had places to eat and spend the night. The people were all more than happy to have someone come to visit. There were many months they didn't see anyone.

Roy fired up the old Powder Puff Model A. We were anxious to hear from Mom and we didn't want to wait until the men got off work to pick up the mail.

Faye returned to Big Creek after unloading the supplies in the shed at the end of Crooked Creek Road. A trail went down Big Creek to the Middle Fork of the Salmon and up Monumental Creek.

Many miners and trappers were scattered up and down the trails. They walked up on snowshoes to pick up the mail for their particular route.

People back in there chose to live a very isolated life for whatever reason. Some lived there because they liked it and will never leave. Some we were told were hiding from the law. Some lived there because they found a cabin or built one from the timber in the area. Their living came from panning a little gold for the necessities of life which were very few, mainly tobacco and coffee. They grew a few root vegetables in the summer and found wild berries and wild game for meat. That was all they needed in life. We learned very soon never to ask questions of anyone, just take them for what they were, how they treated us.

One very special gentleman, a trapper, who we were especially fond of was Wilbur Wiles. Wilbur was a hard-working man and he got more out of life than tobacco and coffee. He kept pretty much to himself but was friendly and hospitable. His cabin was always clean as a pin. Wilbur had the reputation for being the best cougar hunter in the country. Wilbur is still there some 50 years later.

Another fellow we were fond of was Howard Elkins. Howard lived on Little Ramie Creek, there was a nice little cabin there. He was a clean person also. From what we understood he was quite a drinking man. We never saw him drinking when he came to Snowshoe or saw him at Big Creek. He was always very much a gentleman. He moved out to Riggins later on and was shot to death on the street by his girl friend when he was drunk and had roughed her up. He was a good neighbor. We were always grateful to him for taking Mom out when she was sick. Roy and I stopped in to see him quite often.

We were getting the little Powder Puff gassed up and ready to go. When Faye got there, we would be ready to take off. The road down Crooked Creek had not been plowed all winter.

When we needed to pick up the mail, we went on snowshoes. Roy decided since there was only about six inches of snow, we could probably drive the car down. We were so anxious to try out that new paint job.

Down that cold icy canyon a lot of unpredictable things could just happen, as we were soon to find out, but with no high banks it couldn't be too dangerous.

It was time to go. We kept track of Faye down the way and when he left Big Ramie we knew how long it would take him so we took off. We were on cloud nine, that little car with the narrow tires cut a pass through that snow pretty easy. She was running good and we didn't have far to go. All of a sudden the bottom dropped out of the road. We crashed and banged, and there we sat with six inches of water running across the floor boards. I couldn't figure out what happened, I was scared to death. I thought he had driven out into the creek, but no we were close to the bank.

Roy opened his door and looked around, the creek had washed out a section of the road and ice had frozen across the wash out and we crashed through the ice. Roy was using some very expressive language. He had probably learned in the mill around those men. I guess he wanted to show me what he had learned and was exercising his manhood. I did not appreciate this at all. I began getting angry at him. I knew better than to say anything so I sat there stiff as a poker, looking straight ahead.

After he quieted down some, I asked, "What are we going to do?" Wrong thing to say, it started all over again.

"Hell, I don't know what we are going to do. What do you think I am? Do you think I can get out and lift it out?"

After just so much of that I had enough. I opened my door, water flooding through like a river. He screamed, "Shut that door. Are you crazy or something?"

I paid no attention to him but the car began to shift a little. I jumped for the bank. I was never good at jumping and I got into water up to my waist, I reached for some bushes on the bank and was able to get my feet on firmer mud and worked my way out of the water. I was still mad at Roy and didn't look back once to see what happened to him. I started walking down the road, looking down at my beautiful knee high, lace up boots, the pride of my life. Water was squeezing out of my boots with every step I took and my jodhpurs were probably ruined. I wanted to cry. I wasn't going to talk to him at all.

My mind quickly went to getting a letter from Mom. With new enthusiasm I quickened my step and soon reached the shack where the mail was. I grabbed the mail bag, jerked it open, and pulled the mail out. I went all through the mail and there was no letter from Mom. My heart sank and my eyes filled with tears. I put all the mail back in the sack and laid it down in the shed. I walked over to the bank of Big Creek, crying and grieving for my mother, whom I thought would never come back. Roy walked up behind me and said with so much compassion in his voice, "No letter from Mom, huh?"

I shook my head. He walked around for awhile and came back over to me, "Why don't we take Wilbur's mail to him?"

Wilbur Wiles, Monumental Creek.

I nodded my head. He had the mail and away we went up over the pack bridge and up Monumental Creek trail. I was still wiping tears from my eyes as I walked behind Roy.

This was so like Roy. So gruff until he thought he hurt me—then he became so kind as a way of saying I'm sorry. He showed it but never said it. He knew I would like to go up here. That was all to make me feel better. He was a softy underneath.

I could never stay mad at him.

Quite a trek up the trail but it didn't seem far to us.

Wilbur was happy to see us and soon had coffee and lunch on the table. Wilbur took us out to see his furs that he got through the winter. He had them stretched over a pile of brush. We played with the dogs and took a few pictures. We said our goodbyes and headed down the trail. We stayed at Snowshoe until the roads were passable. I helped in the cookhouse and Roy worked around camp. He took the cat down and pulled his car out and fixed the wash-out. Every day we checked to see if we could make it out, we had our things packed and we were ready to go. We heard that most of the snow was gone at Big Creek. That was music to our ears.

We just couldn't wait any longer, we were on our way. We had quite a time on Crooked Creek, but we expected that to be the worst part of the road. When we turned the corner going up Big Creek road, we shouted for joy. We saw a lot of bare ground on the sunny hillsides, it was so beautiful, we felt so good. We thought that was the best day of our lives.

The farther we went the more bare ground we saw. It was more open country and the sun melted the snow faster and dried the ground. We were enjoying this so much, we meandered along looking for fishing holes. We were so anxious to see Big Ramie Hole. We climbed the hill and right on top, the highest point on the road, was the only place we could see that famous fishing hole. We stopped and got out, Roy took his glasses and looked down. He became so excited and said, "Man, you are not going to believe this, those white fish are as big as salmon, and there is so many of them. That hole is so full I don't know how they can get around each other. It's alive with fish. Just look."

He handed me the glasses, I could see what he meant. We dug around and found our fishing gear, hiked down the steep bank to reach the hole. We caught fish like we never had before, we fished until nearly dark and decided we'd better get back up that steep bank while we could still see. We reached the car and drove on down the road. We weren't exactly sure what we were going to do but when we came to the old Big Ramie cabin, we decided to cook some fish—we were starved. We built a big fire in the fire place and roasted our fish, the big room got warm and cozy. We decided we'd spend the night and sleep on the bear rug in front of the fire place. It was badly worn, but we sat on it roasting our fish, thinking it wouldn't be too bad. Roy went out to the car and got our bed rolls while I was looking at some books I spotted on the shelf. "Roy I found four Zane Grey books. Shall we read?"

We fixed our beds in front of the fire place and I read by the light of the fire until way late in the night. Then we snuggled down in our beds and slept. We woke up late. The sun was up, we thought it must be time for breakfast so we roasted some more fish. I got the book and read. We couldn't leave until we got all these books read.

We spent several days there. When we were out of fish, we'd go fishing. We hiked around exploring the area. It was so beautiful there. The cabin sat down in the hollow and there was a bench above the cabin. We saw deer there every day. The warm sun had brought up luscious green grass that must have looked mighty good to the deer after a long hard winter. They weren't the least bit afraid of us, but then it would take a lot to move them out of the Garden of Eden.

Big Ramie creek came down the draw at the bottom of the hill. The road going up the hill went through the creek. The water in the creek was ice cold, it came from the snowy mountains up behind. There were trails leading to Ramie Flats where fishing in the summer is fabulous. Chicken Peak Look-Out, Crosby Lake, Camp Creek, Chamberlain Basin, it was the gateway to the back country, a hunter's paradise.

Roy decided I needed a lesson in driving. There was a little level spot just in front of the cabin. He thought that would be big enough for the beginner. We noticed some stuff stacked by a bush, covered with a tarp, but we didn't pay any attention to it. We got into the car and he showed me how to start it. I turned on the key and pressed on the starter. The car was in reverse and he didn't say I couldn't let my foot off the clutch, so of course I did. The car started lurching backwards. He began to yell at me, "Stop, stop the car."

"How do I stop?"

"Put your foot on the brake, what do you think it's for?"

We continued to lurch backwards, I put my foot on the brake but we kept going back. It was still in reverse and the brakes were not good. I couldn't see where we were going but I felt the car climbing over something back there and I was up in front trying to figure out what went wrong. Roy was still yelling his head off. The car tipped and settled back down, we had run over something big and the motor died. Thank God.

He looked relieved and said "Why didn't you stop it?"

"I didn't know how." He looked at me for awhile thinking about all this and said, "Oh. Let's go read." That was the end of my lessons.

Before we left the cabin we looked under the tarp that was so securely tied down. We saw a little cook stove that we had run over but it wasn't hurt too bad. Someone would have to straighten out the frame.

We began to think about a letter from Mom at Big Creek. Could someone be looking for us. We doubted that but since we had finished the books it was time we moved on.

We drove into Big Creek in the early afternoon. It was bustling with activity that day. Horses tied to the hitching rail, a wagon or two. Clusters of people visiting here and there, they liked to gather there in the spring after being isolated all winter. Some were catching up on the news, some came to pick up supplies, some were there to catch up on booze. Whatever the reason it was good to see that many people. They all acknowledged us and asked about news from the mine.

Dick Cowman owned and operated the store and lodge. He and his wife and two little daughters lived there year round. Mrs. Cowman came from Boston, she was quite a lady, she dressed and talked like a Bostonian.

The men shied away from her. She would not tolerate any rough language or rowdy men in her dining room. It was quite a contrast, the ruffians outside and Lady Cowman inside. It was strange to see a woman of her caliber in this country, but I was fascinated with her. Every chance I had to visit with her I took advantage of. She operated the hotel and cooked for guests. We always wondered how Dick talked her into coming to a place like this. She seemed happy and content, she changed some things but also tolerated some. She was quite a lady.

Dick took orders from the people in the area and made the trip into Boise once a month to pick up supplies and fill their orders. They came in with a saddle horse and a pack horse or two. Some only had packsacks to carry back their orders. We were one of the few that had a car.

The post office was in the store where the clerk could take care of both. The Cowman's were very efficient in supplying the needs of the people back here. They were great people and very successful. They were there several years.

Roy and I walked into the store to check the mail, there was nothing. My heart seemed to stop, was I ever going to hear from Mom again. Tears welled up in my eyes and I walked out and got into the car for fear someone would see me cry. Roy was in the store for a while and when he came out to the car, his eyes were moist also. We missed her so much. Neither of us said a word as we drove up the road. We came to the forks in the road, wondering what we should do, we sat there for awhile, finally deciding to go up Logan Creek. We really didn't want to go there but we had no place

else to go. We didn't know if Fred wanted us there, he sure didn't tell us when he left. This is the only one thing we could do. Right then we both felt like a man without a country. We drove on up the road.

*Bertha, Fred,
Rose, and Donna.*

66

Chapter 3

"Country Bumpkins"

We drove slowly uncertain of what we should do. We had never been to the cabin. In fact we had never been up Logan Creek. We had no idea how far it was to the cabin.

Logan Creek was beautiful, the dusty road just ambled along through the big trees. It was so quiet and peaceful. There was several abandoned mines along the road. Most of the buildings were fallen down probably from the snow in the winter. The only evidence of life was a cabin being built, obviously to replace the old one. It was in a beautiful spot down by the creek in a little meadow. There was a horse grazing in the tall grass by the creek. We didn't see anyone around the cabin, so we went on.

As we drove, we could hear the wind in the tops of the trees. What a lovely melody it played. This was so different from Snowshoe country. You would never guess you were only 22 miles from there.

We soon came to an open flat with three to four foot jack pines covering the area. There must have been a fire through there at one time as jack pines will not reproduce like other trees.

From the heat of the fire, the little seeds in the tiny cones will burst and cover the ground and soon there are little jack pines popping up all over. All about the same size. It looked like that is what happened here.

We saw two cabins on the flat. The upper cabin was considerably larger and in much better repair than the second one which was down by the road. I wasn't sure if this one could even be considered a cabin. It had dirt on the roof with grass and bushes growing all over it. We looked inside. The floors were dirt, built up some or maybe the cabin settled. It was a little higher than the outside. The windows were covered with boards nailed together, looking more like barn doors. They had hinges to open and close the doors, or shutters as they probably were called. We pushed open the door, from what we could see laying around, Fred lived there. We didn't see any of Mom's things so we gathered she was not back yet.

We were disappointed and bewildered not knowing what to do. We went out and got into the car and drove back down Logan Creek. I wasn't sure where we were going but it really didn't matter.

I was so glad I had Roy. If it were not for him, what would I do. It was too painful to even think about.

We started up Profile hill. After about two miles the car boiled dry. We stopped and looked around until we found a spring down over the bank. Then we began looking for a bucket. There was no such thing. Quite often if you found a spring, a bucket or can would be there left by some very thoughtful person. Roy gave me his hat, "Here take this and go down and get some water while I get the radiator cap off. It's so hot she will probably blow."

I agreed and hustled down the bank with his ten gallon hat which didn't hold more than a quart and a half. Climbing the steep bank and stumbling around, the water slopped over. I didn't have much water and Roy was not to happy, "Why didn't you get more than that?" I just looked at him as I puffed and panted. I took the hat and went down again, getting about the same amount this time. I made several trips and the water in the radiator didn't even show. The next trip I handed him the hat and told him I would watch to see if the radiator blows. His radiator was more apt to blow than the car. And it did, quite a few times before we got to the top. He decided that if he would stop and let it cool down when it got hot, it wouldn't boil dry. It took a mighty long time to make it to the summit.

We sailed down the other side. He shifted down but it didn't hold us back too well, our brakes were not too good. We stopped in Yellow Pine and got gas and water. We drove on toward Cascade, the hills were even steeper than Profile. The car was getting hot and boiling dry. We did pick up a can in Yellow Pine, so getting water was easier and faster. I filled the can and held it between my feet on the floor. It slopped all over my feet. There wasn't much left to put in the radiator. It would boil dry as fast as we put in the water. We were not getting anywhere. Roy decided to wait till dark. Traveling was new to us, so we didn't think too much of this. We just did what we had to do to keep going. We decided it was not much fun to travel.

When it cooled down after the sun went down, we tried it again. It was a bit cooler, the car didn't heat up so badly. We arrived in Cascade about dawn. We stopped at a station and had to set there until they opened. The attendant found we had several holes in the radiator. Roy got some stop leak and we thought all our troubles were over, not by a long shot! It helped but it was going to take more than that. We stopped at every station and bought more stop leak. One man told us to break eggs in the radiator. He got a dozen eggs and put them all in the radiator. It didn't help for long, that was the worst mess, egg foam boiling out of the radiator all over the motor and the front of the car and left a strange looking trail behind us. The smell was terrible. Roy bought up every stop leak in Horseshoe Bend before we started up the hill.

It must have been 120 degrees in Horseshoe Bend. It was so hot when we stepped out of the car, it burned our feet right through our shoes. Roy bought a tire patching kit and a pump, just in case. We hadn't had any tire trouble but it might be a good idea to have it.

The Horseshoe Bend hill was much different back then. It was terribly steep, narrow, winding and had sharp corners. It seemed like it was 50 miles long. Well, maybe it was a little shorter but to a couple of hillbilly kids with an old car on a hot day, it may have seemed worse than it was. "I doubt it." We weren't used to the heat and it was stifling to us.

We just got started up the hill and we had a blow out. Roy got out, jacked the car up, took off the wheel so he could get the tube out. He patched the tube, put it back in the tire and put the tire on the wheel, pumped it up, and then the wheel back on the car. He was wishing for some shade but at noon time it was hard to find.

We just got started and a police car pulled up behind us, followed us a ways and turned on the siren. We stopped and he came up to the drivers side and asked, "Where are you folks from?"

Roy answered, "Big Creek."

"Have you lived there long?"

"About two years."

The officer said, "Did you know the car license is supposed to tell me where you are from?"

We looked at each other and I wondered how in the world could that tell him anything. Roy said "Oh."

"Do you have a registration for the car?"

"No."

"Where did you get it?"

"My stepdad gave it to me back at Snowshoe."

The patrolman said, "I'll bet it has been there a long time. Where are you going?"

"Boise."

"Well you go on to Boise, get it registered and purchase some new plates before you come back. By the way, don't paint your license plates any more. That is what identifies your car. Good luck kids." He drove around us and up the hill.

We had no idea how to get the car registered and get new plates for it. I'll bet he died laughing when he got out of sight.

We had never been stopped before and we were pretty nervous but we sat there for awhile until we quit shaking. We didn't know license plates were so important—in fact we didn't know what they were for.

We started up the hill again. We hadn't gone a mile and we had another flat. Roy got out and fixed it. The weather was hot but his temper was getting hotter with every flat we had. That cursing was starting all over again. I didn't like that but I couldn't walk home so I kept my mouth shut.

I guess the hot pavement was hard on tires, because we had one flat after the other. It was dark when we reached the summit.

Roy vowed if he had another flat he would leave the tire off and run on the rim. It wasn't long until we were running on all four rims. Sparks were flying from the wheels on the pavement. We got near to the center of the road so we wouldn't set a fire in the dry grass. There was very little traffic so we didn't worry about someone running into us. We did meet a car when we were going down the hill. They must have seen us coming for miles, because they began slowing down a long ways before they got to us.

We pulled way over and stopped when they went by. They crept up slowly to see what we were and very slowly went around us then speed up to get out of there.

We drove on into Boise on the wheels with all the racket and sparks. We didn't arouse a policeman. We found an all night cafe at the bus station. We sat down in a booth and ordered a cup of coffee. We were hungry for sure but we thought we better save our money to get back home one way or the other. Roy began to unveil his plans to me. He said, "You stay here. There are some people sleeping on the benches, waiting for their bus. You can lay down and rest until I get back. I'm going to find a place to trade off that Model A and get something that will run."

"Do you mean I have to stay here alone?"

"You won't be alone, look at all those people here, you'll be alright."

There wasn't anything I could do about it, I was so tired, I had my place all picked out on the bench right beside a nice looking mother. I hoped she was nice anyway. The benches looked a lot like a feather bed to me, and I went straight for them when Roy left.

Roy returned several hours later, he was so excited, he couldn't wait for me to see this new car. "This is a Plymouth sedan and it is nothing like the Model A. Just wait till you see how it rides, it even has an overdrive. I traded straight across. I got the best of that deal. This has four good tires. We'll make it home fine."

So I left my feather bed behind and took off for the mountains. We stopped at a little store on the outskirts of Boise and got some lunch meat, bread and milk. We were famished. That really tasted good.

Oh this was great. We could go about 35 miles an hour. It didn't heat up and it was much easier riding. We did find that it took more gas though, but what the heck. I felt so good riding in such a pretty car. The lines on this car were more round and the Model A was like a square box. We really enjoyed the trip, just sailing along, until we got to Warm Lake that is.

The car began sputtering and chugging, then died. Roy got out lifted the hood and was dumfounded by what he saw. He assumed since he worked on the Model A he could work on any car, but this car was completely foreign to him. This thing really died and it never ran again that we knew of.

I crawled in the back seat and went to sleep. Roy slept in the front. Sometime during the night we heard a truck coming up the hill. Roy stepped out to flag down the truck. We were glad to see Dick Cowman. He said he would be more than happy to take us to Big Creek.

"But," he asked, "What are you going to do with the car?"

"I'm going to leave it there."

Dick was concerned, "But someone may steal it."

"I left the keys in it if anyone wants it."

He never went back, we don't know what ever happened to the car. Roy decided the Model A was a much better car than a Plymouth.

When we got to Big Creek, it was early morning so we took off walking up Logan Creek. It is about a 10 mile walk so it took us awhile. When we walked into the yard, hot, tired, hungry and dirty, I heard little Donna's voice coming from the cabin. I ran to the door, Mom was working on cleaning up the place. I stood and just looked at them for awhile and my eyes filled with tears. How those two people could make such a change in my life. I felt happy for the first time since they left. I realized how much I loved them and what little meaning my life would have without them. My heart over flowed with joy and love.

Mom turned slightly and saw me standing in the doorway, "Rose," she cried, "Where have you been?" She came over and took me in her arms and held me while I cried, her arms felt so good to me. Little Donna came and wrapped her arms around my legs.

Mom asked, "Why are you crying?" It took a bit of time to get the words out, finally I answered, "I thought you were never coming back."

To that Mom responded, "You silly thing."

Roy came in the door, he was greeted in grand fashion and he said, "Mom, I'm starved."

Mom always said, "Every time that boy looks at me he's hungry." He didn't disappoint her. She had food on the table in a few minutes and we sat around and talked. I wanted to know about her health.

"I'm fine now, it wasn't a heart attack. I was just wore out and I can't go back to work for a year."

"How did you get home Mom?"

"Tom Nevitt hired a plane to bring me to Big Creek, and Dick Cowman brought me up here."

"I'm so glad you are back, I don't want you to ever leave me again."

Then Roy told them about our trip to Mile High. He told her everything that happened from the time she left. It was so good to see her feeling so much better. She was like a real mother now.

There was a wall tent set up beside the cabin and all of Mom's things that she had stored at Snowshoe were in the tent.

Roy fixed a place in there for a bedroom for himself and both dogs. Jim wouldn't be sleeping with me any more.

I slept in the top bunk in the cabin, Donna slept in the lower bunk. The folks slept in the double beds which sat beside ours, there was about three feet in between them. At the end of the folks bed, sat our beautiful old round oak table in front of the window. There was a small cook stove sitting in the corner by the door. Boxes were nailed to the wall for cupboards. Pots and pans hung on nails back of the stove. Mom's Singer sewing machine sat at the end of my bed and beyond that in the corner was more wooden boxes for cupboards.

Mom wet the broom before she swept the dirt floor so as not to stir up dust. It was packed so hard it felt and looked like cement.

Mom had an old steamer trunk, that she had carried around every where with her. She had all her treasured pictures and keepsakes in the trunk, she also had old dresses and table clothes and doilies that she had made. She found enough fabric in there to make curtains for the cupboards, she put tablecloths on the table and doilies on every thing. Her stove shone like a mirror. It didn't matter where or what we lived in, she had it fixed up like a dollhouse in no time.

Fred had made a trip to Snowshoe to get Mom's things and had made some attempt to organize things before she got home, I was glad for that. He also picked up our dogs and brought them with him. Mike Marinoff said he would take care of them until we could get them.

It seemed like our stepdad was attempting to make amends, it pleased us considerably. I was especially happy for Mom.

He must have left some things at Big Ramie and hauled it up later. He had apparently made a trip to Snowshoe and then got the things from Big Ramie while we were out. It didn't dawn on us until Mom made a remark about her cook stove frame being bent. Roy and I stood looking at it, then we looked at each other. Oh! Oh! When we were outside I asked, "Roy, could that have been Mom's stove that I ran over at Big Ramie?"

"Well, if Fred unloaded some of the stuff there before he went up Big Ramie hill, and he may have done that, I think it is the same stove. I tried to straighten it out, but Mom knew the frame was bent. Don't say anything, whatever you do."

In front of the cabin was a lean-to porch. A gas washing machine sat under the porch and tubs hung on the wall. A trough of sorts was laid across the front of the porch where samples of ore were kept. Each one was very important to the prospector. He had to remember where each one came from, so no one dared move a rock.

Mom lived in that old shack like it was a mansion. Everything had its place and was kept in its place. She washed one day of the week, ironed one day, baked one day and cleaned one day. I asked her, "Mom, why do you have to do all this to an old shack?"

She stopped and looked at me, "You never have to be ashamed, if you do the very best you can with what you have to work with." I have always remembered what she said that day, it became my own guideline for living. Mom was respected the country over for the way she made a beautiful home out of whatever we lived in. She made herself just as beautiful in actions as in character.

Axel Falkenburg lived in the cabin up above us. He was a nice fellow and quite a frequent visitor in the evening. Axel also had a claim somewhere up the canyon, that he made his living from. A very meager one I'm sure, as with most miners.

One morning bright and early Axel came running to the house, bare footed, pants and shirt barely hanging on. He had a bad case of Bull Fever. He had shot an elk through his kitchen window while he was in the wash tub taking a bath. He needed help, Fred and Roy went up to help him clean and skin the animal.

The weather was much too hot to keep it long. As soon as it cooled out we ate till our hearts were content, then Axel cut it up and Mom and I canned it. We filled a washtub with quart jars of meat and cooked it on that little wobbly stove for four hours.

We had another one ready when that came off. It took a good hot fire a long time to start the boiling then keep it boiling hard. We washed jars out in the yard in an old iron pot, heated on a fire to keep the water hot and boil the jars before we packed them. This was a night and day job until we got it all canned and safe from spoilage. It was so hot in that cabin, we could hardly breathe. It was worth it all, that meat was wonderful, and we needed it.

As summer progressed, more people were around; fishermen, miners and visitors. Everyone stopped to say hello and have a cup of coffee and a piece of cake or cookie. We visited with everyone and was happy for the company.

Several mines were running then and no one was a stranger. People traveling by horseback or foot over miles of mountain trails to go to town maybe once a year. They stopped at every house or camp they came to. They were fed and offered a place to bed down. This was a courtesy of the back country. Everyone honored it because they knew they may need it sometime. No one ever locked a door. Someone may need to stay there. They left it like they found it and the wood box was left full.

The Moscow Mine was on up Logan Creek road about ten miles, which was the end of the road. Several of the McCoy family lived and worked there during the summer. They made frequent trips to Big Creek store in their old truck to buy groceries and beer. They seldom stopped at our place going in, but the happy bunch would pile out from all over the truck on the way back. They were pretty rough and wild after they had a beer or two. They always brought plenty for everyone, but at our camp they didn't find many takers. I usually preferred to disappear into the cabin. I was very uncomfortable around rough and rowdy people. Our family was a bit more dignified than that, everyone was uncomfortable, however they remained hospitable.

Another frequent visitor was Napier Edwards, coming up about dinner time, two or three times a week, bringing a gift of a lard bucket of milk. We would have been happy to get the milk, but he never washed the bucket and green cream was caked around the rim. He carried it to our house without a lid. Needless to say Mom threw it out, the dogs wouldn't drink it either.

Napier's father, William Edwards, a miner, brought his family in over Elk Summit, through Warren. Napier was just a baby, he was raised and educated by his mother, who was a school teacher. He was not lacking in intelligence, but in social education he was deprived critically.

The Edwards family established the townsite of Edwardsburg in about 1889, which became the headquarters for the mining district with a Post Office and a grocery store. Edwards ranched and trailed in cattle to butcher for the miners.

After his folks died, Napier was no longer able to take care of the business. The post office was moved to Big Creek town site. The other businesses ceased to prosper and were closed.

For years he seldom left the home place. Many small mining towns sprung up in the area, but he kept to himself unless someone stopped to visit. Throughout the summer, he could be seen farming his land and harvesting the hay. His farm machinery was horse drawn. His farm animals consisted of the two horses and several cows, which had been interbred for so long, they were all white with no tails. A generous hunter took pity on him and brought in a young Hereford bull. That made the difference, it took several generations for them to look like Herefords with tails and red faces.

Napier grew a little garden and fished, but his first love was reading. He was current on anything you wanted to talk about, he was a radical. He never threw away a piece of reading material. He had a narrow path through his house. His personal hygiene was not the best, it was hard to be cordial when he was close.

In later years he became more social, he carried the mail from Yellow Pine to Big Creek once a week. He drove an old jeep, we got out of his way when we saw him coming.

Napier had a grudge against the Forest Service. He continuously complained about them. In his complaints about the Forest Service, he made frequent contact with the law makers in Boise during the legislative session, he came nearly every day. If he couldn't see someone, he waited in the hall by the door. He sat on the floor and went to sleep. He made quite a picture sitting there with his old overalls tucked down in his wool socks and high topped tennis shoes. He had a long gray beard and long hair. People became so familiar with him being there, they walked on by not noticing. This went on until he died.

I remember one day when we lived on Logan Creek, in about 1942, we went to the store and were waiting for the mail truck.

We had heard that Napier had sent for a mail order wife, and low and behold she was on the mail truck that day. Everyone in the country was there, news travels fast even where there is no media. Napier was there with his horses and wagon.

She was a sight to behold when she stepped out of the mail truck, a pretty thing, dressed in white leather skirt and vest with white boots and hat. She had a beautiful white satin blouse with big billowing sleeves. She looked like she stepped right out of a magazine with her lovely blond curls hanging down her back. Napier's eyes nearly fell out, but so did hers when she saw Napier. He was not a pretty thing.

I actually felt sorry for both of them, with everyone standing around watching them. After the greeting they drove off in Napier's wagon. She didn't look too happy. She sat just as far over on the other side of the seat as she could get. We were spellbound, and then all of a sudden laughter broke out and those men laughed until they cried. Then we wondered which one of these guys set this up. I wondered whose picture they had sent her. She apparently didn't stay long. We heard one of the guys who was at the store that day went calling on them the next day. She left with him and was never heard from again, that I knew of.

Living on Logan Creek was not too exciting, but my dog Jim and I were great pals. We roamed around fishing and exploring old trails and cabins. My 22 pistol was always on my belt under my jacket. Target practice was one of my favorite sports. I got pretty good at it. I never let anyone know I had a gun. I didn't want them to think I was a tomboy. But there were a lot of animals there and I may need protection. With Jim it was doubtful, but I thought he may get into trouble protecting me. Mom never worried.

In my wanderings, I finally made it to the cabin we saw in construction when we came up here the first time. The fellow who lived there was Red Potter, he was a mighty fine person. I made my acquaintance and he went on working. He told me to have a seat on the chopping block. I was making the conversation as I thought with him working he may not care to talk. I was wrong, he began to tell stories, one running into another and it went on and on. I became so engrossed in the stories, I lost track of time. Red looked up and said, "Say it's going to get dark on you before you get home." I jumped down from my perch and Jim and I took off running.

I yelled back, "Good night, Red."

He yelled, "Come back again."

We ran all the way home, supper was over and I got a bit of a scolding for being out so late.

I went to Red's place quite often and watched the house come up, board by board. It was a nice little cabin when it was finished. It sat in a little meadow near the creek. As I listened to the stories, I looked around at the beautiful setting. It is still in my memory today as it was then. Red noticed that I had an eye for beauty (as he put it), "You kinda like this place don't you Rose?"

"Yes I really do, it's beautiful here, with the meadow and the creek." He shocked me with his next words.

"Well, I won't live long enough to wear this one out, so when I'm through with it, it will be yours." I thanked him, but I was very doubtful that it would ever happen. If things would have stayed the way they were then, it was feasible. We moved away and I didn't return for many years and by then it was all tied up with family, claim jumpers, etc. The thought was all that mattered anyway.

Red told me about his illness, he had rheumatoid arthritis.

By spring every year he could hardly walk because of the cold and he didn't get enough exercise. He said, "That's why I keep that old horse. As soon as I can get over the pass, I go over on the South Fork and soak in the hot springs for about a month. I camp right there and soak 16 hours a day. I wouldn't be walking if it weren't for that." I never saw Red again after we left, he died of a heart attack when he was gutting an elk. He was buried on the knoll by his house. There is a white pipe fence around his grave. We became good friends and I still miss him.

Fred packed all of our things in his truck and moved us to Boise, so we could go to school. He kept what he needed to live way back on Logan Creek. I wondered how he existed in the winter. We moved into a small one bedroom house on Washington Street not far from the capitol. Somehow we managed to get by there, it didn't take long for our money to run out and we didn't hear from Fred. Mom went to work at St. Luke's Laundry department. We skimped by somehow. Roy went to work at a service station and gave Mom some of the money.

We lived across the street from a little grocery store and I worked some there, not anything regular, but just when she needed me. I took the money to the bank, I swept the floors and occasionally I clerked. As I learned more about it, I worked more.

With what money I earned, I gave Mom most of it but I found a riding stable where I could rent a horse for 25 cents an hour or 50 cents for a half a day. I found the way to the foot hills, I rode back by the Veterans Hospital and up the hill. I felt much better about Boise. I loved riding up there and getting out by myself. I also went to a movie once in a while. The Rio and the Rialto were side by side and they both had double feature on Saturdays. It cost 10 cents for two shows, you couldn't beat that. Occasionally I rented a bicycle to ride. I loved the Depot and rode up that hill to set on the lawn and look over the city. Ed came home that fall and left right away for the Navy. Mom was in tears when he left. The war was horrid with the Japanese planes on suicide missions, and all the ground battles were just as viciously fought. Of course the Navy had to meet them on the ocean and that was just as terrifying and dreadful. The one thing that distinguished these fighters from any others was that they cared nothing for their own lives. They had specials honors in glory if they died killing another. Our country was in a state of shock, with our boys having to face such insane fighting tactics. The Japanese were ruthless, showing no mercy for anyone including themselves.

Roy was pretty restless after Ed left but he was only 15 and would have to wait two more years. With two sons over in the Pacific theater, Mom just didn't know how she was going to endure that. There were tears when she got letters and tears when she didn't. The boys weren't worried about people here and how they felt. They had to concentrate on their patriotic duty to their country, and of course we were proud of them for that. They would not have been able to do what they had to do, thinking about home and someone crying for them. So, all in all, it was a tough battle.

The day came that I dreaded the most, going to school. There were hundreds of kids. I was sick with fear. I was so shy, I didn't know how to talk to these girls, so I tried to ignore them by not looking at them. If they looked at me, I wanted to die. I was embarrassed about my clothes. They had such pretty things, I had about three outfits. I hung back trying to stay in the back ground, trying not to be conspicuous. We were required to take PE. I didn't have the gym clothes to wear, so I played ball in a dress. I got some shorts from a friend and was able to take part in tumbling. I did fine until the teacher said something to me in front of the other kids. I sulled up and wouldn't even try.

I liked sports but when everyone went in to shower, I went into a stall to dress. There were no doors on the stalls.

I washed my face and hands and combed my hair, then went to class. One day the teacher was there when I came out of the stall dressed. She told me to take a shower. The first time in my life I had ever defied anyone but I did her. "No, I will not undress in front of anyone."

She said, "You will or you will not take PE."

I repeated, "I will not undress." This was terribly embarrassing in front of the other girls. I went to my class mortified. The word got around and all the girls laughed at me wherever I saw them.

I did well in my classes after I got over a lot of the self consciousness. I was beginning to enjoy the challenge of the assignments. I finished that year and I was happy for it to be over. I walked home alone and I walked to school alone. I didn't think I was like the other girls and did not want to be around them.

A lady we had met in Kooskia, through her son who was a friend of Roy's, moved to Boise and she and Mom had kept in contact. She and Mom became good friends. I became friends with Norman, her son. He went to the same school but I never saw him there. He came to the house with Roy quite often.

We were also visiting with the boss' wife and family from Snowshoe. Her husband was still back there. He came out quite often to visit his family. Through those two contacts we got acquainted with others.

Roy was dating a girl named Bonnie Brown. She lived in the Belgravia Apartments with her family. Bonnie and I became friends and did quite a few things together. Roy still worked at the station. Bonnie was a wonderful skater and she and Roy went to the skating rink quite often. They enjoyed skating together.

Donna was happy there, her school was right across the street from our house and she made friends easily. She played at the school grounds on the swings and merry-go-round.

When school started again, my misery began again. The first day of school the principal came into the room and sat down close to me and said, "Rose we have received your records and you are not eligible to continue school until you take the seventh grade over. You did not go the required number of days to pass the seventh grade, so you were not eligible to go to the eight grade." My heart was sinking; I couldn't believe what I was hearing.

"Do you mean, I have to take the seventh and eighth grades over again?"

"Yes that is right."

"I finished all my books and I received good grades, I passed."

"I know all that but that is the rule, you have to go a certain number of days to be eligible for the next." He hesitated momentarily, I couldn't speak, I was so close to tears. He handed me a slip to take to the office and register for the seventh grade. He left the room. I picked up my personal things and walked out and went home.

I walked down the alleys, afraid the truant officers would see me and take me back to school. The school I hated, anger built up in me as I walked, I was angry at the whole system, not any one person, but everybody connected with it. A defiance was building up in me. They were wrong doing this to me. I wanted to strike back, but I didn't know how but it would happen. All of this just added to my self consciousness and my poor self-worth. I knew now I was a nobody. I must be dumb, ignorant, and yes stupid. I wanted to be educated and I wanted to do something with my life. Now what could I do; I knew of no way to fight this, I was defeated. I could see nothing in the future for myself. I began withdrawing and was sulky. I was ashamed.

Jim was tied up in the backyard by the coal shed. As I came near the shed, he came to meet me. His greeting was the most precious thing to me right then. It pierced through my anger and touched a familiar string in my heart. I reached down and hugged him. I knew he was the best friend I ever had. I went in the coal shed and sat down on a bucket. Jim came and laid down at my feet. He seemed to know how bad I felt and was very sympathetic.

I needed that. That old dirty coal shed felt good. Just Jim and me, I wanted to stay with Jim. There were no threats here. I sat there brooding, not knowing what to do, I just knew I was not going to take those two grades over.

I can't remember ever talking to Mom about it. I didn't want to put anymore on her; she was having a rough time. As far as I can remember, she never knew anything about it or why I refused to go to school.

Our home situation got worse. We got behind on the rent. We didn't know what to do. She couldn't make any more money anywhere else, so we were about to move back to Logan Creek. My stepdad was not sending any money to Mom. Annabelle Riksem was aware of our situation and asked us to move out there with them for the time being. They had a nice large home and there was room for us. We were happy to have a place to live. Mom continued to work and gave Annabelle most all of everything she made. I could see there was no future ahead for her either. We just existed from day to day.

Roy dated Bonnie until he was 17, he then joined the Navy.

He left a pregnant girlfriend at home. Her folks insisted he come home and marry her. He was not happy about that. He became bitter with Bonnie, denying the baby was his.

He went back and left for overseas duty as soon as his basic training was over. Bonnie and I became good friends and I felt like if I could do anything to make life easier for her, I would.

Roy gave Bonnie his name to save her from disgrace, but he soon met someone else and the marriage to Bonnie was dissolved. I really felt sorry for Bonnie, she loved Roy. I gave her all the support I could. I stayed with her after Gary was born for some time. I was crazy about Gary, he looked just like Roy. Bonnie stayed in her parents home until she married again. I lost track of them after a time. I didn't see Gary for several years and I thought it would be better if I left them alone to begin a new life.

Living at Annabelle's house posed another problem for me. Where could Jim and I go to hide? I couldn't see my way out of this, so I went to school. I went into the seventh grade. I got physically sick when I walked into the room. My head was swimming and I was sick to my stomach. The teacher recognized that I was sick and asked me if I wanted to leave the room. This got the kids attention again and there I was a spectacle before the whole class. I laid my head down on the desk for a while and I felt better. I wasn't going to walk out and make a bigger spectacle of myself. The whole day was misery for me.

I was tall for my age and I knew I looked much older than the other kids. When we left the room for lunch, I could see that I was a head taller then any of them.

I wasn't going back. I had to find a way to get Jim and go somewhere and hide. I went back to the coal shed the next morning. No one was living in the house and with the door shut, no one would know I was there. I took some books with me and read. On weekends I left Jim at home and went downtown.

I was fascinated with the old structures like the hotels, the old post office, the Medical Arts building, and the old theaters. Many days were spent just walking, it was quite satisfying. I couldn't get in trouble here. One day I walked around the capitol building, walked through the park and looked at all the flowers.

I walked by the old post office and across the street and by the drugstore on the corner. I stopped to look at the paintings on the windows. There were some great looking ice cream dishes. Banana splits, strawberry sundaes, and root beer floats, 10 cents, WOW!

I finally got enough courage to walk in the drugstore. I stayed pretty close to the door but I was looking around. I sized up the sweet young things behind the counter with short skirts and ruffled aprons. I looked over the counter and saw stools to sit on. I waited for awhile hoping to see someone order a root beer float so I would know how to eat it. No one did and I was beginning to feel uncomfortable, so I walked out. In the days that followed, I must have walked by there 50 times looking at the root beer float. It looked pretty simple, it was in a glass with a spoon and it looked like ice cream on the top, yes I would eat it not drink it. I finally got a dime working for Annabelle. I was ready to try it. I walked in when there were not very many people in there. I sat on the end stool. I really didn't want to be there, but oh did I want a root beer float.

The girl promptly came to take my order. I tried to say it confidently and polite and not show my ignorance. "Root beer float please." There I did it. I tried to watch her but she was out of my sight. She brought this tall glass of bubbles with ice cream on top. There was a spoon, but there was also a straw. Now what was that for.

"That will be 10 cents." I promptly laid my dime down on the counter. Looking this thing over, the spoon? I was to stir it. I picked up the spoon and began to stir briskly. I wondered why she didn't stir it. I couldn't drink it through a straw with a big lump of ice cream in it. The glass began to overflow and flow and flow all over the counter. The girl saw the mess I had made and came running up with a cloth in her hand, "Why did you do that?" The other two girls were also wiping and it was still flowing all over. Very soon I had the attention of everyone at the counter. I sat there, what could I do but drop through the floor or float out the door. I knew I couldn't move on my own. The waitress took my glass and returned with another float. "Now don't stir it." I thought about this. I decided to drink the root beer and eat the ice cream. I was an adult before I realized I was not the first one to stir a root beer float.

One evening after Mom came home from work, we were getting ready to sit down to dinner when the door bell rang. Two men in suits and a lady came in and introduced themselves as truant officers. They asked for Mrs. Erickson, Mom said, "I am Mrs. Erickson."

They asked for me, I stepped forward and said, "I am Rose."

Mom began trembling and said, "What have you done?" I didn't answer, just looked at the officers. I was so ashamed.

I couldn't have felt any lower; right then and for the next year. Not once did I try to explain or defend myself. I saw myself as they were accusing me. A law breaker, a delinquent, a criminal.

I waited for them to tell Mom what I had done. I couldn't look at her. The reflection made me feel lower yet. At Mom's response, I was reduced to an absolute nothing. She said, "Well, I can't do a thing with her." I was shocked at her response. I couldn't believe this.

They asked, "Mrs. Erickson would you like for us to take her into custody until we can decide what to do with her?"

I looked at Mom, my heart was breaking. She said, "Yes." I couldn't take my eyes off her. I didn't know she felt this way about me.

The officers said, "Get your coat Rose." I got my coat and looked around at Donna and walked out the door.

They took me to jail, shut the door and locked it. I stood there, I was in such a state of mind, I really wasn't aware of anything. I was in a stupor. Someone said to me, "Come over and set down." I looked around and saw three women, much older than I. I went over to the table and sat down on the bench. One of the women tried to make conversation but I wouldn't answer, I just lowered my head. I sat like that until the lights went out and I laid down on a bunk. I didn't close my eyes all night. I got up several times and sat at the table.

I was so ashamed to be here. I had never considered myself to be a bad person, but there was a lot of people who thought I was. So maybe I was. My self esteem went lower with every minute I was there. One of the ladies was still trying to make conversation. She sat down beside me and said, "Don't take it so hard, it won't last very long. You know you remind me of Veronica Lake, your hair is so pretty and it waves down your face just like hers."

I raised my eyes to meet hers and said, "Thank you."

Her words had quite an effect on me. One of the very few compliments I had as a girl and it did lift my spirits a little.

I was there for three days. Three days of my shame pouring out on the inside of me. The lady truant officer came to see me.

She said Mom had brought my clothes and she was going to put me on the bus for Cascade and I was to catch the mail stage to Stibnite to stay with Aunt Clara. I could help take care of her family as she was going to have surgery in the Stibnite hospital. I knew I didn't have a choice. I would be a prisoner for the rest of the winter. It was so hard to leave Jim, but I knew Donna would take care of him. I would like to have had him with me. He always had a way of lifting my spirits.

I sat looking out the window of the bus, trying to sort everything out in my mind. The one thing that kept coming back to me was why had Mom done this. She shouldn't have said "I can't do a thing with her." that wasn't true. I had never disobeyed her. Why didn't she tell them I had never been in any trouble of any kind; that I had always helped her. I never even spoke sharp to her but I had always tried to take care of her. I never complained. I got good grades in school and I did most of Roy's homework. I did these things because we were told when we were kids that kids were to be seen and not heard. In other words we never had a choice, we did what we were told to do.

I knew Mom had a very low tolerance to anything controversial. She had a hard time dealing with everyday problems. It was like she ran from the adversary to take the quickest and easiest way out. It was terribly hard for her to forgive or forget. If I missed washing a frying pan after dinner, it would get me weeks of punishing by ignoring me completely.

My childhood suffered most from lack of communication. I didn't know how to express myself because we never did that. I knew Mom had hard times. I believe she suffered because she couldn't talk about her problems. Therefore, the suffering went on down the line to everyone in the home. I'm also sure she did the best she could under the circumstances. Her whole life was passionately devoted to making a living for us kids. That seemed to always be under the most difficult and complicated circumstances. She could not allow anything to interrupt her course because that was the most important thing in her life.

If one of us kids had a problem where we needed her, during a particular bad time for her, she took the quickest way out. And that was not always the best for us. A little encouragement, a kind word, some support, or even discussing the problem would have been so much better for us but that didn't happen. She shot us down. I don't know how she felt after having done this. Did she suffer or did she block it out of her mind? I think she was scarred as a child and never healed.

I loved my Mom dearly and I truly believe I accepted her the way she was, forgiving her whenever I was hurt by her. It did hurt terribly when she turned away from me. I felt this was her problem that caused her to do this to us kids.

I'm sure mothers have problems with one or another weakness. There is not a *perfect* mother!!!

Chapter 4
"All Things Work Together....."

1942

My trip into Stibnite was uneventful and boring, probably due to my state of mind. I ached inside thinking of what Mom said to the truant officer. As the bus pulled up to the recreation building, my cousin Budge was there to meet me. Budge (as we called him) always had a big smile to go along with his happy visage. He, like Aunt Clara, always seemed to lift my spirits.

Aunt Clara was the same old happy go lucky person as before. She was glad to see me and that made me feel even better. Aunt Clara could do that, she was happy go lucky and never took anything serious. No worries, just living from day to day. After my experience of recent times, it was good for me to be with her. Her three older girls were married so that left five kids home, Aunt Clara, Uncle Kirk and myself. There were eight of us in a little box car cabin with three small rooms. The cabin was shaped like a box car, and it was on skids so it could be moved. It was temporary housing until other houses were available.

The company had a hard time keeping up with the housing demand. They were running full bore as the government demanded.

Stibnite began operation in 1927 when the Bradley Mining Company was formed. With the invasion of Poland by Hitler, and the U.S. Bureau of Mines' decision to augment the nation's strategic mineral reserves, antimony and tungsten became the chief minerals produced in this area.

Stibnite's antimony and tungsten were strategic metals needed in the war. Stibnite produced nearly 95% of the country's antimony supply. These elements were in alloys to produce armor-piercing shells, filaments in lamps, x-ray tubes, and radar equipment.

Stibnite soon became a boom town of nearly 1000 people, with a school house, stores, hospital, over 200 homes, and a recreation hall. Stibnite had a major milling facility, but after the war, the tungsten was gone. Bradley continued to mill low grade gold and gold-antimony ore. Smelter problems plagued the operation and the antimony market collapsed. By 1955, the plant was dismantled and moved to Riddle, Oregon. Most of the houses were moved out to Yellow Pine, Cascade, and McCall.

Aunt Clara didn't question me about my problems. I didn't know if Mom told her in the letter. I doubted that because she seemed to assume that I came up to help her when she had surgery. That was the way of our family. We just didn't ask. If someone wanted to tell something about themselves fine, but we never delved into someone else's affairs.

Life was easy there and the cooking was simple, pancakes every morning. Throughout the rest of the day, everyday, we had biscuits, gravy, potatoes, beans, and homemade bread. We had an egg once in a while, no vegetables, very little meat.

There was one bedroom with a double bed for the adults and a small bed for the youngest kids. That left three of us to sleep in the bed. Budge slept on the floor. There was a table and a few chairs in the front room and a big heating stove. The kitchen had some makeshift cupboards, a stove, a bench for the water bucket, and a wash pan. That was all that was needed. The girls helped with the dishes after supper.

I usually walked up to get the mail when it came in once a week. Stibnite was cold, very cold. It belonged in Siberia. There were times I didn't think I was going to make it home. The wind blew all the time out in the open where the landing strip was, and over the roads going every direction from mine to mills and smelters. It got 50 below sometimes and stayed that way for days. I had the better boots and coat, so I did those chores. It was a couple of miles up to the store.

Summers were beautiful there. The elevation was probably 7-8,000 feet. There were so many beautiful wild flowers, especially wild roses. The air was so pure and clean, when you could get out of the dust from the trucks running back and forth.

Aunt Clara's operation went well. She rallied quickly and was soon home and in full recovery. It was nice being with her, she was the complete opposite of my mother. For the short time I was there it was good, and I needed that.

I couldn't have existed there much longer. The crowded conditions were getting to me and it seemed that their poverty was a condition brought on by themselves. They had as much money as anyone else, but preferred to spend it on something other than food and clothes for the kids. This bothered me a lot. It wasn't like my home.

Budge, or Donald, Aunt Clara's boy, was my age and was the oldest child there. I had always liked him. He was a good kid. He had been beaten so badly as a small child he was retarded. Mentally he did not progress after about 10 years old. He didn't learn to read or write, and finally the schools gave up. He was so kind and sweet to everyone. He had a great sense of humor, he loved laughing at himself. When Budge got older he did develop mentally to some degree. He got married and had three beautiful daughters and one son. He made a living for the family and kept them in a decent home. Most of the other kids in the family are quite successful.

I stayed there until Donna was out of school in the spring, when Mom moved to Yellow Pine to operate a restaurant. I joined them to help out. The only welcome I got was from Donna and Jim, they were glad to see me. I was happy to see them. Mom treated me very coolly but I ignored it . She eventually got over it.

We lived in a one room tourist cabin not far from the restaurant. Yellow Pine was a busy place then with the mass production of ore at Stibnite. Ore trucks were on the road 24 hours a day. We opened at 5 a.m. and closed at 10 p.m. It was too much work for just the two of us.

Mom contacted Aunt Clara to come down and help in the restaurant. They made a hasty move into an old log house south of town. Kirk went back and forth to work at Stibnite. He rode with someone else who worked up there and lived in Yellow Pine.

Between the three of us working we made out fine. We had more business than we could handle, but we got by.

Jim followed Donna around when I was busy. Gradually he became less active and laid by the back door waiting for me to come out. I didn't have much time for him, and I was sorry for him. One day I noticed a swelling on his neck, it grew fast. It was soon so large it was hard for him to carry it around. I was afraid I was going to lose him. There was nothing I could do for him.

I walked down to Aunt Clara's house one day and he followed me, when I got ready to go I called and called, but he didn't come. I walked around searching for him and the other kids looked for him too. Every day

I went out and called and walked around looking for him. I finally found him laying under a bush in a swampy spot, where he had apparently found a place to lay to cool his fever, since he had been gone for two days. I expected this, but that didn't help the pain I felt in losing him. My first dog and he was so loyal to me, I loved old Jim, I cried and cried. I missed him terribly, I felt lost without a dog at my side. I was a long time getting over the loneliness from not having him at my side.

That summer a family moved out of Stibnite and left their dog behind in Yellow Pine. He was a mean and vicious animal.

Mart Earl, owner of the restaurant and bar, put him in a back room in the storage room back of the bar. He couldn't leave him loose. I suppose he intended to shoot him because no one could get close to him. When he was with his family he was fine. He was half Chow and half German Shepherd. His name was Kubi. He was a beautiful dog, but he wouldn't let anyone in the door to feed him. I believe he had been abused and locked up a lot of the time. Mart and Bonnie were going to starve him out, they thought if he got hungry enough he would let someone in to feed him.

I couldn't stay away from him. I went to the door and opened it a crack and talked to him several times a day. At first he lunged at the door, growling and barking. I opened the door a little more every day, until he quit growling and barking at me. I finally decided I would feed him and give him some water. With the food and water in my hands I went to the door and began talking to him. I opened the door wider and continued to talk, He was doing okay, so I pushed the door open enough to get the pans through the door and coaxed him to come and eat. When he saw the food bowl he picked up his ears and looked very interested. He got up and ate when I sat the food down, and he drank water. The next time I went to the door he wagged his tail, so I opened the door. I fed him every day and spent more time with him each day. I slowly began to pet him on the back while I was talking to him. One day I snapped a leash on his collar. The street was fairly empty that day so I took him out. I picked up the leash and opened the door, I told him to come. He got so excited, but he was still dubious about coming through the door.

When we got out on the street he tore loose from me and took off running up the street. He was heading for Stibnite, I called and called to him to come back. When he went around the corner, I thought I would never see him again. After a while here he came trotting back to me and walked at my side, he never left me again. We became friends. He was a fine companion, however he was a one man dog and he was my dog.

Bonnie Earl asked me if I could stay with her kids evenings and nights when I wasn't working. I was happy to earn some money and I liked the kids. Besides that, I could have Kubi with me.

Bonnie raised Chows and sold them so she was very fond of Kubi and understood the Chow nature.

One night we were all in bed, the lights were out I was just drifting off to sleep when I heard the window in the kitchen slide open. Kubi heard it too, and he jumped up on the counter. The intruder saw him coming, and backed off, and ran towards the gate. Kubi couldn't get through the window so I called him to the front door, and when Kubi hit the gate, the man was closing it. Kubi was crazy to get out, but I was afraid of what he would do. I did not recognize the man.

I was walking Kubi on a leash a few days later when a man came around the corner of the building. Kubi barked once and went after the man. I held him back and yelled "No," to him. He didn't get to the man but he sure wanted to. The man ran down the street and Kubi didn't let up until the man was out of sight.

I recognized the man to be a local family man. I immediately thought about the man who tried to come through the window. Bonnie stepped outside then and said, "Kubi found the intruder."

I kept Kubi locked up inside the fence unless I took him out for a walk on a leash. One afternoon, he didn't act like he felt very good. He was moping along slower than usual. Suddenly, he coughed and blood came up. He was in agony. I sat down on the ground beside him. Several people had gathered around as he had become quite popular. He loved kids and played with them inside the fence. Adults walking by stopped to talk to him and pet him. He was a different dog than when I got him.

People were squeezed into a tight circle around me and the dog. He vomited more and more blood and he was hurting bad. He looked up at me and whined. I pulled him up on my lap and wrapped my arms around him. I cried as I talked to him, I knew he was dying. Blood was running out his mouth and was all over me but I didn't care. I was hoping I could comfort him to some degree. I couldn't do anything else for him.

The people were murmuring something about being fed broken glass. He was getting very weak, so weak he couldn't cough. Blood was coming from his nose and mouth, his eyes were on me. When I talked to him he cried a low kind of whimper. He became weaker by the second, until he closed his eyes. He was gone. I sat there holding him. I didn't want to let him go. My heart was breaking.

A couple of men came and took him from me and said they would bury him. I let him go reluctantly, but I didn't want to get up, I was remembering how lonely I was when Jim died.

Bonnie came and took my hand, "Come on kid and take a shower, get cleaned up and you will feel better." I followed her to her apartment. Donna brought me some clean clothes. I showered, but I couldn't wash away the hurt.

Bonnie was sitting on the couch when I came out of the shower. "Say kid, I think your Kubi is the daddy to some puppies we are expecting in a couple of weeks. You can have the pick of the litter." I was so thrilled I ran over and gave her a hug. I could hardly wait. Two weeks seemed forever. One day Bonnie sent for me. I ran up the street to the house and into the garage in the back to see the pups. I just knew one was going to look like Kubi. I looked and looked for a resemblance. The only one that didn't look like the others was a chocolate pup, he even had chocolate eyes, chocolate feet, everything on him was chocolate. He was bigger than the others and longer legged. I held him and looked him over and said to myself, this little guy is going to be all right. I named him Kubi. I could hardly wait to take him home, I went to see him every day and held him. By the time I did take him home, he knew who he belonged to.

Bonnie took in a young girl who was in trouble and she stayed with the kids part of the time. We traded off, until she got farther along and then I helped her with the work.

I was a little nervous about taking little Kubi home because he had been sleeping with me to keep him quiet. I didn't think Mom would put up with that since we all three slept in one bed. When she worked long hard hours, she wasn't very tolerant with such things.

I made him a nice warm bed in a box and hoped he would sleep all night. As soon as the lights were out he began to cry. After a little of that Mom said, "I have to get some sleep if I'm going to work tomorrow." I waited. "Get up and get that pup and put him in bed on your side." He went right to sleep.

In the wee hours of the morning Mom sat up in bed and screamed at me, "Your dog wet on my hair!"

"Oh no!!" I jumped out of bed with Kubi in my arms. "What do you want me to do?"

"Well, you can start by building the fire, carry in a couple dish pans of water and heat them so I can wash my hair. Then you can change the bed and tomorrow you can find another place to sleep with that dog." Oh boy, I was in trouble this time.

The next day I put a cot in the storage room behind the cafe and Kubi and I moved. I boarded up the doors so he couldn't get into the cafe or outside. He sat in there, he cried, he howled, he barked. I didn't know what to do, I was about to give up.

Bonnie came to the rescue again. She said I could put him in the garage during the day with the others and go get him in the evening when I finished working. That worked out better for everyone.

Kubi grew up to be a fine dog. He was a good family dog. He knew all the family by smell and bonded to each one. In years to come he could live with anyone of the family and be perfectly content. He never made friends with anyone outside the family. He was a good watch dog, but he never bit anyone. He warned them, and they would stop in their tracks until someone came out, then he would just walk away. He was a playmate, a protector, and a loyal friend. He lived a long and happy life. He was 15 years old when he died. We mourned his passing like a member of the family.

─────────────

My stepfather, Fred, was still on Logan Creek as far as we knew. We hadn't heard from him since he left us in Boise. Mom wrote him once to ask for money. He didn't send any money or answer the letter. She assumed it was all over for them, but we were making enough money to live on, and Mom was feeling better being out from under the stress. I was glad he didn't come back.

One of our regulars customers who worked at Cinnabar began to notice Mom. Clyde Osborn was his name. He talked to Mom a lot and sometimes after the cafe closed they sat in there and talked.

He was such a nice fellow, soft spoken, gentle and friendly to everyone. He was a handsome man with his hat cocked to one side. He dressed in fine western gabardine clothes that were made to fit. He was a gambler and he drank quite a bit. Mom was very leery of that, but you couldn't help but like him. He was one in a million.

He and his family owned the largest sheep ranch in the state of Oregon at one time. After his father died, his wild bunch of brothers began partying and took Clyde's wife to town with them when Clyde spent most of his time out in the hills with the sheep. Clyde came in off the range late one fall, and soon learned the family had gambled and partied them into debt. His wife had been running around on him all summer and she wanted a divorce. She got the divorce and Clyde left the area. He had three children, two daughters and one son, whom he would come back to see quite often and then leave again.

He was accustomed to living with plenty of money, a nice home, a big ranch and all the finer things of life. It was quite a transition for him to adjust to having nothing. He did not adjust. He became defeated. He started drinking and gambling. He went to work in mining camps where there were big poker games every night. He had hopes of gaining back some of his wealth. He did become quite prosperous and that was about the time he came into out lives.

During our dinner rush hour one evening, Clyde was sitting at the counter eating. My stepfather Fred burst through the door. Obviously he had been drinking. I think everyone saw him but Clyde, he was sitting with his back to the door. Fred came up behind him, grabbed him by the back of the shirt, jerked him off the stool, and hit him with a terrific blow in the face. Blood spurted from his mouth and nose. Fred continued to pound him while Clyde was staggering around trying to get his balance.

Someone came up from behind Fred and said, "Give him a chance Fred and let him get to his feet." Fred stepped back. Clyde was stunned and after getting his balance and blinking his eyes, he looked up to see the face of the man who was smashing him. After getting his eyes focused, he went at Fred with both fists flying. He was fast and he could get around on his feet. Fred was also fast, both men were built about the same, slender and strong—pretty well matched. People were scattering out of the cafe every which way. They fought covering every inch of the floor and began breaking up furniture. Tables and chairs were crashing. Mart Earl came in and broke it up. Both men backed off, neither saying a word. Clyde didn't know who he was. Clyde went back to the counter and asked for a cup of coffee.

I was shaking like a leaf. I had been standing in the doorway watching, Mom standing beside me. I had heard her yelling at Fred, and several times she had started to go out there, but someone had pulled her back.

I served his coffee and spilled it all over the counter. Fred was standing there looking at Clyde, puffing like a mad bull. He certainly lost all of his dignity then.

Fred walked into the kitchen, grabbed Mom by the arm and jerked her through the dining room. Mom was crying "Don't Fred! Please don't! Let me go!"

Over and over again those frantic words I heard as I ran after them screaming at him, "Fred leave her alone!" He began kicking her. She fell down and was trying to get up, he'd kick her again. "Fred stop! You are hurting me," she screamed on the verge of hysteria. I wanted so much to make him stop. I ran up to him and for the first time in my life I asked him for something. "Please stop kicking and beating my mother and let her go." He ignored me.

Mom screamed at me, "Get back Rose he will do the same to you." I couldn't get back, there was no one to help Mom.

Somewhere, over all the screaming and cursing, I heard Donna. She was crying, "Don't hurt Mom, please don't hurt her."

I looked back and she was running down the street after us. I stopped and waited for her.

Fred continued to hit her and kick her. Donna and I were coming up on them again, we were both pleading for him to quit. Mom called over her shoulder, "Girls get back, stay back—Oh God—please help me." Fred was shoving her down the road and kicking her. When she would slow down or fall, he'd jerk her up on to her feet and shove and kick her again.

Donna and I did keep a distance from them as it seemed that it would incite him to more violence when we were begging him to quit. We wanted to stay close to Mom. He was letting up on her, after walking and walking, and we got closer to the mill camp. He was behind her and pushed her in the direction he wanted her to go. We all walked into the house, a house he had been living in and working at the mill.

Fred pushed Mom into the bedroom and onto the bed. She lay there sobbing. Fred walked into the kitchen where Donna and I were sitting. He said to me in a snarling voice, "Where is that pistol of yours?" I wasn't going to tell him. I just looked at him. I felt frozen inside, I was so frightened. He said, "I'm not going to hurt anyone, I just don't want that pistol around. Get rid of it. I never want to see it again." He told me more about himself right then, than ever I could have guessed.

We gradually moved our belongings down from the cabin and cafe. It was a much nicer place to stay. I continued to work for Bonnie so I stayed in town two or three nights a week to take care of the kids. I either stayed with Aunt Clara or went to the camp. Kubi walked with me back and forth to town. He was a lot of comfort to all of us. He loved Donna. They played and were great buddies.

Mom quit the cafe and closed it down. She was so embarrassed by what had happened she wouldn't go to town for a long time. She was more or less a prisoner in Fred's house.

Aunt Clara talked to me one day about the fracas. She said, "I knew it was going to happen."

"How did you know?"

She proceeded to tell me that Fred had been coming to see her since he went to work at the mill. He would bring beer and they drank together. He told her not to tell Mom. She also said she told him that Clyde had been coming around and talked to Mom a lot, and she thought Clyde really liked Mom.

I began scolding her, "Aunt Clara you were the cause of Mom getting beat up and Clyde too. You had no reason to say that."

"I know that now. I thought of that when I saw what he did. But he told me their marriage was over. I believed him and thought that was why he was coming to see me. I just drank too much that day and talked too much."

"Aunt Clara, how could you do this, and what about Kirk?"

"Oh he knows, he doesn't come home much anymore."

"I can't believe you did this to your sister." I was so hurt about her disloyalty to Mom. I lost respect for her right then, but as time went by I forgave her and loved her anyway.

"I have always liked Fred and he liked me, I knew he wanted me." Aunt Clara was not pretty, she never took care of herself or tried to fix herself up. I suppose she was flattered.

She often told things about Mom that were not true. I always felt like it was to make herself look better. She was jealous of her. Mom was a very pretty woman and was good at everything she did. She had a lot of pride and it showed. She had a lot of emotional problems, but I figured she never had a chance to get well having to live the way she did and work like she did.

Clyde disappeared. He never came back there, but we did hear from him again on down the line.

That fall Mom moved to Boise again. When she left, she told Fred she wanted a divorce. Aunt Clara went to court with her and testified what Fred had done with her and what he had done to Mom. The judge granted the divorce.

Mom may be able to support Donna and herself, but I knew she couldn't support me. There was no chance of me getting back in school. As bad as I hated Boise schools, I wanted to go to school more, and I would have, but I had to work. I went to work in the Troy laundry with Mom. Donna went to school.

Mom began to go out on Saturday nights with some couples and single friends. They all loved to dance, for the Scandinavians, dancing was a very important part of their life. Donna and I would like to have gone as we always had, when there was dancing.

This was different though, there was drinking in the group. And though I never saw Mom drink, I thought she probably did. This went on most of the winter. At a dance one night she met a fellow she had known in Yellow Pine. He worked at Stibnite. He invited himself to stay with the party and danced mostly with Mom. Mom's only interest was in dancing with him and he was an excellent dancer. They cleared the floor many times for them, and played songs especially for them that they danced well to.

Sandy began calling on Mom at home. She tried to discourage him from anything other than dancing. He would not be discouraged. He became more and more possessive and would not give up. He began to show violence. Mom was afraid of him—and she didn't know what to do.

In the meantime Donna heard from her dad. He had rented a small apartment about a block from our apartment. Mom was disgusted about him being there, wondering what he was planning.

One evening Sandy came to our apartment drunk. He began immediately hitting Mom and threatening her. He also had a gun. Mom turned to Donna and said, "Get your Dad." I don't think Sandy heard her. Fred stormed up those stairs like a bull, jumping three steps at a time, I saw a rifle in his hand when he got to the top of the stairs. Fred was cursing him, Sandy was afraid and began backing toward the stairs. Fred ran after him and was swinging his fist at him. He never laid down his rifle. Sandy ran across the street and up the alley, by Fred's apartment. Fred fired a shot but didn't hit him. After that, we lived in fear all the time, and Fred sat in a chair by his window with the rifle beside him. We were afraid to be alone. Fred began spending more time here than at his home. He and Mom got married again. Mom continued to work supporting Fred and Donna. I went to stay with Aunt Clara who was now living in Cascade. I didn't stay there long as Mom opened the restaurant in Yellow Pine when Donna got out of school for the summer. Mom couldn't make enough money in Boise to keep her going year around and this was the only way she could get by.

Fred went his own way again. We didn't know where he was for sure. We thought he was probably at Logan Creek, working his claims. I think they both realized this marriage was one of convenience and it seemed to disintegrate as they went their own ways. A divorce came quickly.

Donna started to school in Yellow Pine that fall. I was excited hoping I could take correspondence. Mrs. Blackburn helped me work out a schedule where I could take my studies home, and she would check my work. She coached and encouraged me, but it didn't work out as well as I had hoped. There was not enough time or a place where I could study.

I was quite a bit older than, or at least I felt older than the other kids, but I joined them for ball games and play quite often. We sometimes went hiking or fishing. In the winter time, playing poker and blackjack around the kitchen table was very popular with the kids. We played with beans, or match sticks.

There was a lot of gambling in Yellow Pine so playing those games came natural to the kids. It was not unusual for kids to go into the bars during the day, that is where some parents were. The Earls liked kids, and would sometimes call all the kids in to have a pop. Kids would line up to the bar and fill every stool to drink their pop.

During the day, if an order came from the bar, I took the food in and thought nothing of it. There was a huge big stove made from two 55 gallon drums near the back door. Kids clamored into the back room around that stove after playing outside in the winter.

I can certainly see how being around the bar, seeing the gambling could influence and draw a kid into a life style of hard living. Thank God we were not there very long.

Mom approached me one day with fire in her eyes saying, "Aunt Clara said she saw you smoking."

"I did try to smoke one day but I don't like to smoke."

"Oh yes, you don't want to smoke in front of me but you will do it behind my back. If you are going to smoke you ARE going to do it in front of me." I think Mom was angry because Aunt Clara told her, as she did seem to like to find something wrong and rub it in like, "See your kids aren't so good either." Mom took a cigarette and gave me one.

I said, "No Mom, I don't want to smoke. I won't do it anymore."

She insisted, "Take one, I want to see you smoke." She lit it and stood and watched me while I tried to smoke. I really didn't know how. I had been around it long enough, but it wasn't as easy as it looked. I choked and coughed, I was so humiliated. After two or three puffs I became so sick. She made me take another cigarette, I really got sick, I didn't ever want to smoke. Instead of her teaching me not to smoke she taught me how. She made me take one every time she took one, which was never in public, because she didn't smoke in public. In time I was no longer sick from it, but I hated it, especially in front of her. I think Mom was so angry, she wasn't making any sense. I had seen Aunt Clara push Mom's buttons a lot like that.

Mom was a good woman despite some of the odd things she did. I believe it was in the way she was raised. She often told of her mother saying, "Don't tell my daughter she is pretty, it will ruin her and she will go to the devil." Even though she didn't approve of what her mother did, she did the same to me. She was different with the boys, if they did something wrong it didn't make them bad. Only girls could be bad. She was no doubt made to feel bad when she did something wrong and was never forgiven by her mother.

Mom hurt me a great deal and that could have had some far reaching effects if I had allowed that to happen. It did take my self-esteem down to rock bottom, but God gave me to her to raise so it must have been in His over all plan for my life. I am who I am because of it. I have always loved my mother dearly. I could not ever be angry with her or resent her. I knew how much of herself she gave for us kids. And maybe at times it seemed like not quite enough, but she gave all she had to give.

Mom bought a restaurant in Cascade. It had been a drive-in called the "Covy." It was a cute little place, on the outskirts of town, at the south end. It would be in the center of town today. It had been closed for awhile so she built it up from scratch and had a real good business. It didn't take long for word to get around about the wonderful meals she put out. We fed all the mill crew at lunch and most of the working people. We became so busy that we didn't have room for all our customers. The two of us ran the place until Aunt Clara came to work. Mom hired her to cook so she could have some time off.

We had a soda fountain and a jukebox. Those brought the kids in the evening. They pushed back the tables and danced. It was a very popular place with the kids, but they didn't bring much money in and it did take a lot of work hours. We also hired some help for the front. Wages and big meals brought an unprofitable business. We were making a living and that was about all.

One night Mom woke me up in the middle of the night to take her to the hospital. She had a terrible headache, she couldn't stand to open her eyes or barely move. I dressed quickly and drove the car up to the door of the house. It was terrible getting her in the car, she didn't talk and I had to move her legs, arms and body to work her body slowly into the car. I could see her cheeks were wet and I realized she was crying but not making a sound.

When I got her to the hospital, I ran in to get help to bring her in. They brought out a wheel chair and pushed her inside. She was in a room close to the nurses desk.

This was the beginning of migraine headaches for her. They didn't have a positive diagnosis for some time. They thought she had meningitis and therefore was limited to how to treat the headache. She suffered terribly for days. She was taken to the valley for tests, the poor thing, the trip was so hard on her.

One evening when I was visiting her, she didn't know I was there.

I was so frightened when she began hallucinating, I had never seen anything like this. I got up from my chair and stood at the end of the bed. She asked me to get the little people off the end of her bed, they made her head hurt. I really thought she was going crazy. I began to cry. When the nurse came in she said not to worry, people did this sometimes when they were in a lot of pain, or it could be the medication they had given her. They had just started the medication so this could be a reaction to it. I was not comforted by the explanation.

I left the hospital walking home. I couldn't get that off my mind. I was beyond crying and near hysteria when I looked up to find God. I didn't see Him, but I began to pray. I didn't know how but I said "Please God, take her pain away, and give it to me if you have to, but take it away from her, she is going crazy from this pain." I yelled out to Him, "Please God Please."

My crying stopped and my pain went with it, I had peace from God. Somehow I knew God had heard my prayer.

I could hardly wait till morning to go see her. I ran up there and ran into her room. She looked terrible, so pale and weak, but she recognized me, "Hello Rose." I ran over to her and barely pressed my lips to her forehead.

"Oh Mom, I am so glad you are better." At that time I wondered if God was going to give it to me. I felt fine now.

Mom was in the hospital for a few days until she got some strength. In the meantime Aunt Clara was trying to keep the cafe open but it was too much for her. Mom told me to close it and put a sign on the door.

When Mom came home, seeing how she looked and felt and how weak she was, I felt the need to talk to God and tell Him I really meant what I said, "Please don't give it to her again, give it to me. I didn't know what I was going to do with it, but I couldn't stand to see her suffer like that.

———

Mom received a letter, one she was happy to get. It was from Clyde, he was working at Deadwood. He wanted to know if he could see her, if he came to town. Mom wrote back and soon he was there knocking on the door. We were all very glad to see him. It wasn't long until he and Mom got married. He called his daughter in Oregon to come up and go to Nevada with them to get married.

Clyde was a good man. He had good morals, very respectable, and honored by everyone who knew him. He was a few notches above the average guy. Clyde and I were the best of friends, and I think that strengthened my relationship with Mom, but she was happy and that made a difference. She had someone who wanted to take care of her, someone who loved and respected her. It made a better person of her. The four of us moved to Deadwood. Kubi went along and was welcome in Clyde's home too.

I was rather lonely there after being in Cascade, being in the cafe I lost some of my shyness. I wasn't lonely long. The boss asked Clyde if I could come to work at the cookhouse. I was glad to have something to do. I was at work the next morning setting tables and fixing lunches. We served breakfast to 50 men. They ran three shifts in the mine so it seemed like we were serving meals all day. There were 3 people working in the dining room. I made good money and had no place to spend it there, so I sent it all out to the bank in Cascade.

When Clyde got off work he stopped in to see how things were going and have a cup of coffee and a cookie. It was pretty nice to have someone looking after me and caring enough to come in to see me. I was beginning to feel like I really had a dad.

Clyde was a private contractor in the mine, and he made good money. He didn't gamble anymore after he and Mom were married.

The drinking stopped until he went to town, then one drink and he couldn't stop. Mom tried to stop him but it only made it worse, so she gave up. It really bothered her though she wasn't happy about that. Time took care of that problem, he went to town less and less and finally he gave it all up.

I will never forget the time when we went to Cascade from Deadwood. Mom had some shopping to do and Clyde went in to have just one drink. She didn't get him out of there until he couldn't stand up anymore. We had to drive back to Deadwood and it was getting late. Mom got him in the car and she said to me, "You drive Rose."

I was shocked. I had never driven those roads, in the winter, I had hardly driven anyplace. I was glad Mom didn't want to drive, she was a terrible driver. I weighed the situation for a few seconds and decided I was probably the best choice right now. I got behind the wheel of the old Model A coupe and sat there looking things over wondering how to do this.

"Mom I have never shifted down going up a hill, I don't know how."

She very confidently replied, "You'll figure it out."

Clyde was in the middle, asleep, laying his head on Mom's shoulder. I was trembling when I turned the key and stepped on the starter. I was so unsure of what to do next. I took hold of the gear shift and put it in low gear, I let out the clutch slowly and it took off a little fast, but it was going. I was a little surprised, my foot was shaking so bad I could hardly hold it on the clutch. I looked over at Mom as she sat there looking straight ahead waiting for me to go. Not a bit apprehensive about me driving. She had all the faith in the world resting on me at that moment. I sat looking at her for awhile and thought this woman never ceases to amaze me.

I would do my best, I can't let her down. She didn't even notice the first time I shifted down. It was smooth, no jerks, the motor didn't die, I was relieved, I thought I could make it now.

It got dark very soon after we left. Oh boy, I had never driven after dark. I did find the light switch and turned them on I was becoming more confident all the time, maybe I knew more than I thought I did. Then a horrifying thought came to mind. The hill—Warm Lake hill was ahead. I couldn't do this, that hill scared everyone. It was so steep and so narrow and the roads were icy and the bank over the side was way-y-y-y down and a lot of wrecks had happened there. Oh Man, I might just have to stop and tell Mom I was scared and I couldn't do it. I glanced over at her, she was still looking straight ahead. She wasn't worried. I knew I had to do it. I drove slow, kept it in a low gear and kept going. I was putting miles behind us. We finally made it to Warm Lake hill. I drove up and up and near the top, we went around a sharp corner and there were lights so bright they blinded me. I felt like I was going over the edge but I got the car stopped. I thought it might be a big ore truck from Stibnite. I knew I'd have to get off the road so he could pass but I couldn't see a thing. I wasn't about to go over toward the edge where it dropped off hundreds of feet. I turned the other way and started up the bank. I felt like we were tipping over but the deep snow stopped us. Whatever was happening with that big thing with bright lights I didn't know but snow was flying everywhere. What was he doing? Then I heard Mom say, "Clyde wake up, wake up there is a big rotary snowplow in the middle of the road."

He raised his head and looked out and said, "Let 'er come." He laid his head down again and went back to sleep.

The lights on the rotary dimmed and everything stopped.

When the rotary and the snow blowers stopped it was a little less terrifying. A couple of guys came around to talk to us, then guided me out of the snow bank and showed me where I could get around them on the OUTSIDE. I knew it wasn't wide enough but they were guiding me through. They were still on the road but I felt like every inch I moved I could feel the car sliding over the edge. Finally the guy yelled "You can go on, you're okay now." There was a nice wide snow packed road ahead of us when we got to where we could see. Whew!!!! I could breathe now.

I was very pleased with the confidence Mom had in me. I was not so self confident. We sailed along with no problems the rest of the way. We arrived home late.

Chapter 5

"Deadwood"

1944

Deadwood was a mining camp located near Landmark, on the Deadwood River. The elevation is high enough to see the full force of winter in the mountains, probably 7 or 8,000 feet. It is hard to imagine the hardships in such a country as this, from the extreme cold to the mountains of snow. It is a beautiful place until it snows, and then you'd be lucky to find your house. The snow was eight feet deep the first winter and from what I gathered from the seasoned ones that was not unusual. We were 26 miles from Landmark.

We had to dig down into the snow to get in and out of our house, making a tunnel, which was hazardous without steps being chopped into the ice. We also had to shovel the snow away from the windows to get any light during the day. The snow was up to the peak of the house and when flying over the only visible sign of a village were the stove pipes sticking out of the snow.

The roads around camp were trails in the winter. It was impossible to keep them clear of snow. The cars were parked for the winter. You couldn't start them and if you could, there was no place to go. The roads were kept open from the mill out to the Johnson Creek road at Landmark to take ore out. After so long a time the snow became too much for the equipment to remove and they were left to snow in and were opened in the spring.

Walking down the roads between the houses, you could look over the top of the houses. The houses were set in the timber on a hillside, there was a lot of wild shrubbery and brush. Down below camp was a big flat that extended for several miles to the lake. Those big Yellow Pines stood tall on each side of the dirt road, which was the only evidence that any man had ever been there. Nothing disturbed the scenery of the beautiful valley. You couldn't find a more beautiful place in the summer time. It was so green, and the area was like driving through a park. The creeks were crystal clear meandering down through the trees. The air was just as pure as the water. The heavy snow fall brought the lush greenery which added to the beauty of the high country.

Even though the effects of time has all but eliminated any sign of the camp, the beauty is still evident where ever you look. The hottest days of summer are cool and crisp in Deadwood. Deadwood camp was one of the better mining camps in the country. There were about 20-25 cabins, all modern with bathrooms.

The cabins were built well and were insulated. One cook stove in the kitchen and a heating stove in the other room were sufficient to keep the places toasty. Since the houses were built on a hill side it was an ideal place for cellars and they were so necessary to store food.

Mom kept the house shiny clean. She enjoyed her home. She made pretty ruffled curtains and was constantly polishing floors and windows. She did a lot of cooking and baking.

There was a little log school house down below the camp. Donna attended school there with about twenty kids, grades one to eight.

The school teacher was a young, very nice looking lady. We saw very little of her, she kept to herself most of the time. One day it was announced that she and the mine foreman by the name of Johnson had got married when they were out over the weekend. Word traveled through the camp like wildfire. Everyone was so surprised, they had never been seen together. We were all very happy for them. In fact our own favorite entertainer, Dale Johnson, is a product of that union.

Donna went to school there. Kubi went with her every day. He pulled her back and forth on her skis. Any place Kubi would find a glove or hat or anything of Donna's, he packed it home and laid it on the front porch. Kubi loved it there. He was always warm, he had a mat of fur to keep him warm, and he was free to come and go as he pleased.

It was a nice little community and a good place to work, pay was good. There was a store and post office in one building which sat in the center of the village. The cookhouse and bunkhouse, all in one, was located up on the hill. It was a huge building, three stories high. The lower floor was used for storage and was dug into the hill side for an insulation effect.

The main floor was the cookhouse and dining room. The upper story of course being the bunk house.

The mail was delivered once a week by airplane, which also served as transportation for the people in all the back country where roads were not maintained during winter. Bob Fogg, a long time back country pilot, was the man we were dependent on as our link with the outside world. The airport was four miles from camp. It was a long, cold, slow ride on a sled pulled by a cat to get back and forth to the air strip. The sled transported passengers and mail and any orders from the residents for Bob to bring on his return trip the following week. This service was a life line for many people in the days before we had modern equipment to maintain roads, or vehicles to travel in snow.

I remember one trip when we were going out, there was a deep layer of light snow on the strip. Bob took off taxiing down the strip, but we didn't take off in the air, we went nose first in the snow. We took a nose dive for sure. We all had to get out and dig the plane out of the snow. Quite an experience.

Before Alaska became a state, this was considered the coldest place in the United States which could be 50 degrees below zero for sometimes two or three months at a time. It's one of the contributing factors that people no longer live there in the winter, but is a thriving summer tourist spot.

Deadwood always kept their employees. They paid good and treated their employees well. They employed about fifty men in the mine on three shifts. Clyde, my step-father, was a contractor. He contracted by the ton, to bring the ore out of the mine. He hired a number of men to work for him. Contractors made considerably better pay than a regular miner, but of course there was more responsibility and expense.

The cook went out for a few days and didn't come back.

Mom was called on to fill in until they found another cook. It was hard to get anyone to come in there in the winter. So Mom continued to cook. There was a bull cook to help her and a dishwasher. The cooking was a tremendous job. There was an early breakfast and a noon breakfast. A third of the crew each breakfast. There were fifty lunches and one big dinner at night, feeding all of the men at once. Bread was baked every day. Cookies, cake and dessert for supper also had to be baked each day. Meat was brought in by the halves. The cook cut meat for that day's meal from the half of beef or pork or whatever was on the menu. Bacon was cut off the big slabs for a day at a time. The plane brought in groceries once a month.

It was very hard work for a woman. They usually hired men for that position because of the lifting, but of course they had no choice at this time of year. I was helping Mom and working in the dining room during meal time. Mom still was not too strong and she was not able to take these long, hard hours. She soon went down, and was no longer able to work. I was asked to fill in for her. I sure didn't want this job, but I reluctantly agreed to do it, just until they could find another cook.

I was not able to do the job right, and I didn't feel good about it. I got food on the table but it was nothing like Mom had put out. The bread I baked was good but not as good as hers. I didn't like not being able to do a good job, but I just didn't have the experience or the endurance to work from four o'clock in the morning until sometimes ten at night. She did take a rest in the afternoon, but I never seemed to get my work done to take a nap. When I was feeling absolutely defeated, the bull cook quit. The boss asked me if I was doing all right, I thought that was a dumb question. I didn't say that however. I did ask the boss if the men could make their own lunches if I put everything out. That was one of the duties of the bull cook. He agreed and at dinner that night he made the announcement that I was doing my best but couldn't keep up the work. He asked for their assistance. They did help, by fixing their lunches, clearing up the tables, cleaning the dining room and anything I asked them to do.

I got by that way for about two months. I thought I was going to die of aching feet. When I went home at night I fell into bed. My feet hurt so bad I couldn't put the covers over them. I made good money and I sent it out to the bank in Cascade. I couldn't spend it here.

They finally found a cook. I was never so glad to see anyone in my life. I slept for two days.

Up the row of houses about a quarter of a mile a man had a blood hound. He kept him penned up most of the time, but we all worried about that dog for Kubi's sake as well as our own. When we went by the house he would hit the fence and roar at us. One day he got out and came right to our house, like he had scoped it out and knew where to find Kubi. He came onto the porch and attacked Kubi. There was a tussle but Kubi was no match for him. We were all hysterical, trying to stop the fight before Kubi was killed. We were almost afraid to even look. The tussle died down and there was some heavy breathing out there. We turned to look. Kubi was backed up to our door and had a hold of the blood hound's tongue, he was pulling and had it stretched out a foot. The hound was pulling and Kubi pulled, you can imagine what that looked like. I thought the tongue was going to give way any second, but it just came out farther and farther. It was choking the hound. All of a sudden the tongue snapped back and the hound took off, his tongue was hanging and bleeding bad. He never bothered Kubi again.

There was a snow slide between Deadwood and Landmark. It blocked the road for a half mile. It was imperative that the roads were open in the spring to get the ore trucked out. When they found the slide they went to work on it. They didn't have any idea it was as deep as it was. They took all the equipment from the mine to work on it. It was fifty feet deep when they had it plowed down to the road bed. Driving through it was like going through a tunnel. It was only wide enough for one vehicle. It gave you a strange feeling to go through it, but the walls were ice so it was safe enough, until spring that is.

The people in the camp had card parties once a week. Everyone looked forward to playing pinochle. One night when they were playing someone saw a fire down on the lower road near the school house. Everyone ran down there to help, but it was too late by the time they got to it. The family who lived there had five children with twin babies. The older kids went to the card party with their parents, but they left the babies upstairs in their cribs asleep. When they found them, they were still laying in a sleeping position. We assumed from that they died of smoke inhalation and never awakened. That was a small comfort for the grieving parents and residents. The parents went out for the funeral and never returned to Deadwood. A sad day in Deadwood.

The war was over and the boys were coming home. Ed, my oldest brother, came home to Cascade and flew in on the plane to see us at Deadwood.

Like most of the boys, Ed was making his adjustments to civilian life and trying to forget the horrors of war. Most were not in any shape to go to work. The government paid them "52-20," $20 a week for 52 weeks, which gave them time to settle in and find work. "Time was spent drinking and trying to forget." Ed stayed in Deadwood for a few days, but it was to quiet, and that was not what he needed at that time. He needed to work out the problems he was facing. After a few days he took the plane back to Cascade.

He was very unhappy when he found out the money he had sent home was gone. Mom used the money to get into the cafe in Cascade. She was pretty desperate at the time. If it had been available to him, it probably would have been spent in the bars.

With Ed in Cascade, I was permitted to go also. We got rooms across the hall from one another in a little hotel. I spent all I had earned in Deadwood, making it available to Ed for what he needed for lodging, food, and drink. I went to work at Edith's cafe making $.50 an hour.

It was hardly enough for both of us, but I realized Ed had some healing to do before he could be accountable. I could not deny him nor did I begrudge him. We lived in the hotel until fall when Mom and Clyde came out.

Ed had seen a lot of action, he was in the medical corp. He was actually in the Navy, but the Marines did not have a medical corp. so the Navy supplied them with that service.

It had been a long time since he had been home. It wasn't so many years, but there had been a lot of water under the bridge.

It took time for Ed to get over the effects of the war, most of his time was spent in that effort. He did work it out, like the strong person I knew he was.

It was spring out here and it was so nice to get out of the snow banks. Cascade was booming with the boys coming home from the war. Everyone seemed so happy, there was a smile on every face. No one met a stranger on the streets, people were talking to people they had never seen before. We were overjoyed the war was over and the boys were finally home. The streets were full, from early morning to late night. I recall dance bands on a truck and people dancing in the streets. It was a festival of happiness. This lasted for several weeks. People wanted the boys to know they were proud of them and happy they were safe back home. There were many who didn't come back. This was their home town's way of saying thank you. Thank you to those who put their life on the front line for us at home. For our families, for our country, where not a bomb was dropped, nor a drop of blood was shed.

Little kids were wandering around looking over each soldier, whom they had been hearing about for the last five years.

The soldiers were courageous, mighty heroes to them, which was well deserved. You could see it in their eyes as they stood looking up at them. Most of the boys had a beer in their hand, of course there were a lot of people around buying drinks.

I have fond memories of the war ending. No more fear of getting a message that your loved one wasn't coming home, no more news broadcasts about the devastation of war, and no more news shorts at the theater, showing all the bloody truth about what was going on over there. We still had two who were not home, Roy and Uncle Tom. They were not in any danger however. They would be home soon.

War brings to mind something I have thought a lot about and I am sure those of my generation have also given a great deal of thought to, so lend an ear as I share this. I think it is worthy of comment. It has had a great impact on my life, and that of my generation.

World War II brought a lot of changes not only in the American family and our personal lives but in the world. Technology advanced at such an accelerated rate, it was hard to keep up. The advancement in ships, airplanes, all terrain vehicles, weapons and ammunition was unbelievable. These things were happening before our eyes, it left people in awe, a state of disbelief.

My generation has witnessed many changes and advancements in technology, more than any other generation in the history of our universe. Nothing could move faster than a horse, people never expected anymore, so the Pony Express carried messages across the country. Now instantly, a message goes anywhere in the world by computer, e-mail, or fax. A dynamic progression of technology from the telegraph in 1844.

From horse and buggy for transportation to jets traveling at 1000 miles an hour. Experience has forced upon our minds the conviction that what has been, must forever be. We are naturally resistant to change, good or bad. Americans in the 1800s had better weapons and a superior knowledge of geography but there were very few advantages over the ancient Greeks and Romans, thousands of years before.

A single generation around the 1840s would have witnessed the invention of the train, the telegraph, and the steamship. Those were huge leaps, made more colossal because there had been only the most incremental technological changes for thousands of years before.

A basic need in all of us is to hold on to what we know is secure. The older we get the stronger the need.

There are many disadvantages in the technological changes of today. One particular disadvantage is that some of us are left behind. Who understands the computers' continual changes? Only the ones who build them. Surely not any of us who were born in the first three decades of the 1900s. It is intimidating to us, but it is forced on us. Especially when every phase of commerce is computerized.

Our banking system is infiltrated and complicated with the newest technology in computer systems. They no doubt will have to update their systems every year. The cost will be prohibitive, as with all industries. Inflation will follow the example set and the rich get richer and the poor get poorer. It will continue to drain our pocket books, whether we endorse these changes or not, we will be pulled into the network.

The world of medicine has made such dramatic and tremendous progress in the last 50 years, it's hard to imagine. It is good, but it has brought up the cost of medical care to a place no one can afford. We depend on insurance to pay and that brings up this crisis we have now in Medicare, and the cost of insurance. Where is all this going? How does your independence feel? We can expect to see technology accelerate at an even faster rate, until the end comes, until the Lord comes again, until He comes to take us home. Then, only God knows.

My heart goes out to all who are affected by so many changes. We are crowding too much into our mind, and that brings stress, the increased stress level that most people accept as part of life these days. Stress has a tremendous negative effect on health.

When life proceeds at a quicker pace, which it is, more so every day, we can't relax, which is the therapy that restores our body. Stress is depriving us of peace and tranquillity. For the older generation this is devastating. For younger people, it is killing them.

The world is on a runaway train. How far do we go before we jump off, and destroy ourselves. Could it be with cloning? How does God feel about this? I don't think it's hard to figure out that it goes contrary to His natural plan for reproduction.

It has been said we can't stop progress and I'm sure we can't, but we must keep our eye on the Lord, knowing this old world can't last much longer. It has been quite a challenge, living in this age of change, for those of us who saw it as it was, and now see it as it is.

Chapter 6

"Innocence is No Excuse"

1945

This chapter of my life is a very difficult one to write. It was a time of heartache and trials, and I suppose heartaches are always painful to remember. To recall to be able to write it, I had to relive every incident with all the anger, the disappointments, tears, and joy. As you read you will understand the emotions I had to bring before my placid comfortable psyche to relive these details. Another painful consideration was that I had never talked or released many of these memories to anyone, and my children did not know most of these things about their father. If they did not have the strong characters they do, I would have been destroying a part of them. I talked to each one and gave them a choice as to whether I should write it all. Each one said, "Mom, you have to write it like it was."

If I were to omit this part of my life, the reader would not feel the hand of God working a miracle in the lives of my husband, children, and myself. My ultimate purpose is to glorify the Lord, to bring a blessing to all who read it. I pray that I can give hope to one who may not have hope, and to help them find the ultimate peace that God has for us.

I was seventeen years old the summer I worked for Edith Christoff at Edith's cafe in Cascade. I looked older and more mature than my actual years. I was shy and very insecure. I tried to be friendly with the customers, but it was impossible for me to even look at the young guys, being so shy.

I didn't want to date until I found the man of my dreams. He would be a sincere, faithful, good natured fellow, and he had to be a cowboy. I loved horses and country life, I was a country girl through and through. I looked only at the guys who wore cowboy hats. He had to be tall, dark, and handsome. You know, like any country girl's dream man. I would not settle for anything less. I also wanted to be the perfect wife for him, and I was going to save myself for him. I had very strong feelings about that. In my immature mind, I felt that if you were intimate with a man, you had to marry him. Since then I also realize two wrongs do not make a right.

I had a lot of chances to date while working in the cafe, but I didn't feel too flattered because there were a lot of guys in town, and maybe half as many girls. I was convenient to ask because I was there every day. I wasn't sure of a guy's motives and what was expected of me.

I enjoyed this life and being with people, but at times it was too much for me. I wanted to run back to my family where I felt more secure. I was very intimidated by all the pretty girls and handsome guys. There was one in particular who really made me feel uncomfortable.

There are a lot of good memories in my life, and I wouldn't trade them for anything, but growing up so isolated and so socially deprived is not a favor done for a child. It is very lonely and frightful when you are exposed to the outside world. Innocence yes, but to a point. A child can be so innocent, he will not know the extent of his rights, and will suffer unduly, not being able to discern when others inflict abuse. I was such a victim.

One of the fellows just back from the war began to frequent the cafe. He was a friendly fellow and rather good looking. He could not be overlooked, for he seemed to fill the atmosphere with his presence. His bold manner was to me, very distasteful. I had never met anyone like him. He was attractive with his levi's cuffed, and a clean, well-pressed, white shirt, black shiny oxfords and his curly black hair. He was well built with broad shoulders and he was over six feet tall. He looked especially nice in his clothes. He had a proud carriage with his head held high and always had a smile. As soon as he started to show me attention, I wanted to run, to get away from him. I was wondering how to discourage him. I certainly had done nothing to encourage him.

He was loud and boastful, and like a lot of service men, he seemed to think that we were indebted to him. Which we were, but it could not be demanded. He didn't hesitate to make demands and when they were not met, he was ready to fight.

The cafe always being full, I watched him interact with others, which showed him to be not too popular. He had to be in control and the center of attention. I tolerated him until all his attention was on me. I tried to ignore him because he frightened me. He asked me several times to go out with him. My refusal did not discourage him, it only postponed the inevitable.

Bill Saleen.

He was there everyday. He was outside when I got off work. He would leave if I went straight home, but either he or his brother followed me everywhere I went. He knew where I went, what I did, and who with.

Finally on a day off, I agreed to go for a hike with him. I thought that would be harmless. An outing sounded so good to me. We walked from town up to where the dam is now. We went over what I later learned was an obstacle course to test my endurance. I guess I passed the test. I climbed up and over the cliff with little effort. I hiked for two hours with him and enjoyed the beautiful country and the sunny day.

Now he wanted to marry me. Oh! No! He said "You are the girl I've hoped to find, and I am not going to let you get away." I couldn't believe he meant that. I was embarrassed. I couldn't respond. I just walked away. I should have stood up to him right then, but really I didn't know what to say. I didn't want to make him mad. I think he took my silence for

115

agreement. Right then I lost the battle. I became putty in his hands out of fear and ignorance.

It wasn't long until he became aggressive and then took advantage of me. I was a virgin, and I feel now it was his intention to take me because of it. He stole it from me, and it meant nothing to him. My protests were nothing compared to his physical strength. I was so ashamed. I hated myself and him for what he had done. I had to marry him now. I would never offer myself as a bride to another man, not being pure. For all the pain I suffered over that, he later denied that he was the first one, and he KNEW. Oh yes, he knew. This was just another way to hurt me, to tear the heart out of me. He was truly a thief of the worst kind.

I was never given the freedom to learn to care for him, everything was controlled by him. I was so dominated, I couldn't think for myself. I often wondered what he could find attractive in a milk-toast type of person like myself. After a terrible summer of courtship, with threats, coercion, jealousy, accusations of no matter what I said, he did not believe me, he had a "source," who did not lie to him, but he would not let me go.

Bill received a check from the government for $500 about the first of December, for retroactive disability pay. He set the date for the wedding for December 23, 1946. I was given the privilege of choosing where. I had always wanted to get married in a church by a minister. The wedding was simple with his family and mine. When I became Mrs. William Stanley Saleen, it was not a choice of my own. It was a very sad day for me. Where had all my dreams gone? Where did I go wrong? I had thoughts then of running away from him. When, was the only question.

Bill gave me a wedding gift that day, just before the wedding. I was very surprised and pleased, but it did not take the pain from my heart. I had never had a watch, I was pleased and told him so. (There must be some tenderness down there somewhere, I thought.)

Bill began to drink after we were married. He went to the bars and drank up the money we needed for other things. He came home drunk about every night. The sight of him drunk repulsed me so. I somehow found the courage to get angry when he staggered through the door asking for help to get to the bathroom. He was sick. I screamed at him, "Don't ask me to help you, just stay away from me." He staggered through the house and out the back door. He came back in, found his way to the bed, flopped on it, and passed out.

Rose and Bill Saleen on the day after their wedding.

I slept on the couch. I laid there thinking about what I had said to him. I didn't know what to expect in the morning. He didn't say a thing. He probably didn't remember it. He drank and got in fights up town. Others would tell me about it. Occasionally, I went to town with him. He always drank too much and was terribly obnoxious. He told his brother Merrill to dance with me so I wouldn't go home. The whole thing was so disgusting to me. I went home as soon as I could. I tried to be asleep when he came home.

Ed and Lois (his wife) came over to play pinochle several times that winter. I was so glad to have them come, as Bill was always more sociable when they were there. I loved pinochle.

I taught Lois how to play that first winter. She played as my partner and she learned as we played. We had some good times. We'd have to stop and make fudge or pop popcorn every so often, or Lois and I would just talk for a bit. Ed was always so good natured, and thanks to Ed, they put up with us. Bill loved to tease Lois as everyone does. She would jump up, run around the table, hit him, and come back and play again. Just as she does now. We still talk about that winter and Lois recalls, "And Rose taught me how to play pinochle that winter."

A few other things I remember when I think of that winter was how Lois cooked chicken feet. She scoured them, boiled them, skinned them and then cooked them some more. Ed and Bill would not eat them, but she made them look so good when she ate them, she convinced me and I ate them with her. I have to say, they were good. She really did well on fried oysters too. She boiled bones and made sandwiches from the marrow. It was good, but I have never been able to eat marrow since. All of those things most people won't eat, she made them look like they were fit for a king and they tasted that way too. We had some good times. I loved her folks, Roy and Granny Elsie York.

After living around Bill's family for awhile, I could see a lot of his problems came from them. Many times I heard his mother Edrie say, "You can't trust anyone, they will lie to you, steal from you and stab you in the back. They are all a bunch of sons a —— out there." I heard her kids mimic that, especially Bill. They hated and mistrusted everyone. They so often would attack me about a friend or family member. I would get so angry, but Bill warned me never to say anything to any of his family or he'd knock the —— out of me. I had to try to ignore it, but it hurt terribly. I grieved for days over what his mother said about my mother. I also learned that Bill's "source" came from his family. All those things I couldn't imagine any one telling him about me came from his home. What a tragedy. Bill was so confused, he didn't know what to believe. He felt safer believing his family.

I always felt like his mother had mental problems, and that did surface when she was older. She caused her family a lot of heartaches and problems, which they in turn passed on to others, hurting and scarring everyone in their path.

Bill's childhood was a stormy one. His mother and dad divorced when he and his two brothers were quite small. His father, Orval DeGrange, had been very abusive to his family. Bill grew up in Emmett, ID. His mother worked in restaurants and the kids fended for themselves mostly. Family members have told me they were ragged little urchins, and they, many times, had taken them into their homes to feed them when they found them on the streets. Edrie married again, to John Saleen. Two girls were born to that marriage. I understand he was a good man. He was electrocuted on a power pole while working for Idaho Power. The girls were quite small when he died.

Edrie then married Red Gibbons and had three more children, two boys and one girl. Red was a great fellow. He took the back seat to a very domineering wife but he loved his family. He suffered a lot for all the injustices in the household.

He was the only one in the family who showed me any respect or friendship. At times, some of the kids would befriend me, but turn on me in a wink, and that happened time after time. I never felt like I had a friend there except Red, and I really appreciated him. Although we didn't talk about our problems, there was a camaraderie as the two outsiders. There was just a special look that said "I understand." Red was killed in the woods by a falling tree. I missed him terribly when he was gone. I thought so much of him. The kids were junior high age. After he was gone, Edrie fell apart mentally. He had been her stabilizing force all the time. It was his kind gentle presence that kept her together.

Bill's grandmother Mina was, to say the least, a colorful lady.

She had lived in Idaho City for years as a widow. She played in a Senior Citizens band playing the drums. They played for a lot of different events. She was an upbeat person and always had a good positive outlook on life. She worked in Portland in the shipyard as a welder during the war. Bill's grandfather Ed Stowell was a blacksmith when they lived in Emmett. He was a crippled fellow with one leg several inches shorter than the other.

I felt sorry for Gram. She was treated as another outsider. When she came to visit the family. She would be hurt, yet never said anything, just hoping next time it would be better. She would usually leave in tears when she came to visit. The kids were allowed to say hurtful things to her, as they did to me. Edrie treated her like an enemy. It hurt Gram terribly. She finally quit going to their house, staying with us when she came to visit. I was hurt for her. To retaliate in any way would be to reduce one's self to their level, and fight with their weapons. I wanted no part of that, nor did most people who were affected by the injustice. I had to take it, for the time being anyway.

We spent a lot of time at their house. I'm sure Bill was more comfortable there. He either didn't know or didn't care how bad it was for me. Bill bought their groceries, one winter, when Red was out of work. We had a charge account at a local store and they had access to the account. Bill was very charitable to his family. Edrie told me one time, after I had made some reference to my mother, that she was a drunken whore, and none of my family was any good, just a bunch of sons a ————. She didn't want

119

Mina and Ed Stowell, Bill's grandparents.

me to mention them again. I felt so ashamed that I couldn't stand up for my mother, but at the same time, I knew she talked from her own poor self image.

One evening shortly after we were married, Bill's boss and friend came to see us. He was older than Bill but was still a young man. We sat in the living room drinking coffee and visiting. Jim was polite to me and included me in the conversation. I could see Bill was getting mad, so I tried to withdraw. I ignored Jim. Suddenly Bill got up and went to bed.

I was embarrassed, but I sat there afraid to do anything. A few minutes later Bill appeared in the doorway in his shorts and said to me. "Get in here and get to bed." I sat there. Jim got up and excused himself and left. I still sat there, by then I was so angry. Bill came back into the room and boomed "I said get in this bed." I flared back at him, "You're not going to order me when to go to bed." He ran across the room grabbed me and threw me over his shoulder and carried me to the bed. I was screaming at him and pounding on him to put me down. "Are you going crazy," I screamed. I tried to push myself away but he was holding me with a death grip. When he got to the bed, he slammed me down on the footboard and drew back his fist. He hit me in the face with all his strength. The force of the blow picked me up and sent me flying backwards and back down on the bed. I bounced up and over the edge of the bed to the floor. I lay there unable to move. I wanted to pass out, the pain was unbearable. My eye felt like it was bursting, the side of my head was pounding. Bill's raging was trying to get through to my consciousness. I couldn't make out what he was saying. I was trying to hear. His yelling was bringing me out of the darkness.

He was standing over me, kicking me, "Get up you bitch. I'll hit you again."

I couldn't move. He continued to cuss and scream. He went over to the dresser and was rummaging through the drawer, "Where's my knife? I'm going to kill you. Did you take my knife? Where is it, I said."

I knew he was completely out of control. I could hear the closet door open. He was jerking down the things hanging in there, "Where is my gun?" he screamed. "I'm going to kill you." He came over and began kicking me again.

I knew I was as good as dead. He was crazy and he was mad.

I had to calm him down any way I could. At that moment a plan began to form in my head. The first chance I had, I was going to run. I was not going to live with this maniac. I would go so far away, he would never find me. Now I had to concentrate on calming him down. I felt better now that I knew what I was going to do and I was in control.

I lifted my head. Oh, the pain was excruciating. I struggled to get on my feet. I had to get up. I felt so weak. I pulled up, inch by inch. I finally got to my knees. Then I reached for the dresser beside the bed, slowly I pulled myself to my feet. I stood there for a few moments until the room quit whirling, and while holding tight to the dresser, I looked into his face, and begged for my life. I instantly hated myself for doing that, but I wasn't going to accomplish anything dead. I was in control, no longer was I going to be the weak little mistress of this animal. Then and there I divorced myself from him. I had to wait until the time was right to get out. I couldn't afford to make a mistake with him.

He was still cursing and yelling. He sat down on the bed with his head in his hands telling me what a no good so and so I was. He didn't know why he had ever married me. He could have married a whore in Germany that was a much better woman that me. This went on for hours. I wanted to sit down, but I didn't know where. I didn't want to sit by him, but there was no place else, so I sat very carefully beside him. I continued to think and plan. We must have sat there for an hour.

He laid back on the bed and finally went to sleep. I very quietly got up and went into the living room and laid on the couch. It was soon time to get up he had to go to work. I fixed his lunch and breakfast. He sat down at the table. Neither one of us had said a word up to now. I held the plate in mid-air in front of him until he looked up at me. I said very deliberately and cold, "If you ever do that again to me, I will find a way to stop you any way I can, and you will never see me again."

He took his plate and began to eat, he did not respond to my statement. When he had finished he picked up his lunch and coat and went out the door.

After he left I went into the bathroom and examined the damage to my face. I looked terrible. My eye was swollen shut, my face was black below my eye on my cheek, and it extended back to my hair line and beyond. I could see the swelling. My forehead was swelled with a big black lump above my eye. I pulled my eyelid back to see my eye, it was so red it really looked like it was bleeding. I began to cry. What a mess I had made of my life. A lady with a black eye? Oh sure, a lady. No! I was so ashamed, I was not going to step out of the house until it healed up.

That afternoon Mom and Clyde stopped by, they were leaving for Nevada to work in the mines. When they came through the door and saw me, they gasped. Mom began to cry, "Rose what in the world happened to you?" I just hung my head. Clyde walked up to me and put his arms around me. He just held me and never said a word. I laid my head on his shoulder and cried. I didn't want to say anything. They didn't push.

Oh so softly, Clyde whispered in my ear, "You will always have a home with us." Through my sobs I told him, "Thank you, that means so much to me." He walked toward the door pulling his handkerchief out of his back pocket, he went out into the front yard. Mom held me and we both cried. She comforted me but we didn't discuss Bill. I really felt loved. My family finally became loving parents to me. I needed that so badly right then.

For awhile I contemplated just making a run for it. Part of me wanted to so badly, and part of me said, "You can't, you have to give him another chance." I also had an inkling that I may be pregnant, then what would I do? I was trapped.

He came home that night carrying a pair of sun glasses and some cake make-up to cover the bruise on my face, which now looked worse and was covering more of my face. He handed it to me and said "Here, put this on, we're going down to Mom's."

I objected fearfully saying, "I don't want to go anywhere. Please don't make me go out."

He walked up to me and looked at me with the most hateful look (which I learned later was the look to force people into submission) "You are going now." Fear gripped my insides. I put on the make-up. It didn't cover the bruises. I put it on as thick as I could, and really tried because I would be walking down main street. The glasses covered some.

I hung my head, but Bill strutted like a peacock with a big smile on his face. I hated him then. Why did I ever feel like I had to be loyal to him and keep my word.

When we arrived at their home, Bill walked in head raised high and a big smirk on his face. After he got everyone's attention, he turned around to me standing behind him and said, "Take them off."

I have never been more humiliated, hurt, disgraced, and yes, angry. These people were the worst kind of trash I had ever met.

I jerked off my glasses and pushed my face out in front of them. They

Mom and Clyde (Dad).

123

had already seen what it was and were laughing, when my glasses came off their laughter became hysterical, doubling over hysterical. I hated them all. I stood for them for a few minutes and looked at one and then another so they could get a good look. I wanted to tear into them, to pound on them, but instead I turned around and walked out the door. They continued to laugh and Bill laughed with them. What a loyal husband.

As I was standing and turning for them, I looked at Red and he got up and went into the other room. He was not laughing.

Bill was drinking more as time went by. When he came home after being at the bar, his demands on me as a wife seemed inhuman. It was torture to me. I could hardly stand to have him touch me. There was no response from me and he was angered by that, which made it all the worse. After he stole my virginity and then denied it, I hated him. How could I have any feelings for him? Why would I want to please him? That hurt me so bad, for what had I saved myself? For this! I wished he had married a prostitute. "Oh GOD! what have I done."

One day shortly after breakfast I began having cramps. They continued through the day, I had not seen a doctor as there was no doctor in town, but I had missed three periods. I was fairly sure I was pregnant. Throughout the day the cramps got worse. I didn't say anything to Bill.

During the night I was in agony and I was beginning to flow. I awakened Bill and asked him to get his mother. She attended me through my miscarriage. She said I lost twins. The trauma of this, along with everything else, I just wanted to give up. I wanted to die. I didn't want to get up, ever. For three days I stayed in bed. I laid and looked at the wall. I didn't want to see anyone. It seemed like my mind was shut off, but that was okay, I wasn't thinking anyway. Bill's mother told him it was time I got out of bed. I knew I had to or else, God knows what. When I got up I was in a daze. It seemed like I was trying to keep my mind shut off. But I kept moving around. I felt like I was automatically doing the things that had to be done. Bill apparently didn't notice, or if he did, he didn't care. I was so weak and depressed.

After a couple months, Bill took me to a doctor in Boise to see why I didn't get pregnant again right away. The doctor told Bill I shouldn't get pregnant for a year. I was very anemic and run down. He gave me a prescription for high potency vitamins. I took the vitamins for a short time and became pregnant. I was sick all through my time with morning sickness and fatigue. I had a miserable pregnancy.

During that time Ed and Lois had a baby girl. Dr. Paterson had just opened his practice there when Lois went into labor. She was delivered at home. The doctor brought a nurse with him to the house. I was also there and helped the doctor, what little I could. The whole thing was a little frightening to me since that was a first for me. She did have a pretty rough delivery. That little girl was over eight pounds. Little Linda was sure a bright star in my life. It was Linda who gave me a will to live. She came to stay with me quite often. She was a good baby, and I loved caring for her. When we moved out of downtown I didn't see her as much, but after I had my own baby, I didn't miss her so much.

In those days we had some very severe winters. Snow was sometimes eight feet deep. It was much colder then, than now.

There were times when the train didn't come in for weeks at a time. The roads were closed to Boise and the groceries were getting pretty scarce on the store shelves. The wind blew and the snow drifted sometimes six to eight feet deep which made it impossible to take any average vehicle out of your drive way.

Little Linda went out to stay with Granny Elsie York quite often. She and Roy lived south of town in Round Valley, and about three miles off the highway. The long lane was a lot of ups and downs, so it was difficult to get a vehicle in and out when there was just a little snow. We all loved to go see Granny Elsie, Lois's mother. She always had something to eat and set it out as soon as anyone arrived. She loved life and she loved the LORD. In fact, she loved everyone and everyone loved her. A few times when Linda went out a big storm isolated them. After a few days Lois would get terribly lonesome and she'd cry and cry all day long. That was hard to see.

This particular winter Bill worked for Ben Hussman at a service station in Cascade. Considering how tough it was to deliver fuel oil, Ben thought it best to get a half-track from the army when they had all that type of vehicle for sale. They had been used in the war and were no longer needed. It came disassembled but Bill got to work on it and got it put together. He was a good mechanic and was familiar with the half-track. Bill was the only one who could drive it. The half-track was also used for emergencies in the community. Well one such emergency was when Linda was at Granny's. Bill would start up the old half-track and we would load up blankets, quilts, and coats to keep us warm.

This vehicle had no heater and no windows. You could easily freeze on a cold night, but we'd bundle up and head out. Top speed was about

Ed McCracken in WWII.

Rose McCracken Saleen.

Roy McCracken in WWII.

twenty miles per hour. That was highway time, but going up the lane, we crept along plowing through the drifts. Bill would have to make a track to push down some of the snow so we could go through with another thrust of the half-track. We would finally arrive at Granny's house. We would be half frozen, but they always had a good fire going and some hot coffee and homemade bread to fuel us up for the trip back home. Linda was always fine and Lois felt better. We made many such trips that winter. We all enjoyed it to the fullest.

Bill came in from work one day. He had been shopping, and after he set the groceries down on the table, he pulled a little box out of his pocket. He said to me, "I never did get you an engagement ring so here it is."

I opened the box and in it was a beautiful ruby ring. The stone was a large square set into a lovely gold setting. It was the prettiest ruby ring I had ever seen. I was stunned. I couldn't think of anything to say. I looked at it for a long time. I took it out of the box and slipped it on my finger with my gold wedding band. It was beautiful together. I looked up at him and as sincerely and honestly as I could I said, "It is so beautiful, thank you very much."

As little tenderness as there had been between us, it was hard to turn it on so unexpectedly. He seemed pleased that I liked it. I could see a little response there and for awhile, I held some hope that things would get better.

Things were a little more comfortable. We had some outings, going fishing out to Horsethief basin, and walking over the hill to Big Creek to fish. We seldom ever said a word to each other. But at least it was better than before.

It was so pretty out there, I loved going out. Some times we'd just take some hot dogs and bread and a sweet roll, and roast them over a fire, and boil some coffee. It was a feast to us. Bill had gone out there with his grandfather for one summer and camped out to cut wood when he was quite young. He said he thought about that a lot when he was in the war. Those were wonderful memories. So Horsethief meant a lot to him too. We caught some nice trout out there.

Another trip we made was to Little Hidden Lake on West Mountain. We started out after he got off work one Friday evening. It was a beautiful warm, sunny spring day.

Bill told me to have everything packed when he got home from work. I packed two pack sacks and put what we needed in them.

127

Rose with Tippy and Kubi.

With my dog Kubi we drove across the fields as far as we could go and parked the car, loaded up our packs and took off walking. We walked about thirty minutes before we got to the foot of the mountain. The sun was going down behind that mountain and it was getting cold. We walked and climbed faster to keep warm, wanting to get as far as we could before it got dark.

The trail was getting hard to follow, obviously not much travel lately, probably none this spring yet. But we knew by a landmark where we had to go. Well, for as long as we could see the landmark. It was getting dark fast, the trail was hard to see. It was getting steeper, and walking was very difficult. We weren't making any headway. We dug into our packs and found our flashlights. We only used one at a time to save the batteries. Walking was so slow in that brush and soon, both our lights were gone. We used the second batch of batteries, but then they were gone, and it was pitch black.

Bill said, "Well this must be the creek that comes out of the lake so as long as we stay close to it we can't get lost.

Traveling got worse and we were soon on our hands and knees climbing up that hill through brush that was laid down from snow slides. Only about four feet of the brush was growing up, the rest was laying down on the ground. We could hardly get through it crawling, but we kept going. Old Kubi was right behind me crawling on his belly, but he never complained, he just kept on coming right at my heals. We couldn't lie down, so we couldn't stop, nor could we find our way out of this darn brush. The brush was getting thicker, and it became next to impossible to get through it. We had to reach out ahead of us and separate the brush to get through.

I had never seen brush grow like this. Thinking about it, I decided what must have happened was during the winter, the snow slid down the mountain, downing the brush as it went, and packing snow over it. In the spring when the snow began to melt, the tips of the brush came through the snow and grew. The bushes were so intertwined near the ground they could not regain their upright position. Consequently a jungle was made on West Mountain.

For hours we crawled. I was so wet and cold, and our packs were nearly torn off our backs going through that brush.

After what seemed like hours we came out of the brush and we were getting a little light from the moon. We continued on until we found a small ledge that we could lay down on. Bill began picking up sticks to build a fire. I opened my pack and pulled out my wool army blanket, laid it down called Kubi to me and curled up around him and went to sleep. I was so exhausted I could have slept anywhere. Bill told me the next morning he was so cold he couldn't sleep. He called Kubi to sleep with him so he could get warm, but he wouldn't leave me. Bill never cared for Kubi and Kubi knew it. Shortly after that, Bill insisted I send Kubi to Mom because he didn't trust him. He was afraid of him. I missed him so much. I cried even when I saw a hair of his. He had been such a faithful companion to me for so long. I knew, though, he would be happy with them for everyone loved him. Any one of the family would have taken him in a minute.

Kubi, 1947.

129

We were up at dawn, rolled up our packs and took out something to eat as we walked. We found the trail and it didn't take anytime to get to the lake.

The lake was beautiful. It was so cold and crystal clear with ice around the edge along the banks. The foliage grew up to the edge of the water. The grass was getting green, it looked like something out of a book. The crystal blue lake, the snow, the green grass, and the sun warming it to make it even more delightful and inviting.

We found an old raft beside the water. We drug it over and put the boards back on it and pushed it out in the water. We jumped on it with our fishing poles. The fish were swimming around the raft, it was breathtaking. I got so excited I could hardly get my pole in the water. Those fish were a good eighteen inches long and so fat. They weren't very hungry though and we had to fish like a bugger to catch one.

I didn't stay interested too long when they were so hard to catch. I was tired and sore. I went back to the bank, found a nice dry sunny spot and went to sleep, with Kubi beside me.

The trip down the hill was much easier. We found the trail and we could see where we came up in the brush. To our utter amazement, we were not more than 100 feet from the trail all the way up. Had we been able to see, we would have had a much better trip up. That was a bit frustrating but it was worth it. It was a hard trip but we had a good time and enjoyed being together more than we ever had. It was encouraging to me.

We made other trips such as this until I was too busy with children. Several years went by that I didn't go anyplace unless I could take the kids. It didn't bother me, I enjoyed the kids. They were well behaved and well mannered from the time they were little tikes. When we went into a store, or went to visit, or whatever it may be, I was rigid with my instructions. They listened and obeyed. I was very proud of them.

I received a letter from Mom saying she was very ill and would probably need surgery. She didn't say what was wrong, but she asked if I could come down. I knew it was serious or she would not have asked me to come.

Bill drove me down. He was not a bit happy about it. Of course he was asked to stay also, but he would not. He went back the next day. When I walked out to the car with him, his anger was very obvious when he said he wasn't coming after me. I could just stay there. I didn't respond, because I knew he would.

Mom's test showed she had cervical cancer. She had surgery in Winnemucca to remove her cervix. When she was barely strong enough she was sent to Boise to see Dr. Popma, a cancer specialist. He recommended she have radium treatments and to start immediately. We got her a room close to the clinic so she could walk back and forth. Clyde and Donna went back to McDermitt. Dr. Popma said her chances were good for a complete recovery. If after five years it hadn't recurred, then they could be fairly certain it would not. She had her check up every year for five years and it did not return.

It was a happy day for the family. I will never forget the horror I felt when I was told she had cancer. I held back the emotion until I was in bed and alone. It was like a dam breaking, my tears would not stop. I cried until I had no more tears, only the pain, and that didn't leave until we got the word from Dr. Popma. I felt like I couldn't go on without Mom. She had

Rose and her mother, Bertha Osborn.

131

become such a companion to me. And after all those empty years of my childhood without ever feeling love from her, as soon as we found a good mother-daughter relationship, she would be taken away. I couldn't bear that. I prayed, I didn't know for sure what to say, but it worked before. I very simply asked God, "Please don't let her die." The only hope I had. He heard me, and I became indebted to Him for the second time when I prayed for my mother. I knew Bill would be very angry if he knew, so I never told anyone.

Bill had been injured in the war, a piece of shrapnel had gone through him. He had a six inch scar above his hip bone and below his ribs and another scar on his back where it came out. He spent several months in the hospital in Germany before he came home. After he had been discharged about a year, he went to the V.A. Hospital for redetermination of his disabilities, which also determined the amount of his monthly payments. He was given a fifty percent disability status. A nervous condition was what he was rated on.

Bill was in the hospital for about a month. He left me to stay with his mother. I wasn't to go anywhere. I got letters from him every day accusing me of going out with other men. He was so angry he was going

Bill Saleen on a trip to Oklahoma.

132

to come home because he couldn't trust me. I wrote to him everyday and told him exactly what I did every hour of every day, but he would write back and call me a liar. I finally had to go to Boise and spend every waking hour at his bedside. He arranged for me to stay nights with another patient's wife and daughter. He still questioned me about what I did. I didn't dare leave their house. It was very difficult being in the hospital with all those men and not look at anyone. I just kept my head down. I didn't look for fear he would accuse me.

I had a fairly normal pregnancy, except for having morning sickness which lasted until the baby was born. I was vomiting on the delivery table. Bill was so anxious for the baby to come.

I went to the hospital early one morning after having pains all night. I had a few false labor calls before so I wanted to be sure this time. I felt pretty sure when the water broke. The pains were getting very hard. I thought I would have the baby as soon as I got there. Little did I know, that isn't the way it happens. My pains got harder and came closer together all that day, all that night, then all the next day. I got so tired, but the pains came too close to sleep in between. The doctor kept telling me that I wasn't dilating. This went on and on. I was getting weaker with every pain. I perspired so much my bed was soaked. I had a sheet that was tied to the end of the bed that I pulled on. When the sheet got so wet and so wadded up the nurse would come in and change it. I worked so hard to have that baby, yet the doctor continued to tell me I wasn't dilating. I became so irritated with him and I asked him, "How do I do that?" He said, "You just do it naturally. It's not something you control, except I think you are afraid and are holding back." I wasn't holding back. If anything, I just wanted to have that baby! He watched to see what happened when I really pushed.

He walked away shaking his head, saying, "You are not doing anything and you haven't made any headway since you came in, but the baby is in the birth canal." He made the decision to take me into the delivery room. The nurse immediately put a mask over my face and I went out. Suddenly I came to and it felt like I was being pulled apart and splitting through the middle. I raised up to see what the doctor was doing. He had his feet braced against the end of the table and was pulling with the forceps. The pain was unbearable, I leaned back as the pain increased with the pull of the forceps. I went out. I didn't wake up until morning which I don't think was too long. The nurse was talking to me saying "Wake up Rose, it's all over, you have a little boy." I managed an "Ohhh" and went back to sleep.

Again the nurse was talking to me, "Rose would you like to see your little boy, I have him right here."

"Yes." As she laid the baby beside me on my arm, I pulled him up close and attempted to open my eyes, I couldn't see him but I could feel him. He was really here and he felt so good. He is mine and no one can take him away from me. I must have gone back to sleep because that nurse was waking me up again with something to eat. She had me turn over on my side, that was hard, everything hurt. She pulled the tray up in front of me and propped me up on my side. I went back to sleep and fell into my plate. The next thing I knew my mother was standing beside me saying, "Rose wake up, let me clean your face. I came to see the baby."

I was so happy that she was there. I was beginning to wake up a little. She had seen the baby and she said he was so sweet, but so tiny. Bill came in about that time and had been to the nursery, they held up the baby for him to see. He came into my room and was nearly in tears. He said, "What is wrong with the baby's head?"

Mom was trying to explain that this happened to him in delivery and it would go back to normal, she had talked to the nurses.

I was alarmed and I said, "What is the matter with his head?"

Bill went out and asked the nurses to bring the baby in so I could see him. They brought him in wrapped up in a blanket and laid him down. Mom helped to unwrap him. I was shocked when I saw him. The poor little fellow had bruises from the top of his head down each side of his face. His head was probably eight inches long and two or three inches across his face. There was a crease around his crown. There were red pressure marks over his eye, across his cheek and on his forehead. His face looked swelled and out of proportion. I began to cry, he looked so pitiful. Bill was angry. He was sure he would be that way always, and so was I sure of that. The doctor came in and explained to us what happened during the labor and delivery. The baby laid in the birth canal too long and the crease around his crown was him being pushed against my pelvis. The shape of his head was a combination of pushing against my pelvis for so long and the forceps. The bruising was from the forceps. He said he was sorry, but it was the only way that baby was going to come out. He said it would take a few months and the head would be normal.

Billy was near death when he was born. He had oxygen immediately and was in an incubator for several days. He didn't have the sucking instinct. The nurses would hold him up to my breast and open and close his mouth as they squeezed a little milk in his mouth. It took a long time for him to eat on his own. Billy weighed 6 lbs. 11 oz. at birth, but he lost quite a bit before he ate by himself. When Billy was grown, a doctor told him after taking x-rays that he had Spina-bifida. I've always wondered why the doctor didn't catch that when he was born.

He was a beautiful baby when he filled out. He had tiny perfect features. His body was perfect, but he had the littlest feet I ever saw. His face showed red marks for a year or more.

And his head was normal in a few months. His Dad was so proud of him. He took him to town to show him off. He doted over him all the time. I'm afraid I was a little selfish with him, but I couldn't help it. I was so afraid something would happen to him. The only person I would let him go with was Bill. Anyone was welcome to hold him when they came to the house, but when they wanted to take him in the buggy and go for a walk, I said, "No."

I was really criticized for that.

If I went out to the clothes line to hang up his diapers, I pushed him in the buggy out with me. He went into every room with me in that buggy. He slept with me usually on my stomach. He cried a lot up until he was about a year. The doctor said it was colic and he would be over that in three months. At six months, he was still crying. The doctor said surely he would be over it at nine months. He was not the average baby. I adored him anyway. It really didn't matter if he cried. I would have been bored if he was a good baby. After the second baby was born, I was glad Billy was my first. I often thought how wonderful I had something that is all mine, no one could take him from me. That gave me the most wonderful feeling. I was complete. Mom stayed for a few days after I came home. I was so glad to have her there. I was so weak and so miserable with the stitches. I had torn badly during delivery and there were a lot of stitches. I'm sure that had a bearing on why I was so nervous taking care of him. I couldn't sit or stand for some time. I was so afraid I would do something wrong or something would happen to him.

Mom got me started on a routine of caring for him.

After school was out for the summer, Donna came up to help me. It was so nice to have her there. She helped with everything. One day she was

Edrie Gibbons, Bill's mother.

doing the washing on a wringer type washer which was sitting out on the back porch. Suddenly I heard a scream from the porch.

I jumped up and ran out. The first thing I saw was that beautiful blond hair hanging from the wringer. Then I walked around to the other side of the washing machine and it was plain to see what she had done. In one tub she was rinsing the clothes and running them through the wringer to the next tub of rinse water. When she reached down to get an article to put through, her hair got caught and was pulled through, and her head was bumping against the rollers and she was screaming. I shut off the wringer and sprung it so the rollers released and she could pull her hair free. I know it was a very traumatic thing for her, but I had to laugh. She was upset with me saying, "That could have pulled out my hair. It really hurt."

Still laughing I said, "I know, I'm sorry it happened, but it was so funny seeing those beautiful blond curls hanging down through the wringer and almost in the rinse water." After the hurting stopped, she did see the humor in it. She tied her hair up when she washed clothes after that.

One day that summer we all went down to Bill's folks place for dinner. While we were there, Edrie attacked Donna about some boy she had gone with. The same old thing just as she had done with me. Donna was dumb struck. Edrie gave dates, times, places etc., and Donna had been in Nevada going to school. How she knew all that, we didn't know. She was going to go to Donna's school, to Mom, and to the law. Donna, needless to say, was in tears. She was also frightened that if Edrie could tell it so convincing to us, someone else could believe her. We got out of there as soon as we could and tried to forget it. I felt so sorry for Donna. But there was nothing we could do about it. Saying anything would only make it worse.

Tensions between Bill and I seemed to ease a bit more after the baby was born, like we had something holding us together. The one thing that eased was him thinking I was running around on him. I didn't have all those accusations to fight. He still did not trust me out of his sight. I just stayed at home, trying to keep the peace. If I had a friend that came to see me or if I went to see them, it ended in them being torn to bits by Edrie and Bill. So to save my friends that misery, I broke off all friendships. I remember one friend who was not going to take that off them and came back with a verbal defense. It ended in a fight that I had to break up by holding them apart. There was one very black eye to show for it. I felt so bad for my friend. But to save her any more of that, I quit seeing her. We are still friends, though, to this day.

In times like this, I didn't know if I disliked them more or myself for taking all that. I was such a coward, barely able to live with myself most of the time.

Bill's brother Jim stayed with us a lot. I got so tired of having him around. He delighted in making fun of me, "I'll bet your shoes are too big for me, let me try them on." And he would laugh, "Who taught you how to cook? Don't you ever wash clothes? I need a clean shirt by six, see that you have it ready," "Take me to town. I need some money." Then he would get in my face and say "I know you don't like it, but what are you going to do about it?" He would laugh and laugh. Bill never said a word to him.

As for Bill and me, I was pleased when things quieted down, but he didn't hesitate to tell me that "he wore the pants." I was careful not to rile him as you never knew when he would explode.

My retaliation in all this was silence, not intentional, but as a natural response to the way I was treated. I didn't talk to him because we had nothing in common. There was nothing to talk about because he made fun of everything I said, and he wasn't interested in anything I had to say. I was a dutiful wife. That's all I gave of myself. I had no feelings for him unless he became abusive, then I detested him. A woman is a responder. If she is loved, she will give love. If she is respected, she will show respect. She will also respond in a negative way. She will not be respectful when not shown respect, unloving when she is not loved.

Our home on Warm Lake Road.

138

Chapter 7

"The Good Ole Days??"

1949

We moved from town to the country on Warm Lake Road, into a big two story house on two acres owned by Frank Calendar. When I went in to pay the rent, Frank told me the house was for sale for $2,500. No down payment and $25.00 a month. I was so excited about it, I told Frank I would talk to Bill. Bill was agreeable so I went in and told Frank to write up the papers. I signed them and Bill was to go in and sign also. I told him it was all ready for his signature. I didn't want to tell him more than a time or two or he would blow up and never sign. He never did sign anyway. By not saying anything, I hoped he would eventually go in, but we lived there 2 years and the payments were just going for rent. I guess he was afraid of making a commitment. I finally gave up hope and didn't say anymore. I just hoped that maybe someday—and if not, so be it. I was very disappointed, but this is what I came to accept as time went on.

This place was right out of the past, an old story from days gone by. The first bank in Valley County was still standing on the east side of the property. It was constructed with cement, at least twelve inch walls, and the partitions inside the bank were the same. The big vault was made of steel encased by cement. Two twelve-inch thick doors were still hung on huge iron hinges. It had been deserted for a long time and vandals no doubt had taken their toll on it. In that state, it still talked to me telling of the transactions of the people, how they were dressed, their hairstyle, the clerks with suspenders and black elastic bands on their shirt sleeves. Even an attempted robbery or two. I loved sitting in there just looking around and day dreaming.

The barn sat on the back side of the property. It was a lovely old barn, just as solid as the day it was built, and it still stands today looking the same. An irrigation ditch ran in front of the barn with a walk bridge over it. The fence ran between the ditch and the house. An old iron gate swung on sturdy posts leading to the house. There was a wood shed and an outhouse behind the bank facing the house.

The house was huge with a big closed-in back porch for storing wood, a well-insulated fruit room, a laundry room, and a kitchen with the hand pump sitting on the drain board of the big wooden sink. A huge wood burning cook stove was in the kitchen. A cabinet was by the stove, a priceless antique. It had pull-out bins for flour and sugar, a cone shaped sifter with the crank on the side which sat neatly up in the corner with a door enclosing it, beveled glass doors on the upper side, and white enameled top that pulled out to make a much larger work space. This was the baking center. There was one large window in the kitchen and the table sat in front of it. A nice place for morning coffee.

We also had a dining room, living room, and one bedroom downstairs. There were four bedrooms upstairs with a big hallway. There were large windows in the living room and dining room, which made the house a cheery place. A screened-in porch went across the front of the house. A picket fence bordered the property on the front. There were flowers, Sweet Williams, daffodils, and irises growing all along the fence. There were drive ways off the road on each end, and a circle drive in front of the house.

Oh how I loved that place. Nostalgia was alive, to be treasured and preserved forever. This was it. It was all right here. That is until winter came. I then realized how much suffering came to those who had not.

The economy was just recovering from World War II. Credit was available to anyone. It was so strange to me, as I had never heard of anything like this, where you could buy something on time and pay interest until you got it paid. Imagine a piece of furniture, a ring, or clothes. Just charge them, make payments, and take them home. Bill brought home a rocking chair that he had bought on time. It was a wooden chair and I didn't know how much I needed one until I got one. We must have paid on that a year. It was the only piece of new furniture I had and I cherished it. I was never one to want very much as long as I had things fairly convenient and I could keep it clean and warm, I was content. The outhouse was not such a problem to me (yet). I had lived many years with an outhouse, and you get kind of a strange comfortable attachment, especially at night when you could leave the door open and look at the stars.

The house was in need of repair, some wall board, insulation, paint and elbow grease went a long way. Red was the one who came out and did these things for me. He worked the first summer, that fall, and the winter when he was laid off at the mill. Bill never did help him much but it didn't seem to bother Red, maybe that is what he expected. I helped when I could.

Bill worked on the dam construction at Cascade, driving Uke, moving dirt with a belly dump. He was making good money. Ed was out of work and talked to Bill about driving truck. Ed was a medic in the Navy and had never operated any equipment. Bill told Ed to come up and ride with him for awhile. Bill was on graveyard shift so he let Ed drive some and showed him what he needed to know about operating a belly dump. Ed applied and was hired as an experienced driver, he drove the same shift Bill did. It worked out great. They worked together until the weather forced them to shut down.

Bill went to work for the county driving snow removal equipment. That winter was a bad one for snow and wind, they couldn't keep the roads open enough. They were trying to keep the highways open and there was no chance of keeping side roads open too. The road by our house going to Stibnite was closed for a long time. They worked night and day to keep the main highways open and were barely able to keep traffic moving behind them. There was a pathway kept open for emergencies from our neighborhood to the highway. I remember watching Bill walking down that path to the highway to be picked up by his partner and the relief driver taken home. I could barely see Bill's head, so the snow was over six feet deep! They sometimes worked around the clock to keep the roads open. Bill was gone most of the time.

Our second son was born the day before my 20th birthday on August 16, 1949. Billy was sixteen months old when Tommy was born.

The doctor had to take him with forceps also but he didn't let me go so long before he started me. Tommy was on oxygen as soon as he was born. They kept him in an oxygen tent until we went home. He was so congested and full of mucus. After I got him home I had to set by his basket constantly. He would just stop breathing and I would suction him. Each time I thought, "This is it, he isn't going to breathe," then all of a sudden, he'd suck in a breath and squall. I was weak and shaking by the time he was breathing again. We went to Bill's folks place so there would be someone to watch Billy because I couldn't take my eyes off Tommy. Bill's sister, Betty, offered to sit one night with him for a while so I could get some sleep. I was so afraid she would fall asleep or not be able to get him to breathe again, but I was so exhausted, I accepted her offer. She sat on the bed beside me and Tommy was just in front of her in the basket. Every time she'd move, I was awake. I helped her with the suctioning and as soon as he was stabilized, I laid back down. I did get some rest, I was so thankful to her. Bill wouldn't come in the room it scared him so bad. This went on for about three weeks, until we got the congestion cleared up.

After Tommy got over this problem he was a darling baby, so good. He had dark curly hair and big sleepy brown eyes. He was always happy.

My life was even more complete with another baby to love. I couldn't leave them a minute, I slept with both of them. Bill didn't object because I kept them close to me so they wouldn't disturb him. If Tommy woke up, I could feed him right there.

When Tom was ten months old I was pregnant again. I was very sick. I couldn't keep anything on my stomach and I became very weak. I just couldn't get through a day taking care of the kids. I had to take them to bed with me. The doctor took blood tests and found that I was very anemic. He started me on some very high potency vitamins. It didn't seem to help much so he had me come in every day for a Vitamin B12 shot. He doubted I would carry the baby full term. I barely kept going for five months. He said I would have to spend the rest of my time in bed. He told Bill he would have to decide which one to save when the time came.

I called my Mother in Nevada. I hated to ask her but she was my only hope. She and Red were the only ones who cared enough to help. But of course, I couldn't ask Red to do something like this, although he probably would have tried. My Mom lived with us for four months with two babies, a hostile son-in-law, very little money, a very cold winter and two wood stoves with wet wood—or no wood. Bill would only cut a block at a time from the eight foot lengths piled by the back door. Family seemed to be the lowest of Bill's priorities. He was more interested in buying cars than taking care of us. We were car poor. He was always trading cars and spending money on those we couldn't afford.

Bill was angry because Mom was there, but there was no choice, no one else wanted to take care of me. So he seldom came home. He wouldn't help her by helping to care for the kids or even bringing in wood. He was so hateful. He would not bring groceries home, so Mom had to scratch something up from the bare cupboards, but she was never at a loss to put a meal together. We had a frozen deer in the laundry room that she could whittle off something to cook. She baked bread until the flour was gone.

The laundry was the terrible chore, carrying water from the pump to the stove, bucket after bucket to heat in a tub. She put the clothes in the tub to soak and she would plunge them to loosen the dirt then scrub them on the board. They were rinsed and wrung out by hand from two waters and then the water was carried back and emptied. The clothes hung all over the house on every piece of rope or wire she could find. She never complained, but I knew how hard it was on her. She had done all this most of her life, but she was older now. I was so ashamed of Bill and how he was treating Mom and his family. I had hoped no one had to know what kind of a man he really was. I don't think Mom was surprised, but it didn't come from me. I was so sorry for Mom. I felt like I was injuring her every morning when she got out of bed. I was so ashamed I could hardly face her.

The one thing she finally got so annoyed with that she blew up and told Bill off about was the wood. It was never packed in, it was hardly ever cut. Mom certainly had the spunk to object to this kind of treatment, and tell him so (only since she married Clyde), and I know the only reason she didn't was to protect me from any more pain. She would rather be hurt or even suffer injustice rather than to cause problems in her kid's marriage.

Most of the time she had to go out and dig in six feet of snow to find some chips. I would call Red when we were desperate, but I hated to do that. Bill was coming to expect him to do it all. We couldn't do without wood. In that kind of frigid weather the old house was hard to keep warm. It was colder that winter than I had ever witnessed. It was 50 below for about two weeks. You didn't dare go outside. The cold would burn your skin and you couldn't breathe. Hardly anyone ventured outside. Cars would not start or keep running if they did. The whole town was paralyzed. All we could do was sit by the fire. If you ventured away from the stove, you were miserable. And we didn't have wood. The stove we had in the living room was actually a coal burning stove. It had a small fire box and the wood had to be stood upright, so you could never get a very hot fire in it. One day all her anger that had been built up was vented on Bill about the wood. She said, "You get wood in this house that will burn and keep a fire going or I am going home and taking this family with me. I wouldn't dare leave them here, they would all freeze to death." He got mad and walked out, we called Red again.

Bill came home and found Red sawing and chopping wood outside. Bill did go out and help him. Later Bill said to me, "You did that just to embarrass me."

I answered "No Bill, we have to have wood that will burn and keep the house warm, we are all freezing." He was so angry with me he didn't speak a decent word to me for a month. He could make my life so miserable, and he did just that most of the time. At least we were warm.

Bill and I had gone out several times during the summer to cut wood. I took the kids and left them in the pickup as close as we could get to them. We cut with the cross cut saw and piled the eight foot lengths in the pick-up. We hauled them home and stacked them as close to the back door as possible. He must have anticipated having to cut one block at a time. That was terribly hard work for me when I was pregnant. I'm sure that was a contributing factor to all the problems that followed during my pregnancy.

The kids were short on warm clothes so Mom got the sewing machine out and made shirts out of Bill's old flannel shirts and pants out of old Levi's. I was so glad I kept everything. She made patterns from paper bags. I kept those patterns and old clothes and made warm clothes several winters for the kids. The clothes were heavy and warm. She knitted heavy socks and caps and made coats out of old coats. I've always felt that Mom earned a lot of stars in her crown that winter. She did tremendous work.

My winter was spent in the bed or in a chair. My condition did improve. I helped with the things I could do sitting down. I folded clothes and did hand sewing for Mom's projects. I peeled potatoes, sorted beans, and watched the kids from my chair. I was used to being very busy and it was hard for me to sit. I became so nervous sitting around and watching Mom do all that work. I crocheted a table cloth with red roses inset around the ruffled edge. It was never used by me, but it now belongs to my son, Merrill, and his wife, Jill, since he was the one on the way when I made it.

We made it through the winter, thank God. I will never forget that one. We were so glad to see February come when the terribly cold weather was past. Things never got better for Mom. Bill never changed. It was all so discouraging to me. I was heartsick. Mom tried to spare my feelings and not complain, but how could she stand it? There were times when I hated that man. There were two men besides Red down there at his mother's place, and two boys that could have helped, but they never came around.

Merton and Julia Louge lived beside us. With six feet of snow in the winter between us, we hardly ever saw one another. I did enjoy them, they were good neighbors. Merton was Valley County Sheriff for many years.

Merrill was born March 12th. His was a fairly normal birth except that I was in a state of paralysis through most of the labor, until he moved to the birth canal. Because I didn't move or talk for a long time, they thought I was resting, with no pains. The nurses turned out the light and shut the door. Bill left. I was coming into hard labor, the bearing down stage. I became frantic when everyone was leaving. I tried so hard to make a sound, none would come. The baby was on its way. I tried again and again to call or scream, yet nothing came out. In the middle of a pain, a low groan came from my throat. The energy I exerted to call caused me to thrust myself forward. It took every bit of strength I had when I called out at the same time. The sound that came from my throat was louder and louder until it became a scream. With the tremendous effort it took to get that sound from my throat and with the force of the pain, I was lifted up and thrown over to the end of the bed. I did get someone's attention. The door burst open, the lights came on, and the nurses came in, "What are you doing, why didn't you call?" I tried to say "baby" but nothing would come. They were pulling me to get me straight in the bed and my body would not straighten out. I was twisted, it felt like muscle spasms all over my body. Suddenly everyone was hopping, "Call the doctor, get the gurney." The next thing I knew I was in the delivery room. Someone put a mask on my face and told me to breathe deep. I was glad to do that. I woke up briefly when the doctor was pulling on the baby with forceps. I could feel the tearing and went out again. Then all was quiet. I opened my eyes and the nurse was saying "You have a little boy, Rose. Wake up, it is all over now." Oh thank God. The nurse laid him at my side. I turned over to look at him, he was beautiful. I closed my eyes and went back to sleep.

Merrill was so active, so robust, and had slender but stout looking limbs. He was so healthy. It was all those vitamins. His dad called him "Vitamin Flintheart." He had dark curly hair and big blue eyes. He was beautiful.

When Merrill was three months old we moved to Moreland, a few miles out of Blackfoot. Bill went to work as a mechanic at the Atomic Energy Plant near Arco. A previous employer and friend, Ben Hussman, helped to get Bill on. Pearl Hussman and I had been friends in Cascade. I was happy to be near her again. We stayed with them until we found a house. They were good people.

Shortly after we moved there, I realized I was pregnant again. I didn't know how I was going to handle that. I was afraid, but I had no choice and after all, I did want a girl.

I could make it. I knew I could, for a girl.

My babies seemed to be a very private thing to me. I shared them with Bill but in my heart they were mine, since Bill had treated me like he did, and did not care about his family like he should. I knew I could not depend on him. I had to protect my children from ever being hurt by him. I needed their love and I needed to love them. They filled a part of my life that no one else could, or did.

As the kids got older Bill became cranky with them. I was not surprised because of the way he yelled at me when the kids cried or made noise. He had no patience with them at all. I tried to keep them out of his way to protect them. I became very strict with them because I could see if they didn't mind me, or became unruly at all, he became very abusive. I put them to bed early and usually had them fed before he came home. He liked taking them to the show because they were preoccupied and were quiet. He was seldom home on weekends, but life was easier when he wasn't home.

Little Billy was fairly quiet. He didn't walk until he was twenty months old. He had to have orthotics to keep his feet forward. His feet turned to the inside and it caused him to fall down. Even after he did walk he was never too active. He was quiet and thoughtful. He studied everything out until he was satisfied that he knew all about it. He was so helpful, so caring about everything that went on. He never expected anymore than he was given. He was such a good person, even as a little child. If a baby cried, he went to shake the bed, or pat the baby, or talk to it. They loved him and he showed so much love for them.

Tommy was quite active but very serious. I thought he felt the stress in our home and it bothered him. He had spells of crying for no reason. He would become hysterical and could not stop. A time or two this happened when Bill was home, and as young as Tom was, Bill whipped him hard, which only made it worse. Tommy would try to stop, then he would sob and sob. It was a heart breaker. Once at a movie Bill scolded him and he began to cry. Bill yelled at him, he then began to sob. I got into the back seat with him and held him. He cried harder catching his breath, but he couldn't stop. He continued to cry all the way home. Bill jerked him out of the car and threw him on the ground and kicked him back and forth. I got out and grabbed Tommy and ran into the house. I took him into the bathroom and locked the door. We stayed there for about an hour. I held him in my arms until he went to sleep, he still sobbed even in his sleep. Needless to say, what Bill said to me when we came out; I didn't care. I was so hurt over Tommy being abused like that.

I thought about it for a long while. I felt like he cried because of the stress he felt. It was there all the time, but it was when he was with Bill that he cried. That extra pressure on him made it come to the surface, and then he couldn't stop. The more stress, the more he cried. I had to do something to help him, but what? The next time it happened, I just quietly told him that he could go into the bathroom and cry until he was finished, and no one would bother him. It worked. He may have been in there fifteen minutes the first time. From then on, when he started to cry, he went into the bathroom until he could stop, and then came out. He wasn't two yet. He was just a baby when Merrill was born.

I knew I had to do something. Bill's stress tolerance was so low and he could be so violent and abusive. I was so afraid for the kids. It hurt, it hurt so bad.

Merrill was a little rascal and he was mighty good at it. He discovered how to get out of his crib before he could walk. He walked at ten months. He was probably six months when he repelled from his crib. After his nap one day he came crawling out of the bedroom with a big grin and not a sound. It was obvious he hadn't fallen. I picked him up and put him back in the crib and watched. He stood up to the side of the crib, he lifted his leg, it didn't reach the top of his crib, but he stretched and pulled, finally the other foot came up as he was pulling, the toes on the first foot hooked over the top of the crib. Those toes turned white as he pulled, he got past the toes and pushed that foot on over, farther and farther until he straddled the top of the crib. He was holding on for dear life with those little hands, he wobbled a bit, then steadied himself, then that first foot began to go down, down, slowly down, his body was coming over following that foot. Suddenly he swung around, hanging on with his little fists. He hung like that and rested, getting his balance after that jolt. His feet were still eighteen inches from the floor. Then his hands let go and he dropped. He landed on his hinder, which was well padded, he got a big grin, whirled around, and crawled off toward the front room. He was so proud of himself. I didn't breathe all that time, I couldn't believe it. I knew what I was in for then.

Too young to know fear, and I couldn't put him in a place to confine him. Along with his fast development came more discipline. He had to learn that when I put him to bed he couldn't get out until he took his nap. That was hard on both of us. I had to exercise more perseverance than he did, and that was tough, he was a determined little boy.

His highchair sat by the fridge in the kitchen. I left the room for a minute and when I came back, he was on top of the fridge. I looked at the climb and it looked impossible. It had to be his determination and perseverance. That same perseverance has taken him through life as a winner. However, he respected my authority enough that he did not challenge it. If he had, I know who would have won.

He climbed up on everything. Many times a day I would find him sitting on the middle of the table. One day he climbed into the kitchen sink. I heard the water running. I ran in there and there was that hinder so close to the hot running water as he was reaching down to pick up a piece of silverware. I slipped quietly over and picked him up before he could move and I jerked him away from the hot water. Again I was breathless. I stopped to look at just how he did this. He pulled out the drawers and used them for steps. I put a stick down through the handles of the drawers and that stopped that.

He wanted to go outside. Every time he saw the door open he raced for it. I was afraid he would get out and I wouldn't see him. We had a ditch filled with water in the back of the house and a busy road in the front. I got some lumber and built a playpen in front by the door. I got sand to put in there and put toys in it, but the first time I put him in, he looked around and began to climb. He stuck his feet in the little cracks and up and over he would go. I took all the boards off and made a solid wall, not even a toe hold. I put Billy and Tommy in there, then Merrill. He looked around and headed for the wall. He began to scream. He became hysterical. The neighbors came running from their houses. I couldn't leave him in there. That was it for the playpen. I tore down the walls to just one board and made a flower bed. Merrill liked it better that way. He climbed in and played in my flowers and on my flowers while I sat on the porch watching him.

I locked all the doors and Billy and Tommy had to have help going in or out so as not to let Merrill out. That didn't make him happy. He just didn't want to be restrained. I ran more miles after Merrill than all the other kids put together. He eventually settled down, or else I was just run out.

Our house in Moreland was so clean inside. It was small, but it was modern. I couldn't believe how it simplified house work. It was a joy to keep up.

As my pregnancy progressed, I was not feeling too well. I had a lot of swelling. My next visit to the doctor revealed Albumin poisoning. My blood pressure soared. More frequent visits to the doctor until I was going in every day. The swelling became so bad I couldn't get my shoes on. I wore overshoes outside and socks in the house. I wore a house coat for a dress as nothing else would go around me. I was miserable. It became more difficult to take care of the kids, the house, laundry, and cooking. Bill was noticing I was slowing down. He was getting terribly annoyed, screaming at me when his meals weren't ready. He did absolutely nothing to help. The doctor had told me some time before to stay off my feet. Of course, I could not.

Life became nearly intolerable. I was sick and so tired. I barely moved myself through the day. I didn't know how I was going to make it through each day. We only knew Ben and Pearl Hussman. She came down to help me some with the house work, but she had no idea what Bill was doing. She mentioned things like was there something that Bill could fix for supper. I didn't say anything about him not doing anything. No one knew.

Moreland was a Mormon community. They had come to visit a few times. Their purpose being, of course, to convert us to Mormonism, I supposed. By then I was unresponsive to everything. They did take the boys to some class they enjoyed a couple times a week. I believe they got an idea of how things were going around there. Before long they began bringing hot meals to the house. Hot bread, cakes, casseroles, and fresh milk. Everything you could think of. I was so happy and so appreciative. I thanked them over and over. I became good friends with a couple of the ladies as a result of these visits and charity. They never insisted that I go to church.

There were yet several months that I had to go until it was time. The doctor had me coming in about every day. Thank God for Pearl, she watched the kids for me when I had to go in. There were times when I was so dizzy and light headed that I was afraid to drive, but leaving the kids at home made me feel a lot better. My blood pressure was so high the doctor wanted to check it everyday. The medication he had me on was not doing a bit of good. By the grace of God (I didn't know it then), I pulled through to almost the end of my pregnancy. With the help of the kids, what little they could do, Pearl and the Mormon ladies, I made it.

The last visit to the doctor, when I still had three weeks to go, he said he was going to put me into the hospital. I told him I couldn't go in now because of the kids. He said, "You don't have a choice, you have to go. I really shouldn't let you drive home now, but I know with the other kids you have to make plans for them." I began to cry. He wanted to know why and I told him I didn't have any way to take care of the kids. He said "Rose you find someone fast." I walked out saying I would.

Bill was so angry when I told him, he bellered like a bull.

He began cursing and screaming about what he was going to do with the kids. If I was any woman at all, I would take care of my kids. I wouldn't always be wanting someone else to do it for me.

I tried to close my ears, and I didn't waste my time responding once. Anyone stupid enough to say something like that would not be convinced otherwise by a few words from me.

Chapter 8

"Rosana"

1951

Bill called his sister, Betty, to stay with the kids until after the baby was born. She was there one day before I went to the hospital. The doctor tried in vain to get my blood pressure down and to take down the fluid my body was retaining. I had about three weeks until delivery time. The doctor wanted me to go into the hospital that night, and they would induce labor early in the morning. I called home and told Bill and Betty that I was going into the hospital. I was worried about Merrill. I reminded Betty how close she would have to watch him. There was a road in front of our house and a canal behind and Merrill was fast, and at only a year old he had no fear.

Early in the morning they took me to the labor room. They were ready with the injection and gave it to me when I came in. The pains started almost immediately after the shot was given. Things progressed fast from one stage to the next. Pains were coming very hard and fast. I was going into the bearing down stage, my body was convulsed with every pain they were so hard. The reaction of my body was uncontrollable. This went on and on until I couldn't take any more. I asked the doctor to do something. He checked me and said, "You are not dilating."

Oh no, not again!! I knew there was a God up there somewhere, I begged Him to help me.

The doctors and nurses were scurrying around. I sensed all the activity in the room, but I couldn't see anything. I was pleading with the doctor to do something. He said, "We'll make this as easy on you as possible, Rose, but it's going to be a while. Please hang in there for a little longer."

Here was the forceps again. With each pain he pulled. I raised up in one contraction and saw his feet braced on the end of the table and he was laying back pulling as hard as he could. His face was strained. The pain was intensified with the pull of the forceps, it felt like he was pulling me apart. I wondered how much pain a person could take before they die. Then my thoughts went to my boys at home, I knew I had to make it.

It seemed like forever and each pain was more agonizing than the other. I was straining and he was pulling, the baby is coming, another pain and another pain until it was finally over. I was so exhausted I just lay there—it felt like my insides were pulled out. It didn't stop hurting when the baby came. I didn't have the energy to ask what it was. They must have known that as no one said anything to me. They just quietly took care of the baby and me. I was awake but was so weak I couldn't lift my head, or speak. I heard the baby cough, a terrible sound, coarse and raspy. They took it away, I didn't see it. When the doctor had finished he came and stood beside me and said, "You have a baby girl." My heart leaped within my chest. I must have mustered up a smile as he said "I knew you would be glad to hear that."

My first thought was, "It was worth it all. A baby girl."

God did hear me, I'm still alive and I have a baby girl. Thank You God.

Little Rosana was a sick baby, her lungs were full of fluid and she continued to cough. She and I had to stay in the hospital several days. She weighed over nine pounds, but most of that was fluid, I lost mine sooner than she did, she didn't lose hers for several weeks. She was a beautiful baby.

I thought I was beyond hurting anymore by his unconcern. I was beginning to expect this of him, however, I guess I felt a little sorry for myself because no one was with me. That is a tough time for any woman and I was no different. I didn't spend the energy to even say anything to him, about not coming sooner. I was trying not to care.

Bill's brother, Jim came into see me the day after she was born, The nurse asked him if he was Mr. Saleen, he said he was, "Well, would you like to see your baby girl?"

He laughed and said, "That is not my baby." The nurses looked at me without a word.

"This is my husband's brother." She excused herself and left the room. Jim was gloating over the nurse thinking that he was the father. He looked at me and laughed and laughed. I wanted to throw something at him. I didn't think it was a bit funny.

Great Gran with Rosana.

Her Dad came in to see her that afternoon bringing the prettiest dress in town, so he said. It was lovely, Dan River cotton with lace trim and a big hoop in the skirt. It was a print with a solid maroon color shirt. It was probably a one year size. This dress had won a blue ribbon at the fair the previous fall. He purchased it at a fabric store where he saw it displayed in the window.

The cough finally subsided, and she was a delightful baby. So pretty and so sweet. We were all delighted with her. The boys were so thrilled about their SISTER, but she slept most of the time; they felt a little cheated because she wouldn't do anything. I had a basket for her which went from room to room with me. The boys stood beside the basket and watched her, Merrill had to push a chair up to see her. He would talk to her in his little chipmunk chatter. When she got older and was taking her bottle lying down, he chattered at her, by the tone of his voice he was asking her permission to take her bottle. He turned his head from one side to another, waiting for her answer. If she was still he'd reach down and pull easy so as not to awaken her. As he took a couple swigs, he kept watching her from the corner of his eye, and if she stirred he would quickly put the bottle back in her mouth.

153

Bill wanted the boys named after his family. Needless to say, this was a heartache to me. I did prevail in choosing one second name. The first boy William after his dad, the second name Clyde was after the only dad I ever knew. Thomas was after Bill's step-father, but was my brother's name also and my uncle's name, Edward was Bill's brother's middle name, but it was also my brother's name. So that was okay. If you are wondering how I got away with that one, well I didn't act like I'd ever heard those names before. So we had Thomas Edward. When the third boy came along, Bill wanted to name him after another brother, I was heart-sick, I just didn't want that. I didn't care for Merrill Edward as a person, I had to give into the first name he wouldn't hear of anything else. So then he chose Lyle as a middle name which went well with Merrill, so I thought that was okay. After it was on the birth certificate I realized it was Jim's middle name. He got me again. It was too late to change it. I became very weary of this name game. My resentment of his family was so strong and to have to call my sons their names was another heartache for me then, but now, those names fit them just fine. In fact those names are their own, and I love them.

Rosana's name is an heirloom to me, being my name and my mother's name, which was Anna Bertina. And Bill's grandmother's name was Mina Belle. "Rosana Belle." I sent Gram a card and told her what I named the baby. She got on the bus and came up to Moreland. She brought a beautiful white voile dress for her. We dressed her up in that dress and Gram had me take pictures. She was so proud and so pleased to have Rosana named after her. Bill's mother's name was Edrie Belle and of course that had to come into play also.

Being the first girl, Rosana was our toy. I enjoyed her so much, dressing her up in pretty dresses and bonnets and things little girls wear. All the neighbors came to see her and Pearl spent a lot of time there. Nearly all the neighbors were Mormons so me having four children in four years was nothing new to them. They were very good to me, helped with the boys and took them to some weekday class and then home for the afternoon so I could get some rest.

I was not getting my strength back. I felt bad, I felt weak and just miserable. But I kept going, those babies needed me. I finally went to the doctor, after taking tests, he told me I had a severe kidney infection. I was to go home and go to bed and take this medicine. There was no way I could stay in bed, I sat in the living room more than usual and little Billy was good to help me as much as he could by bringing me diapers and so on.

I had hoped that Bill would help when he got home from work. When he came through the door and his supper was not on the table he blew up, started throwing things and screaming at me that I was lazy. He left and went to the restaurant to eat and didn't come back until it was time to go to bed. I fixed the kid's supper and put them to bed. I was also in bed when he came home. He had his lunch fixed at the cafe and ate breakfast there, which was fine with me. Taking care of him was more work than all the kids together.

One Sunday afternoon Ben had Bill come up and help him cut up some board scraps that he had used in building his house. He wanted to use them for firewood. Pearl called and asked us all up for dinner that day also.

Pearl and I had such a good time together, so I was glad for the opportunity to spend the day with her. When we had dinner ready we called the men into eat. Billy and Tommy had been out also in the spring sunshine, in fact they would rather stay out than eat. I went out after them and got them washed for dinner they scarfed up in a hurry to go back out. The men wanted to rest over their coffee for awhile.

I was standing at the sink washing dishes and looking out the window, into the yard where the boys were.

The men had thrown the board pieces into a pile when it came off the saw. The stack got quite high and boards were thrown every which way, it didn't look too sturdy. While I was watching, Tommy came down the path going by the stack of boards. I saw the pile slipping, I screamed, "Bill the boards are falling on Tommy!" He jumped up and ran out to the pile—I was right on his heels.

Bill looking around didn't see him and he yelled at me "Where is he?" Panic was written all over his face, I pointed to where I had seen the boards falling on him. "Right there." Bill reached down with one hand and lifted the boards, reaching under the boards, grabbed Tommy with the other. He was laying on his stomach. Bill was holding the back of Tommy's coat dragging him out. Tommy hung from his coat, his body was limp. The breath went out of me when I looked at him. No! No! Please God no. Bill stood, holding him not knowing what to do. I grabbed Tommy from him and began to tear off his clothes. He was covered with blood. But I couldn't find any deep wounds, mostly scrapes and scratches. Tom began to move in my arms. He gave a jerk and then opened his eyes.

We rushed into the house and Pearl had some clean towels ready, Tommy was hit so hard he regurgitated and defecated. I took him to the sink and cleaned him off some and we wrapped him in the towels. Bill and I rushed out the door with him to take him in and see if he had any internal injuries. The emergency room doctor checked him out and said, "Other than the scrapes I can't find any thing wrong with him. He is one lucky little boy. I am going to paint him with methylate to disinfect these and that's all he needs." When he finished "painting" him he was red all over. There were very few places that he didn't have a painted scrape.

When the scabs began to form they caught on his clothes so I kept him in shorts as much as possible. If he was outside, people in cars slowed down to see him, they would have to stop and ask what had happened to him, the methylate accentuated every mark. He was miserable for awhile until all the scabs came off. They didn't leave scars though.

I was still not feeling well, I just couldn't get over that kidney infection. The doctor said I was just so run down I had nothing to fight with. I took medication, but I couldn't throw it off.

Bill was getting impossible, he couldn't have me sick and unable to take care of him, and he was not going to take care of the kids nor cook.

Bill told me he was going to Horsethief Basin to go fishing. I told him I couldn't go, he said "Fine you stay here I am taking the kids." I knew that he meant it, any other time I would have welcomed it but I didn't feel like I could or should and Rosana was so little, she wasn't ready to camp out. There was still snow up there and I was sure it was very cold at night and in the morning. Bill told me he was going to take the boys and I could stay home if I wanted to. He said "I think they would be better off staying with Mom anyway if you are going to be sick and can't take care of them." I got ready and went along. Most of the time I stayed in the car and kept Rosana in the car. I did get out when the sun warmed up some. At night I slept cold and I couldn't get warm all day. I began to cough, just a dry hacking cough. Bill was mad when he had to take me out. He took me to his sister Betty in Boise and left and said he was going home and I could find my own way home.

I was fevered and chilling. I thought I had more complications from the kidney infection. I went to a kidney specialist in Boise. When I laid down on the table, I could not stop coughing. I apologized and he said, "I don't like the sound of that cough." He called another doctor down who was in the same building. They took x-rays of my lungs and found I had pneumonia. I took more medication, and he gave me strict orders that I was to go to bed and stay there. I was not to leave Boise because any change of altitude now could be very bad and possibly even fatal.

Betty was with me and heard all this. She said the kids and I could stay with her and Bill, her husband. She did great taking care of the kids and me. I was there two weeks or more. When the doctor said I could go home but I had to continue complete bed rest. I knew I couldn't but I didn't tell him that and I didn't want to put Betty out any more than I already had. Betty called Bill and he came after me. He was like a crazy man, with me and the boys. We walked on thin ice for several days. I kept the boys away from him as much as possible.

I tried to fix his meals, do dishes and take care of the kids but I was weak and after being up for a while I felt dizzy, like I was going to faint. I would have to lay down for a while and get up and do a little more. Instead of better I got worse. I continued to get worse until one day Pearl came down and took me to the doctor again. He scolded me for being up and not taking care of myself. He said "At this rate you are not going to be around to raise your kids."

I really got a lecture. He said it was going to take a lot more time and medication to bring me out of this now. The doctor wanted to put me in the hospital but I couldn't go. I went back home and went to bed. I just let Bill rant and rave, and tried not to pay any attention to him. When he went to work I would get up and feed and dress the kids. Billy was a lot of help to me, at four years old that was very special. I couldn't have made it without him. I sat in a chair in the kitchen and told him just what to bring to me or what to do and we got along. He tried to keep watch on Merrill but that was even hard for me. Tom was able to tell me when Merrill was doing something he shouldn't be. I sent Billy to get him out of or off from whatever he was into.

Billy was a very special little boy, he was very kind and considerate to everyone, he didn't back talk, argue or get angry.

He and I had a very good relationship until his grandmother, Edrie, told him, "If you don't like what she tells you to do, just don't do it, if that makes her mad, you can come and live with me. You don't have to live here, if you come over to my house Toby and Ken will play with you all the time, and we will make ice cream and go fishing and all kinds of fun things." I could see Billy taking all this in, he would look at me with a questioning look on his face. I told him "That isn't so Billy she is just teasing you." He heard it often enough that it sunk in and I could see it in his behavior. A

157

separation began between him and I. I no longer had the respect and obedience from him. It hurt me so, but I thought he would forget it, instead he was very disappointed that I wouldn't let him go live with them. That lasted for a long time, I could see it in his face, when he would get upset about something. It was like, "You have cheated me out of doing what I wanted to do." The poor little boy, what a terrible thing she did to him and me. It was better when we moved to Moreland and he was away from that. I could see him coming around.

One evening Bill came home from work and he started in with the same old thing. I was in bed and the kids were in bed. He tried to get me mad or scare me into getting well, and began with "I'm leaving, I'm going to quit my job, I can't work and take care of the kids and do the cooking and take care of you too. You are some wife, sick all the time. I have wanted to kill you for a long time. But I wouldn't have to do it myself. I could just refuse to let you get medical help. If I had done that long ago you wouldn't be alive now. I should have done it." He left the room for a few minutes and came back. "Next weekend I'm leaving and I am going to take the kids away from you, you can't take care of them anyway, I'll take them to Mom." When he said that I went into a panic, I didn't say anything but my insides were churning and my mind was spinning. I had to do something now.

Bill went out of the room again, I heard him go to his car. When he came back again he had a gun, he aimed it at me saying "I should have done this a long time ago. What's the matter are you scared?"

I felt so disgusted with him, so repulsed, "Just go ahead Bill. I don't care, I'm so tired of you, kill me, and you'll go to prison. The kids will be wards of the state and they may even be better off than they are now." He looked at me for a long time and said, "You won't do anything about it I know you, you're too scared to do anything." I said very quietly, "You might be surprised." He said "What did you say?" I turned and looked at him and said loudly, "You might be surprised." He stood there not saying anything. I turned my head away from him.

Bill lowered the gun and he was more angry than I had ever seen him. He walked up to the edge of the bed like he was going to hit me with the gun. I turned around and gave him a dirty look and turned my back to him again. I said "You do as you wish, I don't care anymore." He left the room and I heard him go out in his car again. I really expected to hear a gun shot, I had had too much of his abuse and I wished he would shoot himself. He sat there for an hour or so, he then came in and jerked a blanket off my bed and slept on the sofa. He left in the morning and by then I had everything planned that I needed to do. I had finally had enough, when he threatened to take the kids to his mother.

I knew that what I had to do was going to be hard, because I was weak and sick. I had to do it because I certainly would not allow anyone to take my children away. I thought things out very carefully and made plans, I couldn't afford to waste any time, every minute counted.

I went through all the kids clothes and laid them in the drawer in neat piles so they would be ready to be put in the suitcase when the time was right. I washed just what I needed to take with me. I folded blankets and laid them in a convenient place but out of sight. Coats and overshoes the same. Everything I would need I laid out.

Bill's check would come in the mail the day after tomorrow. The thought came to me like a thunder bolt. If Bill ever caught up with me, he would take the kids and I couldn't do a thing about it. Just like he did one time when I visited my folks after they moved to Oregon. Bill was mad as usual when I left with my brother, home for a visit from Bermuda. He gave me permission to go when my brother was there then he got mad.

Jim drove him down to Oregon. Jim was the one who was Bill's legal adviser, so he thought. At least Bill took his advice. They drove up to my folks house in the car and simply picked up the kids and drove away. I went crazy. I jumped in my stepdad's pickup and tore after them and was right on their tail and I would have stayed there until they stopped. They did stop and told me if I would go home with them, they would take the pickup back and I could pack and they would wait for me. The only way I would agree is to have the kids in the house with me when I packed. So I went home. I had not intended to stay when I went down there. Remembering all this, I was glad for an extra day. I knew what I had to do.

I called the prosecuting attorney and made an appointment to see him the next day. I wanted to have a restraining order put on Bill so he couldn't take the kids away from me.

When I went in to see him the next day, I told him "All that matters to me was to have the kids safe." He explained the only way I could do that was to file for divorce. I explained I didn't have the money for divorce. He said all that was necessary was to file. He asked me a lot of questions and I told him everything. I told him about my health problems. He called my doctor and asked him to come over so they could discuss these things. Between the two of them a plan was put together for me. I was happy for that, I didn't know if I could hold out for all this. The prosecuting attorney filed a divorce action. He said if I didn't want to go through with it I could just withdraw it later. However it would prevent him from taking the kids away from me. He also filed a restraining order.

I guess I was surprised that they believed me but they didn't doubt me at all. The doctor gave me medicine to take with me. The attorney phoned my mother and asked her to meet me at a certain place. He called ahead to Sugar City and reserved a cabin for us to stay in. He gave me an assumed name to use which would be in his files and the doctors files. He gave me a map of just how to get there and how to find the cabin. I couldn't believe it. I didn't expect that at all. I didn't pay a cent to him, he said "Save it, you'll need it." I explained that I could be ready when the check came in the mail. Everything was set, I could take off tomorrow.

That night everything went as usual. The following morning as soon as he was gone, on the bus and gone for sure, I pulled the suitcases out from under the bed. I pulled open the drawers and carefully laid clothes into the suitcases, I needed to make room for everything, I didn't have an inch to spare in the packing. I put everything in the trunk of the car, then got the kids up, dressed them in the clothes I had kept out for them. We were ready to go.

I needed to pick up a few groceries from the store, I put them on the charge account. The PO was in the store so after shopping I got the mail out of the box. Whew!! It was there, I got it cashed and put the cash in my purse. I filled the car up with gas, went into the house and called the attorney. He was happy that everything had gone as planned. He told me where my mother would be and that she had called him last night and all was set.

I drove off down the road, into Blackfoot and beyond. The rest is something of a blur. I think I caved in from the pressure I had been under. I really don't recall anything after I picked up my mother. She took over the driving and took us right to a cabin in Sugar City. Oh what a relief! I was still afraid. After a few days when I got rested and caught my breath I felt much better. We called the attorney collect every day. They had the county and state police alerted for Bill. He told me every place he went. He said Bill had hired a helicopter to go over the area to see if he could spot my car. He hired a lawyer and was attempting to file for divorce and get custody of the kids. He was running around in a car he rented, sometimes all night looking for us. He was displaying some bizarre behavior, drinking and driving, making scenes in bars, etc. Jim had been with him part of the time.

We stayed there for about two weeks. I felt much better and was fully rested. The attorney told me he thought everything was okay now for us to go on to Oregon. I told him I wanted to go back and get some other things from the house. He said he would give me a report on where Bill was and what he was doing, before I left Sugar City. I called the next morning, he said Bill had taken the car and gone to work. So he felt everything would be okay.

We drove to Blackfoot and on out to Moreland. The house looked the same as when I left it. I got a few cooking pans and towels, sheets and bedding and a few more clothes. I packed that car like a sardine can. I put Rosana's basket in there for her to ride in and two boys in back and one in front. They traded off. Before we left I wanted to go see Pearl, I couldn't leave without her knowing. So we drove the few blocks to her house. We all went in, and the boys were playing with some things Pearl had given them. I didn't want them to go outside for fear Jim might pick them up. I knew Bill was working and it would be several hours before he came home. Pearl was fixing lunch for us. Pearl was shocked by all that had gone on, she said "Rose I didn't know you were having trouble and I certainly didn't know this about Bill."

I told her "I have not told anyone until I talked to the attorney, I didn't want to give Bill a bad name. I hoped he would someday straighten himself out. And he would never have had a chance if people knew what he was really like. I have given up hope now. I think he is crazy and I just want to get away from him and get the kids away from him. I certainly do not want his folks getting my kids. I guess I would do anything to keep that from happening. I am going to Oregon and get a new start, I know it won't be easy but I'm willing to do anything."

Pearl was in tears, she said if only she had known, I told her no, it was better this way.

There came a knock at the door, Pearl opened it and there was Bill. He pushed the door open and when he saw Mom he said "I should have known you would be at the bottom of all this."

From somewhere I got courage, I marched toward the door pushed Pearl back and pushed Bill back out the door, I told him, "You get out of here, don't you blame Mom for anything, it was you and you know it, just think about what you have done to me and your kids." I said to him "Go to the back yard so Pearl's neighbors won't hear." I marched ahead of him and when we got out of earshot of everyone I turned around and let him have it. I told him everything he had ever done, what his family had done, how he didn't care how they treated me. And what a life I had living with him. I wasn't going to live that way anymore. He was never going to take the kids away from me, they were mine, all he had done was father them. He tried to get in a word now and then but I raked him over the coals for everything he said. I think he met a new woman out in the back yard. He acted pretty dumb founded, he wasn't prepared for this. He tried to talk me out of going, I said "I told you I am going to leave you and go to Oregon and I'm not going to change my mind. If you try to stop me, all I have to do is call the police. I have got you covered all the way around, Bill. Nothing will change my mind. When you threatened to take the kids to your mother, that was it for me. I am no longer afraid of you, I will never be afraid of you again. And no one will ever take my kids away from me either."

Mom told me later we were out there about two hours and it must have taken me that long to get it all off my chest. I was feeling better all the time. I began to run down, he tried to take advantage of that and bully me into not leaving him. I charged him like an angry lioness, he pulled back. He asked me if I would stay the night so he could be with the boys for a while. "I will stay the night but Mom is sleeping with me."

He wanted to take the sleeping bags outside and sleep with the kids. I warned him that every cop in the country was watching him. He had better not try anything.

I didn't sleep well. I was so afraid he would take Billy and Tommy and run.

The next morning we were up and ready before the sun came up we ate and we were loading up in the car. He stood out beside the car and was crying saying, "Don't take my kids away from me, please don't take my kids." For the first time I felt a twinge of pity for him. Then the boys watching him were really torn up over that scene. Billy said "Mom, why are you taking us kids away from him?"

I said, "Billy I just think it will be better for all of us, I'm sure you will understand later on. Please just trust me." I knew I hadn't convinced him of anything. He was crying and it broke my heart. I cried for Billy. There was not a word spoken for a long time. I didn't feel good about what I had done, but at the same time I knew I had to do this. If I gave up now, oh what is the matter with me I can't. This has been a long time coming, it is the only thing I can do to keep the kids and myself safe. Nothing would change if I didn't go through with this. All I felt for that man was contempt and yes, hate.

It hurt so to see Billy, he felt so sorry for his dad, I don't think he has ever forgotten the way his dad cried and asked me not to take the kids away from him. Would he ever forgive me. I didn't know what to say to him. I couldn't tell him what his dad was really like and the things he had done to me and what his grandparents were like, how that would affect him and the other kids, that they may be caring for him if I didn't take him away. I wanted to tell him, I just couldn't live knowing that they would raise any of my children. Oh! how I wanted to tell him those things, but I couldn't.

The trip went well to Oregon. We stayed all night in a motel in Bend, the long trip was too much for all of us. Mom took us to breakfast at a restaurant. We enjoyed that. Everything went better after that stop. I think we had something else more refreshing to think about rather than that tragic scene we experienced the day before.

We arrived in Myrtle Creek that afternoon. I hadn't seen the property the folks bought on South Myrtle. It was beautiful. Covered with trees and a creek running through it. There was a lovely garden spot down by the creek. They had it all planted and some things were ready to eat. Even though it was just May. There were shady spots so inviting, to set and meditate by the creek. The framework of their house was sitting on a flat at the crest of the hill, with a spectacular view of South Myrtle Creek and the country road winding along the creek. There was a lot of foliage along the creek, but it was fairly open at the turn of the road, where our view was.

Dad had set up a tent with side walls and a wooden floor, it was fixed up very nice—covering on the floor, a set of steps going in. It was under some pine trees so it was cool most of the day. They had electricity for a light, a stove and a fridge, but also a wood cookstove beside it for heat and cooking on rainy days. They had a double bed and dressers, a table and chairs and water piped just out the door. There was the bench, with a wash basin and the bucket of water. It looked and was so homey and convenient. Mom didn't really care when the house got finished, she was happy there. Dad told her she would care when the rainy season hit.

I can still see them sitting on the steps in the evening as contented as could be. It was a beautiful sight to see. It represented a lot of things to me. Things that she had put behind her and I was so happy for her.

Dad had the rafters up, the roof on and the outside walls, no windows in but for the time being that was going to be where we slept.

Donna and her new husband, Darrell, had also got a piece of land on South Myrtle and were building a house. Darrell and Dad traded off work to help one another with the difficult projects. They both worked at the mill so their time was rather limited. I found myself enjoying the work on the house also. I didn't try anything unless Dad was there, but I helped him a lot. Mom said if I helped him she would do the cooking. That suited me fine. He was so good to work with, never out of sorts, easy going, not too speedy, always had time for a break when Mom would bring over the coffee pot and the cups. He appreciated my efforts. I don't suppose the work was so great but he would call me in the morning and say it's time to go to work. That made me feel good.

I was so thankful that this man came into our lives. He seemed happy to have us there. The kids were happy, they had a lot of playing to do up there and down in the little creek that ran behind the house. They made forts in the bushes, fishing poles out of willows and fished in the little stream called Ben's Branch. Dad got them set up with hooks and showed them how to find worms and put them on the hooks.

Old Kubi was in his delight, he really took to the kids, and followed them all around and they played with him; he would fetch for them. They loved Kubi, Billy being the oldest was most fond of him and he would follow Billy. There was a trail leading from the house down the hill to the garden and creek. The kids loved running up and down.

Mom and Dad were so good to all of us. They had beds set up in the new house for us and one corner fixed up with shelves and blankets up for partitions. Donna and Darrell had another corner for their sleeping room. Little Rosana slept in with Mom and Dad. Mom was really bonded to Rosana because she was with her so much. That bond was forever.

I didn't have any plans about what to do. The folks said not to worry as I could stay with them as long as I needed to. It seemed like I couldn't concentrate on anything at that time. They understood that and said don't worry about it now. Mom had seen so much hard times that she did understand.

It was so nice just to be contented, to go to bed at nights and not be afraid. To live again is what I did. One very vivid memory of when we were there was when we went to bed and listened to the frogs and watched the moon through the trees and there was peace. The boys always had a lot to talk about, what they had done all day, how many frogs they found, about the fort they were building and so on and on. Little Merrill lying beside me in the big bed, wasn't going to be outdone for anything, so he talked to me too, in that cute little chipmunk chatter. His voice would raise and lower like he was asking a question and wait for an answer. He had all the tones right for a good dialogue but I couldn't understand a thing he said. It was so sweet. Donna and Darrell could hear him too. We'd lay and listen sometimes for an hour. I was actually disappointed when he learned to talk. We were all enjoying being together but we knew it was not a good idea to spend the winter this way. Winters are rainy, damp and cold, nothing but rain for months.

I didn't hear a thing from Bill, and that was fine with me. Billy didn't ask anymore questions and I didn't bring it up either because I just didn't know what to tell him. I couldn't tell him the whole truth, so I felt it was better not to tell him anything.

Darrell heard about a big house up the creek that was for rent. We went up to look at it. There was a big garden planted and an irrigation system in place. Fruit trees galore, there was everything there we needed. There was a big grape arbor with a beautiful crop coming on. It was like someone had set it all up for us. The house was big. We started moving in and we seemed to find what we needed for furniture. We used the downstairs and there were still several rooms upstairs. Darrell went out and got some wild meat, we ate from that and out of the garden. We bought milk from a neighbor and baked bread.

When we began to can we had to rustle jars. Mom was the president of the H O A club (Help One Another). She put out the word and we got offers for jars and for garden produce from the ladies and many referrals for this and that. We gleaned all summer. We picked tomatoes and halved with the owners. We gleaned many orchards, gardens and got most everything for very little cost to us. We'd bring home three gunny sacks of corn at a time or tubs full of green beans.

Donna was expecting at this time but it didn't seem to slow her down. Mom came up and helped us after Dad went to work. She was a lot of help with the kids. Of course the kids had another wonderful place to play, they loved it up there.

One evening just after dinner we were sitting around the big table in the kitchen drinking tea. One cup had just been filled from the hot tea-kettle on the stove. Merrill was playing, and short as he was, he reached up to the table and got his little fingers inside that cup and pulled it over on himself. That boiling tea went down his front. He began to scream. I knew he was burned bad. I jerked his clothes off and got the shortening and applied a very thick layer over his chest, stomach and groin area. I held him and walked with him through the house and back and forth.

He was laying across my arms still crying and I was crying, Donna was crying and Mom was crying. It was so sad to see that little baby in such pain. Mom wanted to relieve me so she took him outside where the air was cooler holding him across her arms. She walked under the grape arbor, back and forth I stood over by the house watching them, I was happy for the break. My arms were shaking, from holding him in that position. I knew Mom was going to give out soon. She went back and forth up and down the grape arbor time and time again. Merrill's cries lessened to a whimper, he was getting tired and the pain was letting up, that went on for a while then he was quiet. I walked up to where they were. Merrill was sound asleep. She walked for a little longer and then we went into the house. I took him and laid him down on the bed. He slept all night. When he awoke in the morning he wasn't hurting. I couldn't believe it.

He was blistered and I very carefully applied more shortening, then took clean sheets and tore them into bandages and wrapped his little body. He looked like a mummy but he didn't hurt. I redressed his burns every evening and every morning. I kept him away from all dirt of any kind to keep him from getting infection. I had to take a rest from the canning, so I could be right with him every minute. I took a job cleaning houses and took him with me. He seemed to understand and did not complain.

After about two weeks I left the bandages off and he was as good as new. He had a mighty pink belly but he didn't have one scar. The skin was very thin and tender so I kept shortening on him until the redness went away. When he completely recovered I went back to the canning project. We canned until there was no more left in the fields to can. Oh yes, did I mention we did this on a wood stove. None of us had a problem with our weight that summer.

We canned a lot of meat also, meat that Darrell brought home.

I worked at odd jobs cleaning so that I could have the kids with me. Mom or Donna took care of them sometimes. Bill had not sent any money but I didn't expect him to. I knew I could do it somehow, with the help of my family. God bless them. When winter was coming on I did go see about getting some welfare, but I was not eligible because I hadn't been in the state long enough. That was fine I didn't want to get it anyway.

We were scraping the bottom of the barrel sometimes but I got enough work to supplement and keep us going. That was all I needed. I didn't want to be a drain on my family, but I had to depend on them.

Donna had a little boy in October. Cutest little feller. We all enjoyed Terry so much. We fixed Donna's room up for her before she came home from the hospital. We didn't have much time after we moved in, we were just too busy canning. And we didn't have much to do much with. It was more challenging that way.

My brother, Roy, was stationed in Bermuda during the war. He married a girl there who had a little girl, Margie. They had a boy, Barry, who was just a little older than Billy. Roy's job continued there for a few years after he was discharged. In 1952 they moved back to the states and moved to Myrtle Creek. Roy got a job at the mill and Angie worked for the telephone company. They needed a place to live so they took over the upstairs. They had it fixed up as cute as could be. They papered the walls and painted and got some nice furniture.

We had a big barrel wood heater in the front room and the cook stove in the kitchen. Roy and Darrell got in a lot of wood.

Little Barry was about five when they came, he had on neat pressed shorts with suspenders and white shirt. I don't think they had any dirt in Bermuda. Barry sat in a chair and played with one toy at a time. He was perfect in manners and obedience. My kids would stand and watch him sitting in that chair. They had never seen a kid act like that. I couldn't believe my roughneck brother had a child like this. When my boys had looked him over good, they went back out to play. Barry watched them through the window. He was never again content to set in a chair. Angie finally gave in, that little boy loved dirt and he got dirty. He got a lot dirtier than my kids. Well, Merrill was a close second. Then Tom. Bill was always very neat. He did the same things but didn't get that dirty. Well, those four boys became inseparable. They were together all the time. We would have to find them to come in to eat.

As winter came along, it seemed to penetrate that house and we were finding it hard to keep the house warm for Rosana and Terry. Angie must have got pretty cold too as she would come down stairs and stuff that old stove full of wood. She went back up stairs and pretty soon I'd smell something getting hot. I'd run for the stove and sure enough it was wide open and hotter than hades.

The post behind the stove was hot, the floor was hot, I grabbed bunches of towels, wet them and hung them on the post and covered the floor, as soon as the towels were hot, I exchanged them with wetter and cooler towels. I shut the stove down and stood right there until it was no longer red. When I got things cooled down I went up and got Angie and brought her down and explained to her that she could burn the house down doing that and please don't do it again. She would say "Oh! Okay" go back upstairs and when she got cool she'd come down again. When I yelled at her she would say "Well that sure heated the upstairs nice but I won't put so much in it next time."

We'd go through the same thing again and again, I'd run for the wet towels. I have always been so afraid of fire and she was not at all afraid of it. Then I figured it all out, they didn't have wood to burn in Bermuda. They didn't need any heat there. They didn't need to water the lawns because the heavy dew during the night took care of that. They scrubbed the top of their houses to catch rain water which they used for the household. It rained every day. Oh! What a life. We had quite a time Westernizing that gal, but we all loved her and she was a very good cook.

One evening in the fall, Roy and Darrell and I were talking after supper. We needed some meat. We got the guns and went out in Darrell's car and drove up the creek. We had a spot light and we did see a nice big buck off in a field, close to the road, so one of them shot. They both ran out to get the buck and I got out and opened the trunk of the car. I jumped back in the front seat and scooted over to the middle. The guys threw the deer in the back of the car and jumped in beside me and we took off flying down the road. Everything was done double time. I thought " Boy that was easy." Darrell was driving so fast though we were sliding around every corner, flying down the straight stretches on that old dirt road. Finally I said, "Do you have to go this fast?" He answered, "Yes unless we want that game warden to catch us." I said "Oh sure, there's no game warden."

Roy shouted at me, "What are you thinking of girl, there is a game warden on our tail."

Darrell said "We saw him when we threw the deer in the trunk."

168

I began to shake, thinking about going to jail, or being fined, with no money I'd have to go to jail. I was also wondering how we were going to get up our driveway. That game warden was not going near as fast as we were. I knew we were all going to be killed.

When we came to our driveway, Darrell took that corner on two wheels, skidded and nearly lost control. He turned off the lights and went around the house to the back, unloaded the deer in the woodshed. Parked the car, ran into the house and turned out the lights, before the warden came into sight, we were all standing and watching out the window. Soon we could see the lights coming slowly like he was looking for tracks, the car stopped for a few minutes and went on slowly. Of course we were all very apprehensive about what he had seen, and could he see the tracks leading up to the house. Angie began to laugh, we all wondered what she was laughing about.

Roy said, "When she gets scared she laughs, the more scared she is the more she laughs." When the warden got out and was looking around our driveway she laughed louder and louder. Roy told her she should go into the bedroom because if he drove up the driveway he would hear her laugh.

We watched him for about an hour and he finally drove on down the road. We watched for a long time after that to see if he was just baiting us. We were finally able to breathe again. But we were not going to take any chances. The guys went out and bled the deer and gutted it, in the dark. They covered up signs with wood chips and hid the deer so it could not be found. We were ready for bed. The following morning the guys got up early and went out to check it. They came in with a sickening look on the their faces and asked me to come out. When they opened the little door into the cubby hole, the smell just about knocked me down. I said "What is that smell?"

They were looking pretty sheepish and said that deer had been shot before and had gangrene in several spots on its body.

That is probably why he was standing in the meadow and so easy to get. They said they smelled something but they just thought he was in rut and they didn't say anything.

We had to have a family conference to decide what to do with it. It wasn't going to be easy to dispose of that thing and leave no tracks. We finally decided we had to bury it, and play Indian to cover the tracks. Guess it worked, we didn't hear anything about it.

Darrell tried to keep meat around, that was about the only staple we couldn't supply. We were existing on a very skinny budget. We had everything we needed, and we took care in preparing meals so we could utilize what we had. It is my understanding that people who needed wild game would not be prosecuted if they got it. I do think it would have been more lawful if we had permission to do so.

Clothing was another area where we had to be very conservative. We shopped in used clothing stores and being very selective we got good articles of clothing. I always took pride in dressing my kids, meaning clothes were always mended, washed, ironed and put on clean bodies. Many people remarked about how well dressed and well groomed my kids were. I told them how I did it, and that anyone could do it with a little extra work. At nights when the kids went to bed I would clean their shoes and line them up along the wall. It was quite a conversation piece to be sure, especially when there were fourteen shoes lining that wall.

I was just as particular about what went on the inside of those little people nutritionally. I read a lot about it and my mother was very nutrition minded. I was strict, determined to teach them manners and to know right from wrong. I was just as strict as I had to be to get the required results. I did not give up until I saw those results that would get them to where they needed to be as adults. This was a passion with me and I didn't let up. I knew I could work as hard or harder than a lot of people and I was willing to do anything to achieve what was necessary, willing to give all I had for those kids but I expected a lot in return from them. That is why if I had to, I used the belt. I gave them every chance first. Even though they didn't believe it. It hurt me worse than it did them.

As winter progressed there was more rain and cold. It was not cold as we know cold in Idaho. It was from that constant rain and nothing ever dried out. It just got wetter until the walls began to mildew. The windows were mildewing and all the clothes if not mildewed were musty smelling.

Rosana had a respiratory problem and she wasn't faring too well in that dampness. We began looking for other houses to rent. They preferred that I find something first before they moved out. I went down to talk to Mrs. Endicott about renting one of her cabins for the winter. Mrs. Endicott was a widow lady who lived on a ranch. She was fairly old and not able to do much on her place. She was a kind and sweet person, and very charitable.

She owned four cabins on the opposite side of the creek from her house. Her house sat in some trees and some of Oregon's finest undergrowth. She had a log home that her husband built when they homesteaded this place. She had plenty of water from South Myrtle Creek which ran through her place for anything she wanted to do. She kept stock on her place, had the hay land leased out, which provided enough hay for her stock. She would never give up, nothing was ever too hard for her. She did need help though with the chores. She may not have known it until I came along but she was glad to turn over the outdoor chores in exchange for the rent of one of the cabins. She offered this exchange, I thought I would have to clean houses for the money to pay rent. This was much more to my liking.

Moving was a job when it came to splitting up the canned goods. It was a heavy commodity and where was I going to put it in the little cabin. Well I put them under beds, under Rosana's crib, in corners under the table. We found places to put it. That was worth a lot to us. We moved in and got settled, fixed it up and it became a cute and comfortable little place. There were other children living there for the boys to play with. Some of the kids were not too easy to get along with according to my boys. I told them, "Just go out there and hold your ground, don't let them run you off." This was a first for us.

Billy came in crying saying, "Mom they are going to beat me up."

I said "They won't beat you up unless you let them."

"But Mom, they will hit me they said so, and I don't know how to fight."

"I can show you how to fight, come in the front room and we will have a fight." His eyes got big and he wasn't sure what was going to happen. I got down on my knees and hit him a couple times. He started to cry, I told him, "You will surely get beat up if you do that. Most of the time if you act like you can fight you really don't have to. That is called a bluff, so come on now, hit me."

"I don't want to hit you, Mom."

"This is just pretend, so you pretend you are hitting me but pretend good so you can learn. First you have to act like you are really mad. You run up to them and they will probably run away. If they don't run, you may have to hit them, so here's what you do. A quick jab to the nose will make it bleed and when they see blood they are whipped, they go running to Mom. You have to tell them though, that they can't tell you where you can play. You can play any place you want to. It is better to stop a fight before it gets started, but if you can't, get it over with as soon as possible. One little peck on the nose will get it over in a hurry. Don't ever start a fight. If you do you will get punished at home. Now you are ready, they are never going to call you a chicken. Okay hit me."

He was doing good but I kept saying that doesn't even hurt. You have to hit harder than that. I punched him. We boxed all afternoon. I told him he was ready to go out to play. His confidence was built up and he was ready for anything.

I didn't tell Billy that I was so afraid for him. I knew being raised by a mother alone was putting a boy at a disadvantage. I had to try to make up for that. I watched at the window. I saw them come up saying something to him. His little brothers were right behind him. Oh-oh, I didn't want to look. I couldn't stand this, they were so big. I knew I couldn't run out and rescue him that would embarrass him and undo every thing, and show that I didn't have confidence in him. I had told him, I knew he could do it. In a few minutes they came banging at the door. I opened it and they were all talking at once. Billy said "Mom I scared them and didn't even have to hit them. I got mad and hollered at them and told them I could fight and they all ran. There were four kids out there. Some hid, some went up the trees."

I grabbed him and said, "I am so proud of you, I knew you could do it." He won the standoff on South Myrtle. He never had any problems after that. They all got along and played together.

After we got settled in the house. I took the kids and went over to Mrs. Endicott's to get the instructions on how she wanted things done. We went out in the yard. She had peacocks that screamed at us, she had some geese that snuck up behind us and pecked us on the back of the legs, but really they didn't peck the kids legs, they went for the bummer. The kids resented that. Mrs. Endicott said "Oh just don't pay any attention to them when they get used to you they won't do that any more. They want to be fed first thing."

We fed them so they would stay away from us. We went out into the barnyard. Mrs. Endicott explained; "This is a cow you will milk, and this one you milk but you always have to put the kickers on her or she will kick you to kingdom come. Don't act like you are afraid of her or she will get real mean. Milk her last because when she blows up she gets the other cows nervous." I was beginning to wonder why I made this deal. I had never milked a cow. I didn't tell her that, I knew I could learn. But I didn't know about a mean cow. Poor Mrs. Endicott—how did she manage all this? She said, "Oh yes I wanted to tell you about the bull, the only time he will bother you is if you are afraid and if he does come after you, grab that pitchfork, I always keep it right here, stab him good and he will leave you alone." I was thinking how am I ever going to bluff those cows, the bull, the peacocks and the geese. She had some chickens that were pretty friendly. They came to meet me but they only wanted to be fed. Well good I didn't have to worry about them.

I asked her where she kept the cows at night, hoping she would say in the corral in back of the barn. She didn't, she said all of the cows stayed with the bull down in the lower end of the field. Oh! Oh, first day I'm going to die. I better leave the kids in the house with her. I don't want them to see me run from a bull. Mrs. Endicott told me not to feed the kids before they came over because it was too early. She would fix them breakfast and me also. I told her that wasn't necessary at all and she wouldn't hear of anything different.

Everything went fine getting the kids up and over there. She was up and had a nice warm fire going. The kids liked her, she was an old school teacher so she knew how to handle kids. I took the milk buckets and went toward the barn, before I opened the gate I stretched my neck around to see where the cows were. Sure enough they were with the bull down in the lower end of the pasture. I put the milk buckets in the barn and got the kickers out and looked them over to be sure I knew how to put them on that wild cow. I grabbed the pitch fork and went to the end of the pasture by way of the fence, so I could make a quick get away if I had to. I got the attention of the cows and they all turned and watched me. I yelled and swung the pitch-fork around and acted real tough.

They didn't act like they were afraid but they did turn from watching me and headed for the barn. Then a frightening thought came to me. What if that bull goes into the barn with the cows, how will I get him out. I began to run staying close to the fence, trying to head off the bull. They all began to run and when they got to the barn they were all together. The cows went into the barn and the bull went right on by. I slipped up close to the barn with my pitch-fork handy, went around the corner and there stood the bull watching me.

My heart was racing so fast I could hardly speak when I tried to yell at him to put in my bluff. He turned and moved a couple steps, then turned again and looked at me as if to say what are you doing, I don't want to take my eyes off you. I slipped into the barn and closed the door. All four cows were in their stalls eating and wasn't that great. Now which one was the mean one. Must be this one because this was the stall the mean one was in before. I locked the head stalls and sat down to cow number one, she moved a little when I washed her udder. I yelled at her and she stood still. Wow! that was great. I began to milk, I got the milk into the bucket but boy was it hard. How was I going to milk four cows, my hands were getting so tired. I remembered my brothers complaining about this when we lived on the ranch, but I always worked in the house, I didn't have to milk.

When I finished the one cow, I didn't think I could do another, but I shook my hands a while and sat down to the next one. Washed her and began to milk, somehow I got through that one. One more down, they were all finished eating the hay I had given them but they all stood just fine. Oh my hands, wrists and arms were killing me. If this last cow gives me any trouble, I'm just going to walk away and leave her. She was one that gave down her milk and stood chewing her cud all the while I milked her. Gee I felt so good about the mean cow being so good for me.

Now I had to take the milk to the house, strain it and put it in the jars for people who bought milk. I felt real proud of myself, I just acted like it was all old hat for me.

The next day was much worse at first because my hands were so sore but after a while they loosened up and it went pretty good. Mrs. Endicott went to the coast to see her son and family for a few days. I told her we would be just fine. And everything did go fine. The old bull didn't attack me, the cow didn't kick me. I couldn't believe I was having such good luck. She was gone for about a week and her daughter-in-law brought her home one morning when I was still in the barn. I had the kids in there with me. I told them what would happen if they made noise and got the cows upset. They were very good, they didn't want to see me get kicked.

Mrs. Endicott came out to the barn to tell us hello. She gave her greeting and talked to the kids for awhile then she turned to me to say something and looked a little startled, "Why do you have that cow hobbled, she never kicks." Oh my! I'm glad I didn't know. We got quite a laugh out of that but we had quite a time getting the cows to go back to their own stalls. We never used the kickers again. The longer I milked the easier it got. I loved being out there with the animals, even the bull and I were getting along fine.

The kids never did trust those darn geese, they would always ask "Mom did you feed the geese yet?"

———————

Mom invited me to come visit the "Club". I could bring the kids and we would have lunch there. I was to bring a casserole or desert. Donna had been a member for a long time, she really enjoyed the members which were made up of the people who lived on South Myrtle Creek. There were a lot of farmers and people who had been raised on the creek. There were people of all ages. They took care of one another, if there was a sickness, death,

*Mom and Clyde
beside the house
they built.*

fire or just anything where help was needed, on the creek they were there. It was a very worthwhile organization.

Mom had been president for some time. I was really impressed to see her in a leadership position. She did very well, everyone liked her. She was good at delegating, but also a good worker. They had some project to do the day of the meeting, which was once a month. Sometimes they worked on quilts, clothes for kids, dish towels or anything for their (Help Basket). People would work on things all year to put into the H O A donation collection. This group had been formed many years before and they were faithful members who never missed a meeting. They took a lot of pride in their organization. I was impressed and did join the group.

I was happy there, I felt like I had been let out of prison. My shackles were gone. It was good being a part of the community. It wasn't easy making a living but I did what I knew I would have to do when I left Bill. I didn't believe for a minute that he would send any money. I was prepared to do anything I had to do to make a living and feel good about doing it. The kids were happy, they had an interesting life. They had family there who cared for them. They felt welcome wherever we went. We did have a lot of outings with and without family. They loved Barry, he was a good little kid and they were all cohorts.

One day I got a message at Mom's to call the Sheriff's office. She came down and gave me the message. I rushed right up there and called. The message was "Your husband Bill is in town and wants to see the kids."

I told him there was a restraining order and he can't see them. The Sheriff said he could if I agreed. I said the only way I would agree is if a social worker was present at all times. I did not want him coming to my house as I didn't want him to know where I lived. The Sheriff asked if we could meet at my mother's. I told him, "My sister lives in town and if you want to call her and ask if it is okay to meet at her house, make an appointment and please be sure to have the social worker there, call me back here. I will come in and be there. I will check to see if the social worker is there before I take the kids in." He said that was fine. He did call back and the appointment was that day in the afternoon.

I was heartsick, I hadn't felt that way since I had left him. I wanted to take the kids and run away. But I knew I should let the kids see their father.

I got the kids ready and drove into town, I called Donna before I went up there, she said a case worker was there and everything was fine. I drove up to the house, Bill came out to the car to meet us. I didn't want to look at him, I avoided it as long as possible. He greeted the kids and told them he had a lot of toys and things in the house for them. Of course they ran to the house. I walked toward the house and Bill said, "Rose, I've just about gone crazy without you."

My response to that was a cold, "I just about went crazy with you, and before you go any farther, remember you came here to see the kids not me, all I had to say to you I said in Moreland. I don't want to talk to you now. You go in and visit with the kids."

He followed close behind me and kept talking to me, telling me how much he missed me and how he wanted me back. Just then the case worker opened the door. She said to Bill, "You come in here to talk, you are not to harass Rose at all. She was good enough to bring the kids in to see you, now you hold up your end of the bargain." Bill ignored her and went on with the same old rhetoric when we got into the house. I went over and sat down on the couch across the room from the kids. They were playing with the toys Bill had brought to them and looking kind of "I don't feel comfortable here, what is going on." Billy was looking from Bill to me and back again. I tried not to get upset with Bill but he just kept drumming at me. The more he said the more he was primed to say, it went from bad to intolerable, and I finally blew up at him. It was obvious that he was there to see me not the kids and that made me so angry. He barely talked to the kids.

"Bill I went through a lot to get away from you, now I am not going to listen to all this and go through this again. I came here to have peace. That is all I want. Now leave me alone."

Then he started in on, "How are you going to support the kids, I want my kids to have better things in life than you can give them."

I was becoming enraged, I said "They have as much now as they did when we were with you. I want to know Bill, did you come here to see the kids or argue with me. I am about to take the kids and go home, I can't take anymore of you. I don't want to hear anymore."

The case worker said "I don't think it's a good idea to do this in front of the kids, you can see that they are nervous about this."

I said to her, "Do you think it would be better to take the kids home?" Bill looked startled and he said "No, no, I have waited for months to see my family, I don't want them to go so soon."

The case worker said, "Okay let's not get carried away here. If you can talk together and be civil to each other you can continue, but you are wasting valuable time because I have to go in about a half hour. And I want Rose and the kids to be gone before I go. So get down to business and say what you want to say."

Bill began to direct his conversation toward her saying, "I have tried everything in my power to get along with this woman but I can't, if that is the way it is going to be then fine, but I want my kids. I have a good home for them and someone to take care of them." He knew how to get to me. I was fast becoming hysterical, I tried to check it, it was impossible when someone threatened to take the kids. I said with a quivering voice, " Whose good home are you talking about, your mother's and is she going to take care of them. I will never let you get these kids, so forget it, Bill."

Again he directed his remarks to her, I was not going to say a word. Let him talk as long as he isn't trying to make me look bad, because I felt like he was building a case for himself in court. He told her what a good man he was, how much he loved his family, what he was going to do for them, and this went on and on.

I listened as long as I could and I said to the case worker, "Wouldn't any woman be a fool to leave a man that was even half as good as he says he is? When he is talking like this, it makes me wonder who that was standing at the end of my bed (I lowered my voice) with a gun pointing at me, telling me he should have killed me a long time ago, and that he was going to take the kids to his mother, when I was too sick to get up and do anything about it. I felt then and I do now that his frustration was that he couldn't go to bed with me."

Noticing the time, I got up and told the kids to tell their dad goodbye, we had to go. Bill started crying, which upset the kids terribly. I quickly loaded up the kids and drove away, with a very sick feeling in my stomach. I said to the kids, "What do you say we go on a picnic, down to the park." They were very excited about that so I drove out on the other side of town and got some lunch meat, bread and bananas. They enjoyed the park and the outing. We drove home after a while and didn't mention Bill again. I think they understood a little better now, but I didn't offer any explanation, I knew they loved their dad. I didn't want to destroy that.

The next few days were full of thoughts of that day, going over and over the things that were said. My peace had been invaded, and destroyed. The old fears and pain came back. It had been so peaceful during those months when we were alone. I had begun to gain some weight, I had color in my face again. Now what had happened to me, my peace was gone. I tried to do the chores and enjoy what I was doing, but there seemed to be nothing that would bring back my sense of tranquillity. My sleep was disturbed by dreams that didn't make sense. My heart was breaking, how could I get away from this pain. I took the kids and went to Mom's, I just had to talk. She listened and said, "Rose if you are thinking about going back to him then I can see why you are in such a turmoil. Is it that you feel like you can't support the kids? We will help you as much as we can. You can move in here if you need to, you know Dad will feel the same way. We don't want to see you so tortured."

I said "Mom do you think that is what is in the back of my mind that I will have to go back to him. I don't want to." I began to cry and Mom cried. We talked for a long time, I felt better. I hadn't made any decisions but I guess just talking about it released the dam of emotions inside me.

In the weeks that followed I began to feel better. I was getting into a routine of things with my chores and I felt like I had picked up where I had left off. One day in the mail there was a letter from Bill, I hated to open it. Everything came flooding back. He was telling me how much he loved me, which I knew was not true and how much he missed the kids, I was sure that was true. He made some beautiful promises which I did not believe, but if only I could believe him. Things would be so different. I folded up the letter and put it away, trying to forget it. There came that gnawing again. I couldn't bring it out and I couldn't keep it in. I felt like I was going crazy.

Donna came up one day and had lunch with us. She knew I was in a turmoil. We talked some, finally I asked her if she would mind taking the kids to her house so I could be alone. I wanted to drive up in the timber where I felt like I could think. I would come in after the kids later on. She said certainly, I got the kids ready and they left. They were happy to get to go to town. I went out in the car and drove up the creek road. I drove slow just trying to gain a little peace so my mind could be fresh and I could work out what was really bothering me. I drove and drove and it seemed like thoughts were working their way to the fore part of my mind. When I felt like I could see clearly I pulled off the road, turned off the car and got out to walk. I walked and walked trying to bring my fears to the surface.

Suddenly I was facing a brick wall, but there was writing on that wall. "You know Rose that you can't go on living like this, the kids will need more clothes. If you go to work then you can't be home with the kids. Could you make enough money anyway to support the kids when they went to school. What will you do when the car gives out, where will the money come from to replace it. Someday you will have to rent a house closer to town. What about food next year. This was a one time thing and it won't be there next year. Mrs. Endicott will not live forever, you cannot depend on that job and that cabin forever. That cabin is too small now, as the kids get older it will get even smaller." When all these things surfaced I felt completely defeated, what was I to do. There was only one thing I could do. I sat down on a log and cried and cried, until there were no more tears inside me.

I drove home seeing more clearly but not liking what I saw. I went into the cabin and cleaned up a little and drove in to get the kids. I didn't have to say a word to Donna, she knew. I knew she preferred that I not say anything. We were as close as two people could be, it didn't have to come out in words, we knew. Mom knew too, it was too hurtful to talk about but we knew.

A letter came from Bill every few days. One day in one of his letters, something was said and I knew what he was going to do. I guess this was it—I had to accept it.

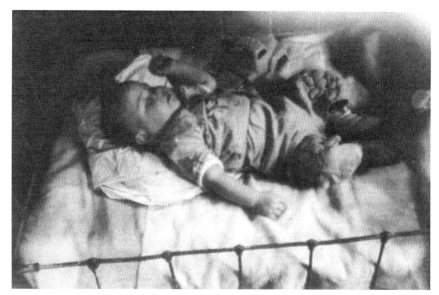

Rosana at Myrtle Creek.

Chapter 9

"Go, or I'll Shoot"

1953

My heart was so troubled during the next few months as I waited. Not wanting what was to come, not knowing just how it would come. I knew it was only a matter of time.

The sparkle had gone out of life for me. For the children, would their life be more secure or would I be subjecting them to abuse or possibly endangering their lives? Bill hadn't changed, I knew that. Nothing had changed since I left him.

Could I even support them; how could I possibly make enough money to live on? I couldn't leave them alone and I couldn't expect that much from my family. I knew I couldn't pay child care and live too. Oh God, what could I do?

One night I had gone to bed to read for awhile. The kids were all sleeping. When I turned the light off the moon was shining through the window and cast a beam across Rosana in her crib. It was so comforting, I was just laying there enjoying it. She looked so peaceful, so beautiful.

I heard a car going up the road. There wasn't much traffic up there so a car so late was note worthy. After a while it came back down. Then I heard it go back again. I got out of bed and looked out the window above Rosana's crib. I watched the lights on the car, it was as though they were looking for something. I reached over and got my rifle from the corner under a blanket where I kept it.

I put a shell in the chamber as I watched the car, driving ahead, backing up, finally coming down our lane. I watched as it came into my driveway, it was a pickup and it was coming much too fast. So fast it came over the log that was laying there. It rammed into the house making a terrible racket, and the house shook. As the car door opened I moved over by the door, just as the pounding began. I waited until they pounded again. The door, which was locked very securely, was a big heavy door made from two-inch rough lumber with a brace on both ends. There was a bar lock with heavy latches so I wasn't concerned about it being broken down. Whoever was there was going to try, by the sound of their pounding. I stepped up close to the door so as not to wake the kids when I spoke, "Whoever you are you had better make tracks because I have a loaded gun pointed right at you. Now go or I'll shoot."

A shaky, nervous voice came back saying, "Rose, don't shoot it's me Bill, please don't shoot, I won't hurt you. I just want to talk to you."

"You had better say what you want to say and fast, I don't want you around here."

"Open the door Rose, just give me fifteen minutes to talk to you."

I was pushing the bolt back when he said, "Wait! Put the gun away before you open the door." I stood the gun up in its place but I did not unload it or put the blanket around it.

I opened the door slowly not knowing what to expect. He stood there for a few moments and asked if he could come in. I pulled the door open wider and he stepped in through the door and reached for me. I backed away toward my bedroom door, where the gun was.

He said, "I am so glad you opened the door, I just had to see you." I pushed him away from me and stood by the gun, reaching over I put my hand on it. He saw what I was doing and backed away. "No, I told you I

Bill and Rosana.

wouldn't hurt you, please trust me."

"I have no good reason to trust you. Just keep your hands off me. What do you have to say to me?"

He said "Can we sit down right here by the table?"

"Okay sit down." I took a chair close to the door and the gun. He sat across the table from me.

He talked and talked and told me how sorry he was for hours and then he said, "Can I stay here, Merrill is out in the pickup, I'll tell him to go on into town and get a room."

"If you stay here, you will sleep on the couch."

He went out the door. When he came back in I said, "What are you planning to do and what is Merrill doing down here?"

"We are going to get a job here."

"Where are you going to stay?"

"I had hoped we could stay here. We don't have the money to get back, and that is Merrill's pickup.

"Oh Bill how could you do this, look at this place. Where could you stay here? You are quite a manipulator, you planned this so you could stay here. You haven't changed a bit."

"Oh yes I have, I've had more than a year to think this over and I can see where I was wrong. I promise I will be better, I will do anything you say but don't send me away, I nearly went crazy there without you and the kids."

I could have said many things. But what good would it do. I shouldn't have let my guard down and let him in the door. I felt the reluctance welling up within me, to even listen. The futility of it all was so evident. I said to him, "Bill I am not ready to go back to you, and I don't want to; go someplace else and stay, I can't have you here. Maybe if you came to see the kids now and then, and I could see that you had really changed, maybe in time I could go back to you. I don't want to raise the kids without a father, but I can't go back to what it was before. My feelings for you are just what you made them to be. I don't even like you. I have hated you for a long time, and I would hate you again. I can't live with someone I hate."

He was pleading "Please Rose, I'll never be that way again. I promise, give me a chance to prove it to you."

"If you don't have any money, do you expect me to feed you and Merrill on what I've got put up for the kids and myself? How could you

Bill. What have you done with the money you've made since I have been here? Don't you even have a car?"

"I really haven't made any money I haven't worked."

"How have you lived and where have you lived?"

He answered, "With Mom. I couldn't work I was just too nervous."

"How do you think you can work now?"

"I will I promise I will, I have you and the kids now and I can do anything as long as I have you to work for."

After about a week of resting up from the trip, Merrill did go out and get a job. He worked over by Roseburg; he had never been very ambitious. With both of them laying around the house I nearly went crazy. They didn't offer to help or even show any appreciation. Merrill had always been a crude person and he made remarks that were too personal. I recall one time he said to me, "Hey, those falsies look pretty good on you, when did you get them." I just ignored him. He said "Huh, I like them." He drove back and

Tommy, Billy, and Rosana.

184

forth to work until he got a paycheck. Bill was just so happy to be with his family he didn't want to leave. I continued to do the chores for Mrs. Endicott and got our rent and milk free. Bill watched the kids and read books.

I finally quit grieving and tried to make the best of it. This is the way it's going to be and that's it. I have to live with it.

After Merrill got a pay check or two, Bill borrowed enough from him to rent a little cabin out in the country at Sutherlin. We moved down there before he looked for work. It wasn't long until he got a job in the woods, driving equipment. We had two rooms to live in there. It was a good place for the kids to play.

We had been there about a month when I realized I was pregnant. It was too much for me at that time, I knew I could never get away from Bill now and I guess I had been secretly hoping. One day the landlady came and knocked on the door, I didn't hear her but the kids let her in, she asked to see me. I was sitting by the window absently looking out.

Merrill, Billy, Tommy and Rosana (in front).

She came up close and spoke to me "Rose are you alright, I have seen you sitting there all morning. You haven't moved."

I said "I'm sorry I didn't realize I had been there so long." She sat for awhile and visited but I was wishing she would go home. I didn't want to talk. She left shortly and the kids went back out to play, I went back to the window. When Bill came home, he wanted to know where supper was. I got up and fixed supper. He went to bed and I went outside with the kids and sat out there on the bridge. The kids came and told me it was time to go to bed.

I said, "Yes it is, we should go in it is dark." The landlady came down several times and fed the kids and talked to me. I didn't remember that she was a friend to Dad's cousins wife, Buster. She called Buster and told her to call my mother.

She gave her a briefing of what had been going on. Mom came down with Donna and took me to the doctor. I was in a fog, I just wasn't thinking clearly. Things seemed muddled to me. Donna took the kids to the park and got them some ice cream while Mom and I went in to see the doctor.

I got the impression Mom had talked to him before I got there. The doctor began asking questions and I answered the best I could, then I told him I thought I was pregnant. Mom was shocked, she said "Oh no." That remark cut me to the quick. I didn't need her criticism, it just added to my own dilemma, and self censure.

The doctor asked me how I felt about that, I said "I really didn't want to get pregnant now."

He said "Why?"

I told him, "I didn't want to be forced to live with Bill. If I am pregnant, I can't leave him." He talked to me for a long time.

"Rose we never know what tomorrow will bring, we just have to live one day at a time. You can handle tomorrow can't you? Then the next day when it comes. Rose, I'm sure that we could find someone to adopt the baby if you don't want to keep it."

I sat up straight in my chair, looking him in the eye and said, "Absolutely not, no one is taking my baby. Don't you worry, I can take care of it." He had a faint smile as he said, "I will give you a prescription for some medication to help you over this hump." He also told me to get myself built up, I was far too thin to be carrying a baby.

I confided to him that I was afraid to have another baby, he of course wanted to know why. I told him about the deliveries I'd had. Just thinking about going through that again scared me to death.

He very compassionately said, "If I promise to stay right with you, I can give you something if it gets too bad."

I answered, "I suppose. But the other doctors have told me the same thing, and then at the last there would be some reason why they couldn't give me anything."

He asked "Why was that?"

I said "My labor was so long and the baby and I were both tired and weak and they didn't want to weaken the baby any more than it was. They wanted me to help as much as possible to bring the baby because I couldn't dilate normally."

"I can see why you are not really convinced right now but I want you to come in every month for now so we can have time to talk about this. I'm sure you will feel very confident when the time comes."

I said "I will try" and we left. When we got into the car Mom said, "I didn't have easy deliveries either and I know what you are going through. You should talk more about what is bothering you. You keep too much inside."

"What good would it do to talk?"

She answered, "It would help you." With just a little sarcasm I said, "Does it help you?"

"I know I have done the same thing. I had no idea you were having the problems you were until that day at Pearl's. She was shocked too, saying that you had never said a word to her."

"Mom it really doesn't help, it only makes the other person feel as bad as you do."

Mom said, "I wonder at times if he even cares." I told her I thought he did. She said, "If he really cared for you he would not have tried to get in bed with me after Billy was born, when I was staying at your house before you came home."

I was truly shocked, I couldn't believe what she was saying. I said "Really Mom. He did that, what did you do?"

She replied, "I just kicked him out of bed and told him never to try that again. I just don't understand those people."

"Mom, did he get out and leave you alone?"

"Yes" She said, "I think he felt pretty foolish."

I had to admit "I shouldn't be surprised the way he stayed out at the bars when we were first married. I couldn't dislike him any more than I do right now."

"I didn't plan to ever tell you that, I'm sorry, I shouldn't have. You have enough on your mind. But sometimes I wonder how a human can take what you do. Rose, please get some help."

We went on down to the park to get Donna and the kids, they were having a good time. We sat there with them for awhile, the kids played and ran and enjoyed just being somewhere different and I felt the same way.

We lived in that little cabin as long as the weather was warm but it was too small when the kids couldn't play outside. Bill was making good money—the best he had ever made, but of course it was seasonal. We did

Clyde and Bertha Osborn.

find a house and moved in right away. Billy was starting school that year and he needed to be on the bus route.

The house was up on the hill in a row of houses. It was in a beautiful setting of fruit trees, nut trees, flowers, rose bushes and flowering quince—I loved it. There was also a barn which is always a kid's paradise. The property went into the timber, they loved going up there but now and then they were run out by the bees. It didn't discourage them, they went back to climbing trees and making forts; it was so much cooler up there.

We had some good neighbors, so friendly, we became quite close and visited every day. The kids had other kids to play with. We mothers talked it over and decided to never take our kid's side against another kid in a conflict. If we got involved there would be hard feelings which we could carry for a lifetime, but the kids would forget it in an hour and we would still be on the outs. That worked good for all of us. The kids got rather upset at times because they thought we didn't care. It all worked out.

I bought milk from a lady down across the road. When I talked to her I knew she was a delightful person, so happy and bubbly. Little did I know what a great role she would play in our lives over the years. She was such a blessing to me and the family. I know the Lord knew then how I needed a wonderful friend. Mary Lou Drake was truly that friend. She was a lovely lady and I knew right then she had something I needed in my life. I had never known anyone like her. We have been like sisters from that day on.

We didn't have a phone and Mary offered hers to us any time we needed it. She also told us if we needed to give a phone number, to use hers and if we got a call she would call us. I said "Mary I wouldn't want to do that, that is an imposition on you."

She said "Why Rose, it would not be any bother at all and I insist." She was like that all the way through. I had a problem trying to be as hospitable to her but she had everything she needed. She never expected anything from anyone, but was so appreciative for any little thing you would do for her. She did so much for others. She told me one day she was a Christian. I wasn't sure what that involved but I knew she went to church. Someday I would ask her about that. I was interested.

All the things Bill had hoped he could be was easier said than done. At times he tried, other times he didn't care. It was encouraging though to see any progress. He was no better at doing things around the place. The inside and outside was my responsibility. That was tough when the family kept getting bigger, and I was pregnant so much. I would get so annoyed with him for not doing anything but laying around and reading. After he got laid off he read all the time. He was in bed most of the day and all night. He would get up and eat and go back to bed to read. At least he was home. I should be happy for that.

Bill was more passive than he used to be. He was not so defensive. In general his mood was better. There were times when without any provocation he would explode. I felt sorry for the kids when this happened. The older they got, the worse they were treated. But there were also times when he treated them very well. He didn't spend a lot of time with them. They were confused not knowing what to expect ever.

When lay-off time came it was hard to live on unemployment and make ends meet. It took exact planning to be able to stretch that money. I made a menu for the whole week, wrote down exactly what I needed and bought only that. We stuck close to that menu, unless someone came to visit, and all the food for a week could be eaten in one meal.

Jim moved to Portland and got married. They came to see us quite often. I really enjoyed his wife Lou. They had a little girl Danny's age, she was so sweet, her name was Robin. Jim and Lou had a lot of marital problems, they were together for awhile and then were separated for awhile. The splits became more serious as time went on. The police were involved in several of their spats. Now and then Jim would be thrown in jail.

Orval DeGrange, the three older boys father, was heir to some property in Oklahoma. Since he was deceased the three boys became heirs. There was a big battle over that before it was settled. There was a large family and they could not agree on the settlement. During the winter when I was carrying Dan it was finally settled. Each one of the boys got about $1500. When Bill got his he put it in the bank. He said that was going to be a down payment on a farm. We were barely skimping by when he got the check, but he didn't touch it. I felt good about that. Just knowing we had a nest egg was a pretty good feeling.

Bill got a message one evening, to call Jim in Portland. He went in town and called. Lou had Jim thrown in jail. He had to have $1200 to post bail bond. Bill came home and told me. I said, "Surely you aren't going to give it to him are you?"

He turned on me yelling and cursing, "He would do it for me. Besides it's my money, so keep your mouth shut."

190

He took the money to him, and posted his bond, Jim jumped his bond and we (Bill) lost that money. Bill was not a very good person to be around for a long time over that one.

Billy in school, that was a great time for all of us. Billy hadn't talked of anything else for weeks. The other kids were so proud of him. I took Billy the first day, signed him up and met his teacher. A very sweet older lady. Billy was just walking on air. He had his desk assigned to him and he had his pencil and tablet. It was time for school to take up, all the parents were going home and the big doors went shut. I watched through the window for a minute and Billy looked around and he let out a scream and ran for the door. His teacher saw this and got to the door about the same time he did. Billy was trying to open the door, she was holding it shut.

I was ready to take him home. I took hold of the door and pulled, she pulled back, Billy was trying to get to me, she was holding him, at the same time she was holding the door from me. She opened the door a crack and was telling me to go ahead and leave, I just stood there. Suddenly Billy went to the floor behind her and was coming through right between her legs. She didn't have enough hands so she clasped her legs around his neck, her dress was draped over his head, he was screaming bloody murder. I felt like just going in and grabbing him no matter what. She said, "Don't do it, that would be the worst thing you could do for him. Just go, go home." I turned and walked away but I kept looking back. The fight was still on. I was crying my heart out walking to the car. I started up the car and drove around to where I could see into the room. I spent the morning sitting there. Poor Billy he had never been away from me and never his brothers and sister. Now he was alone and he was scared to death. I watched, I couldn't see Billy but I could see the teacher and could just about tell what he was doing by what she was doing. I thought at the time, this must be by far the worst part of being a mother. I went home, seeing that he was settling down. I can see the humor now but I didn't then.

I went to the school to pick him up. I didn't want him to go home on the bus, he had enough for one day. I was walking to the room when he came bounding out, a face full of smiles. I was just a little hurt. I said, "Well how was school Billy, how did you like it?"

Still smiling he said "Oh I liked it Mom, I wish I could just stay. We had so much fun and I have a lot of new friends. And some girl friends too."

That little fellow taught me a lot about little people. He was the first to do everything and I had to learn from him. It was much easier on me when Tommy started to school.

After Billy had been in school a few days he was bringing home his papers, I saved every one. They piled up and up then for Tommy, then Merrill. I had boxes of papers under all the beds, I couldn't get rid of one. Until we moved that is. One paper Billy brought home and showed me when he came in, "Look Mom, the teacher wanted us to draw a picture of our family." He was so proud when he showed me. There was a bed with Daddy reading in it, there were four kids standing by Mom who was mopping the floor. I was embarrassed by it but Bill wasn't so I didn't let it bother me.

My Mother gave me her "doctor book" *Modern Medical Counselor*, by Pacific Press 1942. I read that faithfully whenever any of the kids were sick. That book saved me a lot of money. I treated the kids the way they suggested and we got by just fine. There were times when I took them to the doctor but the book helped me to know when it was serious. A fever over 104. A ring-around on a finger nail, such as Merrill had when the neighbor boy bit him. I treated it and the infection just grew from bad to worse, I took him into the doctor. He took a hold of the thumb nail with an instrument like pliers and pulled, it didn't come off and he quickly pulled again. Blood and matter flew all over me, the table, and the doctor. Merrill screamed, and I screamed at the doctor. He said that was the only way he could have taken it off. If he had told us what he was going to do, he would not have got it done. That hurt Merrill terribly bad, for hours after. We never went back to him. It did heal and the nail grew back, but we were both the worse for wear.

It became well known that I treated the kids' illnesses and the neighbors called on me quite often for everything from bee stings, to colds, to nausea, even to stitching with butterflies. We had a lot of poison oak. The one thing I told the mothers before I began was that they go out. The kid was used to being babied and would scream with her in there, not wanting me to touch them. They would settle right down when I'd say, "Now that's enough of that, sit up here and be quiet or I won't even try to fix it, you will have to go to the doctor." That's all it took. I did the same with my own kids.

Danny was an easy baby to carry but I got huge and it was hard to get around. Little did I know that I was carrying Dan'l Boon the second. Time was getting close and I was getting pretty apprehensive about delivery.

The doctor kept his word about talking to me, which did help but not enough. One day in January I began to have cramps early in the morning. I got up and did the normal things, packed my bags, did the laundry, cleaned the house and anything else that needed to be done.

It had been raining, flood waters were coming up. Bill was going to take the kids to Mom. That evening about seven, we had the kids in the car and he was taking me to Roseburg to the hospital. He let me off there and he drove on down to Myrtle Creek. I went in and checked myself in. I thought it was early as my pains usually lasted longer than 12 hours and they hadn't been too bad yet. They got me ready, prepped me and put me in the labor room next to the delivery room.

I was having pains 5 minutes apart but wasn't dilating. I asked if they had called the doctor. They said no, they usually waited until the pains were harder and coming closer together. I thought well I guess they knew what they were doing, but where was all that help I was going to get from the doctor. The nurse turned out the light and went out the door. The pains were getting harder but I thought I would wait, I didn't want to bother them. I probably laid there for an hour and I was getting a bit nervous. All of a sudden a pain hit and wouldn't let up. I rang for the nurse, no response, I rang again, no response, the pain was getting harder and it was constant. I really thought I was going to have that baby alone.

That was very frightening to me. I kept ringing and no one came. I finally started hollering and ringing the bell at the same time. With the lights out in there it was pitch black, and I couldn't reach the light. Then all of a sudden the door flew open, the lights went on and the nurse was rushing. She lifted up the sheet and checked and rang for another nurse and told me not to bear down the baby was close.

She said, "Why didn't you call me?" I told her I had been ringing and yelling for an hour. She said "A patient from across the hall came and told us you were. We were busy." They took me into the delivery room and got me all ready, and said they wished the doctor would get here. They thought they might have to deliver this baby themselves. That didn't make me feel too secure. The pain was still steady but it felt like the baby just couldn't come out. It was agonizing. Finally the doctor came in the door, he checked me and said "Are you ready Rose, it looks like you are going to have a baby." I couldn't answer but I wanted to kick him. They waited around for a while longer and the doctor was reading my chart and looking a bit concerned. I was still in that same pain, it wouldn't let up.

He began to insert the forceps, and the tearing, and the snipping and he pulled and pulled. He pulled so hard he nearly pulled me off the table, he had his feet braced against the table, his face was strained from pulling so hard. The baby's head came but he took the forceps off and continued to pull to get the shoulders out. And then it was over. Thank God it was over.

The doctor told me later "You were not going to give that baby up, I really had a time getting him out."

I said, "It has been that way every time, and why is that?"

He thought awhile and said, "I don't know, you just didn't dilate after you got so far and it wasn't far enough for the baby to come out. I hope I didn't let you down too much. I really expected to help you a little more than I did. When you get that close there is nothing we can do but pull and I know that hurts. I'm sorry."

I told him, "Well it's all over now, and I guess I didn't need that much help."

After he had finished up, the nurses took me to my room. The doctor came in and told me what a beautiful baby I had. He told me goodnight and left and the nurses brought this big lumberjack baby into me. I laughed when I saw him and said "He has to be called Dan he looks like a Dan." He had a big round chest and arms like a man. His legs looked powerful. He was the sweetest looking baby. It was like he reached out and took a hold of my heart and he has never let go, he has been a precious son. And he was the most peaceful baby. He was never demanding, it was like he knew he was going to get what he needed so he just waited. He seldom ever cried. He was a joy to the family. I had a little crib I put in the front room and when anyone would walk by he would turn and grin. He watched the kids and of course they were talking to him all the time. Billy especially stood by his little crib for hours holding his hand and talking to him. That picture is in my mind's eye as if it were yesterday. Some things are so precious you can never forget.

Bill came back from Myrtle Creek the next day. He didn't want to be there when the baby was born, he said. I was hurt, I hoped he had changed, especially in consideration of others. Oh well!

Bill was slipping back into the old mold. It was hard on me and the kids also. It was one thing having him around the house all the time, but he was a raging bull around the house when he was not working. Nothing pleased him. He complained all the time and was mean about it. I was getting to the stage where I thought I was going to lose my mind. One day

Bill went to town and I went into the bedroom just to be alone. The kids were watching something on TV so I took advantage of that and took some time for myself. I lay in there on the bed and I thought. Now I have five kids and I'm going to have to live like this forever. I can't take this forever what am I going to do. Someone switched on a light in my mind. I was listening to see what would come next. Ask God for help! I said "God can you help, I just can't take this, I need you. I know I should go to church but I don't know where to go. Will You please send someone to help me and show me God."

My thoughts and prayers were interrupted by one of the kids, I went into the room with them to take care of the need, the request slipped my mind for a time.

They say pride goeth before a fall, but it is a terribly hard fall when you can't pay the bills and then have to go back to the doctor and ask for more credit. I guess I had a poor man's pride because it was very hard on me to live like that. A constant worry gnawing on me. Bill had complete control of the money. He only paid when he had to, or he would give me just enough money to buy groceries and account for every penny.

He did the shopping when he wasn't working, even buying the kid's clothes. He wouldn't shop frugally, he would overspend on one thing and we would go without on other things.

I'm sure it was hard on Bill too but he could blame it all on me, so it couldn't have been quite as hard on him. The one thing he hated to pay was medical bills, and there was a lot of them. We did have insurance sometimes, but not all the time. Our debts to doctors and hospitals was tremendous. They never turned me away. I think they understood what the problem was.

Billy became very sick, we took him to the doctor but they couldn't find what was wrong with him. He became weaker as time went on, he kept losing weight until he looked terrible. The health department became interested in this as it was not diagnosed, and we were probably referred because of our low income status. A nurse came to the house once a week to monitor his condition. She was working in conjunction with the Dornbecker children's hospital in Portland. The sickness leveled off for a few months and we were hopeful he was getting over it. It was only for a little while. One evening I watched him come up the driveway to the house. It was a steep little pitch, but he had come up that same way hundreds of times, but this day, he would walk a few steps and stop and rest. I went down to meet him, he said he was all right but he was just tired. From that day he became worse, every day. I called the nurse and she came right out. She checked him over and then called the hospital. They wanted us to bring him right up. We took him up the next day.

Not knowing what was wrong with him, we felt terrible leaving him there to return home. He didn't mind, as much as I thought he would, the doctors and nurses were giving him a lot of attention.

The doctor said they were going to run tests and if they found anything they would call us, if he got worse they would call us. They promised to keep in touch.

The one thing that I had in the back of my mind was Leukemia, but I was afraid to even mention it. There were a lot of sleepless nights filled with prayers for Billy. Praying came easier to me now. I got a lot of comfort from it.

Mary spoke often of prayer and these remarks were rubbing off. Billy was in the hospital most of the winter a very sick little boy, but a diagnosis was never made. We all agonized over this, our household was so sad and heavy with fear. I was so consumed with this worry, I couldn't think of anything else. It was hard on the kids at home, I was sorry for them. I tried to be more cheerful, it wasn't there. They went to Mary's a lot and that really did help them.

We got a call from Billy's doctor at Mary's house and she ran out and called to us, it was the doctor in Portland. I took off running down through the field over fences and across the road to get to the phone. I really don't know if the anxiety was from fear or hope. It was good news, Billy could come home. He didn't know yet what was wrong with him but they could still run tests on the specimens they had, but Billy was gaining a little weight, he looked better and felt better. Oh what a happy day! I was on cloud nine, I couldn't wait to tell Bill. He was as happy as I of course. We, in our ecstasy, actually sat down and talked for a while. We found that we both were so worried about Leukemia, neither had said anything to the other.

Bill went up to get him and the little kids stayed home with me. It was getting pretty hard to keep Danny confined that long, that was a long drive up and back. With me in the family way it wasn't a pleasant trip for me either.

Billy did fine when he got home, he continued to improve until he was a little bit pudgy in fact.

The doctor made arrangements for Billy to come back up when he got stronger and have his tonsils taken out. Bill took him up during the summer as I was a new mother of a sweet baby girl.

Dan was three and a half years old when Janet was born. He wasn't a baby long. He developed fast and was a very healthy little boy. He was as good-natured as any child I'd ever seen, he was a big eater, and as long as we could keep him filled up he was happy.

Janet was a tiny baby weighing five pounds at birth. The doctor and I both thought this would be a breeze but at the last, just before delivery she turned to come breach. That was a hard delivery and again the forceps and the tearing and all those stitches. I was beginning to feel that I was plagued to have hard deliveries. She was a beautiful baby, her hair was dark and curly, tiny little features. Her head and body just fit in the palm of my hand. It was so unusual for me to have little babies and it was so fun to care for her.

I do believe Janet was born with a sense of humor, I had never seen a child like that. She would burst out laughing at just about anything, when she was real little. I remember one time when she was about 10 months old. She had eaten her lunch but she wanted another hot dog, I said wait until I get you washed up. I cleaned her up and changed her diaper and took her into her crib. I laid her down and handed her the hot dog. We went through

Janet.

this same ritual every day except it was her bottle I handed her. She lifted up that hot dog and looked at it, then looked at me and she burst out laughing. She laughed and laughed and of course I did too. I went in the kitchen and got her bottle and brought it back she was still laughing and holding her hot dog. Then she handed me the hot dog and took her bottle.

One day the kids thought it would be real cute to put Rosana's doll wedding dress on Janet. We put it on her and it just fit, she looked so cute. We took several pictures of her. The kids had so much fun with her. She was just like a little doll herself and she was fun to play with. She loved that attention. Before they saw her, they were told she had long dark hair. Tommy was so disappointed because her hair was not hanging down her back.

Mary and I had become very close by the time Janet was ready to come. She was such a help, so concerned, just as would be expected of her, being the good Christian she was. I hoped I would never expect anything of her, but she was always there when I needed her. She actually gave her own needs to give to others. It seemed like she went beyond what anyone could ever expect. She was a perfect example of a Christian.

She was so excited when I went into labor. I had some work to do before I left and she was beside herself, she came to the house every few minutes. She said, "Now Rose don't wait too long because I don't know anything about delivering babies, I had mine in about an hour. I laughed at her and told her I had plenty of time. I don't think she believed me but it turned out just about the way I told her it would. I didn't have quite the fear with Janet, but they began to mount up and I was very apprehensive my last month. But the thought of the baby always made me feel warm and comfortable. I have to be honest in saying I was not overjoyed at the thought of all the work and confinement of a baby, diapers, bottles sleepless nights and all that laundry. If it had been by choice I may not have had so many, but the joy far outweighed the drudgery. They gave me more happiness in my life than I ever dreamed of.

However, I knew I had enough energy and I was able when I was well. I enjoyed my babies so much. There always seemed to be room for one more and enough love for a dozen.

I wasn't bothered by having several children as some people said they were. I felt like the only time I would have to apologize for my kids is if they were out of line. I knew if I had twenty kids and they were clean, well groomed, polite, respectful to adults, respecting other people's property and not being rowdy, I could always take pride in them.

I was never ashamed to take my kids anyplace. I was proud of them. We were often invited to other's homes for dinner. People were amazed at how well mannered they were. I assisted them at the table if they needed it but mostly they were not reprimanded and therefore not embarrassed. When we went to a restaurant they showed perfect manners. They stayed in their chairs and ate their meal just as the adults did. They got a lot of attention, people couldn't help but watch them. They often were complimented. The kids were obviously happy and not afraid. With them willing to follow instructions we were able to go places and do things that we could not have done otherwise. We always had a little talk before we got out of the car, however.

One day, when Danny was just a baby, two ladies came to the front door and asked me if I was interested in reading the papers they had. They looked like something I would be interested in and I took them and thanked them. They came back the next day. They asked if I had read the papers, I told them I had, did I like them, yes they were interesting. They offered to come in and explain other things to me, things from the Bible. Oh! (here it was. God must have sent them.) I thought to myself. Oh yes, I surely was interested. We made an appointment for one day a week to have Bible study. WOW! I was on my way.

They seemed to be very nice, but not as nice as Mary. I took out the Bible I had received one year for Christmas from Bill's sister, Betty. I looked it over to familiarize myself with it, before they came. I didn't make much headway. The first studies were pretty standard. Time went on and I began to wonder about these people. They showed me in the Bible where you were not supposed to worship any graven images. According to them we were not to salute the flag, (a graven image) I didn't get the connection, I asked questions and wrote down scriptures we had read. The next thing was we were not supposed to kill, everyone believes that, okay, well they did not believe in war, that was mass killings. I couldn't see that because someone had to protect our freedom. Did they expect someone else to go to war for them and do their fighting. Again I took down scriptures and read both ways from every scripture. I listened, and read all the references they gave me and more, always more. This went on for several months, I became quite well versed in the subjects they were so strong on, but I was always in opposition to them. I was so afraid of doing the wrong thing, I thought I would know when the right thing came my way. Here I had two messages and I didn't know which to follow. God had put Mary in my life but I didn't recognize it until I saw how futile this other thing was getting. I wasn't prepared for Satan's interference. I was to close too the forest to see the trees.

I was talking to Mary about these things and she told me how she believed and she backed it up with scripture, not one, but several scriptures. She told me that 1 John 4:1 was a good scripture to read. "Do not believe every spirit,...but test the spirit, because many false prophets have gone out into the world." I thought a lot about that and it opened some new avenues to me. I studied every reference to that scripture to test it. Mary never pushed, she only answered the questions. It didn't make any difference in our friendship if I accepted her theories or not.

Jack was going to church with Mary, he had been raised in a Christian family, but the rebel came out in him every so often. Bill and Jack became friends and fishing buddies. Jack was the first real close friend Bill had since I had known him. We started having outings together, taking the kids. We were going water skiing, water surfing, swimming, picnics and getting together for dinners and card games. Bill had never wanted to do anything like this. He was having fun, and so was I. He would plan some of the outings and I was pleased, I loved being with Mary and Jack but most of all I loved doing things with all my family. It was a new world for me.

Bill and I became more compatible, we could enjoy being together, talking with one another and planning things together.

Sutherlin's annual celebration was "Timber Days". All the loggers participated and joined in the parade. People came from miles away to see the tree topper's compete, or a log rolling contest. They had chain saw competition, axe throwing, tree cutting with saw or axe. It was a big event for Oregon, the timber state. Bill was anxious to drive his log truck in the parade. He polished it up until it shone like new. He took the boys in the truck with him. This was a great thing for Bill, I had never seen him so interested in anything.

We were all getting ready to go to the parade. I dressed the kids up with new pants and shirts, they were all slicked up and so excited. Bill took the boys and went down early to get the truck warmed up and I was to go down after I got the girls ready. I was dressing and I realized my shoes looked terrible. I really should have some new ones; would I have time to run down to the store and get some before the parade started. I dashed down and found a pair of loafers I liked, put them on and went to the parade. The kids looked so good in that truck with their dad and they all waved. I was proud of them.

I wasn't able to stay very long with the little kids so I came on home. Bill stayed longer with the boys and came home quite late that day. They all came in tired but still excited about the day. The boys went out to play. I was sitting in the living room when they came home. Bill came in and sat down. He noticed my shoes. "Where did you get those shoes?"

"I went to the store and got them before I went to the parade, my others looked terrible."

He jumped up and came for me, he was so enraged I thought he was going to hit me, "I didn't tell you to get shoes, take them back."

"I can't take them back, I have worn them." I tried not to show my fear of him.

"I said take them back, you had no business getting those shoes. I have never allowed you to get things without me being there. Take them back right now."

He stood over me as I tried to reason with him, "Bill, that will be so embarrassing, I know those people at the store. Please don't make me take them back."

"Get your butt up off that chair, take off those shoes and take them back, right now, do you hear me, take them back."

I became so angry I felt like I wanted to pound on him, I jumped up and screamed at him, "I am not going to do it, you can't ask me to do such a thing."

His face turned white with anger, he growled, "You do it, or I will bodily take you down there and you will give them the shoes."

I ran into the bedroom, I had to get away from him. I was angry and he was angry, something was going to happen. I felt a little more freedom with him since we were communicating, I wouldn't dare show any anger at one time.

It is not good for anyone to get that angry, it would be too easy to do something very foolish, that would not accomplish anything but hurt everyone. I was mad enough to kill, for a second and I felt ashamed. I shut the door and leaned against it, breathlessly saying to myself, "You've got to get a hold of yourself, breathe deep." I felt like I was suffocating. I had never felt such anger in all my life.

Someone had to give in and I knew it would not be him. I did what I had to do. I sat down on the bed and took the shoes off, cleaned the dust from them and put them back in the box. I didn't really want to drive the car, feeling the way I did. I walked by him in the front room with the shoe box in one hand and my purse in my other hand, and went out to get in the car, I stopped just before getting in and prayed. It was so humiliating to go into the store, but I did it and I really think God gave me the strength to do it and to come back to the house and face Bill, when I really didn't ever want to see him again. Bill was laying across the bed sleeping when I got back. It was never mentioned again. There was a cold war going on inside me for a long time. It finally passed. I couldn't forget it, not for the shoes but for his unreasonable demands just to show he was boss. He didn't seem to feel good about himself unless he was in control.

I was so afraid he was slipping back into the old mold. How could I live with that again. "Oh, God, please!"

I realized that with the children I had now, I couldn't support them, there would never be a chance for me to get away from him. Yet I could not stand the thought of living with him. Then I remembered something the doctor had said. "You only have to live one day at a time." That would be the only way I could go on. I vowed to never look beyond today, and I lived with that.

I think Bill may have shocked himself at what he was capable of as that seemed to be the real turning point in his life.

He decided we needed a bigger and better house. We found one on second street. It was a fairly new place, it was downtown close to the school. A white house with a garage, four bedrooms, one bath, utility room, kitchen, dinning room and living room. There were hardwood floors, except in the kitchen, dining room, bath and utility. A nice big yard. It was really a nice place. Bill was proud and so was I. We began entertaining, having game nights or pinochle, always with a big dinner. I would make a canner full of chili, with hot bread. Many people yet remember when I made donuts or maple bars for some of our gatherings. Bill enjoyed hosting these parties. It was so different for him. He became friends with people he worked with and through Jack and Mary. The kids were happy and they seemed to take pride in our new found social life.

Bill's next big surprise was a washer and dryer. First one for me. It was wonderful. I no longer had to get up at four o'clock in the morning to wash, nor did I have to always get up before daylight to get the house work done before the kids woke up. After they got up there was no time for anything else. Getting everyone dressed and ready for the day was a chore in itself, the kids never went outside without clean clothes, face and hands washed and hair combed. Baths were at night. After the kids were up and dressed, I bathed the babies and was able to take my time with them. I fed them and that was our special time. I had a schedule and I followed it faithfully, otherwise I would never have been able to keep up with it. As it was I had time to enjoy myself and do things for myself. Keeping my hair fixed and looking as good as possible. This new house and the washer and dryer made it all so much easier.

Bill was changing, I was almost afraid thinking he might backslide again. I could see a difference every day.

Living downtown, it was much easier to go to church. We lived about a block away. I was going with Mary but I wasn't sure yet what my preference was. I was doing a lot of studying. Things were seriously getting to the place where I would have to make a choice. The weekly Bible studies were just getting to be a matching of wits. I couldn't believe any of what they taught. The more I studied the more I knew what I wanted. I started studies with Mary's church. The Neighborhood Church of Christ.

I was afraid of making the wrong choice. I had churning in my stomach when I thought about it, so I hung on to both.

The church was having a revival; I attended several times and really got a lot out of it. That was feeding my soul, I loved it. I was telling Bill about it when I came home. He grew very interested, then I was showing him things in the Bible. It was all coming together for both of us. When I showed him that God loved us and would take care of us, that He would answer our prayers and take us to live with Him after we left this earth, He had a place prepared for us by Jesus, Bill really became interested. He started attending quite regularly with Jack and Mary. I stayed home in the morning so he could go, he took the boys so they could go to Sunday School. He stayed home in the evening and I went, taking the older kids if they chose. I was ready to make a commitment and accept the Lord, but I was afraid it might affect Bill adversely, so I decided to wait for him.

During the revival the minister and the two evangelists were making home visits to members and prospective members. When they came to visit me I was ready with the questions I wanted to ask, before making my decision. I asked them about forgiveness, salvation, tithing, baptism. The deity of Christ and the Trinity. What I needed to know was what that church was teaching.

I learned enough to make my decision. The thing that seemed so important to me was, I wasn't joining a local church organization. I wanted to be assured of my salvation, accepting Christ as my Savior is the only way, and to believe in what He died for.

Christ established the local church that we may have a relationship and fellowship with other believers where we can worship together and find fellowship, teaching, counseling and minister to our special needs. Where God can use each of us to impart those blessings to others. Why must I go to church? There is a scripture that tells me not to forsake the assembling of the saints.

I had to be assured my salvation would carry me through the rest of my life and was honored by Christ in any church I came to worship in. I had read about that in the scriptures and I wouldn't settle for anything less.

Once I started studying I wanted to know more and more, there were so many things I didn't understand. I soon learned that God does not reveal to us anything we are not spiritually ready to digest. It became a passion to me I had to know more, more, more. I continued on that quest for months and months. I learned how to use references and cross references and concordances. I also found that book learning was not enough, I had to wait for the spiritual discernment.

I was fascinated with learning the Bible. I was telling Bill all I learned, he was anxious also to learn, but reading the word is much more effective spiritually than hearing the word. He did not become as impassioned as I was.

Bill's new world and friends were a joy to him, it was like he found out for the first time that it wasn't like his mother had told him. He loved these people. What grew from this love that he showed was something wonderful, people loved him.

He worked with a fellow at the mill who had been making whiskey and bootlegging. He was caught and was going to spend some time in jail; he mentioned to Bill that he hated to leave his dad and mom they were old and didn't have much and neither one of them knew how to read. When this fellow went to jail Bill took over the responsibility of this old couple. He not only picked up and read their mail to them, but took them to town to get groceries or to the doctor. Anything he could help them with he did. The little shack where they lived was not more than twenty by twenty feet. When Bill saw this shack he figured it was going to fall in around them before their son came home. He talked to his boss at the mill. They gave him heister loads of two by four seconds. He built them a house. He stacked them together and made four inch walls on a large room to attach to the existing house. He made it comfortable for them, putting in a big heater and electricity for lights. It wasn't the most beautiful thing but the old people thought so. They were so pleased. Bill became known around the community as a very charitable person. He was well respected. He was a happy man. I was a happy woman. I was almost afraid to wake up some mornings for fear the dream would go away. It did not. God's power in the life of a man can transform him into a new creature.

Our children were happy with our new life, and their new Dad. Bill did special things with Billy and Tommy, things the little ones were not yet able to do. He took them fishing and hunting. Merrill was usually able to do just about everything the others did. Rosana was special to him too. His first girl.

Danny had his own special place in his Dad's heart. He was young yet, to go very much, but that little Dan'l boy sure thought he was big. Janet was very special because she was born after his transformation. There was a new song to sing. He learned how to love, his family, others and he learned to love God. He also learned how to show his love for me. He became a tender sweet husband and lover. We were also good friends.

We were very happy, and all I could think was it was a miracle of God, to change people that way. If you have never seen it happen, then you couldn't believe it.

Bill did special little things for the little kids, like leaving things in his lunch bucket so they could run to meet him and get a cookie or something he had saved from lunch. If he didn't have anything he would stop at the store.

There was always a Santa who came to the house after they went to bed on Christmas eve. He would go in debt to have a good Christmas for the kids. He talked to them to find out just what they wanted Santa to bring them, then he would do his best to get it for them. The Christmas of fifty eight was most memorable, he shopped and shopped not wanting to miss anything. He got logging trucks for the boys and tractors, play guns, everything any boy would want. Merrill was six years old that Christmas.

He was tired and anxious this one Christmas eve, he crawled up on the couch to set with me. He was feeling sort of melancholy, thinking about Christmas and about the things he had asked Santa for and he said, "Mom, I really don't care what I get for Christmas, but I'm afraid if I don't get a Teddy Bear I am going to cry." I thought Oh Oh, who would ever think of that. I wiped his tears away and said "Santa always tries to get everything you want, and he will if he can."

He said, "But I just want a Teddy Bear Mom. Nothing else."

After he was tucked into bed I told Bill what he said. Bill jumped up and ran out saying, "I wonder if the stores are still open." He came home with the biggest Teddy Bear I had ever seen. That was all Merrill saw under his sock. He grabbed it and hugged it and yelled, "Mom, he did get it." He slept with that Teddy Bear for years, until it fell apart.

In back, Merrill, Tommy, and Billy.
In front, Danny and Rosana. February 1958.

206

Bill always talked to the kids like there surely was a Santa, he wanted them to believe it. I think that was one of the very few joys he had in his life as a child.

Tom came home one day just before Christmas and said, "Mom I found out today at school that there really isn't a Santa."

I whispered to him not wanting the other kids to hear, "Don't tell your Dad." Of course don't tell your Dad that you don't believe there is a Santa is what I meant.

He backed up and looked at me his eyes as big as dollars and said, "Okay I won't." It was dropped and I forgot about it.

We continued with our very active lives and with a new focus in our life, even our money seemed to go farther. We were eating better. I had always been interested in nutrition and read everything I could find on the subject. Now I was in charge of buying groceries. I took a lot of pride in

Billy and Tommy, April 1959.

feeding my family good and nutritious meals. Bill having a year around job really made a big difference in our lifestyle.

We were becoming more active in the Church but Bill never mentioned making a commitment or receiving the Lord as his Savior. I felt like we were safe so I wasn't too concerned except I thought it would be good for us as new Christians to make some kind of a public committal, as a testimony to others and something for us to anchor to. I did continue to wait on him to take that step of faith.

When Janet was four months old I was pregnant with my seventh child. I was happy about it, except for the fear of delivery. I could pray now, I could ask for help and knew I would get it. I had a healthy pregnancy. I was very active and in a much better emotional state. Mom was going to come down to take care of the kids and do the cooking for Bill so he could continue to work when I went to the hospital. Mom and Bill were on very good terms now as well as with the rest of the family. It was so good for me. I really felt good about everything. I had it all. The children, the Lord, a good husband, a happy home, and my family, what more could a woman ask.

One thing that really helped us to make a change was we left yesterday in the past, and lived for today. I will have to admit though there were times when I remembered and it was enough to make me sick to my stomach. But I would have to forget, this is what the Lord had given to me and this is the only way it could be, I could not raise these kids alone. They deserved better than that.

Another helpful tool was when one got angry that one said his peace, the other kept quiet and listened. The other was afforded the same courtesy. Bill had quite a few up on me but that was more his nature and not mine. I hated getting angry, I avoided it if at all possible. Bill would soon be over his outburst and then it was forgotten. He didn't get as angry as he once did.

One such incident was a time when the garbage stacked up in the back yard too long. I had mentioned to Bill several times we had to get that cleaned up. There was no pick-up at that time so we loaded it in a trailer and hauled it to the land fill. This particular time some dogs got loose and spread the garbage all over the yard. I didn't see it, I was busy on a Saturday morning and Bill, loving to read, was still in bed reading his book. There came a knock at the door, when I answered it a policeman asked for Bill, I said "He is still in bed, can I help you."

He said he would rather talk to Bill but since he was not available he would talk me about the problem, "Your neighbors called the police and asked if we would see to it that you cleaned up the garbage in your back yard. "I was terribly embarrassed and I began to apologize. He said "That's alright Lady, but we will expect you to get it cleaned up today since it is a weekend and your husband is home."

By the time the door was closed I was burning at Bill. I marched into the bedroom, stood looking down at him laying there and said, "You had better get out of that bed and get out there and clean up the garbage. A policeman was just at the door telling me the neighbors complained about it and we had to get it cleaned up today. Bill I have never been so embarrassed in all my life, I have asked you time and again to do that and you just put it off, now look, what do our neighbors think of us." He began to smile, I said, "What are you smiling about, I can't see anything funny about this, it's disgraceful."

He replied still smiling, "Yes I agree it is and I will clean it up, but it is so funny to see you mad. I've never seen you like this."

I stomped out of the room, not daring to stay any longer or I would have thrown a shoe at him. I fumed for a while and finally, with a lot of prayer and determination on my part it wore off. I didn't say another word about it. When I got my work done, I went out and helped clean up. The kids were helping also, not willingly but with my insistence. I didn't blame the neighbors when I saw what the dogs had done. It was a terrible mess and I was sick with embarrassment. I went from neighbor to neighbor to apologize to each of them.

I could see a change coming in myself. It was slow because I was packing a lot of hurt, anger and put-downs. I was actually becoming an individual. I felt different about everything, I was more outgoing and had a lot more self confidence. It makes a difference when you feel loved and you are treated fairly. Bill being away from his family made a big change in him and in our marriage, I'm sure.

Bill didn't make a complete turn around overnight but any stride was good and I was willing to wait since there was hope. I had hoped the kids would realize more of his change. In the meantime the boys took some pretty hard thrashings, I had to step in, I couldn't stand it. I'd try to stop him. I would pull the boys away from him if it got too bad. I feared for them, and wanted to grab them and run, but that would only make him more angry so I stayed back unless he went too far and I stepped in.

Most of the time it was not their fault, it was Bill's rotten temper. I think a lot of times the kids didn't know what they were getting beat for. This was the worst for me to tolerate in the later years of our family life. I had been the recipient of those temper outbursts before for many years, then when the boys were old enough they got it, I felt terribly guilty about that. If only I could have done something, anything.

Chapter 10

"The Doctor Came At Dawn"

1959

Since prayer had become such a precious and estimable family resource, changes were happening, and considering the enigma our family had suffered, there were many more yet to come.

We struggled through one day at a time. Our trust was in God. Bill was tearing himself away from the old man, it was painful, but I could see him struggling. Seeing him try was enough to give me hope, even though we suffered through this time with him, I felt like with God it would happen. I was so full of hope.

The winter seemed to drag on and what a hectic one it was, with the timber industry on strike, the workers were haggling with the company and union. The Teamsters were attempting to come in and convince the workers to change unions, so there was a lot going on and paranoia was running rampant. No one knew who was on what side. Many times when the men were at meetings, the wives would get threatening phone calls and sometimes crank calls or screaming in the background. It was fast becoming a big problem to all of us. Bill was out on strike the better part of the winter.

Janet was having some severe ear problems. She suffered with earaches, the kind that we were up all night with. It would finally break and drain and she would get some relief for awhile. Sometimes she saw the doctor everyday, she got shots and took antibiotics by mouth. Rocking her and holding warm packs on her ear seemed to be the only thing that would relieve it.

Danny was also sick a lot that winter, he had strep throat and couldn't seem to get completely over it. We discovered that the doctor hadn't been giving him antibiotics long enough at one time to kill the strep germ. I took

211

him in several times but the same thing was happening time after time. The doctor decided to do a blood test and found he had rheumatic fever. More antibiotics and complete bed rest for two months. If he got tired or played too hard he would have a fever again. As active as he was it was hard on him but he was good to understand and do what he was told.

The summer was hot and it was especially hot for me, expecting a baby in August. We went to the river often where the others could swim and play in the sand and I could sit in the shade, it seemed like the only place I could get cool. Mary brought her kids down and we always had a good time. Mary and I loved each other's children like we were sisters, and I guess we were. Janet needed Mary since I was low on energy that summer. We grew very close in those months Mary helped me so much. She was sent from God I know.

I don't know if it was because I was on my seventh child in ten years and was very tired or if it was the heat, but those last few months were very difficult. I was not anxious to go into labor, I feared that terribly. As the time drew near I became more afraid. I prayed, but I couldn't seem to get the peace I needed so desperately.

The time finally came for me to go the hospital. It was late, about ten o'clock when I decided the pain was not going away. The hospital was quiet and the halls empty. We went to the front desk and were registered. Bill left me there and went home. I felt sure he would stay with me this time but he did not. It hurt me more now than before. I was afraid, lonely and depressed as I was going down the hallway in the wheelchair. It was torture knowing what was to come. I felt like I was going to my doom. Bill didn't seem to care, if he even knew I was so frightened. It would have helped me so much having some support.

The nurses got me ready and in bed in the labor room. The pains stopped then so I tried to relax and rest. I dozed off, and awoke with a start when the pains began to get serious again. I hadn't made much progress in that time, but I felt like it was really doing some good now.

Dr. Hudson had promised to come as soon as I got to the hospital. He did come, with his brother Lynn who was in practice with him in the same clinic. I was glad to see them and it did make me feel a little less fearful to see the two of them. He may have suspected something wasn't quite right or was it just reassurance for me.

It was getting along in the afternoon and even though the pains were coming hard and fast I was not making a lot of progress. The nurse said after examining me, she was going to call Dr. Hudson in to examine me. He told me there was a problem, the baby had turned and was trying to come breach. He said this baby was much too big for me to have breach. It would take me hours and then it was doubtful if I could have him, as big as he was.

They left the room for awhile and when they came back in, it was explained to me that they could turn the baby but it would be terribly painful for me. It would only last a few minutes compared to the hours of labor I would have if they didn't turn it. I asked if they could put me to sleep. No, they needed me to help and it would be too hard on the baby, they couldn't do that, he was sorry. I was frightened. I began to tremble.

They explained just what the procedure was. It all sounded so simple but I knew how painful it was just to get an exam during a pain. He would wait until I had a pain and then with his hands, he would turn the baby. Dr. Lynn Hudson would stand right beside me and talk to me about what was happening and he would help me all he could. I find no words to describe the fear I had. I knew it was going to be bad. God knows that normal child birth is bad. Right then I would rather have died.

They knew I was terrified and did not tarry. When the time came, they asked if I was okay, I said, "Yes. Go ahead."

"Please God, help me." The pain was coming and he was ready. I felt the terrible pain as it intensified with this manipulation to the point where my head was swimming, the room began to whirl round and round, "Oh God let me die." I felt a terrible pull against the pain. I couldn't bear the pain any longer. An agonizing scream came from my throat that I didn't recognize as my own, then everything went black.

I have no idea how long I was out, but when I awakened the room was quiet, the door was shut and I was so thankful it was over. I turned my head to see if anyone was in the room.

A man in a white robe was standing beside me, leaning against the other bed. He seemed to have been there for awhile, waiting for me to awaken. "JESUS." I recognized Him before He spoke. He was only about three feet from me. I was elated. I felt like I was in glory. I lay basking in a beautiful aura that surrounded me. I had no doubt that it was Jesus. He looked like the pictures I had seen of Him, which may not be accurate but He knew how I would recognize Him. A warm comfort came to me like when the nurses wrap you in those warmed blankets. I lay still watching Him. I did not have a pain during that time. He said to me, with a passion in His voice that said as much as His words when He spoke, "Rose you will never have to go through this again." And He was gone.

Just a few words, but they meant so much to me. Jesus was there, I was not alone. I would never have to go through this again. Had He come to tell me this because I had just asked Him to let me die? Thank you Jesus. Oh! Thank you Jesus. I was trying to remember everything, just how He looked and what He said, did He say more—no, not another word. Oh how wonderful. I wasn't sure whether my elation was that Jesus came to me or for what He had come to tell me. For both reasons I'm sure. This is an experience I will never forget.

I was in deep thought when the doctors walked in. Dr. Dale walked over and took hold of my hand he said, "I'm so sorry I had to do that, but it will save you many hours of labor. How do you feel now?"

I said, "My labor has stopped." He answered my questioning look and said, "I expected that, that baby had a hard time too. He also needs a rest." He listened with the stethoscope, then said, "He is okay, he is a big strong baby, he didn't want to turn. If he had not been so strong and healthy I may not have attempted to turn him. I hope he doesn't turn back, sometimes they do. Your pains will start again soon." He patted me on the leg and said, "You did great."

Turn back? NO! I was anxious to get this over before he did turn back. With a prayer on my lips I waited. The pains started very soon. The procedure must have dilated me as it was a much faster delivery. There was pain and it was not over in a snap, but it was much easier. I was so happy when it was over I cried, thanking Jesus and the doctor over and over.

I was very tired, but my elation was so great I was anxious to go home. Donna came to pick me up and Mom stayed home with the kids. Steve and I were ready when she got there. We went straight home. I could hardly wait to see the kids and Mom to show them our new baby and to tell them about Jesus visiting me.

Steve was healthy, happy, and the very essence of peace. He weighed over nine pounds. He was a mother's dream come true and for a seventh child, he never gave me a minute's problem. He was a pretty little boy, blonde hair and brown eyes. He was kind and gentle, and his brothers and sisters adored him. His dad thought he was special too. He was so special to me, I wanted to enjoy him to the fullest. Knowing he would be the last, the last baby I would ever have.

I learned later that "7" signifies completeness with the Lord. God planned for me to have seven children. There must be more to this than I am seeing now. We are no doubt very special to Him. I have not told very many people about this incident. I didn't want to throw my pearls to the swine.

When we drove up to the house, we were greeted with a wallop. Billy ran out to the car and very excitedly yelled, "Mom! Merrill set a forest fire up on the hill when they were playing wagon train." Of course I could see him trapped in the fire. "Where is he?" I demanded.

Billy said, "He's okay. He's in the house. The police will probably arrest him."

I was getting more frantic by the minute. Donna jumped out of the car and ran into the house. I followed her carrying Steve. We found Mom hysterical.

"Oh I suppose I'm going to get the blame for this, but how was I to watch them all." She was watching my six and Donna's three, but only for an hour or so, we certainly didn't blame her. "I did the best I could. I suppose Bill and Rose are going to have to pay for all this. Oh my, I'm just sick about this. What shall we do?"

Donna was attempting to calm her. "Don't worry Mom, I will go up and see how bad the fire is and bring the other kids home and I'll talk to the police or firemen to find out just what happened." Mom thought that would be the wise thing to do.

She was settling down some.

With that under control for the moment, I had to show off this new baby. I gave him to Mom so I could hold Janet. She was so glad to see us. She was still a baby herself at just thirteen months old. She needed to be loved, and it felt like I hadn't seen her for a month. She looked so big. It was so good to be home. I felt better after hugging all the kids. We waited for Bill to get home from work to deal with the fire.

Janet started mothering Steve right away. She knew I brought that baby home just for her. She mothered him the rest of his life and he didn't mind, he tolerated anything she did. He was very good to her. But why shouldn't he be? She did his laundry and cleaned his room when it got to the point that I couldn't stand it any more. I would put my foot down saying, "You don't go anywhere until you clean your room." He would tell Janet he was going to get in trouble with coach Pancrats if he didn't get to football practice. It worked.

Danny and Janet's health problems quieted for the summer. It seemed like they were holding their own and hopefully building some resistance.

We went out on the river a lot with Jack and Mary and other friends. We had some great picnics. I sat in the shade with Steve and watched Janet play in the sand. It was hard for her to walk in the sand and stay upright. Her legs were too short and she got so frustrated. I brought her a walker, thinking that it would be foolproof. I was watching the swimmers and skiers and boaters. Suddenly, Janet caught my eye and she had tipped over the walker and her face was in the sand. She was struggling. I ran to her and when I picked her up I could see her mouth was full of sand. I began to dig it out. It was packed hard, way down her throat. She couldn't breathe. I dug frantically, but was not getting much out. She still was not breathing. I ran to the water, knelt down with her and splashed water into her mouth and throat. She finally coughed and made herself an airway. She was okay, but she got sand in her lungs. She was pretty sick for a while with pneumonia, which is the only way to get any foreign body out of the lungs. She got rid of it all and no ill effects.

When all the facts were in about the fire, we learned that Merrill and Rosana were up on the hill just above the house and were, sure enough, playing wagon train. They would travel for a few feet and stop and circle the wagons and build a fire in the middle of the circle. They would travel a few more feet and do the same thing again. They always put the fire out before they moved on, but sometimes it must not have gone out. The fire did very little damage. Only brush was burned, thanks to Billy and Tommy who went to look for the kids when Grandma sent them out. They found them and the fire and ran back home to tell Grandma to call the fire department.

The kids were worried about what Bill would say. He did give them a hard scolding. I don't think they forgot that very soon. Someone told me the police thought it was Bill and Tom. Since they were older, I knew it would go harder on them. I was going to tell them it was the little kids. I surely didn't want them to get the blame when they didn't do it. Bill would not let me do it. He said if we admitted blame for the fire then we would be liable for sure. If they came to us about it then we could tell them. He said, "Let sleeping dogs lie."

Winter came early, and with it came the welcome times of card parties, pot lucks and get togethers. Our circle of friends was getting larger. I believe Bill knew everyone in town. He was very well liked by the people he worked with, people in the church, people in general wherever he went. I was so proud of him. After all these years of hating people, mistrusting them and not wanting to be around them at all. What a change, thanks to God.

I felt so different about myself, about Bill, and life in general. I was a better wife and a better mother. I felt whole and complete. Having the Lord in my life was making such a difference. In fact He made all the difference. He changed Bill and He changed me. He took the bitterness away and gave me peace.

The children were accepting the change in our lives of going to church, praying, giving thanks, reading the Bible and Bible stories. Those were the most obvious changes as we lived fairly clean lives. Other than smoking, Bill hadn't drank for a long time. His cursing was very conspicuous, however.

In my own family, we did not use bad language or cursing. My stepdad may have outside, but not in the house, nor did my brothers curse in the house. My mother followed the teaching of her mother except she did drink some alcohol on holidays when it was brought to the house by guests. I never did see her drink too much. It hurt me so to see her drink at all. I always felt like she was too dignified for that.

Bill and his family were cursing people. They didn't drink at home that I know of. Cursing was such a way of life with them, they couldn't seem to talk without using vulgarity and obscenities. After being around them for a few years I picked up some bad language. I used it in front of my mother once and she turned on me scowling and said, "Ladies don't talk like that." That was the end of that for me. I smoked from the time I was fourteen until I became a Christian. I did not smoke in public because I was ashamed of it, but I had the addiction. After I gave my heart to the Lord, I gave it up. There was one person who I give credit to, who helped me more than anyone. He said "Rose if you say you are trying you will never quit. You have to be able to say I quit, then you will do it." I never touched another cigarette. I am still beholden to Roy York, Lois' dad, for that. I've used that piece of advice many times in my life for myself and others.

Mom had always wanted to be a nurse, so when she was settled in life and her home was completed, she went to school and became a Registered Nursing Assistant. She went to work at the Community hospital in Roseburg. She drove from Myrtle Creek everyday. She was a terrible

Mom, going to work.

driver and I worried about her, but she never had any problems. She was a good nurse, she got a lot of awards and an exceeding amount of recognition for her work. Mom was very competent in every way, and was exceptional in her compassion for the sick. Her patients loved her. She was given the most serious cases on the med floor because of the excellent care she gave and she was so responsible. She could be trusted always to carry out every order in detail.

Her arthritis was getting bad. There were times when she didn't know if she could make it out of bed, let alone work. But she forced herself and after she got to work and walked for awhile she limbered up. It was pretty hard for her those last few years. She finally had to retire. Then her health just deteriorated. She couldn't get around anymore and then she became very depressed and dependent. The last few years of her life were not happy. We took care of her as long as we could but she eventually had to be put in the nursing home. She hated that and it broke our hearts.

My sister Donna was living down South Myrtle Creek a couple miles from Mom's place. She and Darrell bought an acreage there and were building a house. This place was one of the prettiest places I have ever seen. Sitting above the creek, where you could hear the creek and see the trees, the bushes and the blackberries were thick on that bank. All along the creek, which paralleled the property by the house, there was an abundance of greenery. The house sat in a spot where the one bedroom nearly overhung the creek and there was shade over that room at all times. The branches were separated enough so you could see through to the creek when sitting by the window. Such a beautiful place to raise their three great kids, Terry, Timmy and Connie. Our families were very close. I loved them all like they were my own and Donna treated us all like her own. We had some good times.

Donna had many flowers planted and also a big vegetable garden. She was a worker and provided a good portion of their living. She had most of it to do by herself. Darrell was not much for outside work. He never seemed to finish a project. The kids helped a lot. They loved their home on the Creek. Darrell worked at a smelter in Riddle, Oregon.

They raised calves they purchased from dairy ranchers on the coast. In fact the dairies were giving most of them away at one day old. Donna took care of those baby calves and fed them on a bottle every two or three

*Donna, Connie,
and Darrell McGarvey.
In front,
Terry and Tim.*

219

hours until they were ready to eat grass or hay. Many of them got scours. She gave them shots and kept them on clean hay with heat lamps twenty-four hours a day. They were much more work than a child. She sometimes had six calves at a time. She built up quite a herd from hand raising those baby calves. Darrell leased some grazing land from the government. He could keep the cattle on that land most of the summer and fall. Donna said this venture never paid off. I asked her "Why do you do it?" She said, "Darrell loves it. He would be devastated if we gave this up. I think it is the "Rancher" status that makes him feel so good."

In later years I went with them to the coast in the old truck to pick up some calves. The three of us sat in the front with the little ones and the other kids rode in the back on the hay that covered the truck bed. We all enjoyed the trip. One time in particular I remember we were just nearing a little town and we smelled the most terrible smell. The closer we got to the town, the worse the smell became. Darrell pulled into a station to get some gas. In conversation with the attendant there, Darrell said "What is that terrible smell here?" The man said, "Gee, I don't know. I didn't smell it until you came." Darrell looked at him for awhile and said, "Is that right." Donna and I burst into laughter. We laughed until we were weak. Darrell looked at the fellow in very deep thought, as he was pulling up the hood. He saw what it was, the battery was burning up. Donna and I could not stop laughing. We would try and then one of us would start to laugh and then we both would get started again. Darrell didn't think it was so funny but of course he didn't see his expression when the man spoke to him, and he did have to replace the battery. We have had fun over that for many years.

They grew hay down on the place and fed their cows in the winter. They also cut hay for other people on shares. Donna and the three kids and sometimes my kids would help. We had a fall roundup every year that was so much fun. I remember one time when they gave me old Nellie to ride. She did great, but we found out later she was blind. Not knowing that at the time, we didn't make it in until after dark. We went down a steep slope where everyone had to be careful because it was pitch black out. Nellie did fine coming down, she didn't even stumble. Some of the other horses did. She knew that place so well that she knew where to go. She had a tender mouth, so she was easy to control. I sure counted my blessings when I found out she was blind. You'd never know she was blind as long as she was on their place. Darrell sold her to a fellow. He put her in the corral and she ran into the fence and the barn and she was getting pretty banged up. The fellow watched her and figured out she was blind. The guy brought her back. Poor old Nellie. She served us well.

Darrell had an Arab stallion. A beautiful horse, he called him Flame. He was a lot of horse for Darrell to handle. They had Flame bred to an Arab mare. The colt was a filly so Donna took her. I don't know that she wanted her as bad as Darrell wanted her to have her. She was a beautiful little filly. Donna hadn't ridden her much. One day when I was visiting, Donna said, "Why don't you go with me up to check the cows? I'll ride Flicker and you can ride Nellie." That was before we knew Nellie was blind. I said sure, that would be fun. We packed a lunch and planned to eat at the old homestead up there. We saddled up and took off. Flicker wasn't doing too well so Donna said, "You go first with Nellie and I think Flicker will follow." I started up the trail and sure enough Flicker came right behind her. I noticed she was having a hard time keeping Flicker doing what she ought. She wanted to eat. Donna would pull her head up and she would crow hop a little. Then she finally settled down.

We got up on top of the hill and it was pretty warm. The horses would have welcomed a drink even though we took the hill pretty slow. I was about fifty feet ahead of Donna and I didn't hear the horse, so I stopped and turned around in my saddle just in time to see Donna sitting on the horse like a broomstick with her eyes as big as dollars, looking at me. Flicker had straddled a bush and was rubbing back and forth scratching her belly. Donna had no idea what she was doing. Flicker looked like she was dancing, but Donna looked like she was going to get bucked off. I began to laugh and told Donna what she was doing. She relaxed and we waited for Flicker. We didn't really want to argue with her.

When we got to the homestead, we pulled up by the old house under a shade tree. We got off the horses and took the bridles off, and tied them to a rail there. They began to eat from the lush green grass. They did fine until Flicker got to the end of her rope. It pulled her and she blew up rearing and bucking. She got Nellie all excited, but Nellie was just trying to get out of her way. Flicker pulled down the rail and took off running across the meadow. Her head high and her tail standing right straight out dragging that pole. She ran and ran and we just stood there watching her. The pole didn't hit her, if it had she'd still be running. She finally lost the pole. We were enjoying the show and she was enjoying herself. It's a beautiful thing to see an Arab run. Donna said, "There's no way we are going to stop her until she runs out of gas, so let's eat."

That was fine with me. Flicker ran and ran. I can still see her running with her tail sticking out behind. She finally did run out of gas and stopped to eat. When we were finished eating we took Nellie out and rode up to Flicker, took hold of the halter rope and she came on over to the fence where we had eaten. She didn't give Donna a bit of trouble all the way home.

That was a great day. We both have some sweet memories of those days. We always had a good time no matter what we were doing. The kids enjoyed one another and helped us with some of our projects we did together.

Bill had been laid off part of the winter and of course he spent most of his time reading. It was about the first of May when he went to work. He drove heister for the mill in Sutherlin. He didn't feel well a lot of the time. He went to the doctor over in Roseburg and had a thorough check up. He told the doctor he thought there was something wrong with his heart. The doctor found nothing wrong at all. Bill was taking the weekends pretty easy, staying in bed most of the time. He complained of his legs hurting. Complaining was something he didn't do, so I was a little concerned. He didn't miss any work.

One night he went out to a union meeting, he came home about nine and the kids were all in bed. He said, "Come in here, I want to tell you something."

I went into the dining room and sat down to the table with him. He laid some papers on the table and began to tell me, "I want you to pay attention now, this is serious. You write all this down and keep it where you can find it. This is just in case something happens to me. You will get enough money to support you and the kids."

I interrupted, "What is the matter with you? Do you think you are going to die? That's ridiculous, now just stop it."

He continued on as if he didn't hear me, "You will get life insurance from the mill and the union. You will get Social Security benefits and also benefits from the V.A. You will probably get more then, than now. It will come all year around. You will make it fine on what you will get."

I sat there scowling at him, "Why are you talking like this? What are you planning to do? Even if I get money, I still can't raise these kids alone. Just stop this, I am getting scared, hearing you talk like this."

He said "No reason to be afraid, you can do it. Do you hear me? You can do it. Now put these papers where you can get to them when you need them."

I was totally put off by this, I just wanted to change the subject. I went into the living room and turned on TV. He came in and sat with me and watched for awhile. Nothing else was mentioned about it and I just dismissed it from my mind. I really thought he was being ridiculous, maybe trying to scare me because he seldom ever talked about things serious.

Bill seemed to be feeling better, I asked him several times and he always felt fine.

One Sunday morning Bill and Jack were getting ready to go steelhead fishing. I said to them, "Are you going fishing on Sunday morning instead of going to church?"

Bill said "Yes." That yes sounded like he didn't want to discuss it. I had to try once more, "God probably won't let you catch any fish if you skip church to go."

Bill came back with, "If He lets me catch fish, then I will go to church." I felt sorry he said that.

I had a heavy feeling in my chest and wished I hadn't brought that on, if only I hadn't said anything. As they were leaving I told them, "Good-bye and be careful. I'll save dinner for you Bill." Jack's pickup and boat were sitting out front in the driveway. They got in the pickup and drove away as I watched them from the window.

They did get home late, they didn't have any luck. So they planned to go back next weekend. I wished they would not wager with the Lord.

Bill seemed to be feeling fine. He got up and went to work. That afternoon about four he called me from the mill. He said, "I'll probably be home late because the boss is taking me to the doctor's office." He sounded so normal, I really wasn't too concerned.

I asked him, "Did you get hurt?"

"No" he said "I had some pains in my chest. I don't think there is anything wrong. My stomach has been acting up since lunch, and I think it's just gas. I have to go. I'll call you from the doctors office."

Thirty minutes later he called. He sounded disgusted when he said, "They have an ambulance out front and they are going to take me to the hospital. I think that's crazy, there's nothing wrong with me. I'll call you from there."

Getting anxious I asked, "Well what do they think it is?"

He answered, "I don't know, they didn't say. They probably won't bring me back so I'll call you to come get me. I'm fine, don't worry. I'll see you pretty soon. Bye."

I was beginning to feel very anxious about this thing. I called Mom. She had just got home from work. I told her about Bill and she said not to worry. They would let me know when they decided what was wrong. She refused to tell me anymore.

Aunt Clara came and she said Mom had called her to come over because the hospital may call and I would have to leave. I would need someone there with the kids. I was glad to see her. I didn't like being alone now. I had a very strange feeling, I didn't know what it was. "Am I afraid or what?" I asked myself.

I knew Aunt Clara would always drink coffee so I made a pot and we sat at the table and drank our coffee and talked about this thing with Bill. I had dinner ready, so I called the kids. Aunt Clara joined us for dinner, and she visited with the kids while we were eating. It saved me from a tense situation. I was glad for her to be with us.

We got the dishes done and sat down for another cup of coffee. Some of the kids watched TV and some went out to play. They asked about their Dad. I told them just what Bill told me and did not offer any more than the facts, not wanting to frighten them or cause them to worry.

I told them it was seven-thirty and I'd be calling them in about eight-thirty, don't go too far.

Bill did call after they did some tests, "I don't think they know anything, but I am going to have to stay here overnight. That's so ridiculous."

I said "Do you think I could talk to the doctor if I came over?" He thought I may be able to. Aunt Clara stayed with the kids. I drove to Roseburg.

Bill was in an oxygen tent. He still maintained they didn't know what they were doing. There was nothing wrong with him. He certainly didn't look like there was anything wrong.

He said "Get my wallet out of the drawer, look in that hidden compartment. There's some money I have saved, to take the kids to Idaho. I want you to get it out and promise me that if anything happens to me, you will use it to take them to Idaho."

Again I was put out with him for talking like that. I said "You say there's nothing wrong and then you sound like you are going to die. Is there something you haven't told me?"

"No, there isn't. But you never know what can happen to you in the hospital."

I said "Oh Bill don't be so silly." I went out to the nurse's station to ask where I could find the doctor. They said he went home, but they would try to call him. They could not locate him, so I told them I would go on home. If they would please have him call me there as they thought he would be in for his rounds later on. I thought about waiting for him, but they had given Bill a sedative and did want him to sleep, they said it would be better for him if he would just rest. I asked them to please call if he got worse and I could come back.

I went back into the room and Bill was getting drowsy so I told him I would be back in the morning if he didn't get to come home. I threw a kiss to him and told him good-bye. He was about asleep when I left.

It was about ten o'clock when the doctor called me, "Mrs. Saleen, I just came from your husband's room and he is resting well."

I thought, do we go through this again. I asked him, "Don't you know what is wrong with him?"

He answered "Yes I know," he lowered his voice saying, "your husband has coronary thrombosis."

I said, "I'm sorry I don't know what that is, can you explain it to me?"

He said, "He has a blood clot in his heart."

I waited for awhile and then asked, "Is that serious?"

"Yes it is very serious, but I just gave him a good physical and he is a healthy man and the clot may pass through and he will be alright."

I said "If it doesn't then what?"

He said "Oh a number of things could happen, but I really expect him to be fine. I will call you right away if there is a change in his condition."

I said "Yes please do, and thank you for calling."

I didn't know what to think, not being familiar with anything medical. Aunt Clara and I talked, I was glad for her to talk to, it made it much easier for me. I would have called Mom but I knew she had to get up and go to work. I would rather not bother her. I planned to call her after she got up.

I called Mary and told her what the doctor had said. She was very concerned and told me she would be right in. When she came, she asked where she could be the most help.

I suggested to her that maybe calling Pastor Whitford may be good so he could get the prayer chain organized and begin praying as soon as possible. She agreed and went to the phone immediately. After she talked to him she told me Pastor Whitford was going to the hospital to see Bill. I became quite alarmed seeing how concerned he and Mary were, however they didn't say any more to me. Mary, in her kind thoughtful way, said, "Rose, I think I should take the kids home with me. We can carry out the little ones and the older ones can just come in their PJ's. I'll get a clean outfit of clothes for them."

I was a little shocked, "Mary do you think all this is necessary? Where would you put all of them to sleep?" She said,

"Oh Rose it will be fun for all the kids and me too. You know how I love to feed them breakfast. And besides if you should want to go to the hospital early in the morning, you can just get up and go." She trailed off as she went into the kids' bedrooms. I went with her and helped her take the kids out. Mary had them so excited about going to spend the night, they didn't even complain about being awakened. When they drove off they all had big smiles on their faces.

I was beginning to think that maybe I should be a bit more concerned than I was. I believed what the doctor said, and I was sure that if something happened he would call. Was I too close to the forest to see the trees?

Aunt Clara and I talked until quite late. She looked like she was getting pretty tired and I told her to go sleep in my bed and I would lay down on the couch, so I could hear the phone if it rang.

I laid down with my clothes on just in case I was called to go quickly. I don't think I ever went to sleep, but I would doze off then wake up with a start. I was trying to rest, but no rest came. I felt so encumbered, not having the remotest idea about what to expect. I had never encountered anything like this, not being around much sickness. It was frightening to me. When the house became quiet everything was magnifying in my mind. I just lay there in a state of fear and dread, waiting for the phone to ring.

I must have dozed off because I woke up with a start when the doorbell rang. It was instant panic. Who could that be? Maybe it was the Pastor. It was still dark. I looked up at the clock. It was four thirty. I got up and walked to the door, I stood there for a moment before I opened it. "I'm Dr. Blinkenstaff, are you Mrs. Saleen?" I answered that I was and he said, "Can I come in please, I would like to talk to you if I may."

I stepped back, staring at him. What was he going to say? I opened the door wider and said, "Yes please come in. Would you like to sit down on the couch here? I will turn on more lights. Can I get you something?"

He said "The lights are fine and no I don't care for anything. Will you please sit down over here so we can talk." I walked over and sat down.

I said, "Is Bill dead?"

He took hold of my hand and said "Yes Mrs. Saleen, he is. I'm so sorry. There was nothing we could do for him. He passed away in his sleep. He didn't struggle at all. He didn't know. That clot stopped his heart. We tried to resuscitate him but it did no good. He was gone. I would have called you but there was no time, it happened so quick. I am so sorry."

I felt nothing. I just sat there. I couldn't cry, I couldn't talk. He went on talking, but I really didn't know what he was saying until he said, "Mrs. Saleen, listen to me. Do you have anyone that could come and stay with you?"

I said "Yes, my Aunt is here." I think he went to call her from the bedroom. When she came over to where I was sitting she knelt down in front of me, crying, saying "Rose I'm so sorry." I didn't respond to her.

"Rose don't you understand? Bill is gone."

Dr. Blinkenstaff told Aunt Clara he would like to talk to me. Is there someone else she would like to call and have them come also to be with her? Aunt Clara went into the dining room and sat down at the table and began to call.

Dr. B. said, "Can I do something for you? I will wait until someone else comes to be with you before I go."

"I don't think I need anything." I said as I looked down at my hands in my lap. Things were beginning to fade out for me. Mentally I was in a fog.

I asked the doctor, "Bill is dead, is that right?" He nodded his head and said "Yes, Mrs. Saleen, that is right."

I asked him what I was supposed to do. He said, "Nothing, other people will be here soon and they will help you with everything that needs to be done. You don't have to worry about anything now, others will be here soon."

I was thinking about going to get him, where would I take him. Then I thought about funeral and burial, I quickly erased it from my mind. It frightened me terribly. I thought about the bedroom where all his clothes were. About the bed where we had slept. I couldn't believe he was dead and all of his things still in there. I thought about talking to him at the hospital, telling him good-bye, throwing him a kiss. How could he be gone? Oh! The kids what will I tell them? They will be so hurt, they will cry. I couldn't stand to see them grieve. The poor kids, how could I tell them? I just couldn't. Fears were mounting up inside me. What would we do? How could we live? The bedroom was the most dreadful to think about, everything he wore, the bed we slept in. Now he is dead. I have never seen a dead person. The more I thought the more horrified I became. Suddenly all that was inside me burst forth and I began to cry. He wanted me to do everything with him. How did he do this by himself? I should have gone with him. I wasn't sure if I was crying for fear or grief. I had never experienced death, except with animals but that was different. It was hard to lose them but they were not spiritual beings like man.

What am I going to do. My thoughts were whirling around in my head. They wouldn't stay long enough to really think about.

The doctor was still sitting beside me. Nothing he or anyone could do was going to change anything. I wanted to cry. People began coming into the house. Everyone was crying and it made me cry more. Mom came in. The doctor must have been waiting for her as he knew her from the hospital. He got up and talked to her. He gave her something for me to take to get some rest. I didn't want to rest. Someone mentioned going into the bedroom to rest. I grimaced, "No I will not go in the bedroom." That emotion was so irrational for me, I had never been hysterical, but I was about to be. I had never thrown a tantrum, I felt like I wanted to. I've got to get a hold of myself. I was ashamed to even think of that, but there were some things I just was not going to do. Going into that bedroom was #1. Here I was twenty-nine years old, my husband was dead. Maybe some things deserved a tantrum. If it became necessary to get my point across, then so be it.

I wanted the kids to come home, but no I didn't want to tell them. They would cry and I couldn't stand that. The poor kids. What are they going to say? They will feel so bad. It isn't daylight yet, they won't be up. I talked to Mom about the kids. I said I just couldn't tell them. Mom said. "Your pastor will go out and tell them and then he will bring them in." What will I say to them? They won't want to come in here with all these people here crying. My heart broke for the kids. I thought about each one of them and how they would feel about this. With each child there came a new flood of tears. Their father was dead.

I was still sitting on the couch but the doctor was gone. Mom asked me if I wanted to lay down and again I yelled at her, "No!" Different ones came to talk to me, but I couldn't talk to them; however I was glad they were there. I wasn't so frightened with a lot of people around. I hoped they wouldn't go home. I just wanted to be left alone to cry. No one seemed offended.

Mom took me over to the other couch which was longer, laid me down, covered me with a blanket and gave me a pillow. When I laid down my head I could smell Bill's hair. It just wrenched my insides. I asked Mom to get me one of the kids' pillows. I really was tired. It felt good to lay down.

Poor Bill. He didn't know he was dying, or did he? He wouldn't want to leave us or would he? I didn't know for sure. I thought about the things he said. This whole thing was a mystery to me. I had better quit thinking, but I couldn't. The poor kids. When I thought of them, I hurt so I could hardly stand it. I cried and cried.

Mom stayed close by me, she didn't talk. That was fine. I didn't want to talk, but I wanted her there. I felt safer when she was right there. There were a lot of other people there. I didn't know who all was there. I'm sure I knew them but didn't see or acknowledge them. I didn't care. I just wanted them close, talking, so I could hear them. It didn't seem so frightening. People began bringing in food. All kinds of food. They would come by and say they were sorry and cry. I couldn't talk to them. I did say thank you to each of them.

Oh, I would be so glad when it got daylight. I knew I would feel better. I wanted the kids to come home, yet I dreaded that. Thinking about the kids was nearly unbearable.

Why did God do this, we were just beginning to have a good family life and God took him away. Didn't He care about us? What were we going to do? I hope Bill went to heaven, but I didn't know for sure. "Oh, Lord God, I pray that you took him to heaven."

What if he didn't, what if—. I couldn't say it. Did I do everything I could have to see that he was saved? I have to know. I turned over and said to Mom, "I need to talk with Lloyd, our pastor, when he comes." Mom told me he was out to Mary's telling the kids now. He would bring the kids in and then I could talk to him. I wanted to be up when the kids came. I wanted to go out and meet them. "Mom, tell me when they come."

I walked over to the door, the car was in the drive way.

The kids were coming in. Oh God, please help me to help them. If only I could take the hurt for them. I would gladly do it. But how?

There they were and they knew, my heart was breaking. I walked toward the car and Lloyd was helping the little ones get out of the car.

Rosana came running to me crying. She hung onto my legs. I put my arms around her and cried with her. Tom and Merrill got out and hung back by the car, not knowing what to do. I walked up and gathered them up in my arms. Then I saw Billy. He was walking away from me. I said, "Billy please come over here."

He turned and looked at me. There was a look on his face that said to me one of two things. "Why wasn't it you?" or "This is all your fault." He kept glaring at me with those hurting eyes, but he didn't come to me. He walked around the back of the house. Oh, that hurt. Why did he do that? Why does he think that? I was holding the other three and they were crying, I couldn't let them go. The pastor was standing there and I asked where Janet and Steve were. He said they stayed with Mary, she will bring them later. I was glad of that because I needed to be with the other kids now.

Danny didn't seem to understand what was happening, which was just as well. He walked around in the yard, not knowing what to do. He watched the other kids and kept looking at me.

What does a child of four years know about death? What did I know about death? I was remembering when my grandmother died, my mother was hysterical. I was so frightened, it was horrifying for me to see her grief. Danny doesn't really understand that he will never see his Dad again. I called him over and tried to stretch my arms around him also. He was looking around very confused. The time would come when he would want to know more about what was happening right now. He acted like he wanted to get away by himself.

Mom came out and asked the kids if they wanted something to eat. They went with her into the house.

I was glad to be alone so I could go talk to Billy. He didn't want to talk, and he didn't want to cry. I wanted to say to him, do you think it was my fault, but I couldn't. I didn't want to suggest an emotion that he may not have. I couldn't help but think of the day in Moreland when we drove away from his dad crying. I remember how he looked at me then. Was he connecting the two incidents? These thoughts caused agonies inside me. I put my arms around him and I cried, and there was a new pain a deep open wound. "Oh God, help this child to understand." We walked into the house and sat down on the couch.

The kids would go outside and then back in to be with me for a few minutes and then back out again. I was laying on the couch, someone had made it out and put down a sheet and a blanket for cover. I wanted to be out there where the activity was.

The bedroom door was shut at my request. I had asked Mom to see that no one went in there. I couldn't go past the door to the bathroom unless someone was with me.

People kept coming. Some would leave and some would stay. Some were doing dishes, some were taking care of the food, some were making coffee and serving. They brought in food for days and helped in any way they could.

I laid on the couch with my back to everyone crying most of the time. I couldn't stop. The kids came in and lay beside me and that was the most comfort to me. Ever since the kids were babies they usually ended up in bed with us before morning. But I didn't care, in fact I loved it. I know how an old hen feels when she spreads her wings to cover her chicks. They were doing the same now and it was very comforting to me. Little Merrill lifted the covers by my feet and slipped in there and laid down. Just like he did when he was little. I would know when he came in, but I never said anything. I slept with my babies on my chest most of the time. I loved feeling them there.

I dreaded the night coming. There was at least one person sitting close to me at all times. That was very comforting to me, even though I didn't want to talk. Sometimes I would reach out and touch them, just to feel someone.

Pastor Lloyd came in and sat down beside me and said someone told him I wanted to talk to him. It was hard for me to bring it up, but I had to know.

"Lloyd, I have to know for sure, did Bill accept the Lord, was he saved before he died?" I dreaded what he might say.

He answered with conviction, "Yes, Rose he was saved. He accepted the Lord. He was a Christian. You don't have to worry." Those were the most beautiful words I had ever heard. "Now I can tell the kids their Daddy went to heaven. Oh, what a blessed relief. Thank you for seeing to it that he was ready to meet the Lord. What a terrible thing for a family or loved one, to have to think about when they lose someone, where did they go. How terrible if I had to tell the kids their Dad was not saved."

Lloyd said "Yes it is, and I've had to tell a lot of families that very thing. It seems that a lot of people don't think about it until there is a death.

Are you ready to talk about funeral arrangements? There is no hurry if you want to wait."

I said, "No, no not now, I can't." And a whole new outburst came forth.

Lloyd held my hand and prayed for us, that my grief be lifted and that God would give me peace in my heart and also for the children. He prayed for a long time and as he talked to the Lord, I could feel a calming spirit settle over me.

There was so much to think about in our future. It was too overwhelming to think about now. I just had to get through this day. I snuggled up to the kids laying beside me and just closed my eyes shutting out the world.

Funeral arrangements were made. Bill's brother Jim came down from Portland and he took that over. He insisted I go to pick out a casket. I didn't want to do that, but with his insistence, I went along. Mom and Donna went with me. It was so difficult and Jim made it more so. We were shown caskets in different price ranges, and I chose one that was not top of the line, but moderately priced. Jim stepped up and said, "I really take offense to my brother being buried in a cheap casket like this. I insist we choose a better one for him." I could not argue with him, at a time like this, I was stunned, but I thought he may have a reason. I said "Then choose what you want Jim." He did. He chose top of the line. The most expensive one. I felt ashamed that I hadn't picked something better. I was thinking about the money. I suffered such embarrassment because of this. But I thought Jim probably wanted to help pay for this if he wanted better than I could afford. An added heartache was something I didn't need right now.

I didn't realize I was in the mortuary until the mortician asked if I would like to view the body. It was ready and laying out so we could go in if we liked. I nearly fainted. Everything was spinning. I couldn't answer him. Someone said, "We might as well as long as we are here." I said "No." and went toward the door. I could feel myself staggering and someone took me by the arm and sat me on a chair. That same someone was talking to me saying it would be so much easier if I saw him before the funeral. I said "No. I want to leave."

When we got out in the car we headed out of town and I said, "Where are we going?"

"To the cemetery." I cringed, I felt like I couldn't stand to go out there. When we got there I was told that we were to pick out a grave site. I wanted to stay in the car. Jim insisted that I get out. He opened the car door and took hold of my arm and pulled me out of the car. I didn't want to make a scene, so I went. A man was there to show us what was available. Jim walked out ahead of us, saying as he walked, "Isn't there something up on this little hill. I know Bill would like this spot. He could get up every night and look down over the valley." I turned around and went to the car. I was so frightened anyway and him saying that chilled my very soul. Jim stood up on the hill and laughed.

The man was talking to my family and Mom came over to the car and asked me please to get out and say if I wanted this sight under the tree. It was beside a baby. I said yes and looked over that way. I covered my face with my hands and began to sob.

I said "Please take me home." We went home.

I was emotionally drained. I was given a sedative because I couldn't stop trembling, inside and out. Mom thought that would put me to sleep, and when the kids came in to sit by me someone told them, "Mommy has to rest now, so go out and play."

I said, "No, let them stay here, they make me feel better than anything else could." Merrill came in and curled up around my feet. Rosana laid down beside me on one side and Danny on the other, Billy and Tommy sat down on the edge of the couch in front of me. I felt so good, like they were protecting me. I rested.

Bill's family from Idaho came the day of the funeral. They went out the back door and sat on the steps. They made no attempt to talk to the kids or to console them. I could understand if Edrie was too overwrought to talk to anyone, but some of their uncles and aunts surely could have comforted the kids. Somehow a message came back to me that Edrie said it was my fault that he died. He was never happy in Oregon. So, was that the reason they were so distant. I didn't have a comment for that, but I said I didn't want to know about any of their remarks. This was very awkward as it was. They were taken plates of food because they wouldn't come in, their coffee cups were filled continuously. And they were invited in the house. As for me talking to them I couldn't, but then I couldn't talk to anyone. If that offended them I was sorry. I had my own grief to deal with and I was doing the best I could. I was more like a zombie than a person.

Lloyd, our pastor came to talk to me. He talked to me about my obvious fear of death. He reminded me that all the teaching and studying I had since I became a Christian was concerning death, preparing for and after death. Our own and the death of our loved ones. He talked to me for a long time. I did feel better, but I couldn't go into the bedroom. I didn't want to go to the funeral. He said he would be there and would help me through it. He told me how many people were praying for me.

"God is waiting for you to call on Him for whatever you need. You don't need to suffer like this. Peace is there for the asking."

I told Lloyd, "I am ashamed to admit it but my thoughts are not on God, but our loss. These things that have to be taken care of. What are the kids and I going to do? Poor little Janet and Steve would never know their dad. Lloyd, I'm ashamed but I can't even pray."

He explained to me, "When a person is in shock it is not uncommon for this to happen. We get so consumed with ourselves, it is hard to focus our minds long enough to pray. But just call out to Him, He is grieving for you all and wants to help. Even though He chose to do what He did, for what reason we do not know. He feels every tear you and the children shed. He cries with you. He has a tender heart for His children just as you do for yours."

I said "That is hard for me to believe. He did this. He didn't have to, He just did. He took the kids father away from them. Do you know what it's like to grow up without a father, or a mother who lives without a husband? It's not easy Lloyd, and with seven kids, how am I going to do it."

"Rose, please understand the Lord will never leave or forsake you. He didn't do this to punish you, it had to be done. There was a reason and He will let you know someday and it will be for the best just as in Romans 8:28, "All things work together for those who love God and are called according to His purpose." Maybe Bill would have had an accident and he would be an invalid the rest of his life. That would be worse than death. There are many things worse than death. We don't know what God knows. It takes a lot of faith to believe these things and I know you have what it takes. God knows your need and the needs of the kids even better than you. He has a big storage of blessings that He will provide as you ask. He says in His word that He will be the Father to the orphans. He has everything planned for you and the kids. You just have to trust Him. Be faithful, bring your kids up in the Lord and they will be able to withstand the forces of the devil. Rose you can do it if anyone can." And he prayed.

The stone in my heart began to soften. I knew these things, but I just had to be reminded. Just as I will have to remind others for the rest of my life.

Time seemed to stand still, and I was surprised when the sun came up in the mornings and the moon at night. The mill whistle blew. Cars went up and down the road. How odd, my world had stopped, but everything else went on as if Bill hadn't died.

I dreaded the day of the funeral to come, but yet I wished it could be over with.

My black dress with the white trim was cleaned. Someone took me to the beauty shop. Elaine asked if I wanted her to cut my hair. It was down to my waist and was hard to care for. Bill had never wanted me to cut it. But I said, "Yes please do what you want with it. I really don't care now."

I got the kids clothes ready. They needed new white shirts but their church clothes were ready to wear. I was gradually getting up and around a little more and I felt better until someone would say something or someone would come to offer their sympathy and it brought on the tears again. The kids were doing better or at least they played more.

Someone asked me if I wanted them to go into our room now and remove Bill's clothes and take them to the good will store. I said yes, but I didn't want to see any of it. I wanted all the other personal items left for the kids, please just put them in one drawer.

It was such a senseless suffering to be so frightened of death and I wish it could have been avoided. But one thing I vowed, was to teach my kids about death so that when they had to face it, it wouldn't become a dragon and slay them. I dare to think of what could have been our fate if we had never known the Lord.

Bill's family was very distant, especially his mother. I know she must have been grieving terribly. I just imagine losing a child would be about the worst thing to suffer. After everything was over I was able to talk to Edrie, She was very cold. We had not heard from her since Bill came to Oregon. We made a trip or two up to see them, but it was a long way and money was short and we never seemed to have a dependable vehicle.

Jim was around the house a lot, more to torment me than anything. He was continuously bragging about his money and power. It was hard for me to listen to. One day he said, "I haven't forgotten about the $1,000 I borrowed from Bill, but I think I'll just give you a bedroom set we have for that money. We don't need it anymore." I couldn't believe that he would do that, when we needed money so badly. We certainly didn't need a used bedroom set. I felt a terrible pity for him. I just turned and walked away.

None of his family offered anything to help with expenses or funeral bills. But I would rather do anything than ask them to help. Instead I paid ten dollars a month forever on the funeral. Jim didn't offer to help with the expensive casket. They didn't offer to spend time with the kids, which would have been good for both of them.

The funeral was terribly hard on all of us. I didn't realize the kids were reacting so to my response, I should have, remembering my Mother's reaction and how it affected me.

I had my grief and they had theirs and we had to deal with that individually. I went with them at my side. I was concerned about them. I knew they would be frightened and grief stricken. I asked that they not see Bill. I had made up my mind I was not going to. Somehow I was moved with the others up to the front of the church and I saw him. I do not remember any more than that. One of the boys said I cried out "Oh, Daddy" and fell to the floor. That must have been terrible for the kids. I don't know who was with the kids or if they made it okay. I'm sorry for that, but I had intended to stay with them.

It was probably the most traumatic episode in their lives and I wasn't there for them. I wish I could make up for that.

Just before we left the house, Granny Elsie said "Come over here honey and sit on Grannie's lap, I want to tell you something." I did as she said, "Now I just want you to remember when you see Bill in that casket, that isn't him that's just an old piece of clay. Bill went to be with the Lord. He is gone and he isn't in that old body, remember that when you look at him." She put her arms around me and hugged me while I cried. I appreciated her so much. She was a person who lived her faith, she was as Christ-like as she knew how to be.

I rode beside my brother Ed to the cemetery. It was comforting. I saw people lined on both sides of the one main street in town, paying tribute. Men had their hats off holding them over their heart. Everyone had their heads bowed. I was truly honored by their display of reverence and respect. The funeral was so well attended. The church was full and they were standing out on the sidewalk and around the church. That meant so much to me. It felt like the whole town was gathering their arms around us and wrapping us in their love. Again I was honored. I was told that this was the largest funeral ever in Sutherlin, Oregon.

The food that was brought in after the service to feed all these wonderful people, I just couldn't believe. Some ladies from the church were at the house getting everything ready, cleaning the house, doing dishes. And they cleaned up afterward.

So many of these people came to the house to offer their condolences, most of them brought an offering or food or a card.

That meant so much to me. My heart just overflowed with gratitude. I like to remember an old fellow who was very shy but came to the house and asked for me. I came to the door. He asked me to come out in the yard where we could talk. I went out with him and we stood under the apple tree. He said, "I could have sent this but I wanted to talk to you. I knew Bill and all I have to say is that I am so sorry for you and the kids. Bill was a good guy and he talked to me often about his family so I felt like I knew you, and it would be alright for me to come and give you this in person. I didn't know if you would talk to anyone yet but I just had to come and say how sorry I am. And I will pray that the Lord will take care of you and the kids."

He handed me a ten dollar bill and walked away. If the president had come it wouldn't have meant as much to me. I will never forget him even though he didn't tell me his name. The Lord knew.

When I sat down to write all the thank you cards, I tried to remember everything and everyone. I was so appreciative.

I didn't want to forget anyone. I wished I knew who the old man was.

Mary had kept Janet and Steve out there until everything settled down. She brought them in to see me and the families, but would take them out again because there was just too much going on for them. They were happy with Mary, and she was in the height of her glory. I loved her so much for her never tiring devotion to me and the kids. She has her reservation in glory. She served the Lord well. He gave her the grace to do it. It was soon time for everyone to go home. That was hard, knowing we would be alone. They each one came to tell us good-bye. As the house and yard began to clear out and the noise subsided, we had another hurdle to climb. Mom and Donna understood and stayed with us a few more days.

Bill's mother came back to the house after most everyone was gone and asked me if Danny could go home with her. She felt like she could give him better care than I at this time. My defenses came to the forefront right now, but I bit my tongue. Danny was there and heard all this and of course he wanted to go. He didn't know her very well but he thought that would be fun. He coaxed. I finally agreed saying I would come after him soon.

Everything in me said no. But I knew the grief she must have of losing her son, and this may help. How could I say no? He went with her. My heart ached as I watched them drive out of the yard. I just was not ready to be without one of my kids. They gave me such comfort. I wanted them right with me. I didn't have a minute's peace until he was home again.

Billy, Tommy, Merrill, Rosana, and Dan in Sutherlin,
shortly after they lost their father.

Chapter 11

"The Long Road Ahead"

1960

A future of tremendous responsibility was looming ahead like a high mountain with unachievable navigability. I did little else but ponder that commission. Day and night I anguished about leading this family through the long, hard journey ahead.

I worried about what could happen to the kids in a plight like this, one that could easily fail. A large family and a single mother. I had seen many families ruined in this type of circumstance. I loved my kids passionately and whatever the final destiny I would be with each of them until the end, never leaving nor forsaking them. There would be no life for me other than my children. I had no idea how I was going to achieve this, except trust in God, and I wasn't very good at that yet. I knew that it was all up to me. Could I take a stand in the lonely life ahead and be a good God-fearing Mother? Could the kids be controlled by a mother alone? Could I be strict enough without being too strict and keep them under control? If one of them broke lose, I could lose him. I had to keep ahead of the problems. I had to keep control.

What about myself, could I keep control of loneliness, and a lack of any social existence? I knew the problems of a single woman socializing with married couples. There's the jealous wife syndrome and the many needs of anyone living alone, let alone a young widow. I would have to distance myself from any personal involvement. I knew there was no possibility of remarriage with a large family such as mine. That in itself was a hard fact to face. I didn't know anything but married life. Doesn't every young woman want and need a husband? I was a twenty-nine year old widow with seven kids. That meant a life alone. Could I accept that?

Could I live with that? I wasn't happy with this situation. Could I toss away all my selfish needs and desires and think only of the kids? I didn't know, I wanted to, but could I? I was already feeling the pangs of what was ahead. No one to talk to. No one sitting across the room in that easy chair. No one to wait up for. No one coming home from work. No one to lay with during those long lonely nights. No one to discuss the events of the day with. A total aloneness. I was so aware of it now, wandering through the house, so quiet, so desperately alone. I lamented over the short time Bill and I had together after we became compatible and loving.

I had the kids, thank God for that. But they cannot take the place of a mate. They couldn't help me to decide what I was going to do with our future. I needed help I had never made decisions. I needed God's guidance, loud and clear. If He was talking to me I couldn't hear. Many nights in the solitude of a quiet house, after the kids were asleep I was overcome by the reality of all this. I wanted to scream. I would walk outside back and forth across the lawn, around the house through the back yard, crying, the ache of uncertainty and fear inside me was swelling and swelling until it choked me. I lifted my hands to Jesus, pleading with Him to take my pain and worry.

It was so hard to sleep. When I did I dreamed that Bill came into a room where I was with several people. He was always in a hurry saying he had to go. I would ask him where he was going, and please don't leave again. I can't stay here alone, I need your help. You have to help me to raise these kids. He would say he had to leave. As he was going out the door, I was pleading with him not to go. He left—and I cried—.

I had this dream for several months after his death. I was subconsciously thinking it was his will to leave us, and until I made peace with that I continued to dream that dream.

One morning I got up early, made some coffee and was sitting at the kitchen table. The lights were off and as usual I was in deep thought. I was weighing my options and suddenly it was clear to me where to begin. I knew I wanted what was best for the kids, a good clean life. I wanted them to have the opportunity to do what they wanted with their lives. I didn't want a decision I had made to be a stumbling block for them. I hoped that if they decided to be the "PRESIDENT," there would be nothing in their past to prevent it. I would insist they go to school, their schooling was not complete until they had at least four years of college. I didn't know how, but that was what I destined for my kids. I may not be able to help them, but there were ways they could do it, and I could help.

There was not a chance for this happening if I led an immoral life, which is where loneliness leads to, most often.

I had a choice of either living for the Lord or living in the world. Which was it going to be? I had to make a choice and live with it. I chose right then and there to live for the Lord, to bring the kids up in the church, where they could learn right from wrong from another source besides myself, where they had a foundation for moral standards so they might choose their mates and friends accordingly. Where they had the help of the Lord.

I made my commitment to the Lord at that point in time. I told Him I couldn't do it on my own. I asked Him to be my strength and help me day by day and step by step, or I would never make it. I knew He would because that was in His will. Any other choice I made would be out of His will. I could take the other route, but it would be disaster for my family. That is not what the Lord wills for anyone.

I would like to say that was the end of my worries, but it was not. It was only the beginning. My kids were wonderful people and I was very proud of them, but they were kids and demonstrated that every hour of every day.

My solitary life was not working out. I could not seem to get a grip on life, it was aimless. According to Dr. Hudson I was suffering from extreme mental and emotional stress. I was taking antidepressants but it only masked the symptoms. Every nerve in my body was like a live electric wire. Oh, I tried to be strong, I had to be strong to face these years ahead.

The kids were grieving. They were terribly unhappy and were unable to really get involved in anything that satisfied them. They were restless and continually picking at one another causing fights and uproars all the time. They were pitiful to me, but I couldn't seem to help them. We rattled around in that old house.

Nothing mattered to any of us. Friends would come and go, kids would come and go but we didn't have much interest in anything. There was so much remembering, so much grief. We could see the pain in each other, and that hurt. I felt so responsible for the kids pain. I wanted so much to do something for them. I remember so well how the kids would walk around looking at things of their Dad's. Like a boat in the front yard he had been working on to restore, his pickup that had been broke down and he was repairing, his tool box in the garage, in the dresser drawer where his personal items were kept. They were remembering, it was painful but it was necessary.

One day Tommy walked up close to me when the other kids were out of ear shot, and said almost whispering, "Mom, I'm sure glad Dad didn't have to find out about Santa before he died, aren't you?" I stood looking at him for awhile before I could answer. I knew I was suppose to say yes so I said, "Oh yes" not having the slightest idea what he was talking about. I needed some time to think. Several hours later it came to me what he was saying. I remembered when he came from school one day just before Christmas announcing he had found out there was no Santa. Trying to talk softly so the other kids didn't hear, I answered him with, "Don't tell your Dad." Meaning don't tell him you don't believe in Santa any more. I think the others knew also, but this was too much fun to give up. He would be disappointed to know even one of the kids didn't believe. But I didn't say all that. If I had, surely someone would hear us talking. It was dropped and not mentioned again until now. I still didn't have the heart to tell Tommy the facts, so he went on believing. I thought it was so precious for him to think that Bill believed in Santa. I never did tell him. When he was much older he said to me one day, "Mom why did you let me think that Dad didn't know that Santa wasn't real?"

I said "Tom I thought that was the sweetest thing I had ever heard. I couldn't tell you any different." He accepted that.

I had absolutely no energy. I couldn't force myself to take interest in our home. I cooked the kid's meals and did the necessary things but beyond that there was nothing. I had always been so energetic. I didn't know how to handle this. I had so much to do. Things would stack up and I was behind in everything. It was driving me crazy. Nancy Laswell came down several times and cleaned my house. I should have been embarrassed, but I appreciated it so much. She was a true Christian friend.

We went to church and Bible studies and Sunday School. All activities the church had, we needed that, it gave us a reprieve for a little while. Every meeting would end with the closing song, "God Will Take Care of You." It seemed to me the entire congregation would sing their hearts out to us. Everyone, especially myself was misty eyed. That song gave me hope and I knew that was all I needed to face the next day. But the next day all that hope was swallowed up by the ugly face of reality.

I just couldn't get beyond the memories in this house. The kids were not making any progress either. I thought about moving, would it help? I talked it over with God. I didn't have a chance to think about what I wanted. Just out of the blue this little farm seemed to show up and fall into our lap. Nothing down and fifty dollars a month. It was so easy I didn't even have to labor over the decision. I felt like God made the deal for us so I took it. (Is this how God leads? Wow!!) I consulted with my family and they came down and looked at it. No one had any objections. Dad said it did need a couple more bedrooms, and he volunteered his expertise. The mill donated most of the lumber.

When our Church learned of our decision, they all came forward to move us, clean both houses, unpack, hang curtains and hook up all the appliances. Different ones brought food for the moving crew.

It took a couple days and it was done. Praise the Lord. I was beginning to see how God worked. Ordinarily someone stepping in and doing this would really bother me, going through my belongings, finding all my secret little messy places, cleaning up my dirt, or just doing my work. I didn't feel that way now. I was in a stupor and nothing bothered me until much later when I thought about how little I did in the big undertaking.

We did feel better in a different place where there were not so many memories. Dad had the rooms built on before the summer was over. I helped him with what I could do. I mostly just wanted to be out there with him. It was so good to have him there. He was so easy. He always had a smile and a kind word. He was the most understanding person I knew. I fixed his meals, but he insisted he go home at nights. He couldn't sleep well away from home. Once in a while if he worked too late he spent the night.

He called Mom and let her know. He was up at the crack of dawn to get started. I can see him yet, sitting on a saw horse with one leg crossed over the other, his elbow on his knee, his hat pushed back, taking a break and smoking a cigarette. That was the time the kids would come by and chat for awhile. I would bring him a cup of coffee and sit with him. We planned a hunting trip while he was there. It was the last one for him.

We had such a good time. Donna and Darrell came along and one of my cousins went with us also. Dad got his deer, but that was the only animal shot. We did enjoy the trip though.

Dad was an independent hunter. He waited for no man. He was like a deer himself in the forest. You never heard him, and until you saw him, you wouldn't know he was around. He had spent a lot of his life out in the wilds, being a sheep man. I had so much respect and admiration for him. He was truly the dad I never had.

Donna and I had some excitement on that hunting trip. If you have ever been in Oregon you know their mountains are really only hills. Darrell went to the top of one of these hills and followed a game trail along the top of the ridge. Donna and I had gone a different direction. We both got back to the pickup before Darrell. We waited for him for quite a while and were getting a little concerned as it was getting along in the afternoon. Darrell was notorious for doing the unexpected. Will we have to sit here half the night waiting? We were scanning the hill in front of us, Donna raised her gun to look through the scope. She did spot him on the trail. I raised my gun and found him in my sights. It was kind of fascinating to watch someone hunt. We watched for some time.

I was looking around over the area when I spotted movement. I told Donna I thought there was a deer behind Darrell. This was quite open country, very few big trees, so we could see fairly well. I was trying to find this movement again so I could show Donna. Suddenly my scope came to rest on this animal. I said, "Donna, I found it but if I take my eye off it to show you, I'll lose it again. If you get Darrell in your sights, go back down the trail he came on and just follow it until you come to this animal." She zeroed in on it just about the time I got a good full length view of it. I said "Donna it has a long tail," and she said, "it is switching back and forth. Have you got any ideas?" She was looking very intently saying "Oh no-o-o."

That cougar followed Darrell all along the top of the ridge and when he started down the trail toward us the cougar came along. It was pretty exciting watching that. Something you don't see very often. When Darrell got to the pickup, we had lost sight of the cougar some time back. We told Darrell about it. He got pretty serious, and said, "I'm glad I didn't know that up there. I would have made some fast tracks off that hill." He laughed about it.

The kids did not find the euphoria I had hoped for on our little farm. They did enjoy the old barn and still tell stories about what took place there. We planted a big garden and a sunflower forest. They had a lot of fun with that. But I would find them more and more in the house watching TV. That really bothered me. I certainly did not want them to grow up that way. I turned it off and we would proceed with a project of fixing fences, or weeding the garden. We did better at the garden than the fence. I knew a lot more about the garden than fixing fences. I was so handicapped at that sort of thing. I couldn't even use a hammer, let alone stretch wire, or dig a post hole.

The boys picked up on that real quick and would begrudgingly help as long as I was there. But when I came in, it wouldn't take them two minutes to get into a big fight. They seemed to think what I wanted them to do wasn't important or necessary that it was just busy work. I realized this was not going to work. Treating them like a mother was not forceful enough for boys nearing teen age who desperately were seeking independence. I had to be mother and father. That was tough. I had to find a way of enforcing the directives. I gave them the benefit of the doubt, but if it took a big stick, so be it. If I sound complacent about it, I was not. It's a hard role to play. It goes against a woman's nature and it was so difficult for me to carry out. Many times I went to bed in tears, feeling nothing but defeat. How I longed to be a tender loving mother. But you can't raise boys that way.

The younger boys were learning from the older ones and did not need the same kind of discipline, that is for a while until they reached that crucial age. I also became aware that whatever they were doing wrong at a young age, was going to be magnified as a teenager. So I had to nip it in the bud early.

We got a goat, oh what a goat. This milk was so good for the kids, and with the nice fresh vegetables from the garden we could eat well. I didn't let the kids taste the goat milk until I had prepared it with ice crystals and poured it in iced glasses. I had already tasted it and I couldn't stand it, but I had heard that if kids got used to it they would never drink cow's milk again. So I wanted to give Tammy, the goat, every chance to keep her home with us. The kids loved her. But if the kids couldn't drink the milk she had to go. As long as the milk had ice in it, they drank it. If the ice melted they would gag. As soon as one gagged they all gagged. Tammy had to go.

We got a calf to raise for meat. We got so attached to this calf, when it came time to butcher it, I knew I could never kill it. I got my cousin to come and shoot it for me. He wasn't a very good shot and he had just been blinded in one eye playing baseball. He shot that poor calf seven times before it was over and we were all witnesses. I was screaming for him to kill it so it would not suffer any more. He got so flustered he was not able to kill it but the calf finally fell down and he put a gun to the temple and it died. The boys were mortified. So was I. No one stuck around to bleed the calf. After I had recovered, I called the mobile butcher to come take care of it. We had it all cut and wrapped and frozen. I had some very funny feelings about eating it, but I didn't mention it to the kids. When it was cooking, I didn't think it smelled too good. It smelled like fresh blood. I could not put a piece to my mouth. I could not feed it to the kids. I had other people taste it and they said it was fine. I tried again and again but I couldn't do it. I ended up trading the meat to some friends for their meat. Volume wise they got the better deal. Do I need to say more? I don't think the kids ever knew.

The boys played jungle in the sunflower patch. They found an old machete that belonged to their Dad, it had notches in the blade and was so dull you could ride to Boston on it—like my Mother used to say, it couldn't cut anything. Now I didn't know they had the machete, but I wouldn't have worried too much if I had known because it was so dull. We had never kept it out of the kids reach because it looked so harmless. But it wasn't a toy either. They couldn't resist when they discovered the jungle in the sunflower patch. Tommy said they had to make a trail so they came after the machete. Now they had seen enough jungle shows to know how to do that. He swung that blade back and forth, far and wide, whacking those sunflowers down. Merrill got in the way. Tom didn't see him and whacked him across the neck. Merrill screamed, Tom looked up and saw the blood. He threw down the blade and put his hand over the cut to stop the bleeding. He was saying "Don't tell Mom, Merrill, I'll fix it, just don't tell Mom. I'll go get a Band-Aid.

Merrill didn't know but what his head was hanging by a thread. But Tom told him to stay there and he did go get a Band-Aid. Merrill sat out there holding it. The Band-Aid covered it. They cleaned up the blood and took the machete back. I still can't believe I didn't notice that on Merrill's neck. They didn't tell me for a long, long time. I still cringe when I think of what could have happened even with a dull blade.

I did everything I knew of to help the boys but nothing seemed to work. Billy still read too much and the others watched TV. I hated to see them set around the house, and grow up to be a sis. I had grown up where men were men, and to me that was to be tough, not a bully, but not be afraid to get tired, wet, hurt and not cry about it. Maybe even a little Indian-like. I would love to have my boys know how to be outdoorsmen, to hunt and fish. I didn't mean casually. I wanted them to be good sportsmen and know the outdoors. I couldn't see how that was possible. It wasn't going to happen. I was sick at the thought of what was happening to them. I prayed about it constantly. It wouldn't be long until they would be running around town like the other teenagers I knew about. I enrolled them in "Boys of Woodcraft" which was a club to teach them gun safety, archery, tying flies and anything pertaining to outdoor sports. Some camping trips were involved in the summer. (I went along and took charge of the entertainment, games, etc.) They did learn a lot but it was not all I wanted them to learn and there was only one way to learn that and that was by doing it. Maybe someday.

They had friends come and stay all night. We had camp fires in the back yard at nights. We fixed hobo dinners wrapped in tinfoil and cooked them in the fire then sat around the fire and ate them. I showed them how to cook over a campfire. We slept out all night, just in the back yard, but it was a learning experience. We went for hikes in the forests. I showed them what I knew about, and told them about animals, birds and bugs. I didn't know much about the latter.

Mary and some of the other ladies in the church were so good about taking care of the little kids if I wanted to do something with the older ones.

We went swimming a lot with Mary, Lathen and Sandra. Betty Peterson also came along and brought her four kids. We would always take lunch and then put all our food together and have a picnic and what a picnic it would be. Out at Fair Oaks swimming hole. We spent a lot of time there and everyone seemed to have a good time. It was a healing time for us but it would always turn out to be the same thing when we returned home. They were so dissatisfied and I knew it was almost too much to expect for them to be happy without a man in the house. It wasn't the same and there was no way I was going to make it any different. Am I a failure? Can't I do what God put me here to do? I guess I didn't know how. I felt so defeated most of the time.

I did try to keep control, but I tried to be reasonable about it. I didn't push too much as I knew it would end in rebellion and then we would have a show down. I would have to win, I couldn't stop until I did. That could be a disaster.

My health problems were still critical. As long as I was out doing something I seemed to get by, but my nerves were fragile and I know they picked up on that. It was hard on the kids. Looking back now I see how my

A swimming party at Fair Oaks in Sutherlin.

Betty, Mary, and Laurie on a rehab day.

mood influenced the aura in our home, even though I tried not to do that. I was hurting and I couldn't change that it was going to come out somewhere.

I was in a panic worrying about the kids. I had to keep control. I couldn't let this get away from me, and that became an obsession with me. I think sometimes I was out of control more than they were. This was all new to the kids. I had never acted this way. As time went on it just seemed to get worse for me, and I was harder on the kids because they were harder to control. We got a cow. Jack was tired of milking cows so he loaned his to us, which suited me fine. I still believed that the kids needed some responsibility.

Bill and Tom traded off milking and it worked better than anything yet. In the winter of course they would be down at the barn after dark. The three boys went together. On one particular night it was Bill's turn to milk. While he was milking the cow, he was talking to the other boys. He had his back turned to the back door of the barn and the other boys were facing the back door. Suddenly a man appeared in the doorway and stood there looking at them. Tom and Merrill were so frightened, they turned and ran without saying a thing to Bill. All of a sudden Bill realized they weren't answering. He turned to look for them and saw the man standing in the door. He dropped the bucket and took off. He was not very far behind the others, but he was mad.

I didn't blame him. He seldom ever got mad, but he was this time. I called the police and they came right out. There was an escaped convict in the area. They came out and covered every inch of our place and went through everything in the barn and over the entire area but found no sign of him. We thought he must have taken off down the railroad tracks when the boys took off. The boys were a little reluctant to go back to the barn after that and so was I. We asked Jack to come down and milk until the convict was taken. But he made the boys go with him so they wouldn't be so afraid to go back later.

When we first moved out on our little farm, so many friends from the church and from the mill came by and said if I needed any help, they would be glad to come out and give a hand. I thanked them but I knew it would be hard for me to ask them. I thought if only they would come out and get the boys motivated it would help so much, or if they came by and did something they saw that needed doing. Not a one but Jack, he came down, starting a project like fixing the fence not saying a word, but called the boys when he went by the house. He took them out and they worked right beside him. They didn't fight or argue, they just did it. That was so good for me to see. I really appreciated him.

When Dad was working on the addition, one fellow, the husband of a friend of mine, came by and had a lot to say about how he was doing it. I tried to be nice about it, but I told him how much I appreciated Dad doing this for us and as far as I was concerned any way he wanted to do it was good enough for me. He didn't have anymore to say.

One day I was perplexed because there was so many things to be done. I mentioned to a friend in confidence about all these guys wanting to help, but never coming back to do it. She spoke as a friend when she said, "I suppose in your situation you would feel like everyone owes you something." I was stunned. I couldn't answer her. It hurt but it was a lesson for me I never forgot. I made up my mind right then that whatever I couldn't get done didn't need doing. I certainly did not expect anyone to help me after that. If they wanted to fine. But I wouldn't ask them. Unless I could pay them.

Jack and Mary were so great to us, there was many a night when Mary would insist that the kids throw their sleeping bags in the car and we all come out and spend the night. She would fix dinner for us and breakfast the next morning. Of course I would help her, but still that was a tremendous task for their family to endure. But they never seemed to think they had done enough. They always wanted to do more. Mary was by my side constantly if I needed her. She had the true Christian spirit and so did Jack and Sandra and Lathen. I thanked God for them every day. I really don't think I could have made it without her. I would have had to move to Myrtle Creek to be with my sister Donna. She was another one like Mary. She never grew tired of well-doing, as is encouraged in the scriptures. How could I have been so favored by God to have two such wonderful blessings in my life?

Danny was growing like a weed. He was feeling fine now and didn't have any noticeable effect of the rheumatic fever. I was always watchful that he was not exposed to other diseases, extreme cold, or fatigue. He was a good guy. He was not in the least demanding. I knew I had named him well when I saw him growing up. He was built like a square block, and he was strong and had a lot of endurance. Dan was easy to care for. Never gave me a minutes worry. He got along with everyone, children and adults alike. Everyone liked Dan.

He didn't have too much fun at Grannies. He was glad to get home and I was glad to have him home.

Rosana was a pretty little girl. She had beautiful hair with curls all over her head. When it got long enough I kept it in long curls. She was learning to cook and she liked doing it independently, that was fine. The boys especially liked for her to bake cakes and make boiled cookies. They didn't last long. Rosana was never any problem to me. She did what she was told, but sometimes she didn't want to. She was so pretty in her fancy dresses and hats she wore to church. Oh! she would strut when she got dressed up. But she wasn't vain.

The boys thought she tattled too much, but any at all was too much for them. She would get terribly frustrated with them if they teased her and she had no chance of reciprocating. The boys stuck together. There was only one of her. She had to tell someone. I seldom had to punish them, but I would talk to them. Rosana never gave in that she could be wrong and that got her in some difficulties. One day the boys put a snake on the steps of the house. When she came running out she saw the snake and screamed bloody murder. It scared her so bad she was trembling. It would have scared me too. I told them not to ever do that again. I think Rosana would have liked to see them strung up by their toes. She felt like she was getting picked on, but I thought they were teasing her most of the time. She was very serious and took everything as a personal put-down. She was really injured, but no amount of talking I did could convince her that they were not serious and of course they liked her. There was a cold war going on most of the time between them.

She was invited to stay all night with Dr. Strout's daughter. She was so excited about it. The doctor was going to take them to a movie. He took them to the theater and left them and was going to pick them up when it was over. This was a pretty gruesome picture. In the plot a lady got her head cut off by her son and it rolled down the stairs. Rosana was hysterical. The management people called Dr. Strout to come and get them. He took them to his house, but she couldn't stop crying. She didn't want the hot chocolate or the popcorn or anything else they offered her, she just wanted to come home. The doctor brought her home and neither she nor I got any sleep the rest of the night. And for the next few months she would wake up screaming at night. When I would go into her room she looked at me like I was going to harm her. She wasn't truly awake.

Finally, one night I sat with her until I knew she was wide awake. We talked and she told me all about the movie. She would be so frightened when she got to the part where the head bumped down the steps. I told her, "Now that really didn't happen, they just made the movie to look like that. Just like they make all movies. They are only pretend stories." We talked for a long time. She tried to believe me, but it looked so real. I sat with her for a long time reassuring her and finally she went back to sleep. She never had another nightmare about it, but every time she saw something on TV that was the least bit scary she would run and get behind a chair and peek out around it to watch. When the bad part was over she went back and sat down in her chair.

Janet was a saucy little thing. She was two in July and you'd think she had staked a claim on the whole world. She was a nervous child though and she would often get upset just over someone getting a scolding or an argument among the kids. Or if I would get upset. When she started one of her crying spells I would call Mary and she would come after her. We planned ahead to do this. She would go there where it was quiet and follow Mary around or sit in Jack's lap. He'd rock her while he watched the news. She would get relaxed and calmed down. I would casually go out there and she would want to come home. She just needed a breather from the hub-bub of a busy household. I believe it was her ears that made her so nervous.

She was as cute as a bug's ear. She was still small for her age and loved to get dressed up with hat and purse hanging on her arm. She strutted like a peacock.

She didn't give me a problem at all. She minded well and did as she was told. She was a very reasonable child, she understood everything I talked to her about. If I explained to her I was going somewhere and she was going to stay with someone, that was fine, but if I ever left without telling her, or if I didn't take time to explain something to her, that was a different story. She could throw a fit.

Janet suffered terribly with her ears. It seemed she was always on antibiotics and going to the doctor. This year was worse than ever. She would scream with pain. I did everything I could for, her but nothing helped. I called the doctor several times a week and told him about the pain she had and what her temp was. I took her into his office at least twice a week. This had been going on too long and she was just getting worse. I insisted that he do something. He told me to bring her in. When he examined her he looked so long inside her ear, then the other ear. Finally he laid his light down on the table and stood looking at me for a long time. He said, "I'm sorry to tell you this but her eardrums have been eaten away by this infection. This eardrum is completely gone. She hears nothing out of it. The other ear is partially gone, it won't be long until she can't hear from either ear."

I was in instant shock, becoming very angry with him, my voice trembling as I screamed, "How did that happen? I have brought her in for you to take care of her. Why did you let it go so far? Can't you do something?"

With his face turned away, he very quietly said, "I have done everything I could do for her. This was an infection that didn't respond to any medication. I am sorry, so sorry. I can make an appointment with a specialist in Roseburg or Eugene."

I was crying hysterically by this time and I said "Yes, do that as soon as possible. How long will her hearing last?"

He said, "Not long, as fast as this has progressed. I'm sure in a short time the other ear drum will be gone."

"And she will be completely deaf." I cried at him.

Answering he said, "I would advise you to enroll her in the school for the deaf in Salem while she has a little hearing. It will be a lot easier for her to learn. The only thing she will know if she isn't given that opportunity is what limited vocabulary she has now. We will send her to the specialist. But I definitely think we should make an appointment to take her to the school in Salem. Of course, they will have doctors there too that will examine and evaluate her."

I left the office carrying her in my arms. She was crying. I held her up to my face crying as loud as she was. I sat in the car for a few minutes holding her until I could get control of myself. I drove home.

This was on a Friday and nothing could be done until Monday. She was so miserable and cried constantly. I just took off her coat and hat and sat in the rocking chair with her. I began to pray, "Oh God no, you can't do this to us. Why would you put a little child through so much suffering and then take her hearing away? I will have to send her away to school. How can I be so far away from her for so long? She is still a baby. That would be terrible for her as well as myself and the other kids. We have lost her father. How much more can we take? I beg you please, please do not let this happen to my baby. You are the only one that can heal her. There is no medicine or doctor that can but I know you can. Please Lord, heal this child. I can't give her up to go away to a school.

The kids would not take this well, just after losing their Dad and then Janet having to leave. How can they handle any more? "Is this fair Lord, to heap all this on our family—" I went on pleading with God, holding her and rocking her, that day, all night. I could not lay her down. Mary came down and got the other kids something to eat and put Steve to bed. I asked Mary to put Janet on the prayer chain. She said she already had when we first called her.

The kids were so sad and so quiet. They just sat there watching her. The pain continued and she sobbed with her head resting on my shoulder. The hurt on the kids faces was so undisguised. I just kept rocking and praying. I must have lost track of time.

Sometime during the night we both fell asleep. When we awoke the sun was shining through the window. Stirring, I could feel the warmth of the sun casting its rays across our bodies. I felt a burden lifted and a calming spirit had come over me. I felt rested. Janet must have got relief from the pain and she slept in the same position all night. I must have been very tired to sleep that long in that position with my head resting on the back of the chair.

Janet was not fevered. I supposed her ear broke and drained during the night and gave her relief from the pain. I wondered if it took any more of her hearing.

Something was very different. I couldn't tell what it was. I moved a little but I had been sitting in the same position so long I was frozen in place. When I moved, Janet sat up looking around and there came a big smile on her face. I said to her, "Good Morning, Sweetheart. Do you feel better?" Obviously she did because she acted like she didn't have a care in the world. But I thought, how long will it last?

She jumped down off my lap and ran into the bedrooms to wake up the kids. I went in the kitchen to prepare breakfast. She was fine the rest of the weekend.

I took her in to the doctor Monday for her appointment. He looked in her ears. He mentioned that there was no drainage. I had noticed that also. He looked from one ear to the other, and he laid down the instrument and looked at her chart. He looked again, walked out of the room and was gone for a few minutes. When he came back in, he looked in her ears again. This went on for several minutes, maybe a half hour. He walked back in the room, sat down in a chair, and began to explain. He said, "I don't know what happened here but there is nothing wrong with her ears. They couldn't have healed that fast. There is no sign of infection in either ear and the eardrums are well and clean. It doesn't look like there has ever been an infection. I don't know whether to apologize or what because this is wonderful, but I couldn't have made a mistake like that. I just don't know what to say."

I was ecstatic when I said to him, "Do you mean she will not lose her hearing and she will not have to go to Salem to school?"

He was shaking his head, "That's right. I just don't understand it. I know what I saw."

I said, "If she is healed, I do understand it. The Lord healed her. I prayed most of the day and all night and our church was also praying. My kids were praying and my family also."

He looked away and said, "I understand." and walked out of the room.

Janet never had another earache. She didn't go back to the doctor for a follow-up. She did not lose her hearing. In fact, when she started to school she had to be seated in the back of the room because her hearing was too sensitive. She heard everything in the room and couldn't help being distracted. Oh, how I praised the Lord. As did all our friends and family. Mary cried with me as we praised Him over and over for that healing. One day Janet was out to Mary's, Mary was cleaning an apartment rental that was vacated because she was getting it ready to rent again. Janet was tired, so Mary laid her down on the bed on her blanket to rest. She crawled around on the bed and then laid down on her blanket and went to sleep. Later, I found a ringworm on her head. I called the doctor. He said, "Shave her head and I will call in a prescription." He said to be very careful or everyone would get it. I had mastered the art of quarantine, not another soul got it from her. What a sad day it was when I sat her on the stool to cut off her pretty curly hair.

Everyone of us cried but Janet. Oh, how I hated to do that. I went to town and got her the prettiest hats I could find. A different one every day of the week. It didn't bother her, she felt like she was just as cute as she ever was even bald headed. We got rid of the ringworm quickly. And all was well. She was still mothering Steve and he still tolerating it.

Rosana joined the campfire girls that summer. I hoped for quiet time away from the hustle and bustle of our home for her. She did enjoy it. I became a helper and a substitute leader for her group. She also took tap dancing that year since I had done that as a child, when I was my mother's only child, before she remarried. I wanted to give her the opportunity. It does a lot for a girl, teaching them grace and carriage and an extra shot of confidence in public performance. Rosana found out very soon that she didn't like that. She became terribly rebellious and refused to do anything. She cried and said, "I want to go home. I don't like to dance and I'm not going to do it." There was no way I was going to make her do that. So her career in dance didn't last long.

She was not a rebellious child, but very mild mannered. She was shy to some extent. But a very good, obedient and well mannered child. So this opened up a new avenue to me and something I had to work on.

Janet missed her Dad. She had a special place in her Daddy's heart and when he was gone it left a void in her heart. But she liked men, which was different with Rosana. She did not and distanced herself. She may have thought they were all going to be like her teasing brothers.

One day I hired a young fellow to mow our front yard. It was more of a pasture than a lawn and our lawn mower would not handle that long grass. Janet was laying on the daveno sleeping and when she woke up and heard the mower, she jumped up wide eyed and looked out the window. She was so excited when she said, "Mom do we have a new Daddy now?"

It just about broke my heart. I had to tell her, "No." She was very disappointed.

My brother Roy came up to see us one weekend and Janet latched on to him. She stole his heart. He asked her if she wanted to go home with him and she said yes. I said, "Now what are you going to do, take her to work with you in the logging truck or is Angie going to take her to work at the telephone office? She really thinks she is going."

He said, "If she will go home with me, you're darn right I'll take her to work with me."

"She isn't two years old and she still wears diapers at night."

"Don't you think I have ever changed diapers, girl? I've got kids. You just pack her clothes and we'll be leaving here pretty soon."

Oh man he meant it, now what, "Swede, I am afraid she will want to come home before bedtime. Then what?"

"I'll call you and you can come after her." He said with a big grin on his face.

I couldn't get out of it now. But I didn't think I wanted her to be gone that far away. She was still a baby.

She went and was as happy as could be. She was asleep when he got home, so she didn't cry that evening. She didn't know she was there until the next morning when he got her up at four a.m. to go out logging. He owned his own logging outfit, so he didn't have any worry about a boss. He dressed her all up warm and took her to the cafe for breakfast. He got a lunch packed for her and one for him. He shocked a lot of people when he came walking into the cafe with a baby. A lot more people were shocked when he had her all day in his truck. She loved it. The only thing that bothered her was the noise. It hurt her ears, but she would just hold her hands over her ears when it was too loud. She didn't complain and she didn't get tired of it. She loved every minute. She stayed there with him for three days. I would call and talk to her on the phone, but she was fine. She and Angie played together in the evenings. Angie bathed her and washed her clothes.

The boys were getting harder to control. I knew they were dissatisfied. They resented me telling them to do something. But if I didn't tell them they sure wouldn't do anything. I worried about that, not only for today but for a good many years ahead. I decided I would make a big chart and put it up on the wall in the kitchen. Then I didn't have to tell them, they could read it on a chart. The chore was listed on the bottom, the name on the side, the day of the week on the top. I had all the names up and all the chores and they had to check the chart every day. They could get their work done early or wait until the last thing. But if it didn't get done, there were punishments listed also. Like no TV, no reading, no friends, no play, confined to their room. This was set and there was no changing, no mercy and no arguing with Mom. I didn't even have to remind them except for the ones who were too short to read it.

This saved me so much hassle, it worked like magic. If only the other problems were as easy to solve. It seemed to me that they were trying to frustrate me when they were at the table or sitting together on the couch. They picked at one another, then yelled out very indignant. I was nervous anyway and this multiplied my problem. I tried everything I could think of to make them happy, but it was no use. I became defeated and just wanted to give up. One day, one of my worst days I sat down and wrote.

My Ministry (1960)

God has entrusted to me seven souls to perfect, yes to me alone.
He has given me these children to raise up in the Name of the Lord.
He has trusted me with a great and wonderful ministry.
Have I been letting Him down? Have I let others come before them?
Have I let self come before them? Have I earnestly used every
    opportunity to teach the word of God?
Have I let this become a drudgery rather than a ministry? Have I chosen
    to show my ministry or the world my better nature? Have I set a
    good example at all times in all things?
Have I given my ALL to this ministry, and know that I am doing the
    will of God?

The answer to all these questions is not favorable. Oh God, please help
me to be a better mother and to give these children what they should have.
Help me Father to remember at all times to avoid doing anything, that
would take me away from my ministry, and this comes first.

My whole life you want devoted to this task, until the day when you can
say, "Well done, my good and faithful servant."

Oh! God! To do thy will.

Lord you have been so good. Could any ask for a better or more
rewarding ministry than to devote ones life to her children? Where could
any find so much pleasure in their work.

I see now Father you ask no more of me than to do this, that I need not
to please man, only you God.

It is not fair to the children to ever do anything that would take from them
the peace and harmony of the home.

God grant me the wisdom and the strength to carry out this ministry in
the way that is pleasing to you. I know God, if I look to you in time of
need you will give me your strength when mine is all gone. Give me the
wisdom to handle all problems, guide me safely in the darkness, give me
peace when I find cause to anger. Fill my mouth with words of wisdom,
that I may never cause one of your little ones to stumble.

In Jesus Name, Amen.

I kept that prayer handy and read it often. I still have it. It is tattered and torn and the lettering is faded. But I remember so clearly the day that I wrote it and just what it meant to me.

Ever so often I would look at the kids and see the problems within them, trying to find a way to make them happy, as I knew I could never be happy or satisfied until they were, but what was I to do. Just keep searching and praying, I guess.

Billy read so much, day and night, I was beginning to worry that it was becoming a substitute for living. Most of the time he was not aware of what was going on around him. That is until one of the boys would tease him. Merrill was Tom's echo. Anything Tom said, Merrill would carry through on. Tom would walk through the front room and call Bill a girl, thinking that Bill was so involved in his book he wouldn't hear him. Merrill right behind him, "Girl Bill." Bill would jump up hopping mad and go after them. Of course that is what they wanted. Bill never disappointed them.

We were offered a German Shepherd, full grown, a wonderful dog. The people were moving away and couldn't take the dog. I took her mostly for Bill, maybe he would get out more. We called her Lady, Janet couldn't say Lady, she said La La. We all loved her. She was a companion to all the kids and she would go everywhere the kids went. They thought it was especially nice to take her to the barn with them to milk. La La stayed outside. She seldom barked, only when there was cause. When it was time for the kids to go to bed, we locked Lady up on the back porch.

One night just before the kids went to bed, a pickup pulled in the driveway, a man got out and came to the door. I went to the door and told the kids to stay back. The man told me he was a brother to the man we bought this place from and that he had left some pack gear in the barn. I told him I had never seen anything like that here. He said he wanted to go look.

We had things stored at the barn and I didn't want him going down there alone. I told him I would go with him. He went on ahead and I got a coat and a flashlight, and walked down. He was looking around. He got mad because he couldn't find them. He was acting and saying some pretty weird stuff. He wanted me to get in the pickup and ride back to the house. I said I would walk and started up the road. He was cursing and got in the car, revving up the motor and came after me trying to run me down. He was driving all over the road, up and down the barrow pits, off the road, just going like a crazy man.

I ran as fast as I could to the house and went inside. I was beginning to remember something I had heard. I told the kids to get under the beds. I told Billy to see that the little kids got under there too and stayed out of sight. Tom called the police. The phone was out of sight of the front room. I locked the door which wasn't much protection, it was all small glass panes. I got the rifle and had it handy, but out of his sight. I stood beside the door, I could hear him outside and he was coming up the steps. He banged on the door and wanted in.

I told him, "I am not going to let you in because you are drunk. Just leave because the police are on their way." He did leave and turned south on the highway.

The police car came in the drive and I went out to meet them. I told them which way he went, and who I thought he was. The policeman said, "Yes he has been in town drinking all day." He left for awhile and came back. He asked me a lot of questions about the guy and his pickup. He was sure he knew who it was. He could get him anytime. The police man told me, "If he ever comes back, don't go outside with him, stay in the house and do as you did tonight. Turn off the lights. Don't take any chances with this guy. He has attacked several women in his own family, and tried to kill them. He turned a German Shepherd on his sister-in-law and the dog chewed her breast off while she screamed and he watched. The dog was destroyed of course."

They picked him up on other charges but they put him in a rehab center. When he was through there he had a prison term to serve for the other crimes and breaking his probation.

All this time we had Lady locked up on the back porch and little Smokey was under the bed with the kids.

The chief of police came out to talk to the kids so they wouldn't be so afraid. He commended the kids for doing exactly as I told them to. The police said the brother who lived here before, hid his family under the bed because he would start shooting randomly through the walls of the house or into the floor. He was completely mad when he drank.

The policemen drove up and down the driveway with the kids so they could say they had ridden in a police car. He blew the siren for them. I'm sure he could see when he came in the house how frightened they were and he wanted to take their minds off what had happened. It certainly did that, they thought that was pretty neat.

Family church camp was coming up. I was anxious to go. We took Lady to be boarded at the Vets Clinic. We were all going and Mary was coming with us. We drove down by Cottage Grove to a camp back off the main road. We all had a great time. We stayed in a cabin. The older kids stayed in cabins with their own groups. Mary had a cabin with me and the little kids, up to Danny. We had a wonderful time. We ate in the main meeting hall where we had evening services also. Having our meals cooked for us was wonderful. We had a campfire at night and all sat around singing and roasting marshmallows. There was nursery class for the little ones. We had classes during the day but we had free time too and just walking around in the forest was so invigorating for me. Camping I love, swimming I love. Walking along the river and sitting down on the bank, gave me such peace. I love every thing about the out-of-doors. Sure made me homesick for Idaho.

One day while swimming, a very nice young minister was giving diving lessons. I told the ladies who I was with to watch this. I told the minister I would like to learn to dive. We crossed the river and got up on a rock which stood out of the water about four feet. He was telling me how to stand and how to drop down into the water, then lift up my arms toward the surface of the water and it would bring me right up out of the water. There would be no need to fear because he would be right there watching. When I dove into the water I swam under the water to the other side of the river. I came up by some bushes so I could stay out of sight. I watched him looking, swimming with his face down in the water looking one way and another. He dove into the water rather frantically and searched. He swam a ways continuing his quest. I could see I had carried this far enough, he was beginning to look very distraught. Everyone in the pool was watching him and relishing the joke. I called out to him, "David here I am, Da-a-avid are you looking for me? I'm right here." He looked around and saw us laughing, He swam for the shore as fast as he could. I knew what he was going to do, so I tried to get there first. He was much faster. He ran up on the bank, grabbed my shoes and towel, blouse and pants and threw them out in the water. Then they all laughed while I was trying to get them out before they went too far down the river. We had some lively swimming parties after that. It was fun.

It was soon time to go home. I wasn't ready, nor were the kids. But we got packed and drove out with the others from our church. The kids were solemn, but very tired. They slept all the way after we got onto the highway.

We got home late that night, so we waited until the next day to go after Lady. I called before we went over and the Vet told me she got sick as soon as we left her. He did everything he could for her, but she died Sunday evening. He said she had liver failure and she must have had it before we got her.

He wouldn't charge us anything for her keep. He really felt bad. I told him the kids were going to be upset because they were very fond of her.

The Vet told me about a dog the kids might like that he had. It was a Border Collie and Scottish Sheep Dog. "He is just a small dog and well mannered and well trained. He had raised him from a pup. I talked to the kids about Lady. Of course they were heart broken. I told them about the other dog, Gus. They were ready to go see him. I told them I would have to see him before I could make a decision.

We all fell in love with Gus. He was mister mellow. We brought him home and he adapted very well to the family. He was a wonderful dog. So good to the kids and followed them everywhere. Bill was especially fond of him. He seemed to favor Bill. We had him about a month when he got hit out on the side of the road.

We all heard the brakes and the dog crying. We ran out there. Billy picked him up and carried him to the yard and sat down with him under the apple tree by the house. He was suffering and it wasn't long until he closed his eyes, laying in Billy's arms. He began to cry. The other kids went into the house. The sight of Billy crying was too much for them. I cried with Billy and for him. He sobbed and finally he said, "Why does God have to take everything I love away from me." I put my arms around him, and we talked for a long time.

This was the first time he cried for his dad, or said anything about his death. I told him we don't always know why God does what He does but someday we will know. "Billy do you remember when the doctor told us that your Dad would be an invalid if he had lived. I don't think he would want to live that way, do you?" "God loves you Billy and he knows how hard it is for you now that your Dad is gone. We just have to trust Him and know He is doing the right thing for Dad, for you and the rest of the family. If we can't believe that God is right in all ways then we have no future. And Billy look, here is Smokey, he will try to take the place of Gus. He wants you to notice him."

"I know God didn't take Dad or Gus just to hurt you. There will be a day when we will know all things. In the meantime He has Dad up there with Him, Dad is happy there and he is well. There are no invalids in Heaven."

Billy reached out and petted Smokey and said, "Maybe we are not supposed to have another dog but Smokey." He did feel better. I could only pray that I said the right things to him. Just being able to talk about his dad helped him. I didn't know if he would ever be able to accept his loss. He grieved silently for a long time.

Billy and Tommy got a paper route (or did I get it for them, no they did). That was good for them and they really didn't mind it. Then I took a rural route delivering in the afternoon. I drove about twenty miles a day. The kids could go with me when they wanted to. It was a little extra money.

One day just before I left on the route, Billy brought Steve into the house with blood just pouring out of his mouth. His tongue was hanging out of his mouth. I could see the blood was coming from his tongue. Billy said he had hooked it on a nail in the barn. When I got the bleeding slowed down enough I could see a big jagged three-cornered tear on his tongue. I called the doctor to see if I should bring him in for stitches. He said he didn't think it would be necessary if the bleeding had stopped. He told me to keep his mouth clean and watch that it didn't start bleeding again. I took him with me on the route and he laid down on the back seat, and went to sleep. Rosana also went along. I liked for one of the kids to go with me to put the papers in the box. It went so much faster. We were about half way through the route when I heard a funny sound coming from the back seat, I looked back there and Steve was struggling, trying to breathe. I stopped the car and pulled him out. He still wasn't breathing. I shook him around, it didn't help. I sat down in the road and laid him across my lap. His mouth was opened and I could see a clot. I took hold of it and began to pull. I pulled and pulled and it kept coming out. It was clear down his throat. I had never seen such a big clot. I got it out and he cried for a few minutes and so did I. Then he was fine. I did not let him sleep on his back again until that tear was all healed and closed up.

I began to think about how easy it was for something to happen to the kids. I quit the paper route. I tried selling Beauty Counselor make-up products. I gave demonstrations on the proper application of make-up. One day I received a call from the school asking if I would come to the school and give this demonstration for the high school girls. I had studied the literature and was quite confident that I knew the product well and I thought I could do it. I had a very captive audience. That was something they were really interested in. Mary went with me to help me to get set up. Everything went well. We really enjoyed doing it. Mary said later, "Rose have you ever done anything like that before?" I told her no, this was the first time. She said, "You acted like you have been doing this all your life. You didn't act nervous or anything."I didn't think about being nervous. I didn't think about anything at all, but from that day on I knew I could get up in front of an audience and bluff it. I had overcome a fear, no not I.

I knew I needed a diversion of some kind, the responsibility of taking care of every single need that anyone had was wearing on me. It was so overwhelming. It seemed like their needs were endless. Even though my responsibilities were doubled I would not sacrifice my standards that I had always held so stringent to. The kids clothes had to be clean and mended. The kids were well groomed and clean. They wore pajamas every night, they went to bed at a reasonable hour (determined by myself). They ate three meals a day preferably at the same time each day. They ate very little between meals. If they did it was something nourishing. I insisted that their manners were impeccable when we went to visit, or we ate out. They were to be quiet and not rowdy in others homes. If they embarrassed me and did not abide by our standards, I corrected them right there, which I know embarrassed them but they were not apt to repeat that offense. They were ultimately to blame for the punishment they received. They understood that. Oh, if only I could get that much cooperation at home. No, I couldn't be that strict at home with them. They needed to let their hair down sometimes. I did have a lot of rules that they did follow.

Steve was about two years old when we dealt with that for all times. We were in church. He was on my lap and he wanted to get down and play around with another child. I sat him on the bench and told him to sit there and I had some things for him to play with. He objected. I whispered to him to be quiet and sit down. Again he rebelled, jerking away from me and trying to get down on the floor. I then told him "Steve, if you do that again I will take you outside and spank you." He looked up at me and did that again. I picked him up and started for the door in the back of the church. He began screaming, "No mamma, no mamma don't spank me. I won't do it again." as we walked through the congregation. I knew if I didn't carry it out I would have to do it another time. So we went outside and I held him and spanked him. He sobbed and sobbed. I felt so bad. That was his first spanking. I held him and loved him and said "I'm so sorry I had to do that but you didn't mind and I told you what I would do, but you did it anyway." I don't remember ever spanking him again. If I did, it was when he was much older and I didn't feel so bad. Steve was such a good boy. He was an exceptional child. He acted like his mission in life was to protect me, and that he did. He was quiet about it, never making an issue. He just stood by watching everything. He reminded me of a secret service agent, and I was his charge. He has always been a wonderful son.

I was getting some of my spunk back, enforcing the rules was much easier. It took consistency and determination.

I was a little more lenient according to age, if they did not abuse that privilege and could act responsible with it. But if anyone got too pushy their rank dropped a little. I wanted so much to do it right for them. I thought a man talking to the boys might help them, but I gave that up as a failed effort. The boys really resented that. So I had to be the sole disciplinarian in my family. It was a chore that was never caught up, even if I worked on it every single day, all day like the laundry, it was never completely done.

The boys were testy, they had to see just how far they could go. When I saw this coming on, I knew I had to deal with it. Knuckle down and get rigid. They soon gave it up.

We took a trip to Idaho before school started. I told Bill I would take them and I wanted to keep my word. So I went to see his mother. Before that visit was over I was ready for the loony farm. Granny had two kids home, Toby and Kenny. Sue was younger but she was working in Seattle, planning to go to Bible College in the fall. She also had two of her nephews, whom she adopted after their father was killed in a railroad accident while on the job. Their mother was not staying home like she should have to take care of them, so Edrie took her to court and got the kids.

I felt so sorry for those kids. They were not treated well at all. They were treated like the hired hands while her own boys laid around. The oldest one was working on a dairy farm, so he got up early and left. The younger one did the chores at home. He never got to eat at the table when we ate. He got what was left and he had to eat while sitting in the woodbox. There was never a civil word said to him. He was yelled at and made fun of every time one of them spoke to him. When the older boy came home in the evening, he had to go to work at home. My kids were treated pretty good for a while and then all of a sudden she would curse and tell them to get out of that chair. They had no business sitting there.

One day I was out in the barnyard carrying Janet so she could see the cows and the boys were doing their chores. I was talking to one of them and Edrie walked out and said, "Don't you think you could grieve a little longer for my son." That didn't deserve an answer. I just walked away from her. From that day on she treated us like we had worn out our welcome. I began making plans to go home and she didn't want us to leave. I had the car packed and the kids were ready to go, when she announced she was going to drive her car and pioneer our way home. She did. She drove right in front of us, sometimes going ten miles an hour and then she'd speed up to eighty. I had to follow her at ten but I didn't have to go eighty and I was glad to see her outdistance us. She would drop back to ten or twenty. Then she would come back to our car every little bit and remind us she was pioneering the way. I doubted she had ever driven this route. I had traveled it many times. The kids didn't want to ride with her. They had seen too much abuse at her home. I tolerated this in respect for Bill and his children.

We arrived in Sutherlin late and we were all very tired. She wanted to turn around and go back. I asked her to spend the night, as she would be too tired. She said, "No I don't want to stay here but I do want you and the kids to go out to Bill's grave with me." I asked her again to wait until morning and spend the night with us. She wouldn't even listen to me. I got the kids in my car and we drove out there. It was very painful for all of us.

The kids were sobbing. I became quite upset at her trying to revive our pain. We were trying to forget the painful memories and focus on the good times. Now the wound was fresh again. Remembering a loved one is not necessarily grieving. We were trying to make it a positive effect in our lives as soon as possible. There were still times when a memory would wound us, many of them, but they were coming less often as time went on. This was not a subject we avoided, we talked about Bill much of the time.

When we left the cemetery we drove home. She drove right on by. She didn't come to tell the kids good-bye, she was just gone.

Chapter 12

"Dad"

1960

I became more active in church. I felt like I really needed to do something. I went to the Ladies' Missionary meetings, I went to prayer service, Bible studies and I was asked to sing in the choir. I loved the choir and I started singing soprano. We had a good first soprano but she didn't want to be the only one singing that part. I said I would like to try it. I worked on it but the higher the notes the more air it took. I had the range but I didn't know how to breathe to get the true notes out. Our minister encouraged me to take voice lessons. He suggested a teacher. I began lessons the next day.

She had me sing for her and she said I had a nice voice and she would be happy to give me lessons, but it was going to take some time for me to unlearn everything I knew. That was a little deflating. I learned to read music and how to reach a note to make them sound whole and true. I worked hard at it and I thought I was doing pretty well. She was pleased and very encouraging but one day she told me she didn't think I would ever become a great singer. Well, I didn't know about that, kinda hurt my feelings. She could see I was a little shaken and I said, "What is the use of me taking lessons then?" She a bit surprised said, "I didn't know you planned to be a great singer. There are so few great singers in this world. I know you like to sing and you add so much expression, your audience will be pleased with your performance. Put the talent that God gave you to good use, please don't be discouraged. I would like to continue to work with you and I know with all your responsibilities it must put a drain on your budget, so I want to continue without charge. I do see a lot of potential. Please say yes, I would be so pleased."

I took lessons for two years. She wouldn't let me quit. I finally moved away. Yes I had picked up some bad habits. The lessons did put me in the place in the choir that I wanted to be. I loved the cantatas. Songs that were more difficult to sing. Singing first soprano in the choir was what I enjoyed most. When I learned how to breathe with better voice control and more volume, it wasn't too hard. I sang a lot and she was right, I was never great. I learned that people didn't expect that much, they enjoyed hearing people sing who had a message.

Our pastor's wife introduced me to different types of songs where expression was essential for the dramatics of the message. She was a wonderful pianist, she played with a lot of expression; she had the talent to make any singer sound wonderful. She could make the thunder roll or make you feel the mist from the ocean, or she could make you cry for your love of Jesus. It seemed like I worked for her and she worked for me. I had complete freedom to sing as I felt the emotion at that moment and she was always right there with me. It was such a wonderful experience to sing with her. We worked a lot together.

I participated in everything in the church. I was so anxious to learn, when I became active again the longing for the scriptures returned. I studied a lot at home, Mary and I studied together. It was good to get back into something to take my mind off my responsibilities. I kept things up as well as I could at home, and now that the kids were back in school, I did have more time. I took the kids that were able to go, depending on the time of the meeting. There was a big play area in the basement of the church. At nights if the meeting was going to be late, I felt Billy was responsible enough to take care of the little ones or oversee the caring for them, as all the kids were good to care for the little ones. Evening Bible studies seldom lasted more than an hour. There was nothing that had to be done for them as they all had eaten. A diaper could wait until I got home, unless of course it was dirty, but that was up to them. Merrill was good at it. The older kids watched TV, and the little ones played. It was seeing that they didn't get into something and get hurt. They made out fine and were not begrudging me going to church activities.

Betty Peterson and I discovered our voices blended well so we began singing duets. I picked up some of those bad habits again singing "Country." I began sliding on a note and a country drag was worked in there. I loved it, that was what I grew up with and you know what they say about the country girl. I was very careful not to do this at practice.

We had a lot of musicians in the church, these country songs drew them in, we were soon making some good music. The church loved it. Everyone loves country, well most everyone. We were getting invitations to sing for certain occasions. When we were asked to bring the entertainment to a church banquet in Eugene at a convention center, this was getting scary. We put a few jokes together and got some good laughs and then our imaginations ran wild. I was voted in as organizer of the group. I made reservations and bookings and got practices together. We practiced a lot at my house since the kids were there, but they weren't too happy with that. I moved the TV in the bedroom and that seemed to work better.

We had all kinds of invitations. We got very busy but we thought it was great to be asked until it became so demanding, we were exhausted. Our families got tired of it also.

We had several singers, soloists, duets and group singers. We had comedian acts, pantomimes, everyone did one or more parts. Sometimes the musicians sang or were in a play. I was the MC, since I had put everything in order, I was the only one who knew who was going to do what. Everyone in the group was so excited about what we were doing, most of us had never done anything like this before and we didn't know we could.

It was really a lot of work but a service to the Lord. We did a lot of Christmas shows at hospitals and parties. We entertained in nursing homes, church camps and did special music for revivals. We were on the go a lot. It got to be too much, we had to turn down a lot of requests. I didn't have any problem with babysitters, the church ladies were great and the older kids were okay to be alone. I just didn't like being away from them that much.

My sister, Donna, did some great skits. She is tall and slim, she played Long Bones and another very short lady played Short Bones. They had a great act and would bring the house down with their vaudeville presentation. We had a box dance that was absolutely hilarious.

Donna played in a L'il Abner type hillbilly act. She was drinking from a big jug that she threw over her shoulder. It was quite heavy and she dropped the jug on her foot. It broke her big toe, she began jumping around and holding her foot in her hand but everyone thought that was part of the act. They laughed and laughed. She went on with the act and finished the show. She had a terrible looking foot for some time. She said dropping the jug was not an act, it was an accident. She was a good sport.

Bill Washburn, a member of our group, called me one day after he had been to a board meeting at the church, saying we should call everyone together for a meeting, there was something we should talk about. I called all the members, we met at my house. Apparently the head elder, Dale Switzer was complaining about us entertaining in other churches, he didn't want us out of our own church. He said when our church doors were open, our cars should be in the parking lot so the community could see we were there. We were pretty upset about it, this was not right. We decided to talk to the pastor. We did want to continue with our music ministry. We had talked about cutting back but for the church to say we couldn't do it was pushing things too far. We felt that we were edifying our own home church and what could be wrong with it. Other churches had encouraged us saying this was such a great ministry and it was needed.

We never missed Sunday School and Church, once in a while we might miss Wednesday Bible Study. Our pastor was very encouraging and went with us now and then to sing a solo, he did a beautiful "Oh Holy Night." The result of our meeting was a unanimous opinion that the elder was out of line in expecting us to give up our music ministry.

Bill talked to the pastor, he said he would talk to the elder. This seemed to open a can of worms. Apparently we were not the first. A lot of dissension about various things came up and was handled the same way. The elder felt that the pastor had no right to interfere, his word was final. Pastor Smith went to the board and discussed this with all of them. The board would not go over the elder's head. It went from bad to worse. People were beginning to take sides, some were leaving. The pastor's hands were tied, he couldn't do anything without the cooperation of the board. The board sided with Switzer.

Shortly after this began the pastor was accused of smoking and was fired, Switzer was the only witness, but he convinced the others. Pastor Smith didn't have the support he needed to oppose this. He left the church, what a loss, he was the only one there who was qualified to be an elder. He was a wonderful minister, very kind and spiritual. We all loved and respected him and his family. Many people were attacked and accused and were asked to leave. Any objections from the congregation got nowhere. When people saw this, they left rather than fight it.

I might mention here that a woman had absolutely no voice or authority in the church. She was not allowed to talk during Bible study or meetings of any kind. They did make an exception for me since I didn't have a husband to ask questions for me. I didn't object to that. I taught Sunday School and was the president of Christian Womens' Society in our church. I took part in every womens' ministry in the church unless it interfered too much with my family. I was perfectly content with men taking care of the business. There really was no need for a woman to speak out in the business matters of the church, if the church overseer was wise and prudent spiritually as he should be in the Lord's work.

This was a time of learning for me. I witnessed first hand what could happen when a person is put into a position of authority when he or she is not qualified or ready spiritually. It is devastating to the flock when their shepherd is cut down. They scatter, wounded and many are lost. Woe to the one who is to blame.

When we saw what was happening we canceled all our programs and stayed in the shadows. I didn't like what was happening and I'm sure a lot of people didn't. A shameful thing to happen in a church but the Lord was not asleep. He has a way of weeding out the chaff.

I dove into the Bible to look for answers, I got books on church government and doctrines. I studied every resource I could find. I got counseling from many sources outside of our community, trying to get some direction on how these things happened and what should be done. I was so disappointed, I had put my trust in this church and had become a part of it. These were God's people, how could they do this terrible thing.

This can happen to any of us at anytime if we compromise our standards, not seeking and following God's leading. When man becomes empowered with authority and is deceived by Satan into thinking he is an "almighty" elder, deacon, or whatever, his authority takes on super-human power to CONTROL the whole church and everyone in it. It doesn't take long for Satan to have control.

In my 35 years as a Christian I have seen this happen more than once. It seems that Satan targets elders because of their authority and women are also an easy target for Satan. Women are more competitive in power situations. We have to be so prayerful and careful. In our work for the Lord we should never feel that we can make a decision without first prayerfully seeking God's direction. If we don't have God's influence, we get it from Satan. This is true in regards to our personal life also.

Many people were dropping out, some going to other churches and some fell away from the faith. Our image in the community was in tragic ruin.

Elder Switzer came to talk to me at home. He said he had heard that I was no longer happy in the church. He said "You are still a babe in the faith and shouldn't pass judgment on anything that happens in the church. I assured him he didn't need to feel responsible for me, I would be fine and I had not lost my faith in God. I tried to be respectful, but it was hard because I no longer had any respect for him. During this discussion I told him just how I felt about everything that had happened. He didn't have much to say. I was sure I would never be welcome in the church again.

If I could have done anything to heal and restore what we had before I certainly would have. But deep down I knew if anything could be done, I was not the one to do it. I loved the church and the people. I wanted so much to have the security the church gave me and my family in our time of need. I didn't feel like I was ready to go out on my own yet. I felt betrayed and so hurt. I missed the fellowship, it was gone and so quickly it had happened. I truly felt like a man without a country. I still had Mary, God bless her, and Betty and several others but things were so different now. We didn't have the tie that binds.

A few days later I got a notice that I was to appear before the board at their next meeting which was in about two weeks. I was so surprised, I didn't know what to expect. I was fairly sure they were going to call me on the carpet, because I didn't think they wanted my advice. I didn't plan on giving any.

I prayed and I cried and I pleaded for God to enlighten me so I would know what to do and say. I left it in Gods hands. Being a new Christian, I'll have to admit my faith was shaken by all that had happened. I continued to pray and study.

My sister Donna a new Christian also, but a scholar if ever there was one, studied with me and we prayed together. She really helped me in research. We both went to counseling from an authority. I called Mom and told her what was happening. She said she wanted to go to the meeting with me. I said "Mom, I don't think they will let you in."

She said, "I'd like to see them keep me out."

I prayed while they were going through their procedures. When they finally got to me, Elder Switzer said, "Rose, from our conversation, I understand that you are very disappointed with the church. If that is so, I would like for you to tell the board why."

I stood and spoke so they could hear me, "I will take my answers from the Bible." (I hadn't planned this, what am I saying). I answered specific questions. They asked why I was disappointed in the church. I opened the Bible to the answer with Paul admonishing the church for unrest and bickering, and proper action to take in those circumstances. They could not disagree with the scripture. I sat down.

The elder wanted me to repeat everything to the board that I had said to him. He asked questions to that effect. Whatever he brought up I turned to a scripture and read, I didn't add or delete anything. Time after time this happened. "Am I right in saying that you think we do not qualify as elders?" I wasn't thinking about where to find the right scripture, I just opened the Bible to Timothy and it was there.

I read to them. They turned around in their seats to watch me. This must have gone on for half an hour. During this time the whole scriptural layout for the church government was read. Praise God. The meeting closed, they told me I was excused.

I knew there were some sore toes, but I didn't do it intentionally, I followed the Lord's guidance. I wondered if their restrictions for women was substantiated after that. I really felt bad. I couldn't believe I did that. I just had to keep telling myself the Lord laid it on my heart and they asked the right questions, to get the right answers. If there had been a man to do it, I would have gladly given him the pleasure.

As we were going to the car, Mom looked at me with a look of disbelief and exclaimed, "How did you know all that? You just turned to the passage without saying anything and read them the answer."

I said, "Mom, I didn't know. The Lord opened my Bible to the right place and laid my eyes on the right passage."

Mom looked at me very doubtful and said, "You are kidding aren't you?"

"No Mom I'm not. That is the truth. You know I would not kid about something like this."

"I know you wouldn't Rose, but is that what actually happened?"

"Yes, it was really like you saw it. Like I saw it, I can hardly believe it myself. Do you know the Lord had a reason for you coming with me today. If I had been alone, I would have doubted this myself. He had planned this all along."

Mom stayed down a few days and we'd wake up in the night and have to talk about this. She was so pleased that she had witnessed this. I believe this was the very thing that convinced her to give her life to the Lord. The more she thought about this, the more excited she became.

We went to church, there was hardly anyone there. The second elder in charge got up to make announcements. Elder Switzer wasn't in church. We had no minister and very few people. We sang songs and read some scripture and prayed and were dismissed. I didn't want to go back.

I learned later that they had a meeting of the whole church and every one of the teachers, leaders, elders and deacons resigned after examining themselves. They were going to study the plan for the church in the scriptures. The church organization was going to be dissolved and then rebuilt from the ground up, God's way.

I thought about this for a long time and decided the best thing for me and the church was to leave. The officers felt very uncomfortable around me. I believe there was embarrassment caused by the incompetency of the officers. In the Lord's work there is no place for an "I told you so attitude." I tried so hard not to reflect that because it was not my work but God's. I earnestly wanted what was best for the church. I very quietly left, trying not to stir up any problems. I had so enjoyed the fellowship there, it broke my heart to leave. There was a lot of healing to do for many people as well as myself.

Elder Switzer moved to the coast and was denied membership in any church. He held his own services for his family until he was humbled and repentant.

The church lost most of the members but the ones that were left rebuilt the church, got a new pastor and kept going. There were a lot of people who were hurt emotionally and spiritually.

Such a terrible thing to happen to the Body of Christ. There was, I'm sure, a lot of mourning.

The kids and I went to the Christian church. We only attended the Sunday Services. We did not take part in activities. I didn't have the heart to do it. We went over to the church Donna was attending and also to the church in Roseburg. Our old pastor was there.

———————

Dad had looked forward to retirement for many years, he had so many things planned. He loved to fish, hunt and do all the outdoor things most men love. He had been working at the plywood mill in Myrtle Creek for several years. Building the house took a lot of his time. He masterly planned everything for this big day to come. He completed all projects that could have pacified him for a long time in his retirement. His daughters and son lived in Oregon but he didn't get to see them very often. They were busy like all family people. He and Mom would go see them on weekends, when they were home. We all liked Wilma and Lavern. We had a lot of family gatherings together.

He was a great man but he worked all his life and didn't know how to sit down and relax or just do nothing day after day. I had never seen him nervous or cranky. I don't believe he was. He loved life and he thought he was making the best of it.

Mom told about him driving the Model A across the desert from McDermitt to Boise, which was a long stretch of nothing but desert. He could see a lot of things to interest him. He could travel 35 top speed, and he scanned the desert for signs of life or a trail, an old wagon road, he would go slower and slower. Mom would look over at the speedometer, 20 miles an hour and going down. She would say, "Clyde, for heaven sake can't you go any faster?" He'd laugh and say, "What's your hurry?" He would speed up for a while and then begin to slow down again. Mom would have to get his attention again and again. So went the trip to Idaho in the blistering hot weather. They had all the windows open and the wind was blowing in on them to make it tolerable. Donna was sitting in the rumble seat with Kubi beside her, singing her way to fame, with the wind blowing her golden blond curls, happy as could be.

Dad's family owned one of the biggest sheep ranches in the state of Oregon when he was a child. There were several brothers and they all worked on the ranch. Dad's father gave equal shares to the kids who worked there. Eventually the boys married and their wives came to live on the ranch. There were several children born into the family. Dad liked taking care of the sheep in the summer grazing land. There was hay to raise for winter feed, lambing sheds to repair, always a lot of work on an operation like that.

Dad left his family and went out into the hills one spring and was gone for several months. When he came back, his wife was going with someone else, his brothers and their wives had been drinking all summer. The ranch was run down, the work undone and everything was in shambles.

Dad packed up what he needed and left. He drank and gambled until he ran out of money. He then took off for the mines. He was a contractor in the mines and made good money, but he was a broken man. He drank and gambled everything up. He always kept his dignity even in that state.

He was always clean and well dressed. He was well respected by everyone and no one had a bad word to say about him.

Our lives crossed during that time. I liked him the first time I met him. He was very quiet and polite. He was a handsome man but he was not interested in women, until he met my mother.

He was not a man who attracted women because he didn't pay any more attention to women than he did men. He still had a lot of scars to heal and he drank a lot. He was hurt bad by his first wife and I think he had a hard time trusting women. Mom was a lot like him, she was a person anyone could trust, and he learned to trust her and love her. She never hurt him, she was a good wife and homemaker. He was a good husband and provider. They had a good life together.

Mom called me early one morning and asked if I would come up and talk with Dad. I said "Of course but why?" She told me he had been very depressed lately and had tried to take his life. He had taken the gun and walked up Bens Branch, which was the little creek that ran through their property. She had called Darrell and he went up to find him. Darrell brought him back. He asked Dad when he found him what he was doing up there. Dad told him he was going to shoot himself. Another time he piped the exhaust into the car and sat in it with the windows up. Mom came home just in time. I couldn't believe this. I was devastated.

I believe right then I gave him up. I knew he wouldn't be long for this world. It was like he was already gone and he was. The Dad I knew was no longer there. I grieved for him as he was a part of my life for such a short time. A part that I cherished as I had never had a father-daughter relationship until I met him.

I took the kids to Donna's and went up to talk to him. I asked why he wanted to do this. He said, "I'm tired of living, I can't work anymore. There's no use living if you can't do anyone some good." Straight forward as usual, he told it like it was. You never had to beat around the bush with him. I talked to him for a long time and told him how much he meant to all of us. But his point was he did not want to live any longer. He didn't want to hurt anyone, he was ready to die. I talked to him about depression and how it made you feel like you wanted to die. I explained to him about medication that could make him feel better. We should go see Dr. Hudson and he could help him. He said "Ok I'll try it." We drove him to Roseburg to see the doctor. We called ahead and told the doctor what had happened with him so he was ready to talk to him when we got there. He recommended we take him to Salem which was a mental hospital. We tried to act casual with him but we were worried. We knew we had to do something now, Mom was afraid to take him home. They at least would protect him up there.

He agreed to go and signed himself in. He seemed to want help. He was up there for three months. Mom and I went to visit him every weekend. Donna went up whenever she could. She had a lot of obligations with her family and the animals and the farm. On the second visit he told us they had given him a shock treatment. We were stunned, we hadn't given a thought to that.

Mom went right to the doctor, telling him that we did not want him to have those treatments, he is terrified now. He seemed to agree.

Mom told Dad that he wouldn't have any more and the next week they gave him another. Dad was like a mad man when we went up the next time. He was very angry at us, he hated this place and he would get out one way or another.

We couldn't take him o ut. We felt sure he would harm himself in this frame of mind. They wouldn't let us take him out anyway. We convinced him that if he settled down and acted like he was better they may not give him another shock treatment. But they did, several times after that. It was some sort of a regulation when he signed himself in, he apparently signed the wrong paper.

It was so painful to see him when he would beg us to take him out. We finally got permission to take him home for Christmas. By then they were finished with this therapy. We felt that he was much worse after that. We knew that we were taking a chance, but he needed something to look forward to. We were all looking forward to him coming home because he did seem better, having something to look forward to. We didn't think he could stay home and we avoided the subject when visiting him. We were concerned about taking him back to the hospital after Christmas. It would be nothing less than impossible to get him back in there.

The kids were so excited about Christmas. We were decorating and preparing for Christmas at our house, making candy and cookies. Hiding gifts and guessing games. School programs and parties. The air was filled with Christmas glee. We couldn't forget to put Christ in Christmas. We hadn't celebrated with Him very long and the effort didn't come natural yet. Each day we spoke to God about giving His Son to save the world.

I was trying to wean them away from Santa but that wasn't easy, so I didn't push it. We planned to open our gifts on Christmas Eve at home and go up to Grandma and Grandpa's for Christmas day. It was hard not to get reminiscent at this time of year remembering how Bill loved Christmas. The change helped.

I had made big plans for Christmas Eve, something different than our previous ones. Living in a new house made a big difference, and we were going to do the majority of the celebration on the eve of Christmas. Donna and her family came down to be with us. We had our spiritual worship before that time, at home and church.

When the night arrived, we sent the kids into the bedroom. When Santa got there, they all came out. Santa was on the porch and had an assembly line passing bicycles into the house. One for Billy, one for Tommy, one for Merrill, Rosana and Danny, Janet and Steve got a tricycle.

The kids were ecstatic over the bikes. Our living room was not large enough to hold all of them. We got them in there anyway. When Santa left he was telling everyone good-bye and the kids were saying thank you and goodbye, when Tom hollered, "Bye Norm." I guess they all knew who it was. Someone in the church helped Norm Peterson find these bikes and they remodeled each one and painted them to look like new. That was the greatest thing they could ever do for the kids.

We took a lot of pictures of the kids with their bikes. We still have the film and it's priceless now. It's so special to watch them open their gifts. Steve was just walking good and he was wandering around trying to watch what the kids got. He was far more interested in their things than his own. They had a great time and it wasn't as sad as I feared it may be. Not near as elaborate as the ones before but I did not go into debt. They would have to get used to that and they did, they understood.

Our road to the barn was a well-traveled road and was the scene of many accidents. Not serious, it was soft dirt or mud. Those bikes amused them for a long time.

We were getting ready with our things to take to Grandma's for Christmas dinner. The kids didn't want to leave their bikes, I understood but we couldn't take them. They took some of their other toys and games to play with up there. However, they were anxious to get back home.

Dad seemed to have a good time that day, he was quiet but he was usually that way. He was so glad to get home, he just beamed all day. We all visited and the kids played. Terry, Tim and Connie were there to play and they always had a good time together. They walked up Bens Branch. It had not rained very much yet so they didn't have much mud to contend with. The little kids played in the house and garage. We did try to keep things fairly quiet for Dad. But nothing seemed to bother him. He was happy and sat mostly watching and wearing a big smile. We felt so good about that, maybe he was better.

We all put our very best into this Christmas dinner as we wanted it to be so special for Dad. Oh what a feast. Mom did the turkey and dressing and it was done to perfection as was everything she ever cooked. The turkey was browned and flavored superbly. The dressing and gravy was the same.

Mom steam cooked the plum pudding in the round cans and made a hot rum sauce to serve over it. This was a dish served only at Christmas time at our home. The last time I ever remember her making it. Her homemaking came to an end after that Christmas and I hated to see that happen, I missed it terribly.

This recipe for Plum Pudding was a Norwegian recipe. It made her very proud to serve it. It brought back a part of her childhood and she, like all of us cherish the ancestry that molded us as an individual.

Mom's ancestry is the only one I claim. I know nothing of my father. His name indicates he may have been Irish or Scottish. He left when I was two years old or less. I don't remember him and I guess I have denied him as a parent. From the way he deserted us and never contacted us again showed that he didn't care for anyone more than himself. I believe that left a hollowness within me, causing me to deny him. I am proud of my Norwegian heritage that came from my mother. She did all she could to provide for us until we were able to fend for ourselves. It would have been great to have a more secure childhood, but it wasn't there for her to give.

We all brought several pies, which was a custom with us. We feasted all day long, and each snack was topped off with another piece of pie. Eleven growing kids could polish off several pies in a day.

The day went well, we had a good time visiting. The men relaxed to the point of a nap here and there, which is nearly inevitable following a meal like that. There was then the exchange of hunting and fishing stories. The women sat around in the kitchen to visit and catch up on family and friends. The kids returned to their games and play outside.

In the evening, Donna and her family and Roy and his family went home. I stayed with my folks that night, while some of the kids went to Donna's and some went to Roy's. Rosana, Janet, Steve and I stayed with my folks. The following day as things began to quiet down, Dad did get a little melancholy. We all did, we felt like it was the natural thing when a family gathering comes to an end.

Apparently Dad was feeling something else, maybe the possibility of returning to the hospital, or the shock treatments, or the futility of his illness, and the illness itself pulling him down into the depth of depression, where there is no hope, no way out, totally helpless, no future. The terrible reality of mental illness.

We gathered ourselves together and were loading up to return home to Sutherlin. I could see Mom was having some anxiety about being alone with Dad. Donna lived only a couple miles down the road and she could be there in a matter of a few minutes if she was needed. Roy lived up the road about four miles, so I couldn't really see the need for me to stay. The kids were restrained to some extent and they needed to get home. Mom needed some quiet time. Dad needed to relax. We said our good-byes and hugs and we left with Mom and Dad waving from the yard as they disappeared from our sight.

We arrived home in the afternoon, unpacked the car and after putting things away the kids found the gifts they had left behind and sat down in the living room with the TV on. They were content and quiet. I was tired and it felt good to be home. We went to bed early that night, but I had a gnawing feeling in my stomach, something was bothering me terribly; but I preferred not to bring it to the forefront of my mind, instead I read myself to sleep.

The telephone began ringing in the middle of the night. I jumped out of bed and raced to the phone. The house was completely dark. I answered the phone and Aunt Clara said, "Oh Rose! Something terrible has happened. Clyde shot himself in the head." She went on, "He isn't dead but they don't expect him to live. He is in the hospital in Roseburg. Bertha is with him. Rose I'm afraid for Bertha, she has gone all to pieces. This is terrible, Rose what are we going to do? Are you coming down?"

The message was trying to register with me but I couldn't seem to absorb it. I felt like I wasn't awake. I needed time to wake up and think. The dark was closing in and the horror came crashing down on me. I immediately went numb, I felt nothing. This was the most terrible, frightening thing I had ever heard of. I was trying to put the picture together. There was so many absent pieces. I sat there without saying anything. Aunt Clara was saying, "Rose, Rose, are you alright?"

I said, "Yes, yes I'm okay." I didn't want her to hang up. I would be all alone and I was so frightened. I said, "Aunt Clara, please don't hang up. Keep talking to me."

"Rose I have to go. I have to call the others." She said, "Don't take it too hard Rose, this is what he wanted. Good-bye."

My eyes were getting a little more accustomed to the dark as I sat there not wanting to move. I heard a voice behind me. It startled me, I jumped clear out of the chair and turned around. Billy and Tommy were standing in the doorway of the hall. Billy said, "What is wrong Mom? Is it Grandpa Clyde?"

I said, "Yes it is, he is in the hospital, not expected to live. Please turn on the light."

"Mom what happened to him?" I couldn't tell them because I didn't want to say it. It was so horrid. I asked Billy to call Mary and to please stay there with me.

I finally collected myself enough to call Donna. She was trying to hang on for Mom, but she was falling apart fast. After hearing the whole story I understood why.

Mary came down and got the kids, I told Billy and Tommy that Grandpa had shot himself and I would tell them the details when I came back from Myrtle Creek.

I waited with the kids and Mary until it got daylight. The shock began to wear off and I don't know that I felt better but was better able to cope. I did want to see Mom. By the time I got to Myrtle Creek, Mom was at Donna's. Dad had passed away, he never regained consciousness.

Mom was laying on the couch, hysterically telling the details over and over. I sat beside her and listened but I could not stay there long, I had to leave as I felt like I was going to vomit. It seemed so horrifying, how did she live through it without going mad. As the story unfolded bit by bit and I heard all the details, as hard as it was to listen to, I had to know.

A lot of people had come, I was glad for so many there.

It happened about midnight when Mom was awakened by the sound of the shot. She heard him fall, close to her bedroom door. She jumped up and turned on the light. A pool of blood was forming on the floor around his head. He had taken the gun from the rack in the hallway beside the bedroom door and put it to his head above his ear and pulled the trigger, only a twenty-two but he knew where to put it.

Mom cried out to him, "Clyde, what have you done, hang on, hang on, I will call for help." She raced into the bathroom to get towels to hold to his head to control the bleeding. After packing the towels around his head, she ran to the phone in the kitchen, dialed an emergency number, before she got an answer, he called to her. "Oh Bertha help me. Mama, Mama please help me." She ran to him and pulling him into the front room where she could have more room to minister to him, she sat down and picked up his head and laid it in her lap. Holding the towels tightly to his head, she tried to soothe him. The telephone was hanging down the front of the cupboard.

He said no more. Blood was pooling around her on the floor, her lap and the towels were soaked. She knew she had to get help immediately. She called toward the telephone hoping someone would hear her, not daring to move. Holding his head and calling out for someone to please come. She called out her name, address and location, pleading for someone to hear her and send help. "He is dying, please hurry." She heard a siren. They took them both in the ambulance to Roseburg. He died shortly after arriving.

There was Mom, her very being pulled apart by this tragic episode, losing the one who had meant the world to her. After her life of hardship and strife, it had all come to this. I didn't see how she could even survive.

The real grief for Dad was put aside by the anguish Mom was having. She repeated the horrible details over and over until we were all saturated with the blood. She couldn't stop talking, on and on with every detail. We thought she had lost her mind and we could understand why. We wanted to help her, take this pain away. We couldn't stop her rambling. It went on into late afternoon and we decided to call the doctor to come out and see if he thought we should take her to the hospital or maybe medication would help. I guess we were hoping he would do one or the other. We knew we couldn't leave her but we were all going nuts.

After the doctor talked to her, I followed him out the door and asked him if he would please do something for her. He said, "No she is doing fine. It is just going to take awhile for her to work this out of her system."

I said, "She has been going on and on about the details of this for hours and hours. I think she is losing her mind. It was a terrible thing for her to experience."

"This is harder on you perhaps than her. Each time she repeats it, she is getting that much more out, that would otherwise be devastating to her later on. Let her talk. It is good for her."

Donna and Darrell, Roy and Angie and I took Mom down to my place in Sutherlin. A change may be good for Mom to get her away from some of her memories. We certainly needed it. The kids stayed at Mary's for a day or two longer. We couldn't bring the kids into this situation and traumatize them like we had been.

Mom did seem to be better down there. We put her in my bedroom and she went right to sleep. We sat in the front room talking in hushed voices so as not to awaken her. The first time we had the opportunity to talk between ourselves. We found ourselves talking about the same things we couldn't stand to hear any more about. We were all very tired and emotionally spent. We unnerved ourselves so completely, we could not leave each other. We were frightened. It reminded me of kids telling ghost stories and scaring each other. But this was real. We weren't getting any better. When it came time to go to bed, I went in to get ready for bed and I crawled in beside Mom. I began pulling myself away from her. I was afraid of her. I could see all those things she had seen and I was reliving them. I became so frightened, I forced myself to lay beside her. It was like she was transferring all that horror into me.

I lay there frozen with fear the rest of the night. If Mom moved, I would just about jump out bed. I was telling myself how ridiculous this was but I couldn't make myself believe it. Daylight did bring more reality and less fright. I was still afraid of Mom. The other kids felt the same way. We did finally separate the next day and I was sure that they, going to their own homes would be helped, but I couldn't get away.

I could see improvement in Mom in a couple days, but I couldn't seem to shake it. Our pastor called to see how we were doing. I asked if I could come in and talk to him.

It was like turning on a faucet and water pouring out. He listened to me very patiently and was very sympathetic, reminding me that I had been through a lot in this last year. These tragedies take a toll on people. I said, "Yes but why do I fear my mother, I can't turn my back to her." I got my first real life lesson on Satan and how he works.

He prayed with me before I left. He said, "I'm sure you will be able to use this experience to help someone, someday." He was right, I did indeed use that to help a poor frightened girl who came to me in tears.

I never again forgot to pray when I felt a tug from Satan.

It wasn't always an instant answer, but it makes such a difference when you know God knows all about it and, 1 John 4:4 "Greater is He that is in me than he that is in the world." (Christ in me and Satan in the world.)

Mom stayed with me for some time and she did recover. She grieved for a long time and she missed Dad terribly as we all did. She told me that he was the only man she ever loved. How sad to see that certain person in your life go down like he did. I'm sure we all grieved for her as much as we did for him.

We did a lot of things together that following summer. We took trips and vacations together. Mom was always at her best while traveling. She loved it and she helped us to love it even more. The kids still talk about these trips with Grandma, some forty years later. Sometimes we just went for fun and we never failed to have fun like up the Umpqua River 15 miles for a piece of pie. The scenery was beautiful and the pie was wonderful. It was so special to all of us.

If you put Mom in a car, that was the end of all her pains and trouble. She never complained, no matter how bad the roads were or how dangerous, she didn't even notice. She didn't notice if you went too fast, or how long it took. You could bounce her around over rough mountain roads, she would just hang on but never complain.

She used to say she never passed a campground without thinking how nice it would be to camp there. She also said she thought if Heaven were like a campground she could be happy there forever. I would say, "For eternity Mom." She said, "Oh I spose."

Mom was close to 54 at that time. Her arthritis was getting bad and she was looking forward to the day when she could retire from the hospital. She sold her house and bought one in Roseburg where she could be close to her work. She didn't seem to have any interest in life except being with us kids. There was a lot for her to take care of with this new house but it was good for her, she didn't think so, but she needed responsibilities as we all do.

I knew she was lonely but she had lost all interest in everything but her work and family. She seemed to be fine while at work but on her days off she became depressed, she wanted us to do something for her. She went to Donna's place one weekend and mine the next. Donna had a husband and farm to take care of and she could not spend the time to take her out. Mom was so unhappy, she cried and complained. It was so hard on Donna and her family. The kids were so good to her and tried to make her happy.

Tim's jokes were not too well received at that time, but he tried. They all waited on her giving her anything she wanted.

When she came to my house, I gave up trying to get anything done and I just took her out; shopping, to see a friend, for a drive out in the country or for a root beer float. As long as she was busy, she was fine. We felt sure it was depression but what could we do. We understood and really did feel sorry for her but we couldn't make her happy. That had to come from herself but she didn't understand that nor does anyone when they are in a state of depression. It seems as though you have to get better before you can help yourself.

It was a terrible heartache for all of us. We could see what she was doing to herself. Her arthritic condition was worsening fast. How long was she going to be able to work? She wanted to sell her house and buy a trailer house so she wouldn't have so much to take care of. We tried to talk her out of it but to no avail.

Donna became interested in the church. She and the kids attended the same church in Myrtle Creek that we went to in Sutherlin.

Mom went with Donna to church up there and with me in Sutherlin. She didn't say anything about her spiritual growth but one day she announced she wanted to be baptized. An answer to our prayers. We all went to her baptism. It was a glorious time to see her giving herself to the Lord. She was a faithful Christian, she started everyday with her Bible and attended church wherever she was. She found a church in Roseburg she liked. The pastor there was the pastor at the church in Sutherlin at one time so she knew him and that made a big difference. She made a lot of friends there. She was more content, and life seemed to take on a new interest for her. We were so happy to see this.

We were making plans to take a trip to Idaho to see Uncle Tom in Yellow Pine. Mom's vacation was coming up and we planned for a June trip, just after school was out. The kids were so happy they couldn't contain themselves. They were making all sorts of plans of what they wanted to do up there. They were getting their fishing gear ready, the sleeping bags and they packed the clothes they needed, of course that took some supervision. We were all so excited we could hardly wait.

On Friday night Mom was ready and drove over to my place after work. We packed that old red station wagon until there was not an inch of room anywhere. We had a car top carrier put on and Mom said we looked like the "Grapes of Wrath" going down the road. She had to explain that, she did and we didn't mind.

I had a good talk with the kids before we left about how to act in the car or should I say how not to act. We talked about eating in restaurants or staying in a cabin or motel room. I explained to them that since there were so many of us, the only way this was going to work and be fun for everyone was for everyone to do as they were told; and if they did not, I would take the next step of Plan B. I didn't want to because all of us would be upset if I had to get physical with them, but they had to understand there would be no horsing around in the car, no arguing, no complaining. I was going to try as hard as they were to be good to them. It could work if we all worked together. We took books and toys for the little ones. I suppose you are wondering how we all got in the car. We did and we fit just fine. Our big '57 Ford station wagon was roomy. Mom and I, of course, were in the front seat and one of the bigger boys sat up there with us. They took turns. Tom, Merrill, Rosana and Dan sat in the back seat. They had plenty of room unless they sprawled out and that wasn't allowed. Janet and Steve rode in the way back. I had packed it with bedding and they had a very comfortable place back there. We had to take Smokey. He was little and he laid on the floor or on the kid's lap. He minded well, so he was no bother.

We stopped often, sometimes just to let them run around for a while. We stopped to get a cold drink or eat dinner. We bought stuff for sandwiches and fixed lunch at road stops. When we stayed at a motel, we got rolls and milk for breakfast. We liked to stay up around Bend, it was cool and woodsy. The kids played outside before dark. We got a room with two double beds. Mom and Rosana slept in one. Janet, Steve and I slept in the other. The boys slept in their sleeping bags on the floor. The clerk could see how many of us there were but never said anything.

Mom and I always got up first and made some coffee. We had to have that before we could get started. We would then get the kids up, they cleaned up and ate and we were usually on the road when the sun came up. The first trip was so fun. We made many more, we all loved traveling with Grandma.

Mom loved to sing, she knew all the old songs and had taught them to me. She had a beautiful voice in soprano or alto. We sang, sometimes the kids would sing with us but they didn't care much for "Carolina Moon" or "When it's Night Time in Nevada." She knew a lot of fun songs too that the kids liked. We sang choruses from church. They liked to sing those and would join in.

The boys played games like slug bug or the railroad game.

"Lift your feet for there's a railroad, a railroad, a railroad, lift your feet for there's a railroad or you'll lose your friend." One would count one color car and the other would count another until we got to the next town, whoever got the most got to sit shotgun.

Billy read a lot. Rosana got way in the back to play with Janet and Steve. The boy's games bored her because they always won. They really enjoyed their trips and they still talk about them.

We got quite a reaction when we went into a cafe to eat dinner. People watched us trail in one after another, you could see them counting. The kids sat down very politely and talked but never too loud. They ordered their own meals but had been previously coached on prices, etc. I ordered for Steve and Janet.

Their manners were exceptional. They acted more like adults than children. They visited with one another and with Mom and me. They were very comfortable with themselves and the family.

We usually had to sit in the middle of the room because the tables were bigger. So everyone could watch us. We ignored it, we knew we were unusual but we were proud and it showed. Many people stopped by our table and talked to us. We got a lot of compliments for the kids being so well behaved.

Of course, they would count again when we left the cafe, and then they could see they were normal kids. The first to explode always was Merrill. He'd let out a war hoop and jump from the top step and run across the lot. The others would follow and after they wore off some energy, we all took our places in the car and were on our way again.

Our first trip from Cascade to Yellow Pine was breathtaking. It had been so long since I had seen it but the only thing that changed was the size of the trees. The roads were still the same, dusty and narrow trails. The kids were spellbound. They never dreamed of anything like this. They thought places like this were only on "Gunsmoke" and "Big Valley." They were a little nervous with the roads but I drove slow so as not to frightened them or myself.

Cox's Dude Ranch still looked the same. Johnson Creek was the same, there was the Bryant Ranch. The old cabins were there. Oh my what memories for Mom and I, the kids didn't say a word. There was the camp ground where we stayed when I had the mumps. Next was what we had all been waiting for "Yellow Pine."

The kids wanted to know where all the people were. We did see a man walking down the street slow and leisurely. We drove on to find Uncle Tom. When we drove up into the yard, he was sitting on the porch smoking a cigarette. He watched us for a while and not recognizing us, he didn't speak. I thought Oh, oh. Mom leaned forward and said "Hello Tom."

He scowled, "Who is it?"

Mom said " It's me your sister, Bertha." She was a bit annoyed.

"What are you doing here?" Still sitting on the bench, he was looking over the car and it's contents. Mom was getting out of the car and walking toward him.

"What is the matter with you, I wrote to you and told you we were coming."

"Where in the h— do you think you are going to stay. I don't have room." There were two Norwegians butting heads.

Mom chirped "We didn't expect to stay with you. Aren't you even glad to see us?"

"Who are all those people in that car?"

"Why Tom, I'm ashamed of you, that's Rose and her family."

"Those are all her kids?"

"Yes, they are all her kids. Don't worry Tom, we aren't asking you

for anything."

Another Norwegian was ready to get in this, "Come on Mom, let's go, I don't want to stay here anyway."

Uncle Tom looked a little foolish and asked, "Where are you going to stay?"

I said a bit sarcastically, "Where we planned to stay, we are camping out."

Mom was still hoping to shame him, as she was storming toward the car she said, "I never thought I would see my brother act like this. I'm sorry I even came to see you. Good-bye Tom." She was getting in the car. Tom got up and moved toward the car. "Well I don't know what shape the cabin is in but you can stay there if you want to."

Mom boiling by now said, "Tom, for two cents I would turn around and leave and never see you again."

"Well Bertha, I can't feed you and put you up, what do you expect me to do. I didn't know what you wanted."

Mom recovering her pride said, "Tom, have I ever imposed on you? You know I haven't, and you're acting like this."

Uncle Tom was going toward the other cabin and said a little sheepishly, "I'll go unlock the cabin."

When he was out of earshot, I said to Mom, "I'm not staying here. To heck with him. I want to enjoy this vacation."

She said, "Now Rose, don't you start in, we can't just leave and never see him again." She was crying, "Please Rose, don't be mad at him, he didn't mean it. He opened the cabin didn't he? Don't let this spoil our vacation. Please let's go in."

How could I refuse her? We got out of the car. The kids spread out, and weren't about to go in the house. I acknowledged them and went in the house with Mom. The house was sparkling clean, wood in the wood box, full water bucket sitting on the bench, wash pan, tea kettle, dishes, pots and pans, beds in the bedroom and the living room, table and chairs in the kitchen along side of a big beautiful wood cook stove. Everything we needed was there.

Mom looked around and said, "Tom, I just don't understand you." She walked up and put her arms around him and said a few words in Norwegian. He answered her and it was all over, everything was fine.

I walked out and talked to the kids. They didn't want to stay there, I explained to them what had happened. They tried to understand, but they were not very happy. They gave Uncle Tom a wide berth for a few days. They asked me about all the good things I had told them about him. I said he was old now and had been a bachelor for a long time. He wasn't used to people, let alone people coming to see him. I said, "Let's just give him awhile and see what happens. I think all of us in one car scared him to death." They laughed but were not convinced.

It was getting late and Janet had already fallen asleep so we fixed the beds and before long everyone was ready for bed. The kids asked if this was how it felt when I was a little girl and went to bed in a cabin; I told them yes and it felt really good to me because this cabin was one I stayed in when Aunt Clara lived here many years ago. Tell us about it Mom. I told a few stories and they were soon sound asleep.

I got up early and unpacked everything for breakfast. I built a fire and got the coffee on. Before it had time to get hot, Uncle Tom was at the door with his coffee pot full of coffee. That smelled so good. I got the cups out and here came Mom—she had also smelled the coffee. Uncle Tom said he watched for the smoke and knew we were up. It was such a great feeling to set with them drinking coffee in this little peaceful corner of the world. I felt wonderful. No stress, no anxiety, this was really peace that we all needed badly.

I started fixing pancakes and eggs and asked Uncle Tom to stay for breakfast. He was willing. As the kids started getting up, they went right for the door to see if we were really here. They turned to come back for breakfast with a big smile. I got a kick out of them, they thought they were in heaven. Soon Janet called from the bed, "Mom, I have to go potty, where is the bathroom?" I said, "It is right out there," while pointing toward the outhouse.

"Where?"

"Right there." I said still pointing.

She said, "Mom do you mean that little barn."

I said, "Yes that's it." She danced all the way to the door. She stopped abruptly, turning to look at me, she gagged, "I can't go in there."

I said, "This is the bathroom. You have to use it, just hold your nose and I will help you." She gladly took her nose between her thumb and forefinger but she still gagged. I lifted her up on the seat and she said in a very nasal voice.

"Mom, I won't come out here, I can't stand the smell."

290

I said, "For years and years people have used these. If you want to live here like a hillbilly, you have to use it. You will get used to it and won't even notice it after a while."

She whimpered, "I'll try Mom."

"I know you will honey. Thank you." And she did.

I watched Uncle Tom with Rosana. He teased her and sat and talked like he did with me. It reminded me so much of how it used to be. So many happy memories came back. I had always thought he was one of the finest men I had ever known. I was special to him, he never said that, I just knew. True he was a little odd, we had to accept him just as he was, not expecting anymore of him than he wanted to give.

It worked out that he ate nearly every meal with us and went most everywhere with us. He had as much or maybe even more of a vacation than we had. He enjoyed the kids so much. He sat on the bench on the front porch smoking his cigarette and watching the kids play. He would chuckle now and then but he never seemed to tire of the kids. I told the kids they would never be sorry for forgiving Uncle Tom. It was good they were learning that now.

The kids played in among those big old Yellow Pine trees. They loved it there, they built forts and tree houses. I didn't hear one disagreement, one argument. They were in the height of their glory.

They had to visit the school, then they came running to get Grandma and me. They said it was like schools in the old movies. I told them that I went there for awhile and Donna went there. Aunt Clara's kids went there too. They were so excited. They said they wanted to go there, but I explained that before the school could open they had to have so many kids to attend and there were not any kids in town.

Not once did the kids have to be scolded. They spent all their time outside and I didn't worry about them. There was nothing they could hurt or that could hurt them. We had some serious talks about the river. I had to go along if they went fishing.

Oh, I knew it was going to be hard on them to leave.

Uncle Tom asked Mom and I out for a cup of coffee at the restaurant up town. He gave the kids money for an ice cream bar from the store. We were introduced to the waitress who was the only one around. We drank our coffee and went over to the store, as is custom there, sat on the bench in front of the store and visited.

The lady in the store came out to sit with us. We chatted for a while and watched one lone man walking down the street. The man was barely ambling down the dirt road which was the only street in the town. I watched him and was intrigued by the way he walked. There was no urgency to his pace, he was obviously in no hurry. He just strolled along. What it must be like to live in a place where no one is in a hurry. This was worth some thought, I needed to see more of this. Well, wasn't this like it was when I was a girl. No there were more people here. Stibnite was running, there was a saw mill, a dairy, a pig farm and a fox farm. Everything was hopping. But what happened? This town died. There was only a faint heartbeat left here. It was neat and I liked it. Why a person could catch up to himself here, just like the man in the street had. He seemed to not have a worry in the world. Nor was there any stress on the faces I saw here. They lived a very peaceful life. The one thing that was missing though was happiness. They didn't look particularly unhappy, but there seemed to be a cloud that shadowed their face.

There was no church here. To my knowledge there had never been a church. God was probably never spoken of. Was the Bible ever opened, I doubted it very much. How terrible to not even be able to worship. Is that what was missing in the faces of the people?

There was no traffic to disturb a quiet walk in the afternoon, except an old mule that sauntered out into the street. No one paid any attention to him, he was obviously at home in the middle of the street, the man just walked on by.

The kids were a little leery but Uncle Tom said, "Oh he won't hurt you, if you are eating something, he will beg." He saw the kids eating and he began to beg and was coming to see if he could get a hand out. It frightened the little ones who came running over to us even before they looked around. We heard the most awful, mournful, groaning sound, that came from the air being dragged back and forth down his big empty pipes producing this god-awful noise, back and forth, back and forth sounding as if it were his last breath. We all began to laugh and the kids turned around in time to see him with his head up, and his lips curled up smelling the air. They burst out laughing. He looked so undignified, so ugly with his lips curled up. We all cracked up laughing.

As the man came closer, Mom recognized him. She said, "Tom isn't that Harry Withers, well for goodness sake it is. He sure doesn't look any different. He never gets any older." Harry came over then and greeted us all. Mom asked him if he still played the violin.

"Whenever there is a dance and they come after me to play. I don't play that much anymore."

Mom asked, "Do you still live in the same house?"

"Oh yes, I'll be there forever. Say Bertha, Tom told me about Clyde, I was sure sorry to hear that. He was a good man." Mom thanked him for his concern and told him how much she missed him.

"There are so few people left around any more but in the late summer some come in. They have cabins here. They spend a month or so and leave again. Earls come in to open up their bar and cafe about the time the people come in. Faye Kissinger and Ivy come in and spend some time each summer. Henry Abstien comes in now and then but he is so crippled up he doesn't get out much. He has ropes hanging down in the middle of his room so he can take hold of them to get around. I think Faye put them up for him. He usually brings him in and takes him back out. Lafe and Emma are still at the Dude Ranch."

He and Mom chatted for a long time about the old timers. He said "There just aren't many of us left Bertha, oh yes Fred is down on Johnson Creek. He bought that cabin down there. He pretty much stays to himself there unless Piccolo Pete comes in and he stays with Fred. He is a ski instructor at Sun Valley. He skis over the hills to Sun Valley every fall when the snow is deep enough and when skiing is over in the spring, he comes back. He sure keeps Fred's house clean and he does all the cooking. He is a pretty good old guy if you can understand him. Being Fred is Swede too he doesn't have any problem with that. Beeney died in 1945. Mart and Bonnie moved out and just Murf and Mary are taking care of the place over there, but it's closed a lot. Donna and her husband, Bud are here part of the time but they take the boys out for school in the winter. They haven't come in yet, it's too quiet here for most of them; but that's the way we like it, isn't it Tom."

"Yeh, you're darn right. We've seen enough of those fights and brawls when Stibnite was running, all that gambling and booze and then people driving back to Stibnite drunk, a lot of them was killed too. No it's just right the way it is."

We wanted to go visit Fred Erickson, after all he was getting pretty old now and he was Donna's dad. Uncle Tom said he didn't want to go with us. We asked why, they had lived together for a long time. He said, "Oh, we don't even speak any more, he's such a cranky old thing, I don't want to be around him."

Mom asked him if they had a fight over something, he said "Oh yeah, but I was sick of him anyway. We had a blow out over frying fish. He always wanted to fry them with the heads on, and I couldn't stand to see those eyes staring up at me out of the frying pan. It's just a waste of grease, and I told him so. He got mad and said he liked to eat them so it wasn't a waste. I just decided it was time for me to get my own place to live. We were both getting too cranky to live with anyone. So I bought this place from old Orville Jackson, you remember him don't you? He died some time ago."

We drove up Johnson Creek to the little cabin where Fred lived. It was a lovely place, a solid old log cabin set in a grove of Aspen trees. A little spring up the draw supplied the water for them and to water the place for pasture for his old mule. He would sit out on the back steps in the evening and play his mouth harp to bring the deer in to eat the beautiful lush green grass.

He was glad to see us and was a lot more friendly than Uncle Tom was, but he didn't think we were wanting to stay with him either. Mom didn't seem to feel uncomfortable nor did he. Just old acquaintances. The kids started calling him Grandpa and he thought that was great. He got a big grin on his face and looked at me. He made some coffee. It took a while because the fire was nearly out, but he stoked it up and soon the coffee was smelling good. Mom continued the conversation she had going on with Harry. She asked him about Bob Beaty. He said, "Oh he is too old and crippled up to come in anymore. He is staying in a cabin next to Emma Bryant's house in Boise. She looks after him now, you know he worked for the Bryants for a long time. Old Bob was a good guy. He worked on the power line when they put it into Stibnite in 1940 I believe. Sure a shame they never took that line into Yellow Pine when it was so close. But the ore that was at Stibnite they needed it in the war, they used it in ships to strengthen the metal, so the government paid to get the power in there. It came straight over the mountain from Cascade, they followed the old Thunder Mountain Road."

I was fascinated with all this. They were things I didn't pay any attention to when I was a girl back here. I knew Stibnite was protected with armed guards at the gate but I didn't know why. After the war was over, of course, they didn't guard it so closely. We talked into the evening and the kids had explored everything on his place. They found that old mule to be a friendly old feller. They talked to Grandpa about how old he was and so forth. Grandpa had owned him for a long time. He said he was not going to live much longer. They wondered why, he said, "He isn't very well anymore, every now and then I find him laying down and he can't get up. His bowels get kinked and one of these days I won't be able to help him anymore. I have to go out and give him a big enema, that will fix him up for awhile."

On the way home the kids had a lot of questions about what Grandpa did to the mule: they decided they never wanted a mule. I told them most mules didn't have a problem like that.

Just being in the mountains had such a tranquil effect. Every day we feasted our eyes on the beauty of it all. As we were coming down Warm Lake summit, we looked out over the mountain tops at a distance so far we could not imagine. Mom sat quietly taking it in. She whispered so softly, "Majestic, Oh how majestic." I believe it was an image she would keep in her heart forever. Then there was the view of Warm Lake from the summit. And Landmark meadows with the lazy little stream stumbling every which way to find its way to the guard station and down the mountain to be the Johnson Creek that we loved so. Going by Cox's Dude Ranch, the Bryant Ranch, the Johnson Creek landing field, and the Ice Hole.

Many years ago I remember the men going to the ice hole and cutting big chunks of ice with a hand saw to store in the sawdust pile behind the town for everyone to use during the summer. Johnson Creek flows on lazily now by campgrounds and the Pioneer Cemetery, then to the Devil's Bathtub where it rushes into the East Fork, never to be our beloved Johnson Creek again. We visited the Carpenter Ranch, where the old dairy used to be when we were there. Julio Eiguren bought it after Jim Carpenter died. We drove up to Stibnite which was only a ghost town now but told a lot of stories, then over Thunder Mountain summit and down the other side to Roosevelt Lake. Down the other side is the most beautiful display of wild flowers anywhere. Just on one hillside where a spring is running through the midst, spreading out to water every flower, there is every kind of flower imaginable and every color. What makes this so spectacular is, it is all done by God's Hand; man had nothing to do with it.

We drove over Profile summit to Big Creek. That place really did some talking to us by bringing back a lot of memories. Some of the names we remembered were: Napier Edwards, Red Johnson, Cye Boyles, Dick Cowman, Eric and Jake Jensen, Wilbur Wiles, Red Potter, Axel Falkenburg, the McCoys. There were many more but after twenty or more years some names slipped my mind. Napier, Red Johnson, Wilbur Wiles, and some of the McCoys were the only ones still around. Snowshoe, Wardenoff and Moscow mines had employed quite a few men and some families lived there. The Forest Service employed a few men. All together it made quite a population for Big Creek area, but you would never believe it now. This was a very quiet place. We didn't even see a mule.

There was so much more we wanted to see but two weeks is not long enough. We wished we could stay indefinitely. It was so hard to leave Uncle Tom and the peacefulness of the lifestyle. We all cried and even Uncle Tom had a few tears. Mom said it was the first time she had ever seen him cry. He said we had spoiled him with all those sourdough pancakes. He'd never be able to cook for himself again. He also told us that we were welcome to come back next year.

The trip home was not as happy as the trip out there, in fact it was pretty quiet. Everyone must have been remembering something of the last two weeks. "Mom I've never had so much fun in all my life. What a neat place." Now and then one of the boys would ask, "Mom, why can't we move up there? " Then there would be a chorus of "Yeah Mom let's do."

I said "No, that is impossible, now just be quiet about it. There isn't even a school there. I don't want to hear anymore about it."

Chapter 13

"The Call"

1961

After experiencing the tranquillity of our wonderful vacation, it was not easy to get adjusted to home again. The kids talked longingly about Yellow Pine. I didn't dare think too much about it or I could get emotional. The real world wasn't too great after what we had enjoyed. It was so satisfying to have our little Sunday Worship and see the people so hungry for the LORD, being fed by His Word. We missed our own church at home, but had we gone back it would no longer be there. The tension and stress were returning.

We had to find a way to make our home a contented one. It was hard on all of us when the kids began to get bored, but who could expect kids to sit around the house. Was I to entertain them all the time? Well if that is what it took then so be it. I wasn't getting much done at home but the kids could care less about how neat and clean the house was; but when it started piling up, I became so anxious I wasn't a very good parent. The kids wouldn't need this extra attention for the rest of their lives. They seemed more important to me now than anything else. We made some calls getting friends to go along and we all went swimming. The kids enjoyed that so much it was hard for them to be unhappy there. We did a lot of things together that summer. I knew the older boys had been very unhappy since their Dad died. They were trying to make the best of it, but now they had seen something better. I prayed about it earnestly asking God to please find a way that they could be happy in their growing up years. It would make such a difference in their adult lives.

The one thing they looked forward to was next year's vacation. We talked to Grandma and decided that when she got her vacation next summer we would go back. She informed us she had a month vacation next year. Oh what happy kids. We would leave the first of June and return the last of June. I really talked to them about: would they be more unhappy after a month of living up there? They agreed they would do their best to be content when they got home.

Oh the kids needed that, how could I ever give them what they needed. They needed to be out where they could feel more independent, especially the boys. The life they were living would be useless to them as adults. Sitting in front of the TV, doing little duties that were assigned to them from a chart, woman's work. They were not doing one thing to develop their masculinity, their self worth. This was a constant challenge for me as a woman raising sons. One day I asked myself, what kind of men do you want your sons to be? I had to have some direction. I wanted my sons to be men who knew how to escape the pressures of life from the stress they would encounter as they endeavored to accomplish the things they desired. They must have college. They all had high aspirations of what they wanted in life and they all knew they had to get it themselves. We talked often of college. They were not to consider anything less. It would be tough on them and it would take every ounce of energy they had to get through. The Veterans Administration and Social Security would pay their living expenses, they would work and pay for tuition, books, etc. The stress they could encounter at this time could take them over the edge. To escape, they could turn to alcohol or something worse unless they knew a better way. If I could only introduce them to the outdoors. Nature has a wonderful way of doing wonderful things for the human mind and body.

They had to learn how to hunt and fish, how to know the ways of the outdoors and the habitat. They had to learn how to build a camp fire in just the right place to keep it burning, what to look for to start the fire, how to cook over the campfire, how to keep it going if they bedded down close for the night. They had to know how to handle all emergencies out there, from being hurt to unfriendly animals. They had to know how and where to set up a camp. They had to know how to catch a fish without a pole for survival, or how to make a sling shot to kill a rabbit. What water to drink and what not to drink. What to take in a first aid kit or in their pocket, and how to use it. How to keep landmarks to find their way back. They had to know how to cut down a tree, and chop wood for the fire, to put chains on the car, or dig the car out of the mud. How to drive on ice or snow. They had to know how to take care of horses for pleasure or work.

They had to learn where to look for an elk and know how to track it, where to shoot it and how to take care of it after it was shot. There was so much to learn, and they would not get it here in this house, in this town, or from me. All their activities were not enough to teach them how to be men as I knew men. A successful man in my opinion, would be the one who could survive the worst kind of stress by knowing an escape as an outdoorsman, but at the same time being successful in business and a good Christian, and teach his children the same.

My boys had to know, but how was I to teach them? I had to use the tools at hand and that wasn't much. I started by cooking over a campfire in the backyard. Taking them camping, setting up tents, etc. We shot guns and they learned to shoot a bow. They loved it but there was something missing. I soon learned that a mother teaching the ways of a man was not effective. I attempted to fill their needs but I really didn't know the needs of a young man. I went on anyway knowing that they sometimes resented me for taking a man's position. They loved and respected me as a mother. I taught them a lot just in our daily lives. I put them in a boy's outdoor club. I encouraged and supported every outdoor sport that was available. I prayed for God's help.

I realized that some of my children may not go to college and I accepted that, but I never told them. When the time came, they would not feel like a failure for not reaching the mark. My love would be no different for one than another.

We picked fruit and beans and walnuts most of the summer. The little kids would go out with me and they enjoyed that. The older kids went out to pick but it was not their favorite thing to do. If they stayed home they had assignments to do, which usually didn't get done. Then to deal with that was a chore.

We were gone for about six hours a day. We got up and were out on the job at six. It got too hot to pick after two o'clock.

We always tried to make it fun. Several of my friends and their kids went along. We'd take our lunch and put everything together and have a picnic. We did have a good time, we made fun out of everything we did. We did everything together. There was Mary, Betty, Helen, Nancy sometimes others—whoever wanted to go. Fruit was fun to pick. We didn't make a whole lot of money, but could have if we had shorter picnics. But the little kids needed to be with us for awhile, they got tired and as a rule went to sleep after lunch. We did get tired. Packing the big bags of fruit up and down a ladder was very tiring, so a rest was welcome, about 10 o'clock.

In the fall when the walnuts were ready, it was cold and the leaves were wet. We had to crawl around in them and dig to find the walnuts. We tried to dress warm but we couldn't keep warm. The walnuts turned everything black that came in contact with them, our clothes, our gloves and it soaked through onto our skin. We were black from head to toe. It was nearly impossible to get that black off. Our hands were black for weeks.

I tried bottled lemon juice just on a hunch. My mother canned tomatoes last to get the stain from her hands, it must have been the acid, lemon juice should work and it did. I called Mary and shared that piece of information. Mary and I were the only ones to venture out into the walnuts. We couldn't find a way to make it fun, we would get so cold and wet. We lasted at that about two weeks. Of course the walnuts paid better than anything else we picked.

Thanksgiving and Christmas were just around the bend. My picking money was to go for Christmas. Mom and I both had a rough time over the holidays. Mom was very melancholy and depressed, as could be expected. I wasn't much help to her. We did what we could for her but nothing seemed to work.

At that time Donna seemed to have the most stability in her life so we leaned heavily on her. She was always so good about it. We spent a lot of time down there.

I battled depression and nerves. It seemed like I couldn't get a life put together for myself. There wasn't time right now for a life for me, why couldn't I accept that. It seemed like a hopeless situation. I felt like I was in prison, walking around looking out the windows but couldn't get out. I knew that unless the kids were getting what they needed, I could never get out of prison. I couldn't do what I wanted to for the kids and they didn't want what I had for them. I believe we were working against each other (not intentionally but it was just happening). My adjustment to the single life was not easy, it was impossible. I was terribly lonely. When I say lonely, that's just what I mean, I was not lusting for a man. I wanted someone to be with, to talk to, to share my life with. Someone to make me feel very special and who was special to me. A best friend, a companion. Someone who would take an interest in our place and fix things, improve things. Someone who would bring a family to completeness. This was no real life for any of us. It was an existence. A father to direct those children's lives, to be their friend. To care with me what happened to them or what grades they got. A boy needs a father to teach him how to be a man. A girl needs a father to make her proud to be a woman. My heart cried out to the women who wanted to be divorced, they had no idea what life is like without a husband, a father, a head of the household.

It seemed to dominate my life, I was aware of it every moment of every day whatever I was doing. I tried to shake it but it hung on. The Bible tells me to be content in whatever situation I was in, so I had guilt also to battle. I thought about if someone came into my life, sent by God, I would be ecstatic. It would wrench me inside to watch a movie where a couple was together, or to see a young couple walking down the street holding hands. If I sat down in the front room I was so aware of the empty chair across the room. I began looking in a crowded room, not intentionally, just scanning the scene everyplace I went. If I saw someone who was a Christian and single, WOW! could it be this one or that one. A fantasy began, of course I thought of that person constantly. Until, for some reason or another, he dropped out of sight. No one knew. They may have suspected but I never told anyone because I knew better. When I got serious with myself, I had to admit that no one, especially a young man who had never had a family, would want to marry a woman with seven kids. Why should I think he would even want to marry me without seven kids. I also thought, they didn't know what they were missing because these were the best kids anyone could ask for. I mentioned a certain handsome single minister to Colleen Smith, our pastor's wife. Not revealing a thing about having day-dreamed about this guy.

She laughed and said, "Availability is the most attractive feature a man can have for a single woman." Whoops, I blew my cover. I realized then I wasn't fooling anyone, I didn't forget that, I was just more careful. This was crazy, but it was sure hard to quit looking. I didn't, I just quit being so obvious, thinking so much. I had to have more self control so I wouldn't embarrass myself so.

I also worried about a wife being jealous. If I was with a couple, I was very careful. Jack and Mary were one exception, Mary wasn't the least bit jealous of me. Jack and I were like brother and sister. We could sit and talk about hunting, he loved for me to tell him about the places where I grew up and the people I knew. He would tell me about his life and places and people. All perfectly innocent. I think God arranged that relationship, because if I didn't have them at that time I couldn't have made it. Betty and

Norm Peterson were special friends to me also. Our Pastor Dick and Colleen Smith were also very special friends of mine and I could be myself around them. But I couldn't mix with a lot of couples (most in fact). The first sign of a woman thinking I wanted her husband, I was gone. I didn't want to be thought of in that way. Donna and Darrell were both good friends to me, I was a lot the same with Darrell as I was with Jack. We could talk by the hour about most anything.

I was taking medication for my nerves and depression. When I could get outside and work, or play with other people, I was able to cope, but winters were so bad. I hated taking medication but I was affected physically, internally. My heart was racing at 120 beats a minute, my blood pressure was high, the tension in my body was causing spasms in my internal organs. Nothing was working right. The doctor said I had no choice but to take the medicine. All our problems were working against each other. There is no house big enough to put seven kids where they won't violate one another's space. They were very territorial, like all kids. School was a blessing but then there were evenings and weekends. We all got in each other's way. At times my situation became so stressful, I could hardly keep from screaming, but for the kid's sake I had to find a better way. What could I do other than what I was doing?

I knew that loneliness was going to be my worst enemy throughout my life whatever I did, and I wanted my life to count for something for the LORD. I prayed endlessly for God to take this situation and make something good out of it. I think we all would have escaped if there was an opportunity. It was just that hard on all of us. But we loved one another and we were going to stick it out. It would get better, the Lord would see to that.

Bill's sister, Betty called us from LA and asked if we could come down for Christmas. She and Bill (her husband) offered to pay for our bus tickets and all of our expenses to go to Disneyland. She asked us to stay for Christmas vacation with them in LA. Oh my! How could I do this? For the kid's sake I had to, they would love it. I could not deprive them of an opportunity like this. I didn't take long to decide. Betty was going to send the bus tickets and everything was taken care of. So the plans began to form. Get clothes ready, wash, iron and pack. We had about three days to get ready. And keep seven very excited kids contained.

As soon as we got on the bus that was it. It was dark and their excitement was reduced to sleep. Janet and Steve didn't sleep much. They sat with me. I don't think they knew there was another person on the bus.

They chattered and sang and talked together and kept all the people entertained around us through the night. We made a stop for breakfast, the kids were still too excited to eat. They drank some juice and had a roll, walked around and it was time to get back on the bus. Several other passengers got on at that stop. A lady sat down behind us with a baby. Janet saw the baby and began a conversation. She asked what the baby's name was, the lady very sweetly responded, "Her name is Tami."

Janet became so excited! Her voice in full volume she said, "We have a goat named Tami." The lady began to laugh, and did not take offense as I thought she might. Beginning with the driver, laughter rumbled right on back through the bus. That started it and the kids, one or the other entertained the passengers throughout the trip. They talked to the kids and made a good enjoyable trip for all of us.

I had never seen such heavy traffic. It was frightening, I was so glad I was not driving as I had toyed with the idea, little did I know what I would be getting into. Betty told me it would be better if we came on the bus. We had a good driver, he darted in and out of the traffic but was not reckless. I seemed to be holding my breath most of the time. The fog was getting bad. The farther we went toward LA, the thicker the fog got. Our driver didn't slow down until he came around a corner and there were cars turned over all over the freeway. People were out trying to slow down traffic but no one saw them until they were too close and they would slam into some other car or truck. It was a nightmare. I could see people climbing and crawling out of the wrecks. They were obviously hurt bad. Some of the people on our bus were coming into LA for the first time also. They began telling the driver to stop and help these people. He got on the speaker and explained that if he stopped he could be hit also. If he stopped at every wreck, he would never get any place, he was following orders to keep on going. He explained that there were people who were much more experienced at this than he was and they would help them. He drove on weaving in and out of the cars and trucks wrecked on the road. I kept expecting something to slam into us. It was a relief to get out of that mess, but I also felt bad for not helping those people. I saw kids and babies and I got sick to my stomach. The kids just looked at me with a horrified look and didn't say a word.

It was exciting to us to see the places we had only seen on TV. When we came into LA, seeing the big HOLLYWOOD sign up on the hill was a real thrill. We finally were pulling into the depot. The people were as thick as many skippers on a small pond, running around here and there. It didn't look like they knew where they were going. They were just following someone in front of them like leaving a big stadium. They couldn't go to the left or right. I couldn't help thinking, "How in the world do we find Betty among all this crowd. People were so packed you couldn't see beyond them. I told the kids not to move, to stay just as close to me as they could. Watch one another and hold hands. I became aware of someone standing in front of me looking at me. I had been looking around that person until she said, "Hello Rose." I was never so glad to see anyone in my life. I should have known she had everything figured out. There she was, we all grabbed onto her. She had a stroller, bless her heart and we put Steve and Janet in it. That was half my worry taken care of. Now I could take care of the other kids. I got them all in front of me and we followed Betty. She walked us right to her car and we felt more safe when we were inside. It took some time to get out of the congestion of the depot but we were finally driving through the residential areas.

We arrived at their beautiful home up on a hill overlooking the city. The neighborhood was all big gorgeous homes. I was in awe. Their home seemed so massive, but she explained that she wanted a place big enough for people to come to visit.

Michael got home from school, it was good to see him, a handsome little boy, but he was more like a stranger, we hadn't seen him for a long time. Becky came straggling in, tired and hungry, dressed like a doll with pretty ruffled dresses. She looked so different. Bill had to work so Michael and Becky stayed home when Betty came for Bill's funeral. Bill worked for MK as an engineer, they had lived in LA for several years.

The kids soon got over their shyness and they all went out at Michael's invitation. There was a high fence around the yard and that seemed safe to me. They found everything imaginable to play with. I wanted them to stay outside as much as possible as Betty was a very nervous person and she wasn't used to that many kids around. Everything started out fine. Betty put the coffee on and we sat down to visit. Little Steve came back in the house and stood by my chair. I asked him "Can't you find anyone to play with?" He nodded his head and said, "Yeah." Aunt Betty said, "Did you find the big trucks and the sand pile. I'll go show you if you want me to." He was worried about something, but I thought with all the kids out there he would be alright. He was not the kind of guy that had to depend on someone else to entertain him. I walked out and called Janet and Rosana. I knew the big boys were too busy to look after Steve. Rosana said to me,

"Mom, we try to play with him but he just keeps walking back into the house."I told Steve to go out there just for a little while and then he could come in. I knew he needed to stretch out after that long ride. He did go out and was gone for about five minutes and he came in and whispered to me, "Mom is God asleep?"

A bit puzzled I answered, "No Steve, He doesn't go to sleep. Even if He did He would always leave someone to watch over you."

"Well, if He isn't asleep, how come it isn't raining?"

Oh Boy, how could any one say it any better. What a commercial for California. He was right. It did rain all the time during the winter in Oregon. I put his fears to rest and he went back outside to play, loving the sunshine.

Betty was ready to take us all to Disneyland the next morning. She rented two strollers. Danny and Rosana held onto the sides of the stroller that I pushed. The others stuck pretty close to Betty. The first day Betty's kids were in school as she thought it would be easier if we only had seven that day. The kids did everything, she had enough tickets for them to do anything they wanted to do. I kept busy counting heads, keeping track of everyone. We did take some time just to walk around and see the beautiful sights, it was fabulous. We had lunch there in a quaint little restaurant. I was glad for the opportunity to sit down. And the coffee tasted so good after a workout like that. We had a wonderful time. The kids loved to look at everything from the Indian village to the trip down the Amazon, where the snakes were in the trees and the alligators were in the water beside the boat. Birds were squawking at us from all sides. The kids rode in the pack train going on a wilderness trail. We went down in a submarine, Steve didn't care for that going under water (they made it all look so real). But he was perfectly content after he saw the mermaids. He watched them the whole time we were down or shall I say, the whole time we were in the submarine.

Betty wanted us to take the trip in space. We all went into a circular room and were seated. The big motors started and the ship just rumbled and shook. Then we were off into space. (The screen projected the scene in space, it looked so real.)

The ship continued to vibrate until we stopped somewhere in space to just look around. A voice came over the loud speaker, telling us what we were seeing. It was so fascinating, so real, it could have fooled me if I hadn't known. Steve was sitting beside me and he began tugging on my sleeve whispering "Mom, Mom," I looked down at him and he was scowling, obviously very worried.

I asked him, "What is the matter?"

"Are we going to be able to find the car when we get back?"

A good question, I had to admit.

I was quite nervous about the kids bothering Betty, her own kids drove her nuts. She was taking this big responsibility on herself for her dead brother's kids, to do something for them, that they would never forget. It was commendable and very special to all of us. I thanked her many times and told her I knew it was hard on her, and I wanted to help her in every way I could. All I could do though didn't seem to be enough. I was beginning to wish I was home. She trembled, even her voice shook. She tried to keep herself under control. I said to her, "Why don't you go lay down for awhile and I'll finish dinner." She said, "No I'll be okay." I knew she was a very nervous person but had no idea she was this bad. I really felt sorry for her. She said the kids were great, I kept them outside as much as possible or playing games where they weren't roaming around and were being quiet. She said it was not really them, but it was just the hubbub and her own kids taking advantage of her in a tight spot. They seemed to not care how they affected her, they had no consideration for her at all. Of course they didn't know, but how could they have got this way.

The next day Betty's brother Merrill drove up with his family. Betty wasn't expecting them and it threw her for a loop. His two girls were sweet little girls and his wife was a dear soul, I loved her. Merrill was a little overbearing with the kids and caused some uproar (only playing but Betty didn't need that rough housing). The situation became more tense and so did I. I was trying to keep all the kids busy and out of the way.

Becky, Pam and Sheila hung together, they had been together much more than with my kids. Becky had everything a girl could ever want in her bedroom and of course the girls wanted to play in there. Rosana was the odd one, they were leaving her out. They locked the door when she went out of the room and they wouldn't let her back in. They whispered to one another about her. I watched all this from the room where I was laying down with the intention of avoiding this very thing. I asked Rosana to ignore it and play somewhere else. Rosana was one who would take offense if anyone slighted her at all. She would whine and cry no matter what I said. She got in a lot of trouble for that during her childhood. She knew they were doing wrong and she was not going to be quiet about it.

Betty stormed into the bedroom screaming at Becky. Becky came out saying they were not doing that, Rosana was lying. The other two girls wouldn't say anything, they stood there hanging their heads. They wouldn't look up. I didn't say anything to accuse anyone. I wanted Rosana to just drop it but she went back in there and it happened again. Rosana was very angry and hurt. She came in to tell me about it. Betty heard her again and came into the room. I knew the lid was going to blow off the house then. She went back in the girl's room so mad she was shaking and screaming at them. Becky still denied it. I pulled Rosana into my room and told her to stay there, not to come out. She really felt violated then. Betty went back into the kitchen and was talking to Latrice.

I heard a little knock on my door. When I opened it, Pam and Sheila each handed me a note on a little piece of torn paper. They asked me to forgive them, they were in the wrong, but not to tell Betty because Becky would get a beating. I looked at those two little girls and wanted to cry and I thanked them for being so honest with me. The only thing they were worried about was Betty finding out. I whispered to them, "I won't tell."

After I pulled myself together and got Rosana settled down, I went back into the kitchen. I knew Betty had lost it when she screamed at me, "If you would teach your damn kids not to lie, things would be a hell of a lot better around here." Oh! I was so angry and hurt. For her to imply that my kids were allowed to lie. (I think anyone is in trouble if they think their kids never lie.) She was cursing my kids, I was stunned at her reaction! I couldn't believe her. What could I say, I couldn't betray the girls, nor could I betray Rosana. I felt like anything I said would be wrong. I walked from the room. Oh! I wanted to go home. I went back to Rosana and asked her to please go outside and play and forget what had happened. I was hurt for her, but I had to make her understand right or wrong she just had to do what I said. She was not happy with me but she knew she had better do it.

As much as I hated to, I knew I had to go back into the kitchen and face Betty and Latrice. I prayed for help so that I could hold my temper. If I could have walked out the door, that's what I would have done. But I was entirely dependent on someone else. I was so utterly obligated. When I went into the kitchen, Latrice tried to be casual but Betty wouldn't look at me. I suddenly got the feeling that I had worn out my welcome. I knew what I had to do. I said "Betty I want to thank you for everything you have done for us. I know it cost a lot of money and I feel bad about that, I wish you hadn't spent so much. I'm sorry things didn't work out. Will you please arrange for us to go home now."

She was startled, she just looked at me and I let her understand that I meant what I said. "I will call, but I don't know when the bus will leave." As it turned out, a bus was leaving in just a few hours. I said "I can be ready." I only took time to throw clothes into the suitcases. I called in the kids and told them to wash up and comb their hair, we had to leave. I went as I was. That was a short stay for all that money, but I knew it would be disastrous if I stayed any longer.

Still I knew, I couldn't break my word to the girls. To this day when I think of them my heart skips a beat or two. They knew I knew, they knew I believed Rosana. I admire them for coming forward, but they had no idea what that little incident cost us all. The hurt, the misunderstanding, the pain that would never go away. When I was unpacking, I found little notes saying, "Aunt Rose I love you, I'm sorry." or "Please forgive me." How could I ever do anything else but forgive them. I hugged them both and told them I loved them before I left. Becky never came to me at all. I cried all the way home. I felt so bad for everyone concerned but most of all for Betty, she tried so hard. I hope she learned that Rosana didn't lie, but I couldn't tell her at Becky's expense.

She did a wonderful memorable deed for the kids, we will always remember her for it. It was never spoken of again. Betty died about three years later. She had some heart trouble and during an angiogram, her heart went into fibrillation and they couldn't get it stopped, and she died right there. The poor soul. Another pain in my already breaking heart, oh if only we could have had an understanding before she died.

I cooked Christmas dinner at home and had the family down. Of course everyone brought pie again, and many other delectable dishes. We had a nice Christmas after all. I had bought and hid gifts for the kids before I left, so on Christmas Eve we opened our gifts and lit our tree.

Time dragged on that winter. It seemed like a day was a week long.

I longed to get back to the tranquil life of the mountains. As soon as the first flowers bloomed, I was packed and ready to go. I got the car serviced and the carrier on top. When Mom put in her last day, we left like we were shot out of a cannon.

When we were getting near Yellow Pine, things looked different somehow. We could see the evidence of activity, here and there it just didn't have the same look. We drove through town and it was easy to see why. There were people all over, kids playing in the streets, dogs running around after the kids. People sitting in front of the store, the hotel, the bars. Some kind of explosion had hit or a hard windstorm. We drove slowly looking at everyone and everyone was looking at us. People were coming out of the businesses to look at us. Boy what a change, was this the same place?

We hurried on down the hill to Uncle Tom's to find out what was going on. Uncle Tom was glad to see us, and we felt that he looked better than he did the summer before. We couldn't wait to start pumping questions at him. Mom started it with, "Tom where in the world did all these people come from?"

He chuckled before he answered. We sat down on his bench in front of his house and he began. "Well there is a lot of development going on, subdividing and building houses. Stibnite is working again, smelting gold out of the old tailings that were stockpiled when Stibnite was running. During the war the government was paying to get that metal but they wouldn't allow them to take the gold out. They were using the metal that came from Stibnite to add strength to the metal used in battle ships, it was very rare so they wanted all they could get of it. That's why the mine was guarded so heavily during the war because that was a strategic metal. They have hired a few men; and after they get started and going good, they will hire more, I had heard talk of this before but I couldn't believe it would ever happen. It seemed that a lot of people have been waiting for this.

"The Pond's bought the store and three families moved in with them to work there. Some of the men though are going to work in the mine. They plan to enlarge the store and have it stocked with a better variety of food of all kinds. Between them they have ten kids. So they will have to open a school with that many kids.

"A guy by the name of Warren Campbell from McCall has bought the houses in Stibnite and is going to haul them to McCall and Cascade to sell. There are quite a few going to be set up right here in town. I think I'll buy one. I am tired of this old shack. In fact I have talked to Ernie Oberbillig about surveying my place. I don't need all this land. I will sell off lots. There's just all kinds of things going on here. This is a boom."

Since he seemed so happy, we didn't want to ask him how he felt about it. We would hear if he was unhappy. I think he was glad there were more people in town. He and Harry had more people to watch from the bench in front of the store.

We decided we had better get unpacked and make beds and feed kids before it got dark. Uncle Tom came over and helped us. He built a fire and put the tea kettle on so we could make some coffee. After a light supper we were ready for bed.

The old cabin was still the same and that blessed peace was still here. The river still rumbled down over the rocks. The birds in the morning were still singing. The sun had the same friendly warmth when I walked out on the porch. Oh this wonderful place.

I spoke at an Idaho Centennial celebration in 1990. I think it may be appropriate to print here as this is where the inspiration was born.

"Ode To Idaho"

In tribute to our great State of IDAHO this Centennial Year of 1990, I would like to tell you what IDAHO means to me.

I am a native of IDAHO, I have lived here all my life.

I have no desire to live elsewhere. IDAHO has everything I could ever wish for. It's the mountains, the deserts, Bear Valley, the Craters, Hells Canyon, the big Salmon, Chamberlain Basin, Pahsimeroi Valley, and just the little mountain streams. Oh!! The peace it brings to my soul to hear the breeze blow in the trees, when riding down the trail, or watching the moon rise over the mountain, or the birds singing at sunrise, to see the deer grazing in the meadow or an old mother bear waddling along with her cubs trailing behind.

There are few places where you can experience quiet, hear nothing but the silence of the snow fall. A leaf quivering to the ground, the trickle of a little stream, the soft sounds of nature.

Yes, that is what Idaho means to me.

Many see the beauty that I see, some have lived here all their lives, others have discovered this little peace of paradise, tucked back and nearly forgotten, and take residence here.

We are hospitable, we welcome you, however my cherished dream, is that Idaho may never become what you came here to get away from.

Uncle Tom came over for breakfast, we lingered over a cup of coffee to visit. The kids were anxious to go outside, they didn't tarry over breakfast.

Uncle Tom told us Fred Erickson bought a little cabin up town and moved in a couple weeks ago. Fred Bachetes bought his cabin on Johnson Creek. I hated to see that go. The people who bought the hotel, Don and Barbara Browning, had two boys. Very nice kids. Don also bought Faye Kissinger's hunting business and was going to take out hunters. He should do pretty good.

Faye and Iva Kissinger had a house moved down from Stibnite. It was set on a lot up on the Circle. They were ready to retire, but those two never would. They moved to Yellow Pine in 1929. Iva had a garden down in the valley, she went out to water once a week. Faye always had something going. I remember he drove into town one day and he called to me from his vehicle. He said "Come over here I want to show you what I found at my mine. The richest stuff I have ever seen." He pulled out his black light and shined it on the rock. Sure enough it was that beautiful purple that I had seen before, scheelite, everyone was looking for scheelite. He went off showing everyone on the street. He sold the mine later on. As I remember the vein wasn't very big.

Faye put in the steel bridge to the Abstein place after a big flood washed out the old bridge. That bridge was dedicated in 1987 which was the last time Faye was in there. He passed on in 1990. He also had the Yellow Pine city water system to his credit. He turned that over to the Community after it was completed. The Kissingers certainly left their mark on the country back there. I had known them since 1941. I knew their daughters Claudine and Betty Lou.

After we did the dishes, we walked up town with Uncle Tom. He introduced us to several people. I liked the Ponds in the store. Two Pond brothers married sisters. Hathaways were the other couple who came in with them, with three kids, a girl and twin boys. They were all very nice people, their kids were all ages, I think the oldest was about ten. One family lived behind the store in the apartment and the other two couples rented houses. The men in the family were all out cutting wood, they knew it would take a lot for winter. We walked up to the hotel and met Barbara Browning and the two boys. Don was out working. I liked Barbara instantly. She was happy and outgoing. Pretty little gal. The boys were nice polite kids. They were anxious to meet my kids who were playing down in the school yard. I expected them to make it up town, but I think all these people frightened them. They had the whole town to themselves last year and this was quite different.

I had brought material along to have Sunday School for my kids since we were going to be there for a month. We went out and found a place under the trees, where it was quiet and cool and very woodsy. I read stories and we sang. We all read from the Bible except the little kids. Mom joined us, we brought her a chair, the rest of us sat on the ground. Just as we finished a song, we heard some noise in the bushes. We all became very quiet and listened, soon we saw some little heads poking around the trees. We ignored them and went on with our worship service. They were there until we were finished. I called out to them asking them to come on over, they ran away. They acted more like little Indians. For the next few days we saw them behind trees and bushes watching everything we did. We would try to call them but they ran away again.

The next Sunday I had some cookies and Kool-aid for the kids after services and we finally coaxed them out offering them a treat. It was the twins and two of the Pond's younger kids.

After they got their treats, we tried to talk to them and they left. This was a regular thing so we just ignored them, but we invited the other kids in town down to join us. To my surprise all but the Browning boys came down. When the little Indians saw they were all joining us, they came out. We were having about twenty kids at our little Sunday School.

Most of these kids had never been in Sunday School. They didn't know who God was so it was right from bare roots teaching. It was fascinating. I wondered if my kids had been so Bible illiterate, just a few short years ago. Knowing what my kids knew and what these kids did not know, there was an eternity between them. These kids should be taught, taught about salvation, and to think there wasn't a church here.

As I became better acquainted with the other new people in town, I realized the mothers were just as hungry for the word as the kids. We talked a lot about the Lord. I felt useful to them, I prayed for them. They began coming to the house. I learned the sisters had been in Sunday School as children, but they were not sure of their salvation. After a few classes Bonnie and Phyllis Pond received the Lord. I was on Cloud Nine, thanking the Lord for the opportunity, what a privilege! The kids were very receptive to the

Sunday school in the schoolhouse.

teaching. They were there an hour early now on Sundays. One Sunday it rained, we didn't quite know where we could have classes. With a little inquiry I found the key to the school. The kids were so excited, my kids couldn't believe anyone actually went to school here. We had a great time and had our picture taken on the steps of the school that morning. Since we got permission, we continued to have services and I will have to admit it did feel more like Sunday School. I could keep a little better order and I am sure they learned more with better organization.

It didn't take long for the word to get around town that we were having Sunday School. So many people came and gave us an encouraging word. To their knowledge there had never been a service of any kind in Yellow Pine. I asked Harry Withers about it and he said, "No I don't think there has been. No one has ever been interested, but I agree we do need one." Even Uncle Tom was agreeable. "These kids need to be in Sunday School."

I thought it was remarkable that there was that much support. The people who ran the taverns were very supportive. They were all disappointed that it was only going to last a short time, so was I. The kids were also disappointed. The townspeople began talking to us about moving up there, I agreed it would be wonderful, but I couldn't do that. I had a home in Oregon and I had a son who was going to high school this fall. They had a solution for every objection I had. Finally I just said "Absolutely not." Money was a big problem. I was paying for my place down there. I didn't have the money to move. "No." Move from a four bedroom, modern home on an acreage. "Absolutely not." How in the world would I do laundry for eight people?" That's impossible. There is no church here, "Nope."

Leave my family, "I can't." There is no doctor, no electricity, how would I heat a house, where would I live? There is no way this can be done, not with a family like mine, no sir.

Mom was getting very nervous about this, she sat quietly listening. I knew she was getting worried. She need not be.

We continued our teaching, it seemed so right. I was going to hate leaving these babes in the faith. I talked to them about continuing, with one of them teaching the little kids. But they were not receptive to that. I was afraid this little work would go down the drain. It really didn't matter if it was little.

Where two or more are gathered in HIS name, HE will be there also. Didn't I read that the very angels in heaven rejoice if just one soul is saved. It really didn't matter how small the work was. June 28, Mom was getting anxious to get going. She wanted to stop and see Ed and Lois in Boise. We packed up and with another tearful good-bye we drove off down the road. The people were standing in the road waving to us. The tears rolled down my face. I was leaving behind something that we all loved. The kids were not coaxing, and they were trying not to cry. Mom was silent. I was trying to keep the tears out of my eyes so I could see.

There was something I was experiencing that was unfamiliar to me. Some thing deep down inside. All I could do was cry. I was trying to push it back. It was like someone was calling out to me. I didn't want to hear what was said. The tears rolled. As time went on it got worse. I have never been so miserable in my life. Am I going crazy? What is that gnawing inside me. What am I supposed to do. I finally had to stop the car. I was sobbing so hard I couldn't drive. Mom and the kids sat looking straight ahead. They didn't say anything to me. They had seen me shed a lot of tears the last few years and they had seen me in agony. They must think this is just another one of those times. They let me cry.

I don't know if I heard Him or felt Him, but I knew He was speaking to me. I was saying silently, "No God no, please don't make me do that. Do you know what you are asking me to give up. Do you know what you are asking me to do, after all God." I got out of the car to walk around. "God are you trying to kill me."

Then I gave in, "Okay God, tell me what you want, just take this terrible agony away." When I got back in the car, I did feel better. Then He began to tell me what He wanted me to do. I argued with Him mentally with the same objections I used verbally with the people back there. There were so many reasons why I couldn't do it. God should understand that. This argument went on and on until we got to Boise. We spent the night with Ed and Lois. I was feeling better, maybe God had forgotten about this. I hope so, it was such a relief. We went to church the next morning with Ed and Lois. God began nudging me again. Then the congregation sang, "I'll go where you want me to go Dear Lord, I'll do what you want me to do." I refused to say those words the first time and again that agony hit me in the chest, I could barely breath. I SANG the words next time. "I'll go where you want me to go Dear Lord," I also sang, "Yes God I will." Then the flood of tears were different. It was a release of self, I gave up self to God. Oh God,is it fair for the kids? Would they be deprived. Oh come on now, the kids would surely side with God on this one, they would be on God's side. I could not fight it anymore. The relief I felt, from giving in. The fight was over.

"Well God," I prayed, "You show me how. There are so many reasons why I can't possibly do this, but if you say I can, I can. You will have to take care of all these things for me. Thank You for taking my agony away." I could feel the heavy load lifting from my shoulders, what a relief. After all, wasn't this the opportunity I had prayed about for the boys? Didn't I see those little kids running around the streets up there who didn't even know the Lord? What about the women who seemed so hungry for the word? Didn't I feel the stress and pressure lift from my back up there? I think I could get well up there. Hadn't I grown up in much this same life style, would it be so terrible for me? Could I really get over this nervous condition and feel happy and content again? Could I be the mother and servant for the Lord I had hoped to be?

There were so many questions about how to do all these things and a panic would strike me in the chest. I would instantly turn it over to the Lord.

Where would we live? How could I get along without electricity and water in the house, a washer and dryer? How would I get wood for winter? Where could we hold services in the winter if the school was not available?

How could we move? Where could we get the money to move? What about my house? What about all the furniture and other things we could not move? The kids would need warmer clothes. WHAT ABOUT A DOCTOR??? Panic.

Did I really want to leave my family? (This would be terribly hard.) How could I tell my friends? Mary, could I even get along without her? How would Billy go to high school?

I had only been a Christian three years, I had been studying for seven years. I couldn't take on this responsibility. I was just a babe in Christ: leading others to the Lord, teaching children, being responsible for the spiritual leadership of the community, and their salvation.

"No, not I but the Lord."

I knew all these things would have to be settled and it was very hard to not think and worry. I had said yes to God, now I had to go. I knew beyond a shadow of a doubt that He wanted me to go, so I was sure He would have all the answers to these problems. In the night I would awaken, and there was a small voice there telling me, "Don't be stupid, you can't do this, it's crazy to even think about it. Forget it. There are too many problems to this ridiculous plan. Who do you think you are, that the Lord would do all these things for you, this is just selfish to try to run away from your problems. Forget it and settle down."

Thinking about it there in the night, I knew everything he said was true. Who do I think I am.

"No, no," I cried, "Satan cannot defeat me. I know God is leading me." Just where do I start? I needed to test the waters.

I wrote to Uncle Tom and told him what I wanted to do. Could we rent his house for the winter. If so, how much?

I got a letter back sooner than I ever thought was possible. We could live in the house rent free as long as we needed it.

I wrote to Bonnie Pond about Billy boarding out for school in McCall. She inquired around and learned that several of the kids from Yellow Pine had done this and it cost about $100 a month. We could do that without rent or lights to pay. I talked to Jack and Mary about moving up there and they were so supportive and offered to do anything they could to help me as long as they could come and see us a couple times a year.

That made us very happy. I talked with all my friends, I was shocked that there was so much approval. This made thinking easier. The ones who were not supportive were my family. That was a heartache. Donna understood why it would be better for me, even though she didn't want me to go.

I went to see my doctor in Roseburg, telling him what I was going to do. Before I could finish telling him, he was so excited and raising his voice to me, "Rose this is exactly what you need. This will keep you out of the sanitarium. I was really worried about you, I had done all I could do for you and I knew it wasn't enough. You just have to get out from under all that stress and responsibility. It's killing you. I am so happy for you, the Lord will take care of you if He is sending you there, you can depend on that. I know you must be worrying about the kid's health care. I will give you what you need to administer aid to the children, like penicillin, and give instructions on how to use it. Your kids are healthy, so don't worry. My brother and I are going to the missionary field this year also. We have set up families going to the mission field from our church, just like I am doing for you. You have my blessings. When you get settled up there, visit one of the nearest medical facilities and let them know you are there, then make arrangements with them and they can be ready for any emergencies."

I was feeling a little dizzy when that was over. He stood and when I was going out the door, he gave me a hug and again gave me his blessings. He told me to come in just before I left. He would have everything ready for me. He didn't charge me for medications or any of the supplies or the office visits.

Next the money to move on. Where God, will I get this money. We had an old Plymouth station wagon sitting down by the barn. The motor was shot and it couldn't have been worth anything. One day, while I was doing house work there was a knock at the door. A man asked if I was the owner of that Plymouth. I said yes but it doesn't run. He said, "Will you sell it to me for $500?"

I stammered for awhile and answered, "Yes, but it doesn't run. The motor is shot in it."

He said, "That's fine, I'll be back to pick it up Saturday with the money." He hurried out to his car and drove away. I was stunned. I went back into the house and sat down. I had to think about this. "Oh God, Oh God, thank you so much."

My house, I advertised it for sale, but we didn't have any buyers. Some of the people who looked at it said they couldn't buy it but would like to rent it. I said I would let them know. I took their name and number. That was an ace in the hole. I could at least start moving my furniture and sorting things out that I could take. Mom offered the storage shed in her garage. Perfect, everything seemed to be coming together. It seemed that everyday another major step was made that brought us closer to putting this giant puzzle together. Oh how I praised the Lord. Many of my friends were calling everyday to see what the Lord had done that day. It was exciting to be able to testify to so many. Some of my friends couldn't believe that there was still a place in the United States, where there was no electricity. Houses were not modern. Cook on a woodstove. I had a lot of explaining to do. One old fellow from the church, Leroy Gerard and his wife who had been very dear to me for a number of years, just were not going to let us go. It was too dangerous where there was no law enforcement in the town. They were so worried and I finally convinced them to just trust in the Lord.

In packing the bare essentials I knew how much room I had in our car and Jack and Mary's pickup. I just didn't know how I was going to get along without a lot of my things. I did want to take my sewing machine. Just how we got all that stuff on top of my car and in his VW pickup I don't

That trusty old Ford.

know. By the time we had the furniture etc. in Mom's storage (several friends and Donna and Darrell helped us with that), we were ready to get down to serious business in packing vehicles. Some boxes were repacked several times because of lack of space but we got it all in and were ready to go. When I told everyone good-bye, it was a sad time. When it came time to tell Mom and Donna and family good-bye, it was very hard. We couldn't say good-bye but with promises of coming to visit, the leaving was bearable. Oh it hurt to drive away. It hurt all the way to Idaho, to Yellow Pine. It still hurts thinking about it.

Jack was anxious to get unloaded so he could go fishing. Mary stayed with me so the boys could go with Jack. Mary was a big help unpacking. We were all pretty excited, the peace was not long coming back after we got settled in. To our great surprise and delight, our woodshed was full of good dry wood. Uncle Tom told us the Pond brothers and their boys were responsible for filling it up. There were eight cords of wood, I was so pleased. Mary and I made a special trip up town to the store to thank them.

We did have a lot of company up there. So many people were fascinated with this little village that was not modernized. They didn't know a place like this still existed. Good fishing and good hunting in this beautiful country. But it was soon discovered by everyone and we had a barrage of people coming and going all the time unless we were snowed in. In the winter the roads got pretty bad from snow or mud and it kept a lot of people out. Of course this was good for the businesses. They couldn't keep enough groceries on the shelves or gas in the pumps. The Ponds had to make a trip out nearly every day for supplies. They were also trying to get some ahead for when the roads closed in the winter.

The Ponds were very congenial and were there for any and all the needs of the people. The older residents seemed pleased that there were new people and services. Getting their mail every day, having fresh meat at the store, fresh produce and fruit, fresh bread, and pastries, ice cream, all kinds of candy; they didn't have to leave town now to get up town services.

These old timers loved to watch people and what was going on up town. There was someone sitting on the bench in front of the store at all times. They loved to visit too, as long as they could visit up town, they didn't much care for people coming to visit them at home. They may not answer the door.

As soon as we were settled, I made a trip out to McCall to talk to the school officials. I did inform them we would have four kids in the Yellow

Crossroads in center, white building on right is the church.

Pine School and one would come to McCall as a freshman in high school. They gave me some names of possible room and board places for Billy. The first one I contacted was the one we settled on. The family of the chief of police in McCall, Bill Acker. Their children were quite small. They had a big German Shepherd dog. Billy loved dogs so I knew he would enjoy this one. The lady of the house was Rose and her husband was Bill, that should make Billy feel right at home. We got everything worked out and returned to Yellow Pine.

The superintendent came into town to check on how many kids were going to be in school there. They didn't have a teacher hired yet but would get right to that. Seemed that a teacher to teach all eight grades now a days would be hard to find but it was just the opposite, they had a lot of applicants who were anxious for the experience.

The next thing on the agenda was to find a place to have our Sunday School since the school official said we could not have church services in the school. We were disappointed but we were not defeated. I walked from one end of town to the other looking at old houses or buildings. I stopped at an old house that I remembered well, which was owned by Mart and Bonnie Earl.

Their family lived there when I was in Yellow Pine in the forties. They worked at the Yellow Pine Bar and Cafe which was a 24 hour a day job, they were in joint ownership with Murf and Mary Earl. Murf and Mary had one daughter Donna, and Mart and Bonnie had six children; one was in college. I was the keeper of the children in that same house. I cooked for them, kept house and watched after them. This little house held a lot of memories for me.

It sat on the corner across from the hotel facing the Stibnite road. It was obvious that no one had lived or done anything to it for a long time. The old gray building paper was hanging down from the walls. The chimney mortar had broken and was falling off, several of the windows were broken out. The floors were in ruin from water, snow and mud. At least an inch of dirt and dust was on the floor. The doors were hanging and had been left open for a long time. There were papers tacked up on the outside of the building, which indicated the building had been used at one time as a polling place where people came to vote. Everything in the building was filthy. I looked around and said, "I think this will do just fine."

I wrote to Mart and Bonnie in Eagle and asked if we could rent it to hold Sunday services there. A fast answer came back with, "Of course if you can make use of it. Do what you want to it and no we will not charge rent." Well good, now we can get busy.

I found very few that shared my enthusiasm. The kids thought it would be impossible to fix it up. I heard several, "But Mom, are we going to have church there?"

"This is what we have and I'm sure we can make it work." The torn paper came down first and the broom helped a lot. After we got it cleaned up, Billy, Tommy and I made trips to Boise in the station wagon to get wall board, linoleum, paint and whatever else we needed. We had to wait until we got enough donations and offerings which wasn't very much. We got just a few things in one trip. I paid for a lot of it (as much as my budget would allow).

One of our visitors in Sunday School, Iva Kissinger was very impressed with the work and expressed a desire to help. Knowing we had a lot of fixing to do and needed a lot of money, took upon herself the task of going to the bars and taking up collections in town. She first took someone's hat and went into the bars, tapped each person on the shoulder and asked them to donate to the new Sunday School. Somehow she convinced them this was their privilege to be a part of the founding of this church by contributing to the initial work here. She collected well over $100. The next day she had gallon jars sitting in each place of business with a sign on it asking for donations.

I was so surprised and thrilled at the attitude of the people toward the church. They were in support 100%.

Several fellows walked up to the church and asked if they could help. They said they were working for stars in their crown.

I enthusiastically said, "You are more than welcome to work for stars in your crown, but you know where you will have to go to get them."

One tall lanky cowboy by the name of Don Caward said, "You mean you don't give them out here?"

I said, "No but I have a road map that tells how to get where they will be given out."

"We will be anxious to see it. How about us tearing down that partition and that old chimney?"

"That would be just great, I really appreciate you fellows coming here to help. You surely will be blessed."

Don Caward and Harry Withers, 1966.

The townspeople seemed to be feeling a part of this work. I was so thankful. That spirit continued until the work was done. One would come one day to paint or sweep or put in windows. They did most of the work. I was always there to help or to encourage. Many of the people came by to see how things were going.

I never passed up an opportunity to invite them to Sunday School. I made it sound very casual and expressed my sincerity in wanting them to come. "This is your church, you know. It is so great that you all are supporting it. I can't tell you how much it means to me and the Lord." Yes, they felt they were a part of the church and they supported it wholeheartedly; except one man, a hired bartender who did his best to talk the guys out of helping. He said, "Run her out of town, she is going to ruin this place. Before long we won't have any bar business." They laughed at him and eventually he came up to help also.

Don Caward brought up a little crew to put the stove in and a pipe through the roof with an insulating box around it. They laid the floor covering also.

We all worked long hard hours. A lot of projects were started and some of the men came along to help. One job the boys and I did, I was wishing for help, was putting up the sheets of wall board. When I went out to get it I gave the room measurements. In putting it up we found that it was a foot too short. On which end? The decision was made to patch the bottom where the seats would hide it. I made another trip to town and got the other foot cut and ready to nail up. I knew it would be a disaster if I tried to cut it. It was never mentioned but maybe they were only being polite.

One of the men working in the mining operation stopped by the church one day and said there were some old theater seats at Stibnite. He gave me the name of the guy to contact. The owner said we could have anything we could use up there, because it was only going to be burned. They had held services there at one time and the furnishings were still there. This was exciting but how do I get these things down here? I had a problem asking anyone to do something for us, if I could possibly find a way to do it, I did it. If they wanted to help, they would come and do it. I was wishing someone would help with this. Since they didn't come around, I figured this was my baby. I would figure a way to get it done. I needed a pickup or a truck. No sooner thought about and it was available. A fellow who was working at the mine and staying in Yellow Pine for the summer had a flatbed in his yard. I asked him if I could use it to take to Stibnite to get the seats. "Oh yes of course," he said he had to work or he would help. I told him my boys would help so that was okay.

Well I had driven a lot but always a car or pickup, not a flatbed truck and not on a road like that. The road was narrow, the flatbed was wide. The road was so rough you couldn't go over ten miles an hour, or the truck would nearly bounce off the road, in places it was straight down to the creek. I felt like I was falling off most of the time, but with much prayer we got up there, found the building and looked everything over. We got what we needed. We began piling it on the truck. It was not an easy chore for any of us, the boys really worked. We put the seats, blackboard, pulpit, benches, chairs, charts, maps of the Holy Land and a few more things we could use. It was piled high. We had brought rope at the suggestion of the man who owned the truck. We tied it over and around and up and down and every which way.

We had an exciting trip back, I thought the truck was too wide for the road. I did not feel a bit safe for myself and the boys. They had not worked on the roads for a long time and they were terrible, especially on the upper end. Those ruts were so deep once you got into them you couldn't get out. I didn't try to stay out, I just stayed in them because I felt a little safer.

The truck rocked over the sidling road where it was the farthest over the cliff. I was sure I could feel the truck tipping over. My stomach came up in my throat, I held my breath and prayed until we rocked back the other way. I fought an impulse to close my eyes. This was too dangerous to watch. I didn't say a word to the boys about being afraid, but they weren't talking so they were probably just as afraid as I was. When we got off the steep part of the road, I could breathe again. I crept all the way back to Yellow Pine. I backed the truck up to the door of the church and told the boys let's go home, I am exhausted, we can come back in the morning to unload it.

Now it looked like a church. It worked like a church. The seats were pretty rough; they had been sitting for several years. We sanded some of the rough places and the ladies sat in those. The boys didn't care. We were very proud of our church. We then started on the two back rooms for the Sunday School rooms. We got tables and benches and cleaned some more. We finally had it ready.

On a Sunday afternoon, we held a grand opening. We put signs all over town advertising it. The kids had their mothers help them bake cookies and the girls served the guests. We had a great turnout. Many of the weekend travelers saw the signs and came out. We had all our books displayed and everything was set up as for church. Our attendance was far beyond what we expected. We had so much encouragement from everyone, we were all so pleased. We were very fortunate to have the community support we did, this was to be cherished as it is the greatest asset a church can have. I know the LORD was pleased.

Until we had the church ready to go, we met in people's homes and outdoors if the weather was nice, or in the church if there was room among the mess. It was awkward after we knew we were going to have a place to meet. Our meetings consisted mostly of worship, singing and prayer.

Rose on the church steps before renovation.

One Sunday after church.

When we began having our services in the church, everyone met in the main room. We had prayer, song service, learning the books of the Bible, memorizing scripture. And we had a lecture or devotion, I refused to call it a sermon. I chose a subject and studied it, got references, and spoke about it hoping to make it simple enough to reach the little ones but challenging for the older ones. It was a difficult thing to do.

I was glad when the time came that we were ready to set up classes. I went out and got material for the teachers to use. They had never done this before so they needed a lot of encouragement but they were very devoted and did a wonderful job. I realized my kids needed a talking to; they had to set an example in class. They were the only ones who had been in church before, so everything was funny to them. They laughed when the little ones would say or do something a little out of place, only because of not knowing proper church etiquette, and knowing nothing about the Bible. If we had share time, you never knew what they were going to say like, Mom and Dad had a fight or Daddy got drunk. I'll admit it was funny but we couldn't tolerate Merrill and Tom erupting in laughter, then all the kids would laugh. It was rude to laugh at someone so serious. We talked about that, they could be the cause of me losing control of the class. I had to control my own, even if I had to embarrass them. These little kids watched everything. It had a double message. It did help the other kids to understand what was acceptable and not acceptable in Sunday School.

Some of the mothers asked what stories their kids told in church after they got wind of this. I told them, "I won't believe what he tells me about you, if you promise not to believe what he tells you about me."

Merrill slumped down in the seat where he thought I couldn't see him and wrote a note to his fishing buddy about where to go after church. When I saw this happen, I stopped talking and looked at him, until everyone in the room turned to see what I was looking at. When I quit talking, Merrill knew something was wrong. He raised up to see if he was the target. He said, "Sorry" and I got back to the lesson. A time or two I had to go further with the discipline. None of the other kids wanted to be disciplined after that. They were much more attentive in classes here than in school. Some of them were impossible for parents to control, but they never gave us a problem.

My kids played another role in the church, they were friends of all the kids. All the boys hung together, and they knew my kids couldn't go fishing or play until after church. They all came to church with the boys.

The girls brought all the little girls with them as they all played together. So it became pretty well ingrained in all of them that church came first.

Curious travelers stopped in to observe, and they were impressed; they wanted to help us with materials and books, etc. Some sent song books, some sent Bibles, literature, chalk, crayons, tablets and all kinds of reading. One church sent us Sunday School papers, the leftovers from their classes. In fact we had a library from all the donations.

We left the church open at all times for anyone to come in to pray or have a private time alone with God, to read or to take out books. We never lost a thing, in fact we gained far more that way. I am proud to say we never had any vandalism. Other places in town did, like the school had all the windows broken out by a set of twin rock throwers. Several homes complained of the same thing.

Red Johnson, who lived in the alley, came out one night shooting his gun up in the air. When everyone turned out to see what was wrong, he said someone was throwing rocks on his tin roof late at night. We knew who it was and they swore he was shooting at them. He was mad at kids after that but he didn't seem to blame my kids, they stopped to visit him a lot.

After having the experience I did in Oregon, I was not in the least anxious to put a name on the church. There was something about a name that I felt obligated us to by-laws and non-scriptural doctrine. There was no reason for a name except for the benefit of people going through town. We opted to put up a cross on the peak of the roof, that was all that was needed.

I had firm convictions that we were there to serve God.

I followed the scriptures as I read them. A name was given to a church to identify the location of a body of believers.

(Romans: Chapters 14 and 15: 1-7.)

We did not discuss do's or don'ts in our classes but we did follow Rom: 14 and 15:1-7 as our guide and as our example to others. I don't believe we should be concerned about what is or isn't a sin in another Christian, only ourselves. There is always the chance that we could cause someone to stumble and fall. I felt like we should let God do the judging especially since He sent Jesus to die on the cross for the sinner.

When Phyllis and Bonnie felt like they were ready to teach, we split up the classes. I took the oldest class in the main meeting room. The classes there consisted of lecturing more or less and some of the people from town found that they also benefited from these lectures. I chose a subject and studied it in depth and spoke on it. I always felt unqualified, but the people who heard, were challenged and grew in the Lord, so it must have been what the Lord wanted and expected from a Christian such as I, with a vision for HIS WORK. The Lord called Gideon, He ignored Gideon's plea of inadequacy. "Go in the strength you have and save Israel. Am I not sending you."

"But Lord," Gideon asked, "how can I, my clan is weakest and I am the least in my family."

The Lord said, "I will be with you." Judges 6:14 (in part)

The Lord usually calls the lowly, rather than the mighty to act for Him.

God can enable us to perform far beyond our natural abilities. All He asks from us is to be willing to go. He can do the rest.

———

We had a beautiful Indian summer that year. The snow held off until way after Thanksgiving. The roads were open late and I made a trip out to bring Billy in every weekend regardless of the roads, as there was snow up on the summits. I said a prayer for a safe journey, and He honored my request. He saw us through some very bad road conditions, mud, snow and ice. There were times I thought this was going to be impossible, but that red '59 Ford station wagon was a hard one to whip, with an angel on each fender, how could we lose. Sometimes I gave those angels a merry little ride. I missed Billy being at home, and I know he missed us. That being a new school, new kids, but he never complained. He lived in three different homes that winter and that wasn't easy for him. I guess he knew we were committed and were going to stick it out. The kids at Yellow Pine were having the time of their lives, and I wanted Billy to join them on weekends.

Two horses owned by Ponds were pastured on Uncle Tom's property and the kids had free reign to ride. The boys were told they had to take good care of them and they did. They had so much fun with those horses, it made their summer especially great. They were given a lot of privileges because they could be trusted.

The Ponds and other men took Tom and Merrill on trips with them to Boise or McCall to pick up supplies. They took them hunting or on horseback trips or fishing. This was an answer to prayer to be sure. They also went wood cutting quite often. I felt so good about the experience they were getting.

The little ones were happy. They were free, no longer underfoot and tied to my apron strings. They were under strict supervision, and they accepted that. Being strict with the kids allowed them freedom they would not have had otherwise. I had to know where they were and what they were doing. They were finding a new world out there. My life was so much better for it. I worked hard but I was content because the family was happy.

One Saturday afternoon I asked Murf if I could set up shop and cut my kids hair in the back room. He said, "Sure, you can use the barber chair back there if you want." Murf had a power plant to run his freezers and refrigerators. I could use the electric clippers there. I had some hand clippers I brought from Oregon. I had planned to use them but I think the kids threw them away after I pulled the hair on their necks out.

The kid's friends came with them when they came in to have their haircut. They thought that was pretty neat, so they rushed home and asked their mothers if I could cut their hair. Before the afternoon was over I cut 27 heads of hair. Twenty-six kids and Uncle Tom; he insisted he pay and gave me a dollar.

We continued to make two trips every weekend until way after Christmas, the roads stayed passable. We just didn't have any problems unless we met Warren Campbell hauling a Stibnite house out on his truck. We were pretty safe. No, he never caused an accident unless it would have been frightening someone to death. We knew when he was hauling out and we made allowances for that.

He drove fast where he could and made good time, sometimes taking out two a day, 75 miles one way. This is hard for people to believe, especially after traveling the roads back there. There are overhanging cliffs and rock bluffs, where he had to jack up the house and move it to one side of the truck. He had several barrels of water in the house that he balanced with. He put his barrels on the short side to keep the house from tipping. Sometimes he could only go a few miles before he had to stop and do it all again, shifting it over to the other side, then move the barrels. Dinger Gray and Sunny Yelton worked for Warren and the three of them did it all. There was a lot of work involved in getting the house ready to go on to the truck, then the unloading. Most of these houses were three bedroom houses. They were well built homes, the government financed the building project, to have housing available for the mine workers.

They came out in beautiful condition, considering the age of the houses, being built in the early forties. Warren only lost two houses, one just on the other side of Yellow Pine and one on Lick Creek.

An area in McCall where many of the houses are located is called Little Stibnite. There must be 50 or more houses there. Warren moved out the hospital and another large two-story house that he cut in half and made two trips. They are still standing some 30 years later.

Stories were in eastern papers and magazines. It was something that will or should go down in history. A tremendous feat this was. Warren Campbell should be recognized for this undertaking.

I was going out one Friday to pick up Billy for the weekend, and we were going up Lick Creek summit when I noticed my gas was gone. I got out and looked under the car and a little drizzle of gas was dripping down on the ground, probably from a rock. I turned the car around facing down hill. One of Warren Brown's logging trucks came barreling down the road. I was glad I was out of his way. Most of the drivers are very courteous and helpful. They were hauling out of Zena Creek.

He pulled off the road in front of me and got out. I told him what happened. "There is nothing I can do here, but I'll pull you down to the camp and the mechanic will help you there."

I said, "Fine, that's great." He already had the chain on my car and on his truck. He said, "Jump in, there is another truck coming up and I want to get to the bottom of the grade before I meet him."

We jumped in and the way we went. We were so close to the truck I couldn't see anything but the back of the truck. I was trying to steer, but it was totally wearing me out. I could barely hold on to the wheel because we were going so fast and so close. I couldn't even guess how fast we were going but it was fast. I would think that speed was suicide on this road. It was steep, narrow and dangerous. I hoped he knew what he was doing. I wasn't walking too straight when I got out of the car. The driver unhooked the chain, I thanked him and he was gone.

The mechanic came out of the shop, he wasn't in such a hurry. He looked at the hole and he told me to go up to the cookhouse and get a bar of soap. He rubbed the soap on that hole and put some gas in it. It worked, he gave me about five gallons of gas and said, "That will take you to Yellow

Pine. Get Tom Nicholas and he will fix it up for you." I offered to pay and he wouldn't hear of it. Tom had the hole fixed in no time. I still made it out to get Billy and bring him home for the weekend.

In late fall when everyone was scrambling to get their elk before the end of the season, we got the fever also. The kids and I went out scouting around to find a place to hunt.

I talked to Dad about where to go. He said, "Well it's too early yet, wait a bit longer and you won't have to go so far. I'll let you know when the time is right. In a few weeks he came to me and said the elk had crossed ———— —— and they were going down to the —— —— for the winter. "If you go out to the —— ranch and watch along the road you will see the tracks. They don't all come across at once, so what you will have to do is follow the tracks of the elk that came down and go back up and you will find some elk. Go now, the time is right."

Billy and I dressed for it and left town shortly, we did exactly like he said to do, there was a lot of climbing but we were in pretty good shape, it didn't bother us much. It was cold and there was about six or eight inches of snow. We saw where the elk came out of the timber and went down just as Dad had said. We back-tracked and we found the place where they had been laying down, we walked around and found fresh sign from other elk and where warm bodies laid in the snow. We hunted for several hours up there and we saw the tracks where they had milled around. We circled the area, we sat and waited but we did not see an elk, even though we felt like we were so close. It was getting late and darkness was setting in, it was getting colder by the minute. We decided we had better start down, but darn it was hard to leave.

We walked and walked. The snow was getting crustier all the time and it was hard to keep our feet under us. We decided we had better find a shortcut but that meant going down a very steep hill. Bill started down hopping over the sage brush and staying on his feet. I watched him thinking I could probably do that. He was ahead of me now by quite a ways. I picked up my speed and tried hopping a sagebrush and down I went. I tried to stop but there was no stopping. I held my gun up in the air and kept on going. I was catching up to Bill now. I yelled at him, "Look out below, here I come." He stopped and turned to see what I wanted, just as I was flying by. He raised his gun, sat down and away we went gaining speed all the way. I seemed to be getting a little colder on the back side, but I was numb and I couldn't really tell what was going on. It was feeling mighty suspicious when I went over the sage brush, but I couldn't stop. We ended up at the bottom about the same time. We stood up and felt our back side, neither of us had any thing covering us in the back. We both laughed and took our coats and wrapped them around us and went home. We had so much fun we didn't care about an elk.

Emma Bryant came to church quite often, it was so good to have her. I had been down to see her several times, we always had such a good time visiting about the history of the country here. I believe she went way back to about 1913 when her husband first came in here and fell in love with the country. She said it was all big Yellow Pine trees then with very little underbrush.

Melvin, Emma's late husband then brought his father in and he loved the country and eventually they went in partnership with Al Hennessey and went into the fox business. They built their home in 1922. Emma said the fox business was a failure, but they never left the country. Emma told about her husband driving the first Model T Ford into Yellow Pine. Many of the children and some of the adults had never seen a car before.

The road from Cascade to Yellow Pine was built in 1917.

A.C. Behne came to the Yellow Pine basin in 1902 and was founder of Yellow Pine. He had the first homestead and he had the town platted about 1924. The streets and their names are largely as he visualized them then.

Behne was not the type man you would picture in Yellow Pine.

He subscribed to the Sunday *New York Times*, a lover of classical music, he was an opera buff, sports enthusiast, and he grew roses. Behne was convinced that someday Yellow Pine would be a mountain metropolis. He died in 1945 and never gave up his dream for Yellow Pine. He rarely left town.

Emma Bryant came to the house before she went out for the winter. She brought me her radio to use for the winter. That was very special to me, I appreciated her generosity. She was so much a lady to have lived in this wild country most of her life. In fact she was a role model for me. She could be as tough as she had to be, nothing was too hard for her. She lived alone on her ranch on Johnson Creek during summer months for many years. She was a very stylish well-groomed lady. She never had an enemy. She cared for people, none was better than another. She loved the Lord and was quite an inspiration to many of us. Emma came to town when there was a celebration, she was very loyal to her home town.

Lafe and Emma Cox were great people. They owned Cox's Dude Ranch about ten miles out of Yellow Pine. I had known them since we lived at Snowshoe Mine. They were living at Mile High and Clark and Beaulah, Lafe's parents were operating the Dude Ranch on Johnson Creek. They are a family that has been highly respected around the country. My personal relationship with them are precious memories to me. Clark and Beaulah Cox bought the Dude Ranch in 1927. The parents are gone now but Lafe and Emma operated it until they sold in 1974. They are still on Johnson Creek, on the old Hanson homestead where they are spending their retirement after 50 years in the guest ranch business. They also have attended all big celebrations in Yellow Pine and supported the community whenever possible. It seems important to them to keep their acquaintances there.

The Reed family history goes back to 1921 when they moved into town to put their eight children in school. Mr. Reed, better known as Dead Shot, had quite a reputation and many stories were passed along through the years. They moved from Emmett to the Reed Ranch on the South Fork which was a homestead. There is evidence of it being quite an operation. I guess they grubbed their living out of the land, to the extent of making the kids shoes out of elk hide. I knew two of the sons, Pat and Billy. Pat was pretty sensitive about the stories that were told about his dad, saying most of them were not true. In respect for the sons, I will not repeat the stories.

Mrs. Reed and several kids moved to Yellow Pine in the winter to put the kids in school. They lived in a wall tent all winter. They had to be tough people, that must have been cold. Pat Reed bought Uncle Tom's house after he passed away.

One Sunday when we were getting ready for church, it was nice and warm in there and the kids were close, waiting for the bell to ring. Lee Green came running in the church and said, "Two of Dad's hunters are coming to church today." I froze on the spot.

"Lee you are kidding me."

"No I'm not. They are coming up the road now. See."

Well I had got used to speaking to women in the church but strange men. Oh boy!! I have to change my message. I can't speak to them on divorce. Oh I didn't have time, they are almost here. What will I do. One of the first things I was taught and I verified it by the scriptures that a woman is not to lead men in a church service. A real panic was setting in. There is no one else to do it. The door was opening. I walked to the door and introduced myself and welcomed them. Both said they had gone to church in the past but had not recently and they thought it would be nice to visit Yellow Pines little church while they were here. I told them how glad I was to have them, and I walked up to the front of the church. I asked one of the kids there to ring the bell and the doors flew open and a rush of kids came in the door and sat down in their favorite seat and became instantly quiet. Our little dog Smokey right behind them and he laid at the kid's feet.

Bonnie and Phyllis came in, saw the two men, greeted them and raised their eyebrows at me. They knew how I felt about teaching men.

We started our song service and in every spare breath I had I prayed that the Lord would give me the words He wanted me to say. I need boldness too God, I am so afraid.

After the little kids went to their classes and we had prayer. I began. I was so glad I had studied this subject well.

I was as prepared as I could be. Now God please help me.

I had a good audience, they hung onto every word I said. God gave me the boldness to bring the scripture to these people and tell them what the Bible said about divorce.

I could see that these men were hungry for the word. I was shocked, that was just like saying sickum to me. I told these people that the only way we were going to keep our children from the vices of this world was to keep them in church. Not send them, take them, begin now to teach them what the Bible says about how to be Godly men and women. I really got fired up and ran overtime. I was shocked at myself, but I thanked God over and over again.

The men were very polite and thanked me for the message and said they were going to give that a lot of thought. I thanked them for coming and saw them to the door and crashed into a seat.

The next fall when the men returned for their hunt, they looked me up, it was on a Saturday. One of the men at the time of their earlier visit to the church was getting a divorce. When he got back home, he and his wife worked things out. They are going to church and going to stay together. The other man said he hadn't taken his kids to church in years; but after this message, he went home and talked to his wife and they agreed things had to change—they had to get back in church. Since they were here he hadn't

Steve, Janet, and Merrill with Chinook.

Steve in front of our cabin.

missed a Sunday. I said, "Praise the Lord. He took the message home to your heart didn't He." They stopped to see me every time they came into town after that and gave me an update. If I was gone, they left a message for me. I still say "Praise the Lord and maybe it isn't so wrong for a women to teach, when there isn't a man to do it. God works in mysterious ways."

Home Sweet Home—Uncle Tom's cabin.

Chapter 14

"The Lord's Work"

1962

A day in the life of a country woman starts early when it is mighty cold. Starting the fire to get the house warm for the kids when they get up, then to fix breakfast. The kids being outside so much had a big appetite, so we had a good hot breakfast. We had sourdough hot cakes quite often. The kids loved them. I always fixed a little extra for Uncle Tom and to make cake or cinnamon rolls. After the kids went to school Uncle Tom dropped in for coffee, but would never turn down a pancake. He was anxious to see what else I was making out of the sourdough. He would drop in again when he smelled it in the oven.

I had the coffee pot on and we sat down to visit. He had never seen anyone make pastries out of sourdough before and he tagged me as the sourdough queen.

I always enjoyed feeding him, he loved to eat, especially deserts. He didn't bake anything, but he sure made good spudnuts.

He seemed happy to have us there, he got along fine with the kids, he had won them all over or shall I say they had won him over. I had given them plenty of warning about him being so particular so they were pretty good.

While the dish water was heating, I went through the house, making beds, picking up clothes, sweeping floors. When the dishes were done it was time to start lunch, if it was cold out I usually fixed a hot lunch. The kids walked home from school which was only about a quarter mile. After lunch dishes were cleaned up, Janet, Steve and I walked up town to wait for the mail. Bonnie and Phyllis took a break from the store and we went for coffee. We always had plenty to talk about. The kids went to play with the Pond kids.

Before I went home I picked up groceries for supper. Since we didn't have a fridge, we couldn't keep much ahead. In one window in the kitchen, the glass had been taken out and a box was built into it. The box opening was inside the house, the box itself was on the outside so things could be kept cool but still be accessible from the inside. It kept things cool most of the time—it was insulated well. During the day in the winter, unless it was very cold it kept well and at night we set things inside, sometimes we just opened the door to the box, to regulate the temperature.

Uncle Tom told about a bear coming, sometime back, to that window because he smelled bacon. He tore the box off the wall, ate everything in it and then was coming into the house through the hole. The man who lived there then had to shoot the bear. The kids were all eyes when he was telling the story. Uncle Tom told the kids, "I want to tell you something that may save your life someday. If you come up on a bear you never know what he will do. They may attack you or they may run away. If one comes after you, he will stand up before he charges, wait until he does and get a good shot at him in the throat. If you hit him anyplace else it won't kill him because he has so much fat the bullet can't penetrate, it will just make him mad and then you are in for it. If you hit him in the throat that will drop him quick.

This bit of advice did save Merrill's life one day when he was hunting, a bear barreling down the hill, saw Merrill and whirled and came after him. Merrill stood still, he thought the bear would go on by, the bear stood up just in front of Merrill and was charging. Merrill raised his gun and shot, he hit him in the throat and dropped him just a few feet from him. He said it was quite a thrill, but he doesn't want to do it again.

The house was comfortable year around as it was well insulated in the walls. The one big bedroom where the kids slept was log and that was very well insulated. Whoever built that part of the house knew how to put logs together. However, in the loft there was sawdust about six inches thick (which was used for insulation when they had nothing else) and it drizzled down into the bedroom. It got in the beds and on the floor, it was a mess. I remembered seeing some ore bags in Stibnite that had not been used. The bags were about a fifty pound size bag, which was several thicknesses of heavy paper. I got permission to get some of these bags and hauled them home. I opened them up and stapled them to the ceiling, overlapping them to keep the sawdust from falling through, which also doubled as insulation.

When we heated the room at night and shut the door it stayed warm all night. I'm sure the house would never pass a fire inspection, but I doubt that any back here would.

The kids changed their clothes as soon as they came home from school, got in the wood, split kindling, carried water and filled the gas lantern. Rosana helped me in the house, with meal preparation, shopping, paying bills, keeping records and all the other household chores. The boys went off to play until I called them to eat. Since we lived down under the hill from town, a holler didn't go far. I had a signal though, two long honks on the car horn. Just like two long rings on the telephone. That brought them home. Everyone in town knew that signal. Uncle Tom didn't mind as he knew it was the dinner bell. We used this signal wherever we went, to call everyone together, fishing, hunting, hiking or whatever. It worked very well. Occasionally I asked one of the kids to give the signal, they couldn't seem to do it right. I tried to show them but they couldn't do it the way I did, it could be mistaken for an ordinary car honk. Seldom did the kids come in if someone else honked, it didn't get their attention, they just didn't hear it. Like on the old telephones—if your ring wasn't long enough it was mistaken for a short. This may sound very trivial, but it wasn't as we used it in emergencies also. If someone got hurt and I had to take them to the hospital, the kids had to know where I was. If I wanted to call them in because we had guests from out of town, that was the only way to let the kids know.

After the dishes were done in the evening, we built up the fire in the front room and opened the kids room to get it warm. Then we sat around the fire and talked or read, the little ones would play games or color. The older ones usually had some project they worked on, they loved doing leather craft.

About 8:30 they got washed up and got ready for bed. When it came time for prayers it reminded them of something they wanted to tell me or something that had happened that day. When one would open up the sharing time, then they all wanted to share. That usually took an hour or so and then they were ready for bed.

I laid out my books on the kitchen table, I got everything in order so I wouldn't be interrupted. I built up the kitchen fire, pumped up the lantern and sat down to study. At times I had four or five lectures I was working on, finding information from my Jameson, Fausset and Brown commentary and different versions of the Bible comparing one with another. Mom loaned me her Amplified that Donna had given her. I used it a lot because I seemed to be able to translate my writings into a more understandable form for people unfamiliar with the Bible. I loved reading or studying when the fires were popping and the lantern was purring. I could hear the rush of the East Fork just below the house. An occasional owl or coyote broke the silence of the night. This was something I looked forward to more than anything. It was such a peaceful time. On designated evenings, usually Mondays, I wrote letters home. Family and friends were all curious about this kind of life and I enjoyed telling them about it. I wrote about what was happening up here, what I did, what the kids did, and what was happening in the church and community. The letters were passed around. I wrote one letter as a continuation of the one before. Sometimes 20 pages were stuffed in an envelope.

We covered all the windows with a heavy see-through plastic. Two layers, one on the outside and one on the inside. We couldn't feel a draft through them at all. One evening while we were sitting by the fire in the front room, I looked up and saw a rat silhouetted between the two plastics and the glass. It was sitting down like a cat looking at us. It wasn't the least bit afraid, I suppose it was enjoying the heat. It was a perfect picture with the moon shining behind it. We tried several times to frighten it away but it would not leave. It probably had been there many times before, enjoying the heat while I slept in the room.

The next day I borrowed a trap from Uncle Tom, he showed me how to set it. I took it up in the attic with a little bait on it. That night shortly after the kids had gone to bed, they heard it snap and then a squeal. They called to me and when I went in there, the rat in the trap was hanging down outside the window. Blood was dripping and running down the window. The kids ran screaming from the bedroom. We shut the door and waited until it was not moving anymore. The boys and I went out and pulled the trap out of the attic and threw it down on the ground. We went back into the house. I covered the window with a heavy blanket so they wouldn't have to look at the blood. After that it wasn't easy to get them back to bed. They had all heard too many ghost stories about dripping blood, and they were spooked. But finally everything settled down and they went to sleep. They wouldn't let me take the blanket off the window for a long time. They thought they could see the blood. I shuddered when I went out the next day to clean the blood off the window. I still shudder when I think of it. I had to be "tough" for the kids sake, not showing my repulsion at such things. I

340

insisted the boys take the rat out of the trap, wash it and return it to Uncle Tom. I had all the rat blood I could handle.

Uncle Tom had some old wallpaper that was an off-white color with branches and red cardinals on it. Since I had been fixing up the house, he thought I might be able to use it. I stapled the paper on two walls of the front room. Man was it loud, but it sure brightened up that room. I made curtains for the windows and hemmed some old pillow cases and made little doilies for a little table and the treadle sewing machine that sat by my bed. We angled the couch to sit nearer the stove and put the overstuffed chair in front of the stove. There wasn't much room left but we could all sit in the evening. Many evenings Janet and Rosana sat on my bed and played with dolls. Steve and Danny usually sat up to the little table and colored or played with toys of some kind. We had hot chocolate in the evenings around the fire and occasionally we had popcorn or fudge. The older boys liked to do the fudge. One weekend when Billy was home, they were making fudge. It was a big batch, they cooked it for a long time and set it in a pan of cold water to cool. The three of them had their fingers (literally) in the pot. They thought surely it should be cool enough to whip. Bill said, "Oh I know its cool." He stuck his finger in it and pulled it out yelling, "Ouch, Ouch! It's burning, get me some cold water."

Tom said, "Oh Bill, it couldn't be that hot," and he plunged his finger in it. Tom pulled it out yelling like an Indian, "It's burning, get me some water to stick it in." Of course he didn't pass up the chance to taste the fudge, when it cooled he put his finger in his mouth.

Merrill watching all this and noting that they were licking the fudge off their fingers, said, "Oh, you guys are just putting on." Down went his finger into the fudge. He pulled it out screaming, "Get me some cold water." They all began to laugh at the other, jump around and roll on the floor laughing and holding their burning fingers.

The outhouse was very drafty, taking the lantern out didn't warm it up much. The kids hated to go out there when it was so cold at night. Standing there waiting for them I had an idea. I still had some ore sacks, I covered everything in there, the walls, the seat, the floor, the ceiling. Then I found some linoleum pieces at the church and tacked them down on the floor over the paper. Uncle Tom laughed when he saw our fancy outhouse. The lantern did much better to heat it. I stacked snow all around the outside to keep the cold from coming up from underneath. That did the trick. Cozy as a bug in a rug.

One night when we were all sitting around the fire in the front room we heard geese squawking. Thinking they were flying over we didn't think to much about it but the honking continued, we finally went outside to see what was going on. Uncle Tom's whole field was filled with snow geese. It was so foggy we couldn't see them too well, but we did see what they were. Uncle Tom also came out to see them. He said they must have got lost in the fog. There was nothing we could do for them so we went back in the house. They squawked most all night, I thought I could never sleep with all that racket. But when I woke up about daylight they were still there. They didn't leave until the sun came out and burned off the fog. We watched when they finally took off, hoping they would find their way. They were way off course up there in our yard. Later someone told us they landed down on the airport. They found some picking down there, but they finally took off and we didn't see them anymore.

Warren Campbell had a big white malamute dog, that he couldn't keep in town, he was a roamer. We picked him up one weekend when we went out to get Billy. He was a beautiful dog, but I had never seen a dog so big. It was a good thing, some of the kids opted to stay home that day because he covered the whole back seat, from one side of the car to the other, there would not have been enough room for the kids to sit. The little ones got in the way back, and Billy sat in the front. The kids loved that dog, he pulled them around on the sled or skis, he was so playful. He went every place with them. The only bad thing was we had to keep him tied up when he wasn't with the kids. They generally had a leash on him. I knew the people up town would not like him running loose. If he got in a fight with their dogs I wouldn't give a nickel for the other dogs life. There was always the possibility of him running deer, as big dogs in a rural setting are bad for that. We tied him so he could sleep on the back porch. If he saw the kids coming or got excited he stood up on his back legs, and his head was up to the rafters.

He weighed 150 pounds. He didn't eat as much as I thought he would. When I first saw him I thought about how much a small horse would eat. I understand though, after a large dog like this gets his full growth he doesn't need a whole lot of food. He didn't eat much more than our little dog Smokey. The kids had a kitten that was just a month or so old. One morning when the kids took Chinook out for a walk, that little kitten was sitting on top of a fence post. Chinook walked up and touched his nose on the kitten's nose and didn't have to stretch to do it. He was so big and gentle. He didn't

342

bother Smokey at all. I took him up to Smokey when we first got him and demonstrated that this dog belonged here too. He was great with him, he didn't even compete for the top dog position.

Georgia Hathaway and I were going on a horse back ride one morning. When we got up it was snowing but we agreed this shouldn't stop us, it wasn't really cold, and the snow was falling lazily in big flakes. It was so pretty, so quiet. I dressed Janet and Steve up real warm and they went with us. Just before we left the house I remembered my camera. I handed Chinook to Steve and told him to hold him until I got back. Chinook bolted and took off, pulling free of Steve's hand. By the time I got outside he was nowhere in sight. I called and called but he didn't come back. We went on down the road on the horses, thinking he would come back later. Steve was behind Georgia and snuggled up to her back, Janet got on behind me, she laid her head against my back and both were as warm and contented as could be. They helped keep us warm, and it felt so good to have them so close.

The snow was hanging on the limbs of the trees and the road was covered. There was not a sound out there and we kept silent enjoying this so much. The kids were covered with snow, it was getting hard for me to see Steve behind Georgia, he was so covered and she was getting covered also. We rode up the old road to the Carpenter Ranch. We thought we should start back but no one wanted to leave. We rode down into the meadow and made a big circle turning around and went back up the hill toward home. When we got back to the road our tracks were completely covered. The horses seemed to be enjoying this as much as we were. They ambled along, making a little scrape in the snow before their foot came down to make a new track. It was disappointing for us to get back into town. We all would like to have gone on up the road, but we thought about a cup of hot chocolate, it sounded pretty good. About the only way we could get the kids off, was a promise of hot chocolate.

We never saw Chinook again alive. We were told that he did hunt deer and kill them, he would sometimes be gone for two weeks at a time, hunting and killing for food. He caught salmon like a bear and ate them. Salmon kills most dogs, but he may have become resistant from being poisoned and living through it.

When spring arrived, people driving down Johnson Creek spotted him on a log jam by a big rock. He had been shot. We felt bad, but beings he was that kind of dog he would never be any good for anything else. We felt like it was better that way. To this day that big rock is called Chinook Rock.

In the fall we all decided to go Christmas shopping before the roads got too bad. Early one Saturday morning we loaded up and went to Boise. We thought since we were there the kids should see their Granny Gibbons. Some of the boys wanted to stay there instead of going shopping. It was okay with her so I went on into town to do the things I had to do. It was getting dark when I got back to their house and they insisted we spend the night. Uncle Merrill was at Grannies and was insistent that the boys come to stay with him and Latrice. Aunt Betty had come to visit, she was going to stay with her mother but she was visiting Merrill and Latrice during the evening. I drove the kids over to Merrill's place and sat down to visit for awhile. It was getting late and the kids were going down one at a time, little Merrill was the only one up.

Uncle Merrill became angry out of the blue and for no reason that I could see violently began a verbal attack on me in a very aggressive and offensive way. He was throwing accusations at me about not providing a good home for the kids. They were starving and I was not taking care of them. I was giving all my money to the church and there wasn't enough to take care of the kids. I was spending all my time in the bars and leaving the kids alone.

I was so shocked I really didn't know what to say. I sat there and looked at him for awhile and looked at Betty and Latrice. They both hung their heads. I said, "What are you talking about?" He was even more angry and was really throwing some terrible abusive charges at me. "And to put it plainly you don't deserve those kids, and we are going to take them away from you."

Again I looked at Betty and Latrice and asked them, "Do you believe this, do you think what he is saying is true?"

Betty had a peculiar look on her face, a half smile and very uneasy, "I guess I don't know what to believe. You would have to prove it to me that it isn't true."

Merrill was still yelling and cursing me. It reminded me so much of Bill when he acted this way. Little Merrill got up from where he was sitting and came and sat down by me.

I was still dumfounded and bewildered. I sat there looking from one to the other. Why would anyone do this, what was the motive? Then immediately I thought about Edrie's brothers kids and how they were taken away from their mother. Whatever the reason I did not know for a fact, all I heard was what she told me. If they were doing this to me why couldn't they have done this to her, and got others to believe it.

I had always thought Latrice was my friend. Betty and I had one dispute in LA but did that cause all this? I couldn't see a connection to anything, I was getting so angry at all of them, I felt like some vipers were loose in the room. I screamed at them, "I don't have to prove anything to any of you. I want you to get this straight, you will not take my kids away from me. If you ever step a foot inside my door, I'll blast you to kingdom come. I mean that, it would be over my dead body that you would get my kids." I was crying by then and beginning to feel the seriousness of what they were saying. I told little Merrill to go wake the kids and tell them to get dressed, we were leaving. He left the room.

I don't know what Merrill told them but it was no time until the kids appeared in the doorway ready to go. I gathered them up to head them out the door. I was right behind them. They got into the car, not saying a word. I was still crying, little Merrill was sitting in the front seat with me, he said, "Don't worry Mom, if they ever came to take us away from you, I will kill them."

Oh no!! What have they done to that boy, to make him say a thing like that. A new ache began in my heart, a child this young is thinking about killing someone of his father's own family to protect his mother and siblings. A double tragedy for sure. What was I to say to him, I had said nearly the same thing. I tried to pull myself together so as not to be so emotional and said to Merrill. "Merrill it isn't good for us to say that or even think it. We would never do that. There is the law to protect us. We haven't done anything wrong. We do not have to worry."

I was telling him that but I wasn't believing it myself. I was remembering when they took Granny's brothers kids away from their mother after he died and how they were treated. Only one stayed with her, the others scattered. They were older than my kids. The fact remains that they did get them, that scared the heck out of me. Merrill was so much like Bill, I was seeing it all again. I told myself I had to stay ahead of them, think a little faster. The first thing I was going to do was get my kids back home and in our house and God forbid that they would ever come after them. I drove all the way back to the cabin that night. The kids slept all the way. The house was cold, I sent the kids to bed as it was warm in their room. I knew I couldn't sleep so I built a fire in the kitchen stove. I made some coffee and sat with my feet in the oven. At daylight I stoked up the fire, barricaded the doors, took the rifle and set it by the bed and laid down under the covers. I was tired but I couldn't close my eyes. I lay there thinking, planning, what should the next step be. What should I do to assure the safety of my kids? I realized with a start, I had not prayed. "Oh God I am sorry I haven't asked you to help me in this situation. I know you can control all things. May I ask that you never let anyone take my kids away. Please show me what to do. Show me where to start. I am afraid to leave my kids to go out and get help. Please, please show me what to do." I begged.

I got the kids up and we got ready for church. Church seemed to calm the raging fears inside me. I hadn't told anyone yet so I had to wait until after church to talk to Bonnie and Phyllis. I kept the kids at my side all day, they were a very solemn bunch, they were worried. I talked to them about what happened at Uncle Merrill's house. I assured them no one would ever take them from me. They were very insecure right now. They were afraid.

We all went to the store and in the apartment back of the store where Bonnie lived with her family we talked. I began to cry, and poured out the whole story to them. They were shocked and wanted to comfort me. They were willing to do anything to help. I told them, "If you could keep an eye out for anyone of their description coming into town. I won't dare send the kids to school, or take Billy out to McCall." We talked for a long time, it was good for me to share with someone, and pray with someone.

After I left the girls told their husbands and the word spread like wild fire. I was hoping it would, I needed all the support I could get.

Phyllis came down to the house and told me that a visitor in town heard the story and he is a lawyer, Tom Graff was his name. He wanted to talk to me. We walked back up town after we had lunch. Mr. Graff asked questions and after assessing the situation, he told me, "I think they are bluffing. You have to run your own bluff. Get me some paper and I will scratch out a letter for you to write." The letter began with "My friend is an attorney and he has advised me that. . . "

I thanked Tom Graff and all the townspeople as they all came forward to protect us. The Pond brothers came were wonderful as were many others. They offered to let the kids stay with them if I needed to go out, or if we were threatened in any way, they were right here to help. That was a big relief knowing that I had all these people behind me.

I did go out about a week later, because I wanted to know if they had started any kind of action with the county. I went to Cascade to see Larry

Shoenhut, the Prosecuting Attorney. I had known Larry for a long time, since we were both teenagers. He also knew the rest of the family. He said, "I have been expecting you." I knew they had been there.

I asked him if he had seen them. "Yes, they came in with a big story about you and I told them they are just wasting their time. They insisted that I write up a complaint. They wanted me to send in a Social Worker to check out the situation. They also want the house that you live in condemned. Jim and Merrill both came in. I told them that they didn't have a leg to stand on as far as you being indecent or an unfit mother. I told them what you were doing up there and that you were a real asset to the community. I told them they should be proud and not hassle you and the kids. They also said something about splitting the kids up, Merrill and Tom would go to Merrill. I can't remember who was going to take the others. I don't like for that to happen to any family, they are so much better off being together."

"Larry, is there anything I can do to be sure they won't be able to do this?"

He said, "Well anything they do will have to go through me and I won't let it happen. There is one thing you can do, get some letters of character witness from where you lived in Oregon and some from the people in Yellow Pine. You see, what they are going on is that Yellow Pine has a name for being a rough town and they think because you live there you deserve the same reputation. Get me some letters and if they push this we'll have everything we need."

"I will sure do that, so legally they don't have much of a chance if we have all this proof. Now I guess the only thing I really worry about is them just kidnapping the kids."

"No they wouldn't dare do that, but I can write them a letter and tell them you came in to see me, that their fears are unfounded and the kids are doing well, and if there is any further threats from them, the County would take action against them. That is more of a threat than anything and if they want to pursue it they can cause a lot of misery. This might just scare them off. What about the house you live in, what condition is it in?"

I laughed, "They are right it is a shack. But we are warm and comfortable, it serves our needs just fine. It is just this winter that we plan to be there. In a sense we are camping in an old house. I will have two boys in high school next year so I can't stay in there. We have made this a missionary experience. We fixed up an old house for a church and we have been holding services every Sunday. After I move out to McCall, I plan to come in on weekends for services. When the road closes we can't come in of course."

"Yes, I have heard what you are doing in there, first time for Yellow Pine isn't it? Maybe this will change the image of that place in there."

"Well I hope so because Yellow Pine doesn't deserve a reputation like that any more. There are some wonderful people in there. They still have parties and dances there but every one goes, the little kids go dance, just like the old school house dances. The Kissingers, the Coxes, the school teacher Mrs. Shiline and her kids, everyone in town goes. The bars are the only place where the community can meet, and they do. We use the bars for church when it is too cold to get the church warm. We used it for an immunization clinic that Dr. Allen set up last fall. They serve meals to families in there so we prefer to call it "Tom's Place" Most of the women up there go to church, most of them don't drink. Their husbands will have a beer or two there but we just don't have the drunken brawls that used to be there. Now they may get loaded when the women and kids go home, I don't know, but they have respect for women and children. It is different Larry."

"Well it sounds like it is, I'm glad you came in to chat and I am glad to hear about the change up there. Now get me the letters and don't worry, we are not going to let anyone take your kids."

I thanked him and shook his hand and left with a much lighter feeling than when I came.

I drove back into Yellow Pine as I was anxious to get back to the kids. I talked with Bonnie at the store and told her what I had found out. She told me later that people came pouring into the store to find out what had happened. I was not offended that they were all curious about this thing, they gave me their support and they were entitled to know. I went to the house and wrote letters to get character references from Oregon.

Letters were quickly returned, and I was so pleased with the results from friends and officials. I sent copies to Larry but I kept the originals, just in case something like this ever happened again. I still have the letters in my file.

The letters that were sent to Granny and Merrill pretty much squelched the whole thing but they still tried to get something stirred up with my folks. Of all things, the family (mainly Granny and Uncle Merrill), denied having anything to do with it and blamed it on someone else. They finally got to my family, saying it began with them. It all blew over but it was so hard for me to trust them again after that. I was afraid to go around them, not knowing what the next thing may be. That was cruel, threatening the very thing that meant the most to each one of us. They said some very demoralizing things about me, but I don't think anyone who knew me believed them. God fights my battles for me. They have never apologized nor asked forgiveness. I don't feel hateful to them, but I can't go back as friends knowing how little friendship means to them. The kids see them and show their respects and I am glad for that, I hope they never hurt them again.

On the summits it snowed every time it rained down lower. The roads were getting worse every weekend and when all the hunters went out over Lick Creek when the season closed they tore up the roads terribly. They had horse trailers and big four wheel drives and they just barreled through. The trailers would slide off and then getting them out was a mess. They had to unload the horses and walk them over the hill. The empty trailers swished around in the snow causing ruts going every which way. The next guy would do the same thing. The locals hated to see this happen because we knew that would close the roads until spring. A slow steady pull would have gained more headway and not been so bad on the road.

The South Fork road was still open, as the only high summit involved in that route was Big Creek and the County kept that open as long as any one was in Warm Lake.

We much preferred the Lick Creek route as it was only fifty-one miles to McCall. On the South Fork route it was seventy five miles to Cascade and another twenty-six to McCall. So it was a hundred miles one way now to get Billy. I kept going out as long as I possibly could. We prayed our way through when there was no other way we could make it. We had mud to contend with on the South Fork road. I traveled in the morning and in the evening, the mud was firm then. If we happened to be early I got out and walked over the bad spot and found the firmest passage through. I drove slow and steady so as not to spin a wheel and dig the car down into the mud. The roads got so bad at one point I was not going to try it. Sunny Yelton was going out so I went out with him, just one more time I could bring Billy in. Sunny would take Billy back to McCall on Sunday. I took Janet and

Steve and we started out early in the morning. We made it out fine but on the way back the frost was out of the mud. Sunny drove up to a big mud hole (I believe it was on Dollar Creek) and plowed right into the middle of it. We sunk in up to the axles. The pickup would not move. I was very annoyed, it wasn't necessary that this happen. We had to wait until someone came along to pull us out. That was the next morning. We didn't have blankets and we couldn't keep the pickup going all the time to keep warm. With five in the cab we were close and that helped. I tried to keep the kids warm. Sunny drained some gas out of the tank and threw it on a slash pile which was very wet. The gas burned and that was about all but it finally dried the limbs enough to start the fire. A Fish and Game van came along and pulled us out. What a welcome sight.

Steve made it fine, when he got bored and warm he took his YoYo out and stood on a rut and YoYo'd down into the rut. He was too short unless he was on top of the rut. That pacified him for a long time. Billy went back out with the Fish and Game car, the weekend was almost over then. I know he was disappointed and so was I but it couldn't be helped.

We drove on down the South Fork road. It was pretty bad, we didn't know what we might find around any corner.

We came upon a sand slide which had come across the road. Again Sunny drove right into it. He bogged down and couldn't move. The sand was pushing against the truck, the sand was full of water and heavy.

I looked up to see where the sand was coming from. I was frightened at the thought of that truck going into the river. We had to do something to save this truck. I again looked up the hill at the source of the slide. I had an idea. I took the shovel and climbed up there until I came to the top of the sand slide and just as I thought, a stream of water was coming into the sand. I went a ways farther and began to dig. I diverted the water to come down away from the sand. I could see the sand shrinking. I walked down the hill and by then it had sunk down six inches on the pickup. I told Sunny, "After that sand dries up a little more you can drive out of there."

He said, "What do you mean dry up." I told him what I had done and he didn't think that would help.

I said, "Of course it will help, come over here and look what it has done already." He walked around and could see for himself. We waited a while longer and he got in the truck and drove out. He laughed at me saying, "How did you ever think of that?"

I answered, "Sunny, the Lord talks to me and I listen."

He shrugged his shoulders and said no more about it.

Sunny was a good kid, he would do anything for us. He was respectful, and honest. I had always liked him.

One day Tom came home from school with a badly infected finger. He was a little reluctant to show me as I had given all the kids warnings about coming to me to take care of any kind of injury, so that it would not become infected. An infection can turn into blood poisoning, and that is very bad. It can be fatal and since we lived this far out we couldn't take a chance.

Tom's finger looked bad, it was red, up into his hand and swelled about twice its size. When he showed it to me I said, "Why didn't you come in when you did it?"

He painfully explained, "I didn't think it was going to be this bad. It's my own fault, I know, just pour turpentine on it."

I said "Tom, when it is infected this bad it is really going to hurt if I put turpentine on it."

He said "I know Mom, just go ahead and do it because it is my fault. I don't care if it hurts, it couldn't hurt any worse than it does now."

"Tom, it will hurt bad, it will burn that infection out. I can soak it in epsom salts, and give you penicillin, even though you don't have a fever, you will have with that much infection.

"Mom just do it, I want to get it over with."

I held his hand over the wash basin and poured the liquid over the wound. He shrugged his shoulders, "Oh that isn't bad." About that time his eyes opened wide and wider and his mouth came open, he blurted, "Oh man, this burns terrible." His eyes getting wider all the time. He shook his hand wildly with a distorted look on his face, he stomped his feet. "I can't stand it Mom. Do something." I held his hand over the wash basin and poured cold water over it. It eased some. I plunged his hand in cold water and held his hand in it.

It began to cool down some. He pulled his hand out, opened the door and shot out into the yard, running as fast as he could go. That must have lasted ten minutes. He came back in the house, "It's cooling down now."

"When it quits burning I will put some ointment on it and wrap it. It should be alright now." He sat down to rest, he was exhausted. He asked for a drink of water.

He said "Mom I will never do that again. I will come in and get it taken care of as soon as it happens."

"That might save your life sometime, just don't let that infection get started, if we pour turpentine on it immediately it will not burn, and it kills all the germs that cause infection. It will never get sore and it will heal in no time. I'm sorry it had to happen, but it wasn't because you didn't know."

That little incident just reminded me how lucky we had been up to now, but I didn't want to put it off any longer.

I made a trip out to talk to the Dr. Allen in McCall about treating the kids back here, he was very cooperative. He made arrangements to set up classes for me and anyone else who wanted to come. Donna Leatherman went out with me to take the classes. She said it was about time she did this, she had been here all of her life.

We went out early one morning and had classes all day. Dr. Allen lectured on burns. Dr. Phlugg on heart attacks, Dr. Nokes on accidents. They were very thorough and gave us some of the equipment we would need in an emergency. The one thing that Dr. Allen told us that I used a hundred times, "Reassure your patient or victim. You could keep a patient alive by making him believe everything was going to be alright. If you allow him to get frightened he can go into shock and you can lose him." We asked questions and had demonstrations of securing a broken limb, clearing a blocked airway, aiding a drowning victim, or a coronary, and in case of a death what to do. We were given demonstrations on how to care for burns, what to do and what not to do.

They made up forms with codes on them for us to fill out when we had an emergency. We were to record the information, then call on the radio. The purpose being to save radio time, lessen the chance of error and for privacy. When the doctors responded, we were to record their codes on the form and then decipher it. It worked quite well, I only had to use it once. I had other emergencies, but I may be too far from the radio, or I may know what to do, or the situation was critical and time would not allow me to make out the form and take it to the radio. I may drive them out or if the roads were impassable we called for a plane. Radio service was available from Oberbillig camp about five miles out of town.

This training saved some lives. I was called to car accidents, heart attacks, one girl had a cut from barb wire on her thigh which was about twelve inches long. An ugly gaping wound where the flesh protruded from the cut. I stitched it up with butterflies after bathing it with turpentine. It healed without a scar. It didn't burn because it was fresh, still bleeding in fact. (Iva Kissinger's granddaughter.)

It was not in the class that we learned about turpentine. In my childhood, it was one of the very few medications in our household. It was also used, by putting it on our neck and wrists to keep the ticks and mosquitoes off us.

Vicks at one time had turpentine in it and was also good in a poultice to draw out infection and it was a little less abrasive. When Rosana was grown, she heard alcohol was just as good used the same way as turpentine. It is true, I have tried it.

Wash day came around once a week. We were very conservative with clothes. The kids always changed clothes when they came home from school. The clothes were hung up as they took them off if they were not soiled too badly. Socks and underwear were worn for two or three days, if possible. If clothes were wet from the snow, they were dried and worn again. It was very important to all of us to look neat and clean. We were not sacrificing our standards in the least, but we had to cut down on the laundry and at the same time keep clean.

We took a good bath on Sunday night in the big tub heated on the stove and a sponge bath in between, whenever we felt we needed it. A sponge bath was from a wash basin, we undressed and bathed and rinsed our bodies. In the summer it was usually a nightly ritual, unless we used Uncle Tom's outdoor shower. On the bank of the river he had set up two 55 gallon drums. One was for the fire with a pipe coming out the top. A hole was cut into the top of that drum and the other drum lay across the hole where the fire burned under it heating the water that had been poured into it. From the top drum of water a pipe ran out onto a platform where we stood for the shower. A blanket draped around the platform gave all the privacy we needed, that is until too many people came into town and we had to give up the shower.

Tom decided he was going to let his hair grow until school was out. When it got down over his ears, he couldn't stand it any longer; we had to cut it.

Uncle Tom's shower.

The boys packed water and filled a wash tub on the stove at night and a rinse tub filled to the top so I could get two rinse tubs from it. The following day I started the laundry early, it usually took all day. I soaked the white clothes all night in purex water, then scrubbed them on a washboard and rinsed twice. If the weather was conducive, I hung them out to dry. In the winter I usually had to bring them in the house to finish drying. I hung them over chairs and ropes hanging back and forth across the room. I was very careful to shake and hang everything up so they wouldn't need ironing. I used a flat iron heated on the stove when I had to iron something. I didn't much like that job.

Living like this seems like a chore of an unattainable magnitude now, but somehow the Lord gave me strength. I actually enjoyed it. I had the energy and the mind set.

Some kind soul left a gas washing machine on the front porch, one day when I was gone. I never knew who it was but I was thankful for it. I kept it in the house to keep it from freezing and so it would start easier. Didn't care much for the smell. Wash day wasn't so long. The boys had to start it for me before they went to school. I had absolutely no skill in anything mechanical.

354

Uncle Tom's smokehouse.

I couldn't handle the gas lantern. I was so frightened of them, I opened the door before I tried to light it, and if they didn't do something just right I threw them out the door. Sometimes the flame would flare up around the top of the lantern as soon as I got near it with a match. Out the door it went. I shouldn't have thrown them so far, it was hard on the lanterns. One lantern had to be hung as it would not stand, it was so badly bent, but it still worked. (We had kerosene lamps when I was a girl.) I could not make myself hold onto a lantern once I thought there was a chance they would catch on fire. The wood stoves were something else, I couldn't throw them out but I never allowed them to get too hot.

I no longer took anything for my nerves, the serenity had worked its magic on me. I was as content as I had ever been. The lifestyle here was undemanding, we hardly needed a clock. Being so in tune to the elements from spending a lot of time outdoors we weren't a slave to time. Life was easy. The kids were as contented as I was. They didn't put any demands on

355

me nor did I put demands on them. We all knew what we had to do and we did it (most of the time). I began to wonder if the decision to move up here was mine at all. It all came about so fast and easy. It was like someone took it out of my hands and did it Himself. He did it to benefit a lot of people. Isn't that just like God. It was a great benefit to eight people.

I hoped that a lot more people were benefited also, through the church. I'm sure they were.

I had to remind the kids now and then about their chores. I remember one time when I woke up late one Saturday morning. I went in to start the fires and there was no wood or kindling in the wood box. I was very irritated, I marched into the bedroom, no boys. I got dressed up in my warm coat and went up town, carrying Tom's belt in my hand. I couldn't see a sign of them. I soon heard some kid's voices up on the hill. I walked up there to find them with their sleds sliding down the hill, through the bushes where the ice had formed from melting snow and running down to make a perfect slide on an obstacle course. They were flying down swaying around bush after bush. Tom, Merrill and Dan, and I believe every other boy in town was there, and they were having fun. I thought about how quietly they must have tiptoed from their room, through my room and went out the door. This was planned the night before, to be sure. They had to get there early in the morning before the sun melted the ice too much. I walked over to the boys and said, "Go Home."

They didn't say a word, they picked up their sleds and walked off down the hill. I was right behind them, not a word was spoken until we got home. The boys were heading for the woodshed, I walked upon the porch, telling Tom and Merrill to come over here. They did so and I gave them two hard swats across the rump. They didn't cry but headed for the woodshed, Dan was right behind them looking back at me like he was expecting me to give him a swat. But I felt like the other boys were the instigators. I seldom had to punish the younger boys, they learned from the older ones getting punished. Rosana and Janet seldom had to be punished. They knew what was expected of them. Steve remembers only one spanking he ever got.

I really got the wood in that morning. Merrill came in with kindling and started the fire while Tom was chopping the wood. When they came in to eat, they apologized saying they were sorry, but they thought they would be back before I woke up. I asked, "You planned this last night and you still didn't get your wood in and you didn't say anything to me so what does that tell me? It tells me that was very irresponsible of you. I don't want it to happen again, and I don't want to have to check to see if you do your chores. Now it is time to forget it, it's over. Let's talk about something else." Our house was pretty quiet that morning. Rosana and Janet were doing the dishes. Tom and Merrill went into the front room and sat by the heater. Tom picked up his belt and said, "When I made this belt, I said I was never going to get a whippin' with it, now it's ruined. He sat there quiet for awhile and said, "Well maybe I'll just cut a notch in it." He took out his knife and cut a small notch up near the buckle. Of course that made me feel bad.

The meetings were going well and more people were coming out. Nearly every Sunday each home in the community was represented in the Church. The children in most cases, or adults, many parents brought their children. My lectures were addressed to more mature audiences now so it took more study and more time to prepare. I was very nervous when new adults came in unexpected. As I said before, I did not feel adequate to do this, but the Lord put me here and I prayed before every meeting that He would take my message however humble and use it to bless someone's heart and soul and ultimately to a saving knowledge of our Savior, and that it would be done to His Honor and Glory. I also prayed for God to send in a man to do this all important work for Him, but He did not do that. He kept me in that little setting for eight years. A lot of souls were saved, a lot were rededicated and experienced a great growth in their walk with the Lord. I believe the Lord sent some of His favorite people in there where they could be exposed to the gospel before they went to meet Him, exposed in a way that was not threatening or embarrassing for them. Where they were among friends and not ostracized for being a sinner.

They learned for the first time in their lives that they were no different than anyone else. We all sin and come short of the glory of God, but Jesus forgives us after we accept Him as our Savior. They could not be "good enough" to get to Heaven, they had to say, "Yes Jesus I believe in you. I believe your blood that was shed on the cross was shed for me, to cover my sins and save from condemnation and hell that I may spend eternity with You in Glory Land." He will make opportunity for you to be taught and that you may grow and serve Him as His messenger to tell others of the gospel message.

Thanksgiving day there was a light skiff of snow on the ground which fell that morning. It was beautiful, and such a day. The whole town was invited to Murf and Mary's place for a potluck. Hunters that had been out hunting and had learned of the dinner, came back to join us for the day, of course all were welcome. We were together in a common setting that seemed to excite everyone, people were visiting, walking around meeting all the newcomers, which pleased them to no end. You would think that we had invited them to our own home. We were all getting to know one another as we worked together, putting the dinner out.

One person was there, who was influential in a pattern our lives took for many years—John Gillihan. He and about ten of his hunters and several guides were not expecting this and were overjoyed with the homecooked dinner on Thanksgiving. John told me about his family and that his wife went to church sometimes, but she had never got him to go. I told him I would like to meet her.

The crowd spent long hours there finishing up the leftovers over the course of the afternoon. It was evening when we all retired for the day and went to our homes. Building up the fires and getting the house warm for the night. Billy was home that weekend and we were a happy family. I did have a lot of twinges of loneliness for my family in Oregon through the day, but I quickly passed them off and enjoyed what was at hand. I had Uncle Tom and my stepfather and all my children so how could I complain. I was very thankful this day of Thanksgiving.

One afternoon the kids went out to the woodshed to cut wood and kindling to be carried in the house. They came running into the house and said, "Mom, come see what is in the woodshed." They were so excited I couldn't imagine what would be there to cause this response. I opened the door and there hanging from the rafters was a deer all skinned out and clean as a whistle. It was fresh as it had not hardened up yet. We were thrilled to death, I cut some steaks off and fried them for supper. I sent Rosana over to get Uncle Tom for dinner. He came in with a big grin. I asked him if he knew who brought it. He said, "Yea, it was old Fred. He brought it down this afternoon when you were up town. Sure surprised me, I've never seen him do anything like this before."

"Well did you talk to him or help him, that must have been hard on him in his condition."

"H— no, if he would have asked, I'd help him but he won't ask me for anything. He won't even speak to me."

"Do you speak to him? He probably thinks you don't like him. Someone has to break the ice."

"Well I don't like him, and I'm happy with things just as they are. Hummp. Break the ice."

I went up to talk to Dad and thank him for the deer. He was so pleased to have done something we enjoyed so much. He told me, "If you let a crust form all over the deer, it will last all winter and it would be just fresh on the inside. Don't cover it, there are no flies out now and it is high enough that cats or dogs can't get it. Just take that rope, untie it and let it down when you want to cut off some meat, then pull it back up again and tie it."

"Okay, I'll do that but why don't you come down for supper Friday night. I'll fry up some steak and make gravy, cook some potatoes and maybe some hot biscuits and a vegetable. I'll think of something to have for desert." He laughed and said he would be there. He wouldn't pass that up.

I also asked Uncle Tom over for supper that night. I was a little nervous because Uncle Tom came over first and was sitting there drinking coffee when "Dad" came in. Was one of them going to leave or maybe wouldn't speak to the other. What an awkward situation, did they really hate each other? Oh my, maybe I shouldn't have done this.

I turned to greet Dad when he came in the door calling him Dad, the kids all greeted him with "Hi, Grandpa." I looked at Uncle Tom, he was looking at the floor. Dad walked over to him and said as he extended his hand, "Hello Tom, it's good to see you." Uncle Tom stood up and said, "Hello Fred, good to see you too." They conversed through the dinner. Mostly about people around the country, and what was going on at the mines. Dad was much better informed than Uncle Tom as he got out more, so Uncle Tom was enjoying the conversation. I had nothing to say I was busy getting supper on the table. In fact the whole evening was dominated by them in conversation. I was so happy the "ice had been broken." Uncle Tom never mentioned my sly little trap. They were never close in friendship but at least they spoke to one another and chatted when they were together. I saw them once in a while sitting on the bench in front of the store.

Uncle Tom told me one day, "I never thought I'd see the day when I'd be talking to old Fred again. I thought we would be enemies for life." I didn't dare say a word.

One morning after the kids had gone to school, there was a knock at the door. When I opened the door, I was shocked to see this tall handsome young man that I had never seen before. He was dressed in a black cowboy hat and boots, Levi's and a blue Pendleton shirt. He had the biggest bluest eyes I had ever seen. He was a very handsome man. He was as shocked as

Uncle Tom and Fred Erickson (Dad).

I was, we stood there staring at each other. Finally he spoke, "I am looking for Tom Hagen."

After I found my tongue I answered, "He lives over there in the little cabin." He nodded his head and thanked me and turned to walk away. I knew Uncle Tom was up town but I didn't say that. This man disappeared around the corner of the house and soon he walked off the porch and up the trail toward town. I watched him until he was out of sight. I wondered who he was.

At coffee one day when I met Bonnie and Phyllis at the cafe, John Gillihan came in. We all spoke and he informed us he had lost some horses. They left Big Creek and headed over this way, he followed their tracks this far but above Yellow Pine they left the road. He was wondering if anyone had seen them. He was worried they had bypassed Yellow Pine in the middle of the night. He was eating lunch and noticed the big jar sitting there for donations for the church. He took out his wallet and thumbing through his papers he found a two dollar bill. He said if I find my horses I will donate this to the church. And in case you don't know why I'm doing this, I want you girls to pray that I find the horses. We said that we would and he left. He came back in the late afternoon with the horses in the back of his truck. He went to the store and gave the bill to Bonnie, he asked her to be sure that I knew that he left it for the church. When Bonnie gave me the bill, it was special to me. Special because it represented contact with the people right where they live. I felt it was a milestone. I hoped everyone would someday know that we prayed for them. That we cared about each and everyone of them, we cared for the good and bad in their lives.

(Can I help. Can I, through my relationship with you, bring you close to our Jesus, will you learn to trust Him and give your heart to Him as I have. I care about your soul, I care about your life and your family and everything that is you. Yes all of you.)

I showed the bill to our gathering on Sunday. I told them what it represented to me and I told them that I was going to put it in my Bible and never spend it, because whenever I looked at it I wanted to be reminded that we must meet people in a personal way to help them, we couldn't communicate with them otherwise. I also told them whenever they wanted to see it I would show them and tell them again what that bill means, and how important it is to us as Christians.

A short time later at coffee, there sat John and his wife, Elsie. He very proudly introduced her and let us know that since we had a church here he was going to move his family up here.

She was sweet and I loved her from the first moment I met her.

Over the years our friendship grew to where we were inseparable in our love for the Lord and His work. Elsie said she had been a Christian most of her life but she really never grew until she came up here. We sang duets together, we worshipped and praised together, we were one in the spirit of the Lord.

With Bonnie and Phyllis I felt the same way, the Lord gave us a special love for one another and it has endured through the years. When we meet now with lines in our faces and grey hair and grandchildren, we know the years have flown by but we still have the same enthusiasm and excitement as we had 35 years ago. The Lord's work bound us together and it is a very special relationship. So many others, who came to the church have been such blessed memories. "Blessed be The Tie That Binds our Hearts in Christian Love."

John and Elsie had a big two story house moved down from Stibnite and rebuilt it to repair the damage that was done from age and moving it.

They painted and worked on it until they had a nice home and Elsie and her family were very happy there.

Elsie married John after his wife died when he was in the service, they met in Texas where she lived, he didn't tell her parents that he had seven children for her to raise. When he was discharged they got on the train on their way to a honeymoon in a home with six wild boys and a sweet daughter. She laughed when she told about some of the problems she had with them. Nothing was ever too big for Elsie. She raised those wild boys and then started her own family. She and John had a son Milton, a daughter Kristy, and another son, Pat. Milton was Merrill's age, Kristy was Janet's friend although she was older by a few years. Pat was more the age of Steve. Pat started out like he was going to be another wild one, but in the end his mother's prayers paid off. He is a good kid, Kristy and Milton are also products of their mother's prayers.

Elsie became another teacher just when we were growing to the point where we needed her. The church was growing and the town was growing. It is surprising how the Lord works these things out.

The family was a blessing to us. They took over where Jack and Mary left off. We stayed with them often, the kids were to go there if I was not home for one reason or another. Going in and out as much as I did, there could be a break down or any number of things that would delay my return.

Through the years that I went in and out on weekends to take care of the church, during the winter months we stayed with John and Elsie most of the time. I brought in fresh produce and things that they couldn't always get in there and that was our contribution to the meals. We were always welcome there no matter how many we had. We brought sleeping bags and pillows so all we needed was the space. She was always genuinely happy to see us.

We had some great singing in church, we sang without music, we didn't have a piano or anyone to play it. We learned that without music we sang louder and couldn't depend on the music to cover up mistakes so we didn't make as many, except when I sang the wrong words, that became quite a joke, but actually I would get so into the singing I would drift away and not notice when I sang the words to a different verse. The singing audience would look up at me, I would grin at them and go on singing. They always had to let me know they heard it. I led songs and my voice became very strong over the years, I really had volume. We all loved to sing and we sang our hearts out. We left the door open when it was warm outside. We were often told that people throughout the town looked forward to Sunday morning and the singing. Campers who heard the singing would often come in.

Our little dog Smokey came wandering through the door when the singing started, I think he knew then the boys would be staying for awhile. He laid by the door and greeted all the latecomers.

We had always hoped to someday have a piano and someone to play it, new people were moving into town we thought we should make plans. We found a piano advertised in the paper. I made a trip out to Cascade to see it and bought it for $50.00. It looked so good in there, it was an antique and a beautiful one. A new one was bought for the church. Now and then someone played but most of the time it sat quiet.

The Brownings in the hotel, Barbara and Don and their two sons Dave and Danny were a delightful family. The boys came to Sunday School, it was a pleasure to have them.

The Hathaways lived in a house close to the church, right next door to Red Johnson. They filled a vital spot in the community. But we still had some good memories. Pat worked in the mines and Georgia worked in the store. Red wasn't a happy neighbor after they moved in. They had the twin boys that I have spoken of previously and a daughter named Pam who was a good friend of Rosana's. The twins were all for themselves, they only picked fights with the other kids and were not interested in playing with anyone. They were very mischievous.

I remember one time Janet was playing in her wagon and they asked if they could pull her, she thought that would be great. They pulled her over to the edge of a steep rock slide and pushed her over the edge. Luckily she didn't get hurt, the wagon stopped on a big rock or she may have been killed tumbling down the slide in the rocks. She got out and came storming down the hill to tell me what they did.

I realized these kids were dangerous, this is more than kid stuff. It would be impossible to be with Janet all the time. I sat her down and explained to her that some people did act like that. We can't do any thing about it but we have to protect ourselves from them. "Don't give them another chance to hurt you, don't be alone with them, but if you should have another encounter with them, act like you are real angry, pick up a rock, a stick, or anything you can put your hands on, scream at them and run after them, just swing your stick or throw the rock at them, (try not to hit them) but do not let them hurt you. Now don't ever do this unless someone is threatening you. If you don't frighten them away then YOU run just as fast as you can, go to someone else, then they won't hurt you. Don't go anywhere alone, stay with other people."

It only took one time for them, it worked. Janet played out her part well. She had the dramatics it took to do it. In fact they were more afraid of her than she was of them. They did some pretty bad things around town, their parents would beat them if they found out. Everyone was reluctant to tell them. I did have them in Sunday School and they did fairly well considering. It was impossible to keep their attention or get their interest. I could never call them by name because they deliberately confused people as to who was who. One was Gary and the other was Dary, no one but their parents could tell them apart so everyone called both of them Twin. I always hoped, by them being there in church, it did some good.

They are still the same as far as I know. When they were grown they got in a fight while drinking in a bar, one beat the other in the head with a bat, he spent a long time in the hospital. I guess he lost a lot of ground mentally, his mother Georgia is taking care of him now. He is no longer able to care for himself. The other twin had a lot of remorse for a while, but it didn't last long. I hope this terrible incident will not all be in vain and some good can come to the boys. I believe it has, be it ever so little.

Tom and Betty Nicholas were residents of Yellow Pine, they owned Tom's place, which was a bar, lodge and cafe. Tables lined the perimeter of the lodge where food was served, or people sat around drinking coffee, pop or beer. A small cafe only having a counter for eight, was next to the lodge or bar. The cafe did a great business as most of the time it was the only one open. With such limited seating, they used the other room for table service most of the time.

Betty did most of the business in the bar or lodge, she hired a cook for the cafe. Tom was a mechanic, he had a shop beside the cafe. He did quite a business in his garage and it was a blessing to the people back there.

As the summer progressed and business was increasing to the extent that extra people were needed. Betty Nicholas hired Myrna and Eddie Raney who came in with their family of one boy and two girls. Eddie sang and played the guitar, he was a wonderful singer and musician. He sounded as much like Johnny Cash as Johnny himself, especially with some songs. He was quite an attraction. People found it easy listening, as they ate or drank or whatever. Myrna was a great cook, very pretty and a lovely personality. She was an outdoor gal and we found that we had a lot in common. She liked to ride, hunt, fish, shoot, hike or just being out of doors was something she enjoyed. I liked Myrna, we always had something to talk about and we did a lot of outdoor things together. All five of them came to church, most of the time, depending on how busy they were at Tom's place. Eddie came carrying his guitar up the road and played for our song service. He was soon singing hymns. He was fairly new to the church scene, but Myrna and the kids were more familiar. Myrna was always willing to help in any way she could so we used her mainly as a substitute teacher. She couldn't always get off work.

Tom Nicholas was such a good guy, I liked Tom, he was a guy that you could talk to about anything. He always had time and he always cared. Tom was a caretaker which was new to me, I always took that position. I really appreciated him. He was like a father to me. In fact he told me one time if he ever had a daughter he would want her to be like me. That made me feel pretty good. Myrna and I would tell him anything and we knew it never went any farther. He was a hard working man and an asset to the whole back country as a good mechanic. Betty was a nice gal but she was not as available as Tom. She was gone a lot or very busy. We all liked Betty, she was good to us. In fact when it got very cold and was impossible to heat the Church building, she set up the lodge to have our services there. She allowed people to stay but no drinking and no bad language. If anyone even said anything, she told them to shush. Most of the people there would turn their backs to the bar and listen to every word. We always hoped it touched someone.

Tom Nicholas broke his leg and wore a walking cast for a long time. The kids started calling him Chester, he even kind of looked like Chester, tall and slender with a big black hat. That came from one of their favorite TV shows "Gunsmoke." It stuck with him for a long time.

Myrna started a leather tooling class. She brought in several kits of different kinds and then she invited the kids to come and she would teach them how to use the different tools and decorate and sew leather. It was a big hit, the kids loved it. Two nights a week my kids went up to classes. They made me a little Bible cover and a coin purse. In fact I still have them. They made belts and wallets for themselves. My boys were older and they were able to pick it up pretty fast. It was a good project for them.

The Brownings moved out and Gillihans leased the hotel. They seemed to be the right kind of people there. They didn't operate it like the Brownings, who were such meticulous people and the old hotel became an immaculate room and board facility. Barbara was a wonderful cook and there was much more style to her management of the hotel.

Gillihans, on the other hand, had the western type hospitality, everything was clean and in order. There were blankets on the beds for spreads. Everything was done accordingly and very plain. The meals were breakfast of biscuits and gravy, ham, potatoes, eggs, and plenty of hot coffee. Lunch may be beans and hot bread. Dinner a big hearty stew, corn bread and honey. John still did the outfitting out of Big Creek on Crooked Creek and up toward Mile High country.

One of John's hunters, Jim Cox, brought his wife and daughter in to live in Yellow Pine. I first met them in the hotel where they stayed until they found housing. I had heard that Olga was recovering from a coma where she lay close to death for weeks. When she regained consciousness she had to learn to walk, talk, everything all over again. She was gaining strength and it was all coming back gradually, she was in the very first steps when she came to Yellow Pine. My heart went out to her, when I saw the condition she was in. She was very thin but had a huge stomach. She could only wear smocks or housecoats. I attempted to talk to her but she only responded with her eyes. That told me a lot about Olga, because what she said with her eyes was more than most people can say with words.

Elsie told me that Olga had been an alcoholic for years. Her liver quit functioning and was hemorrhaging. Somehow they pulled her through and she had a second chance at life. Elsie said she probably wouldn't live long. The doctors told her if she ever drank again it could kill her in a matter of a few hours. I became very close to Olga as time went on. She finally began talking and doing all things she did before she was sick. I asked her if she would like me to pray for her, tears came to her eyes. I asked her if she would like to come to church. She said "I have never been in church."

"Olga what do you know about the Lord?"

She said, "Nothing." She looked frightened.

I told her I had a lot of wonderful things to tell her. I said to her, "Are you afraid to come to church?" She nodded her head. I told her I would come after her this coming Sunday. When I went to pick her up she was in a pretty clean little house dress, a sweater around her shoulders, her hair slicked back. She carried a little hanky in her hand. I couldn't help but cry when I saw her. I put my arms around her and we cried together. I told her how happy I was for her to meet the Lord.

After a few times of me going after her she came by herself. Always with her hair slicked back, a fresh clean dress, her sweater over her shoulders and a hanky in her hand. Olga came to church from then on. She accepted the Lord. I became so fond of her. I told her about the Lord and read to her from the Bible. She was so proud to have made her turn around and was living like a Christian. She was proud to be a lady. I loved Olga, I wanted to stand by her until the day she died. I spent a lot of time with her. She talked to me for hours at a time and what a horrible life she had. The pain both physical and mental was enough to drive anyone to drink if they didn't know the Lord. This gave me an insight into the hearts of many people I knew here. Never again did I say why do you do this to yourself, but what is your pain. Oh, how they needed to know the Lord. I knew God loved them just as much as He did me. He put me here to introduce them to Him, these precious people.

I spread the love of God everywhere I went, it was easy for me to say, I will pray for you. I understand your pain. Everyone has pain of some kind and they want to hear that someone cares. Oh, what rejoicing in the countenance of their being when they knew God had heard and answered. Then they believed. They needed the hope so badly. I continued to pray for them and talk to them every chance I got. Just anywhere they happened to be I would talk to them about the Lord. In the bar, the store, the street. They were not offended nor did they ever shun me. They knew I was there to tell them what they needed to know, what they wanted to know. The position I took on drinking was as follows; Let God be the judge. He sent me here to minister to these people not to judge them.

One day I was talking to Elsie out in the street when the man with the beautiful eyes walked up. He was still handsome but he was a little dirty from work on a cat up at Stibnite. He walked up and greeted Elsie, she shook his hand and said, "Ray you are getting fat, I didn't think I'd ever see that."

He drew his head back and responded, "Well if that isn't a case of the kettle calling the pot black." He laughed and she laughed. They never forgot that little encounter, when they saw the other. They would laugh and say, "Who's the kettle now?"

After their little joke, Elsie said, "Ray have you met Rose?"

"I haven't been introduced to her but I met her when I went looking for Tom Hagen. She came to the door and about scared me to death. I wasn't expecting a good looking lady at Tom's house. But I asked around town

367

Ray Thrall, Dad, and Rose at Tom's Place.

and found out all about her." He looked at me all the time he was talking with those big blue eyes. I could feel my face flushing and I was very uncomfortable. Elsie saved the day when she said, "Rose this is Ray Thrall." He took off his hat and offered me his hand. I shook his hand and said, "Hello Ray, it's nice to meet you."

He responded, "Well it's nice to meet you at last. I thought you were going to stay hidden the rest of the summer."

I stammered again under that steady gaze, "Well I've been here all the time."

"I know you were but I spend most of my time in the bar at night and work during the day." He knew he was embarrassing me and he was enjoying it. "I live right there next to the Church and I hear you every Sunday morning. In fact I can't leave my house until Church is over."

He really had the best of me and I found out later why he enjoyed this so much. He was so shy, he could hardly talk to anyone unless he had a drink or two and that was most of the time.

Everyone liked Ray. He was as honest as the day was long. He was generous and good hearted. But he was his own worst enemy. He seemed to not want to drink himself into a drunken stupor. He would all of a sudden disappear, so no one saw him drunk, but if he was friendly and talkative, he was drinking you could be sure.

His language was bad when he was drinking. He would embarrass a drunken sailor, so ladies stayed away from him when he drank. When he was sober, he was a perfect gentleman.

He had been in the war and received a head injury. He had some kind of plate in his head. Apparently, when he was coming home, he had a seizure in the plane. He had never had one before, but they told him he may have them from now on. Or he may never have another. As far as anyone knew he never had another. After he got home he went back into the wilderness and hibernated. He lived at Big Ramey cabin on Big Creek about 15 miles from Big Creek Ranger Station.

Ray was a very proud man, he didn't want anyone to see him in a seizure. He took a violin in with him and learned to play it when he was back there. The one thing he didn't learn was timing. He would have been good if he had the timing right. He played "Boiling down the Cabbage," "Yellow Pine Stomp," and "The Big Ramey Hop." There was no timing but fast and faster. He had a lot of requests for those tunes.

He had played classical piano before he went into the war. He had forgotten a lot of what he knew, but when he played it was fascinating to see his fingers gently caress the keys so lightly his fingers hardly moved. He seemed so familiar with the piano. To watch him, you felt like you were seeing a great maestro at work, but he would never finish the song. He would suddenly stop and get up saying he had forgotten. It seemed painful to him. He was definitely in his own world when he played, it was like he was afraid of losing himself in that piano. What he did play was beautiful and haunting. What he didn't play was the unfinished drama of his life. I could see a very polished gentleman in Ray. He tried to extinguish that person and bring forth just the opposite, a crude cursing drunk. That wasn't the real Ray, and when he was the gentleman, I enjoyed him and admired him greatly. He was intelligent and a very skilled person at every thing he did. I couldn't tolerate him as a crude drunk.

One week night I was helping out in the cafe cleaning, as I often did. He was in the bar, I could hear him talking. He came into the cafe, sat down on a stool and said, "Do you have anything to eat?" He didn't appear to be drunk or even drinking for that matter.

"Yes, what would you like, I can fix you a steak, the grill is still on, or a hamburger. Tell me what you want and I'll tell you if I can fix it."

"Well give me a cup of coffee, for right now and let me think about it, while I talk to you."

I walked over to where he sat and perched up on the stool that was behind the counter. He began as the gentleman, "I will be going out in a few days and I will be staying in Idaho City with a couple guys. I wanted to talk to you before I left. I really have enjoyed having you in town. You are the one good thing in my life. I think of you all the time when I am not here in the bar. If there was any possible way I could straighten out my life I would and then I would like to tell you more. I don't think I'll ever be any different, I wish I could believe otherwise."

He did it again, I felt my face burning, I was embarrassed. Get a hold of yourself. "Ray, I thank you, I am honored by what you say."

"You are honored. You are honored by a man like me telling you these things. I am the one who is honored."

"Yes, Ray I am honored, I believe I see the real person in you. You try to hide it, but I see someone whom I admire very much. Do you want to quit drinking? Is that what you mean? I can give you help and get the information of who can help you in rehab programs and such. If you are serious, I will help you."

He reached out and took my hands and held them in between his hands. "Will you write to me, I do need some help. I would love to hear from you this winter. I know you think I have had too much to drink, I haven't because I wanted to talk to you. I want you to believe me. I have never been more serious in my life. I care a lot for you."

"I will believe you Ray and yes I will write to you and give you some names of people to contact. I can't tell you how happy it makes me that you want to quit drinking. I will pray for you everyday." My heart was pounding so hard, I was breathless, but I had to hide this. "Here is a piece of paper for you to write your address for this winter." I was pulling my hand away, he wasn't letting go. I stood up and said, "What can I get for you to eat?"

He let go of my hands and said, "Really I am not hungry, I ate just before I came over. I just wanted an excuse to come in and talk to you. I am sober Rose."

"Okay I believe you, and I am even more honored. Do you believe that. Ray the only way you can conquer that alcohol is to accept the Lord, so He can help you. Will you take Him as your Savior now. Do you understand enough about the Lord to accept Him."

"Yes I do and I will accept Him as my Savior. Is this all I have to do? I'll miss you this winter but I will look forward to your letters." He got up and walked into the other room.

"Ray, that is all you need to know right now, I'll tell you more about it later." I heard the outside door open and close when he left.

The next spring when he came in, he came to me right away and thanked me for the letters. It truly meant a lot to him.

But he had not followed up on the leads I gave him. He got involved in a job at Idaho City and really didn't have time. He told me, "I didn't answer your letters either not because I didn't want to, but I didn't have any progress to report. I was ashamed."

I looked away from him with a feeling of disgust and he said, "I don't blame you. You kept your end of the bargain but I didn't. I will though, I promise you."

"Okay Ray. Welcome back to Yellow Pine. It has been quiet around here without you. I'm glad you are back."

He put his arm around me and gave me a little squeeze across the shoulders and said. "You are some woman. You are."

Ray dug ditches from his property to the church and hooked us up to his water line. I asked him how we were going to pay him for water and he said, "You are not, I just want to do something for the church." I thanked him sincerely. He put in the pipes and faucets and hooked it all up. He also paid the power for the church after it came into town. I would always ask him to come to church. He never refused but he just put it off. He and Don Caward came together one time. Don was sure the roof would fall in but it didn't. I felt sure they both would have come if the other guys couldn't see them. They didn't want to be razzed.

One Saturday afternoon I walked to town to get my mail. Ray was in the store, he was holding what looked like a bottle of whiskey in a paper bag. I greeted him and asked him if he was going to come to church tomorrow. He said, "Well I won't be able to."

"Why not?" I quipped

"I've got a bottle of whiskey here and if I drink that I won't be in any shape to come to church. I probably won't be able to get out of bed." He laughed.

I asked, "Well why don't you give me the bottle and I'll keep it for you till after church."

He stood looking at me, he finally responded, "Would you really give it back to me if I went to church?"

"Of course I would. If I say I will, I will."

He looked at me so serious, "I believe you would." He handed me the package and left the store. I don't know who told but everyone in town knew within an hour.

Ray went home, he didn't go to the bar. They went on with their party and during the night someone came pounding on his door. There had been a wreck up toward Stibnite and would Ray go up and take his cat down to get the car out. He went, and when church started the next day he wasn't there. I really thought he chickened out. That afternoon I was down by the store and he came out to talk to me. He said those guys set him up so he couldn't come to church. I told him that was too bad but I would give him back his bottle.

"No you won't, I made a deal, you keep that bottle until I come to church. Those guys can't tail me forever. I'll do what I said I would. Now you stick to your side of this deal."

Well I did and I had that bottle for quite a while hidden in a safe place. The guys didn't take their eyes off him on Sunday mornings. He finally made it. He was almost too late but he came charging in. He stayed until after the kids left and asked if he could try out the piano. He sat down, played, and the sophistication returned to him. You would never believe he was the same man. "It's a little out of tune but not too bad. Would you mind if I come over to practice when no one else is around? I can't practice in the bar."

"You are more than welcome, just come anytime you like, the doors are always open. Ray I didn't bring the bottle with me to church, so I will have to bring it up later if that is okay."

"It sure is, we kept a deal didn't we?" He reached out and took my hand.

That first Christmas was different, so different. I didn't know how I was going to handle this. The kids didn't show a sign of missing what was in the past. My family was very much on my mind. But I just had to get over this and get into something. We put up decorations at the church and at the house. As I was trying to think of something to do for the community, I thought about caroling. "Oh yes, dress the kids up as Biblical characters and take them through town, stopping at everyone's house." Oh, what an idea. This would be wonderful. I sat down and designed the greatest little Christmas Caroling Cantata. We had a lot of work to do and in the morning I would go see all the ladies and get some more ideas and some help. We had five days to get this ready.

I got the kids all together and told them we had a lot of practicing to do. We did work hard night and day but this was very effective. I had six kids up front who dressed as Bible characters and the rest dressed in white sheets over the head and body. They would carry song books, open in front of them just for effect as they would have to know the songs by heart because they couldn't see, it would be too dark.

The characters would act or pantomime every song we sang. Adults held lanterns up, one on each side, we would walk singing and then stop to pantomime the song and the lantern holders would walk toward the center to hold the lights up for the play. Several other lanterns were around through the carolers. We first went down through main street. Then we went to individuals homes. All turned out to see and some even followed us. We went over to Red Johnson's house, the house was dark, we stayed a while longer there in the dark alley in the front of his house. That was probably his only Christmas message. Then we went on up the alley to Hathaways house and up the street. It worked out so well and the kids did wonderful. They were serious and reverent. But I'll have to admit the actors were superb.

When we sang Silent Night, Mary picked up the baby and walked around with it looking up into the sky. Joseph walked beside her, first one and then the other held Jesus and rocked Him back and forth. He went to sleep and they laid Him in the crib very gently, smiling so sweetly at the baby. Then they knelt down on each side of the bed and bowed their heads and prayed. The lanterns moved back and Mary and Joseph remained in that position while the light faded away, until the song was over. We did several songs and they were equally effective, yet so simple.

So many people told us how they liked the play. They thought it was so effective. I asked people to please tell the kids. Red Johnson walked up to me the next day, with a big smile and he said, "Say I thought the angels were singing outside my house last night. I thought for sure they were coming to take me away."

A Christmas surprise for us was a box of Christmas goodies from Donna and Mom. They baked all kinds of cookies and breads and made many candies. It was a big box stuffed full. It must have weighed forty pounds. We enjoyed that for a long time. We rationed it though, we brought it out every evening before we went to bed and had two or three pieces. That was so much work for them. It was certainly appreciated. The kids still talk about that, thirty-five years later.

We had a little Christmas tree decorated with home made decorations. We really felt like pilgrims. We had some nice gifts under the tree and everyone was happy.

After the Lick Creek road closed for the winter, we went to the South Fork to sit in the sun and fish for white fish. We called that the banana belt, it was so much warmer down there because of elevation. It was only twenty miles or so from Yellow Pine but the difference was amazing. Uncle Tom went with us a lot. He loved to fish. He smoked the white fish as they are pretty bony to cook. We sure enjoyed those smoked fish though. Driving down the East Fork before we got to the turn off to the South Fork the road was shaded from the steep banks. Ice didn't melt all winter. After so long the road got pretty bad with ice running across and building up over the road. Washouts were quite common. A little stream coming down from the hill above the road would wash during a bad storm and form a rut. As water continued to come down through the rut, it would become bigger and deeper until you couldn't get a car across it. There were always rocks you had to watch out for.

One particular Saturday we went down the East Fork heading for the South Fork to fish and have a picnic. The road was blocked with an ice build-up about four feet high at the upper end. With the water running over it, it was very slick and the car would slide off into the river if we drove over it. I looked over the situation and possible ways to get across. I needed some loose dirt, but no the dirt was all frozen, we couldn't loosen it. I turned around and went back home and got a bucket of ashes from the stove. We went back down and sprinkled half the ashes down where we drove across. The ashes would run off quickly with the water running over it, so I couldn't waste any time. I told the kids to get out of the car and walk up higher where it was not quite so slick, they made it fine.

Lick Creek sledding party.

I was a bit apprehensive but I had better go before I thought about this very long or I would back out. I started the car and began to move forward slowly and carefully, I did not want to spin a tire or it would take off the ashes and become very slick. If I started to slide, I may not stop and that cold river was on the driver's side. I kept the Lord's name on my lips until I was safe on the other side. I went over without a bit of a problem. I could breathe again, but I knew I had to go back over it. I didn't say anything to the kids about being afraid, I don't think they were. We went fishing and had a good day. Needless to say, I felt much better after the return trip over the ice. We put the rest of the ashes on and didn't have any problems.

With spring coming and warm weather we did have some washouts on the East Fork. The kids wanted to go fishing again on the South Fork and those warm spring days were so inviting. There were two washouts we couldn't cross so we put our little bridge down. This wasn't as frightening as the ice. The only thing I had to worry about was driving off the boards or the boards breaking. Again I prayed for the Lord to help me cross this bridge safely. Praise the Lord! We put the 2 x 6's back in the station wagon and went on to the next washout. Until the county came in to open the roads we carried our bridge and a bucket of ashes everywhere we went.

We considered ourselves most fortunate to have been there most of the first summer. We experienced the fall, the winter, the wonderful spring and another summer. God had surely blessed us. We lived every day to the fullest.

A family camping trip.

Chapter 15

"Springtime in the Mountains"

1964

Spring is always a beautiful time of year, but here, it is spectacular. So many exciting things happen. We were so close to nature we watched as the tiny buds formed on the bare limbs of a bush. Every day we counted the new ones and their extraordinary response to the warm air and the sun. They had waited so patiently for spring to arrive, waiting with the new growth just beneath the surface ready to burst forth. They could wait no more.

The landscape turned from white to green right before our eyes and yet we didn't see it happen. We rushed out every morning to see what had occurred this day, but it had happened just before we arrived. How secretive was nature how sly these miracles did come about. The snow suddenly went from solid to liquid, routing little streamlets to make their escape to the river, so anxious to get on their way. Where there was no escape they formed a puddle for little boys and poly wogs to play in. Is there ever another time of year that is so captivating as spring. I guess spring is the same everywhere but in the busy life we just don't take time to watch.

We not only enjoyed spring in our own backyard but the whole countryside. We walked down the trails and beside the river, watching for new signs of another season. One of the most dynamic shows of spring came in the middle of the night when a loud rumbling noise woke me from a sound sleep. Could that be thunder, hardly the right time of year. What could it be, something was falling, snow slide, no, there is no place that close with snow. It was coming closer, what on earth. I sat up in bed, I was trying to remember where I had heard this deafening, thunderous roar. One loud crash jolted my memory back to Monumental Creek many years before

Rosana, Steve, Rose, Merrill, Janet, Dan.

when we stood by Wilbur Wiles' cabin on Monumental Creek saying good-bye, that same roaring, crashing, awesome sound. The ice breakup on the river, where huge pieces of ice, as big as a house come crashing, rumbling, breaking up in the narrows. You don't have to see it to experience this powerful force at work in nature. It is frightening in a splendid way to remind us once again that God is in charge.

All winter we saw smoke from a chimney as the only source of life from these little cabins and houses around town. I could always imagine the occupants sitting in an easy chair, legs curled beneath them or stretched out on a stool, reading a book, not caring if they were neighborly. Did they greet their friends when they hurried to the store? They pulled up their coat collars and pulled down their hats and walked hunched down in their coats hurrying to get home by the warm fire. They only saw the snow at their feet.

When spring came, so did they come out of their cabins, happy and greeting their friends. A new world out there, one of sunshine and hope for another new season awaited them.

I had not yet learned the habits of the old timers. I loved the snow falling on my head and blowing in my face. The distance was not so far that

I couldn't get home to the fire quickly. My feet stayed warm until reaching their destination. I lived for contact with nature and a happy hello to my friends.

The winter passed quickly, but it would not have—had I hibernated. We enjoyed the season and were entertained by the resources and recreation that were at our back door. In every possible way, we played. We enjoyed life to the fullest. We absorbed the beauty, which etched itself on our hearts and we have carried it around to recall at any moment for our pleasure. The seasons so close we couldn't ignore them for a moment. It was a wonderful year. One to remember.

We held services in "Tom's Place" mostly all winter as it was too cold to get the church warmed up in just a few hours. If we could have kept a fire all night, it would have been warm but the stove was not that safe nor did it hold enough wood.

We tried to keep the same worship pattern as we did in church. We had communion, our singing, Bible classes, messages and special music. We had share time for the kids to talk to the class about anything that was on their hearts. No we did not feel a contamination from this, our place of worship, but we felt happy to be able to bring this place and all the people who were here, an hour with Jesus Christ.

There were people there who would never have heard otherwise. Those who very reverently turned their back to the bar and listened to every word. It may have been, if we chose not to hold services in the lodge that we would not have been able to have services at all. Most of the places in town closed up for the winter. Tom's Place was like a community meeting place. The only one in town. We were happy to have the availability and we made good use of it. We were very appreciative of the owners to welcome us there.

Entertainment for the winter was a get together every Saturday evening at "Tom's Place." We had potluck dinners, card games, or just visiting for the evening. Sometimes we played the jukebox and danced which was always fun to remember the dances from our teen years. Jitterbug was the thing then. Every man dancing had a different step for the jitterbug and it was up to the ladies to learn each one if we wanted to dance.

Only the locals were in town now and it was pleasant to have such quality time together. Dad and Uncle Tom came out most Saturdays unless it was too cold. With Dad's lung problems he had to be very careful. He only lived about a block from "Tom's Place," Uncle Tom had a little farther to go. Dad's health had a lot to do with him moving to town but he was also Justice of the Peace, appointed by the governor. Harry Withers stayed in town all winter, as well as Fred and Millie Bachettes. Fred and Millie lived on the upper end of town next door to Harry Withers.

They were lovely people and had a beautiful log cabin that was kept in tip top condition. Fred was a boss at Stibnite when it was running.

In the early spring the first attraction for visitors was steelhead fishing. The county opened Big Creek summit first. Then if the South Fork road was passable, here came the fishermen. The South Fork river banks

Dad, "The Judge."

were lined. They camped in tents, campers and some slept in their vehicles.

This was the sport that was tops on everyone's list. They loved it. They fished the South Fork on down the Rebillet Ranch road. A lot of the people came into Yellow Pine to get warmed up and stay in a nice warm room or cabin. Then back to the river early in the morning. They could always envision someone else catching that big one and it drove them daffy, they couldn't wait.

On one spring day Kenneth and Clarence Pond went steelhead fishing. They brought back two very large fish. It was a weekday and very few outside people were in town. In the apartment back of the store we had a fisharama. I cut the fish in bite size pieces, breaded it, and deep fried it. Bonnie and Phyllis made a dip with mayonnaise, grated onion, chopped olive, fresh lemon juice, grated lemon rind, and paprika. That was so good, everyone in town came down to the store. Everyone loved it.

With the Steelheaders came the Fish and Game. I walked into the store one day and coming out the door was a nice looking guy in a uniform. He was dressed so immaculately, you had to notice him. He spoke to me and as soon as I found my tongue I responded. He smiled with the biggest, warmest, most beautiful smile I had ever seen. I thought I was in love and I didn't even know his name. We stood and looked at each other for a moment and he very politely introduced himself. His name was Frank Watkins. I told him my name. We chatted for another moment and he excused himself, saying he had to go to work. He said he would be back in that night and hoped he would see me. Since it was a Saturday night, we would be up town for our social. I became quite excited and then reality. No chance.

I walked on into the store and Phyllis was working. I asked her about this fellow. She said he had been in a few times last year, and he was a very nice guy but she didn't know much more than that about him. I did take a little extra care that night fixing my hair and dressing. We took our food for the potluck and walked up town. I looked for a green van, there was none in sight.

We put our food out on the counter, everyone stood around in a circle, I was asked to say the blessing. The kids were told to fill their plates first. I helped the little ones get their plates ready and seated them at a table. The older kids went to sit with some of their friends. After I got them settled and eating, I fixed my plate and sat down with the kids to eat. I was sitting with Myrna and her kids. Eddie was busy and was not eating yet. When we were nearly finished eating, the door opened and Frank walked in. Everyone seemed glad to see him and called out their greetings. He looked around the room and saw that I was sitting there and came over to speak to me. He was very polite, I introduced him to Myrna. The kids were anxious to meet him I think because of the uniform. I introduced them.

I pointed out my other kids around the room. He didn't seem shocked like people usually did at the nice round number of seven. At least he didn't show it if he was. He went to fill his plate and sat down at the counter to eat with some of the other guys. This was a nice guy. I was sure of it.

After we cleared up the dishes, some folks played cards, some of the kids played games and Myrna got out the leather craft. Janet and Steve played with Myrna's kids, they were coloring and drawing pictures. Someone played some songs on the jukebox. A few couples got up to dance to work off their dinner they said. Myrna and I were sitting there talking, more people were getting out on the floor. Frank came over to ask me to dance. He was a nice dancer, very smooth and easy to follow. We talked on the dance floor and I finally got to the all important question. "Are you married Frank?"

He answered, "Yes, but I am getting a divorce. I have been separated for about a year. I have two sons who are in high school. Now how about you?" I couldn't help feeling happy that he was getting a divorce. I thought that wasn't very Christ-like.

I quickly dismissed my nudge from God.

"I am a widow, I have seven children. I came up here to start a Sunday School. It has been very successful, I really enjoy living here, the kids love it. I have one son in McCall boarding out going to school. I am going to move out for school next year because Tom will also be in high school. My stepfather and my uncle live here. I live down over the hill in Uncle Tom's house."

"You mean Tom Hagen is your uncle, I know him. He is a great guy. Who is your dad?"

"Fred Erickson, everyone calls him 'The Judge.' "

Frank said "Yes I know him well, I take my violators to him. He does a good job. Well the song is over, shall we sit down?"

We sat together by Janet and Steve and the other kids. We danced a few more times and he excused himself and said he had to get up early in the morning. "Good night Rose."

"Good night Frank."

Frank.

I thought about him more than I wanted to, he was so nice. But this is impossible. Don't get your hopes too high Rose. How about just being friends. Yes we are very comfortable together.

Sunday was warm enough to be at the church, it seemed so good. Everyone seemed happy to be back in there. We had it nice and warm. All the kids were there and Phyllis and Bonnie had their classes. I did my class and I felt so free to speak my heart. I didn't realize until then I had been inhibited being out of the church. I hadn't realized how much I missed the church. It was so good to be back.

Bonnie, Phyllis and Myrna asked me if I would consider changing class time around so they could be through with their class in time to hear my message. We discussed different ways this could be done. We came up with a plan that pleased them so I went along with it. The only difference it would make to me was I had two separate things to study for each Sunday. That was fine, I had plenty of time. The older kids stayed in after their Sunday School class for the message. At first all I could think of was they'd rather be fishing. So I had to make this message more interesting and challenging. I gave it a lot of thought and decided to do object lessons and work the message into that and include the kids in the object lesson. I got a book on object lessons which was a great help; and I got another book on nature lessons using the animals, fish or plants from our own back door, and tying them into the Bible. The kids loved that. I alternated the two subjects. It was interesting for everyone.

Now that the roads were open all the folks wanted to go out for some fresh scenery. I was anxious to see Billy but I was going to wait until Friday night, then he could be in for Saturday and Sunday. The kids were anxious to see their big brother. They all went out with me. We did a little shopping and had a hamburger and milkshake. Billy was anxious to get back, he had missed being home. We had a good weekend. We enjoyed just being together. I did a lot of cooking. That seems to be the thing mothers do to show they are glad to have them home. We all talked about when school was out and he could come in for the summer. It was hard to take him out again and leave him, we had all had enough of this being apart.

I hadn't seen Frank since the night of the supper. It was doubtful that we would have anymore suppers because customers were coming in now that fishing was open. I was sitting out on the porch one afternoon and Janet and Steve were playing out there with their trikes, enjoying the sun. I heard a car coming. I was watching to see who it was, very few cars were out around town. It was green, could it be, surely not. It was and he drove up in the yard. He got out of the car and spoke to the kids and walked over where I was sitting. I spoke to him and he sat down on the porch beside me. We exchanged greetings and he began, "You know the Coxes don't you? They are going to have a square dance at their place Saturday night, my boss is coming in for that and I wondered if you would like to go with me. We would all go together in one rig. What do you think?"

"I would love to go if I can get someone to take care of the little kids. Bonnie or Phyllis probably would but I can't say for sure. How late would we be?"

"We can come home anytime you want to. You just say the word."

"I have known the Coxes for a long time, since I was a little girl in fact. Oh I would love to go."

He smiled and said, "Well I didn't know if you dated or not. But I thought it wouldn't hurt to ask."

"I haven't dated, no but I'm not opposed to it. I love to dance. I have danced as far back as I can remember. We had dances in the school houses, and at home or wherever there was room, my folks were Scandinavians, they love music and dancing. We danced when there was only enough room for one couple at a time." Frank chuckled.

"See if you can get someone to take care of the kids and I will drop back down before the weekend."

He got in his car and drove away. I couldn't believe it.

Who would ever believe that I have a date and it isn't anything like I thought it would be. It was so easy talking to him and I wasn't nervous until he left. Now I'm so excited. Janet said, "Mom who is that, what did he want?"

I said, "Don't you remember I introduced you kids to him when we were at Tom's Place a week ago. His name is Frank. He asked me to go to the dance with him at Coxes."

Both kids looked startled, "Are you going to go?"

"Yes if that is okay with you."

"I guess, will you be gone long?"

"No I don't think so, I am going to ask Bonnie if you can stay with her until I get back."

"Oh," I didn't think they were too excited about it but they didn't object. When the other kids got home I told them about it and they seemed pleased. Just one more obstacle.—She said yes, she would be happy too. She was also happy that I was going out with Frank, he was such a nice guy. Everyone liked him. Oh great, but I wouldn't allow myself to think beyond Saturday night.

Merrill found the fishing was good down below our house.

He tied a fly and went down to try it. It wasn't long until he came back with enough for a meal. From then on he was up at daylight tying a fly so he could go fishing. He was so excited to get down to try his fly, he never tied more than one. When he'd lose it, he would come back and tie another. Nearly every morning he got enough fish for breakfast. On Saturdays he fished nearly all day. Tom was a fisherman, but he did think of other things. Terry Leatherman was an ardent fisherman also, he went with Merrill a lot but none was as zealous as Merrill. If it got him up early you could be sure he was very fond of it. He loved to sleep.

One day Merrill, Tom and Terry didn't go right back to school after lunch. They followed some bees and saw that they went into the walls of Uncle Tom's cellar. They decided they should get those bees out for Uncle Tom. They were sure he didn't want them in there. One of them had heard someone talk about smoking the bees out. They got some kerosene out of the lamp and splashed it in there between the logs where the sawdust was. They lit it and went back to school. Surely the bees would leave now, they didn't like smoke. When they came home from school they had a big surprise. The cellar was on fire.

Oh my, this is the thing that I have been hoping would not happen. To destroy something of Uncle Tom's. What was he going to say or worse yet, do. I was sick to the ends of my toes. The boys were too. They packed water and got the fire out but it would just start up again after a little while. I worried about what was he going to expect me to do to them. That was my biggest worry. How would I punish them after causing such a costly disaster. They were so sorry, what should they do. I didn't know.

Uncle Tom came home, we had to tell him, as much as we hated to. He yelled at them, I cringed, "How in h— did you do that?"

Then I said, "Uncle Tom, you punish them any way you want to, I don't know what would be just punishment for this." He looked at the boys for awhile, all the mad was draining out of him, you could see it. I don't think he had ever punished a kid, but like most people he had a lot of opinions about kid's punishment.

"Well you have to fix it. You dig out all that sawdust, and then when you are sure the fire is out, you haul sawdust down from the sawdust pile and fill it up again and put the logs and boards back up. Can you do that?" They all nodded, they would have done anything to make him happy.

When he walked away they looked at him as if to say, "Is that all there is?" We all expected more than that. We were ready for it.

It took a long time to get the fire out of the sawdust but he kept watch and checked it often. They took Uncle Tom's wheelbarrow and shovels to the old sawdust pit where they stored the ice many years ago. They hauled and hauled but they never complained. Uncle Tom reminded them how much sawdust he wheeled over there. When they finally got it all put back together again, he did the inspection—it passed with his approval. That was the end of it with him, he was satisfied that they got the punishment that fit the crime. I figured he would be mad forever. I learned something wonderful about Uncle Tom. He could forgive.

Uncle Tom did a lot of work on his place. The one thing that fascinated me was a rock wall he built along the road going to the North on his property. The rocks were as big as a gallon jar, which would have been pretty heavy to bring from the river in the wheelbarrow. He put them together so carefully, the outer surface was flat. Every rock had to have a flat side which would have been hard to find. I never did ask him how many loads he pushed up from the river at one time. The wall was a quarter of a mile long. It must have taken a long time. Everything he did was done like that. He never had any conveniences to work with, just a wheelbarrow and a shovel. Those years with Uncle Tom were pleasant years when I came to know him and appreciate him even better. I talked to him about my problems, he was so sweet and understanding and he always took my side in everything. Not that I expected that but that was unconditional love. We seldom find that wonderful treasure in life. I had always wished Mom was like that.

Saturday evening came and I was ready to go when the green van drove up with Frank driving and his boss sitting beside him. They both got out and came to the door for me. The kids were all there and after Frank introduced me to his boss, I in turn introduced all the kids. Pete Horning was his boss. A very jolly fellow but he could also be very serious. The guys passed a few words with the kids and we were off to the dance.

We talked on the way up to Coxes, general conversation. We all agreed that Johnson Creek was the prettiest creek in Idaho. We talked about the Coxes and what great people they were. About the parents Clark and Buella. I mentioned that I had worked at the ranch when I was about thirteen years old. They wanted to know what the ranch was like then. "Not much different than it is now. It has always been beautiful. They didn't have electricity yet, the power line was going into Stibnite about then and I think Coxes had it run over there at that time. It was after I had gone home. Buella was a wonderful cook. The whole family has done such a great job at that ranch, they are just the kind of people to run a place like that and have had such a great success all these years."

We drove into the parking lot and hardly found a place to park, it looked like we may be late arriving. We walked toward the house. There were so many people there. The lodge was full, the porch was full, and a band was set up outside where a large platform was built to dance on. We walked over there and watched the dancers. They were all dressed in square dance finery. The lady's dresses matched the men's shirts. They looked like professional dancers. Something you could see on Lawrence Welk. It was fascinating to watch. I leaned over to speak to Frank, "I can't dance like that."

He leaned back toward me saying, "I can't either. I don't think Pete can either." The music was so loud out there we walked toward the porch. We found an empty table and chairs and sat down. We sat watching and enjoying everything that was going on. I wondered where they were all going to sleep. I didn't think there was enough room at Coxes. They were a long ways from town if they were planning to go back to Cascade. Pete saw a table where punch bowls and other bottles were sitting and asked what we would like to drink. Frank said he would have a beer and I said punch or pop or whatever they had.

Lafe and Emma came out the door and spotted us sitting there. They came over to greet us. They were so busy with all these people they only had time to say hello. Emma said "Be sure to mix, I think there are people here you all know. Get into one of those dances."

Pete thanked them and said we were doing just fine. Frank said "I think we could dance better if we went back in Yellow Pine, what do you think?" I agreed and we went to the car.

I was a little bothered about what Emma might think of me being here with these men. I tried to push the thought back out of my mind. It gnawed on me but I was trying to reason with myself, I have a right to go out with someone. Even if he is married, he is getting a divorce. There is nothing wrong with that. I think it probably looked worse than it was. Everything was okay.

I was glad when we got to Yellow Pine and went to Tom's Place. The activity took my mind off what I was rolling around in my head. Frank and Pete got another beer and brought me a pop. We sat for awhile and Frank asked me to dance. Of course I was anxious to dance with him. We glided onto the floor and I was getting some looks from the local people that bothered me. Good night! Didn't I have a life of my own. This was my own business.

Frank was talking to me and it finally registered what he was saying, "What's wrong, you look bothered about something."

I said, "Well I haven't been out with anyone since Bill died, it is kind of a strange feeling."

"I know. Do you want to go?" I nodded and he went over to talk to Pete and we left.

He drove slowly down by the school house and down our lane to the house. He said, "I'm sorry I didn't mean to make you uncomfortable. It is pretty new to you isn't it? Would you rather that I didn't come back?"

"Oh no, I don't mean that, I like being with you. It's just being out like that I guess." We sat in the car in front of the house and talked for awhile.

"Frank, what about your marriage? How long have you been separated? Have you filed for divorce?"

"Well, we haven't got along for years. I am out on the job most of the time and I take assignments where I have to live away from home. When I go home to see the boys, I stay in the camper. We would have had a divorce a long time ago but she is Mormon and she is really fighting it. I am trying to get a transfer into another part of the state and then I will get the divorce. Is that what is bothering you?"

"Yes I guess it is. I feel guilty about it. You are a married man. I hope I'm still around when you are free."

He looked over at me and smiled. "I do too. In fact I think I will look you up."

"I would like that. Thank You Frank, I hope I didn't spoil your evening. I will see you later."

"Wait a minute, is this it, you don't want to see me anymore? Can I come down and visit you once in a while?"

"Yes of course that would be great. Yes, I do want to see you. It isn't that." I felt like I was getting nowhere trying to explain. I looked away. I realized then, I had to say what was on my mind to this man. He seemed to know anyway.

Now I did it, I should have said no I don't want to see you again. I've always had a hard time misrepresenting myself. Seemed I had to say what was on my mind.

"I think I understand and I respect you for it. You can't live a double life can you? Good Night Rose, thanks for going out with me. I enjoyed being with you."

Now look out, what are you feeling, don't tell him any more. "I enjoyed it too and thank you so much. Good night Frank."

I went into the house, my heart was racing, I like this guy a lot and he likes me. I leaned back against the door. "Oh God, what is happening to me. He is such a nice guy, does it have to be so wrong? Can you make it right God. I know what your word says about divorce. Unless there is adultery and I doubt it if she is a Mormon. Oh God please understand. Help me, I feel like I am in a trap. Please, Please God I beg you. In the name of our Savior I plead. Amen."

We received a letter from Mom saying she was ready for her vacation. Donna was bringing her up to Ed's. Could I pick her up there. We worked getting the house cleaned and ready for Grandma. This was exciting. I was so anxious to see Mom. The kids had also missed her. We began planning things to do that she would like. We walked over and told Uncle Tom. He was pretty elated about it and his unusual way of showing it was he grabbed Janet and gave her a dutch rub. She was screaming and trying to get away from him. He laughed and laughed and when he finally let her go, her hair was standing on end and then he did laugh. We all laughed and Janet was mad because everyone was laughing at her and she went home, stomping her feet all the way. I said to her, "Well I'm glad someone else is getting it now. That's what he used to do to me."

Uncle Tom said, "Darn, I almost forgot." He was running for me. I took off after Janet and ran into the house and shut the door. He didn't pursue that any farther but he was really laughing now. I had almost forgotten what a tease he used to be. When Janet saw me running from him she laughed too.

Frank came walking down the road one evening, the kids came in to tell me he was there. I walked out after laying my book down. "Well Hi. How nice to see you. Come on in or would you rather set out here on the porch."

"Out here is just fine, it's so nice out." He sat on the top step and I sat down beside him. " I hope it's alright that I came down."

"Oh Yes, of course, I'm glad you did." The kids kind of drifted away, not intentionally, but their play took them elsewhere. "How is everything with you?"

"Just fine, with you?"

"Fine." Wow, this is awkward, here I thought we could talk. I thought this was a guy that I didn't feel shy with. Now look. If I don't think of something to say quick he will leave. Maybe he should leave. No I don't want him too. "Could I get you a cup of coffee or something?"

"No thanks, I just finished supper, Myrna cooked me a good steak for supper. She is a good cook. She seems like a nice girl."

"Yes, she is a good cook and a nice gal. I really enjoy her. She has some good kids too."

He looked around at me and said, "I thought I had this rehearsed but I forgot what I was wanting to say. Let's skip the small talk and get down to business. I have to make a horseback trip up on the mountain above Yellow Pine. Would you like to go?"

"I would love it, when?"

"Tomorrow about ten in the morning, if that is alright with you. We should be back about two or so. That is a real pretty trip, we follow a road most of the way up. So it's pretty easy riding."

"I'll be ready at ten. Do you want me to come up or do you want to come down here?"

"I'll come down here. The horses are down by the school. I'll take the trailer down and saddle them up there and come on over here. I make quite a few trips like this to check for feed or count deer or elk population. I need to check on that mountain right there," as he pointed over the town to the east, "for what is growing up there and that tells us what kind of animals will populate that area during what seasons."

"That sounds interesting. I didn't realize all that was necessary to find what animals were where and when. That is fascinating."

"Yes it is very interesting work. Some people think all we do is run up and down the road trying to snag someone on a violation. That is a small part of the work. In fact my theory is if they see that the officers are out and around they won't be so apt to break the law. I don't like to ticket anyone. I think a lot of times people get so excited they forget to count their fish, then when we stop and count them, they are shocked to find they have too many."

"I will talk to Bonnie or Phyllis to see if they can watch the little kids. The bigger kids will be in school. Oh I am so anxious to go, I haven't done anything like this for years."

He stood, put his hand on my shoulder and I automatically put my hand on his, then thought I shouldn't have done that. I took my hand down. He smiled and said, "I'll see you in the morning." He walked back down the road. I watched until he was out of sight. He walks so proud and so straight. He is such a handsome man. My heart was doing funny things again.

It didn't take long to make the arrangements. I began wondering what I was going to wear. I looked and looked and couldn't decide. I went in and looked at my hair, shall I wash it, no it will be too frizzy tomorrow, I'll just put a few curlers in it. I had some Wellington boots which were real comfortable, I'll wear those. I turned around and went into the kitchen and sat at the table. What are you doing Rose? This isn't good, be careful. Oh

God remember my prayer the other night. I wish I were stronger, why am I so weak.

Seemed like days until the next morning and I was spending a lot of time getting ready. Finally 10 o'clock came. He was punctual that's very good. Gee he looks good on that horse. He is a good rider. I raced out the door, I couldn't hold my excitement. I embarrassed myself. I noticed he must have felt the same way. Well, I thought he was too dignified to get excited. I thought I was too.

I walked out to where the horses were, I smiled at him and said "Good morning." He came back with a big smile and a very hearty greeting.

"Are you ready for this?" As he was getting down off his horse.

"Yes, I am. These are good-looking horses. Are they yours?" He was walking around front and tying the halter rope on to the saddle.

"No they belong to the Fish and Game but they are mine for the summer."

I took a hold of the reins and the saddle horn and pulled myself up and into the saddle. I was glad to see I had the shorter horse. My legs are short and sometimes I have to find a stump.

The horses were ready to go. They turned sharply and we were off. Frank pulled up on his horse and said "That's enough of that, we've got a long ways to go, you better take it easy." The horses slowed to a walk and we leisurely went down the lane. It felt so good to be on a horse again and riding down this beautiful old road shaded with acres of overgrown yellow pines.

We road up Johnson Creek about two miles past the rock slide and started up the trail which had been a road from a mine at one time. We didn't talk much, we were enjoying the ride and the scenery. Frank was right. It was just about noon when we got up there. We dismounted on a grassy knoll overlooking Yellow Pine. It truly looked like a lush green lawn. The grass about three inches high.

We walked around the edge of the opening looking down at the community and identifying certain houses, Uncle Tom's place. Frank showed me his house. In surprise I asked, "You have a house here, where is it, I can't tell which one you mean."

"See that little white cabin down there on the edge of the hill. It is not far from the Judge's house, just come out on to the street and go down two houses. It isn't mine, it belongs to Fish and Game. I'll be staying in it for the summer. When other officers come in they will also stay there. There are several bunks in there."

"Yes I see now, you do plan to stay here all summer?"

"Yes, I will go out for meetings once a month, and that's about all unless I have to go out for court on some violation. That would be the ones that the Judge does not take care of, when they contest it. They don't do that often though, they just plead guilty and pay the fine. It is much cheaper in the long run. Of course if they are not guilty, they won't pay the fine. I'm generally darn sure before I give anyone a ticket."

We sat on the edge of the hill, looking around, enjoying the view. It was a wonderful place to be. I was beginning to wish I had brought a lunch, but that was the farthest thing from my mind when I was getting ready to go.

Frank got up, walked over to his horse and took some thing from his saddle bag. He came back over where I was sitting and opened up a small bag. He took out some rations and we had lunch. He even had a small thermos of coffee. That was a wonderful meal but even more so because we were together. I told him how nice it was to bring lunch and coffee. He said I always have a lunch with me, these do not spoil. After a time or two getting very hungry, I don't forget to repack the pack as soon as I get home.

We began to exchange backgrounds to find out more about each other. We talked for probably an hour. He got up and picking up from the lunch he said, "If we get home by two, we are going to have to run the horses all the way."

"Is it that important that we get there by two?"

"No but I try to be punctual. I think you are the only one I told two o'clock. You probably told the kids and they will be looking for us at two. I don't want to get on the bad side of them already."

"Well, let's take a chance and not run down that hill with these poor horses."

"You don't think they will be angry with me?"

"No I am sure they won't. I appreciate you being concerned and I also appreciate you being punctual. But I don't think you are the kind of guy who runs horses downhill."

He smiled at that and said, "No not hardly."

He reached down taking my hand and helped me to my feet. I was directly in front of him when I was standing. He looked at me and I looked away. He put his hand under my chin and lifted up my face. His face was so close, his eyes focused on my mouth, his lips barely touched mine. I wanted more but yet I didn't. He put his arms around me, I laid my head against his shoulder. He held me that way for awhile and then whispered to me. "You didn't want me to do that did you?"

I whispered "Yes and No."

"What does that mean?" He drew back and looked in my eyes like he was trying to learn what I was feeling, but not saying.

"Frank, I am very attracted to you. I don't play games. And I don't go out with married men. I am a Christian and I am suppose to be setting an example in this town and to the world. This is a hard situation for me because I really like you. I have never known a man that I could feel so comfortable with. There is something different about you."

"You make me feel very guilty, I should just have left you alone. I don't want to hurt you, nor your testimony. Please believe me I am not playing games. Since the day I met you in the store, I haven't been able to get my mind off you. I feel very deeply about you and I know I don't have the right to say that now. Rose, I am getting a divorce, does that make any difference?"

"Yes, to me it does, but will the people in this town believe that. Frank, please let's wait until you get the divorce. I just can't do this. I am happy when I am with you and in agony when I am not, thinking about what this looks like to other people and I am very concerned about the Lord. He is my Master, my Father, I hate to disappoint Him. He has done some wonderful things for me and the kids. I love the Lord, He is expecting a lot from me. I can't disappoint Him."

"I know Rose, I have a strong faith also. I have not been able to even go to church since I married Shirley as she is a Mormon. I can't become a Mormon, I can't believe that way but my boys are Mormon. I can't hurt them. I want to get a divorce and get away from this and it won't hurt the boys so bad then when they don't see me going to their church. I see the meaning of unequally yoked now. I thought it could be worked out. But it has been a living hell. There is no end to the hurt it causes."

"While we are talking, I can't help but wonder how you feel about my seven kids. Most men run from that and don't want anything to do with it. You didn't seem shocked when I told you, like most people. I am proud of my kids and I would never do anything that would risk their future. I realize that men would worry about supporting a family, I don't blame them."

"To be honest with you I like kids and I love a big family. I don't think it would be a problem to me. I don't make a big salary, but you must have some kind of support, you have taken care of them this far."

"Frank do you realize what we are saying, we talk like we are having big ideas about a future."

"Well I think it is good to get these things talked about at the beginning of a relationship. It is good to be honest with each other."

"We had better go." I was turning when Frank took my arm and turned me around and said, "May I kiss you?" My eyes must have said yes because he didn't wait for an answer. He again kissed me tenderly, he held me for a while. I couldn't respond. I couldn't encourage him. I couldn't pull away. I stood there as long as he held me, it was wonderful. "Let's go."

We rode down the hill in silence. I was thinking about what we were doing to each other. Is this just going to cause us both misery. Where else can it go? I knew I could become blind very easy. I prayed that God would not let go of me. Please stay with me Lord. Help me through this. I know in the end it will be you and me. I have to be strong. I am not strong enough. God help me.

Even though we didn't talk we were communicating. Every so often he would reach for my hand. I put my hand in his, he squeezed it and smiled at me. I smiled back. " I'm happy, are you?"

"Yes and No." He said he understood.

When we arrived at the cabin, he got off his horse and came over to mine. He reached up his arms, I hesitated and he said, "I'll be good really. But it's not easy." He still held his arms up so I slid off the horse and into his arms. He put me on the ground and drew back and said, " Thank you for a wonderful day."

"You are very welcome, but I should thank you and I do. This was so great. I will never forget it. That beautiful mountain top. The scenery, the whole thing was out of this world. Thank you so much Frank."

"Can we do this again? Not to the same place but some of the other places I have to go. Pete told me when he was here, there were a lot of places that needed to be checked. I have to do a beaver check on Johnson Creek below Dead Horse. Would you like to go?"

"How could I refuse? Trail riding is my favorite sport. Let me think it over. Bye."

"Bye." He walked away leading the horses. I turned around when I got up on the porch, I watched until he was out of sight.

My heart was singing, there was so much hope here in this relationship. I would never dream that I could have so much in common with anyone. Our likes and dislikes were so similar. We were so compatible. "Is it possible that the Lord sent him here for me? It isn't God's way of doing things, is it? God if this isn't your plan, why did you put us to together. You surely knew we would fall for one another."

School was out and the kids wanted to go with me to pick up Grandma at Uncle Ed and Aunt Lois' place in Boise. We picked up Billy in McCall and took him with us. We were loaded but that's the way we came to Idaho so we could do it again.

It was so good to see all of them. I couldn't believe Linda and Tom. Ed's kids, were adults. Linda was driving the car and she was as big as I was. Tom was bigger, he drove too but he wasn't supposed to. He was an adventurous kid. Mom looked great, she was so happy to get back in Idaho. She gave her report of the family in Oregon. Everyone was fine.

Lois was getting supper, I told her not to try to fix something for all of us. We can go to McDonald's. She wouldn't hear of it. They also insisted that we stay all night. I said "Where in the world would you put all of us?"

Ed said, "Come in here and look. This is Lois' new sewing room but it isn't finished yet. See all these pads on the floor. That's where the kids are going to sleep and you can sleep in Linda's room and Mom can sleep in Tom's room. Now I don't want to hear any more about you not staying all night."

Lois fixed a big pot of chicken and noodles, a big salad and fresh bread. They had a big picnic table in the back. The kids sat out there to eat and the adults ate at the dining room table.

We had a wonderful evening. The kids had a great time, the kids were flying about from one thing to another. Linda was driving them around in the car and they were so excited to go, especially since they didn't have to have adults with them. I was concerned but Ed said, "Oh they will be alright, Linda is a good driver." Lois' response to that was, "She might be, but she doesn't drive me." We all laughed because very few people ever drive Lois.

We finally got the kids all settled down and went to bed. I heard them laughing and giggling most of the night. Sure enough when I went in to wake them up so we could go, no one wanted to get up. They did though and we had a nice quiet drive home. We stopped in McCall to get a few groceries to take back in. Mom didn't want to stay long because she was anxious to get in there. Sure enough when we got into the timber she started

O-O-ing and ah-ah-ing. "Look over there Rose isn't that beautiful. God just didn't make another Idaho, this is the prettiest state in the Nation. Oh, look at those mountains way over there in the distance, they are so majestic." She was quiet for a few moments and then, "That is such a pretty campground. Every time I go by a campground I think how nice it would be to stay there."

"Mom, maybe God will have a campground for you to live in when you get to heaven."

"Well, I wouldn't want to live there alone."

"I'm sure there are other people who feel that way about campgrounds. I do, I'd come and live with you."

"I'm not ready to go there yet."

"I think you will be when the time comes."

"Let's talk about something else."

We drove into Yellow Pine and around the school house, down the old road to the cabin. When we pulled up into the yard, Uncle Tom came out to meet us. He and Mom embraced. They were happy to see each other. They both remarked how well the other looked.

"Tom I will go over and put my stuff away, why don't you put on the coffee pot. I'll come back over to visit you while Rose is getting dinner."

After supper we did the dishes and the kids went off to play, I had noticed Mom being rather sullen, so I wasn't surprised when she said, "Rose, Tom said you were going out with someone."

"Well we went for a horseback ride and down to the Coxes to a dance. We didn't stay long because the place was so crowded. I have never seen so many people."

Mom was looking rather stuffy and somber "Who is it?"

"His name is Frank Watkins, he works for Fish and Game."

"Did you know he is married?"

"Yes I did know that."

"What, you knew that and you are going out with him?"

"Mom, he is getting a divorce."

"Oh sure, that's what he would tell you. I'll bet he never gets a divorce."

"Mom, how can you say that, you don't even know him. He is a very nice guy. I care a lot for him."

"Oh, I suppose you do. Why don't you face the truth? He is not divorced and he won't be because he is playing it safe. He wouldn't marry you with all these kids. What on earth are you thinking of? What about the church here? What are these people going to say? How do you think the Lord feels about this?"

"Mom I am not a child anymore, and I can make my own decisions. I would appreciate it if you didn't bring it up again."

She started to cry, "I just don't want to see you get hurt and I know what will happen."

"You don't know, you are not God. I talk to Him about it all the time. I will leave if you don't quit talking about this."

She stormed out of the house crying heading for Uncle Tom's. I was sick. Here it is, its just the first of it but it won't be the last. She is the toughest critic I've got. The worst thing about it, I know she is right. But I knew before she told me. Does she think I am a child? It hurt, it hurts bad. I was especially hurt about Uncle Tom telling her. I went for a walk down to the East Fork bridge. I didn't think I would see anyone that way. I was standing on the bridge just watching the water, when a car pulled up behind me and stopped. It was Frank. He got out of the car and said, "You were very deep in thought, is something wrong, or did you just lose your best friend?"

"Well kinda, my mother came in today for a visit and Uncle Tom told her I was going with a married man." His face went white, his eyes showed instant pain that extended across his face.

"Oh Rose, I'm so sorry. I won't come around anymore. You were right. We have to wait until my divorce is final. If we care for each other as much as we think we do, then it won't go away. Will you wait for me?"

"Yes, yes I will wait." My emotions were brimming over the top. He stepped over toward me and we went into each others arms, clinging to each other. Then his lips found mine with a crushing kiss that caused my heart to break.

"Rose, I love you, please wait for me. I have to go before someone comes. I will see you around town and we can speak, can't we?"

"Yes, of course we can speak. I will wait."

He jumped in his car and drove away toward Yellow Pine.

I was so shaken I could hardly walk. I sat down on a rock up on top of the hill. Tears would have been welcome now but they wouldn't come, I felt like I was frozen. I needed some way to release this pain inside me. I began to pray. I pleaded with God to understand. I said "God I hope you don't look at this like Mom does. It sounds so sinful the way she says it.

Frank and Uncle Tom.

Please God, try to understand. Don't let me go, help me through this. Stand by me. In Jesus Name, Amen."

I was able to go on back up to the cabin. I felt better. I felt like God did understand. When I walked up to the cabin, Mom had evidently been watching for me. She came out of the house in a rush, "Rose! Where on earth did you go. I've been worried sick about you. Don't you do that again. You tell me when you are going and where you are going. I don't like sitting here by myself."

I walked on by saying casually, I walked down to the bridge.

"Well couldn't you ask me to go with you? I hope the rest of this vacation isn't going to go like this. What are you mad about? Frank I suppose."

"Mom please be quiet about it. I don't want to hear any more. Let's drive over to Big Creek tomorrow."

"Oh yes, let's do. Now that's better, it isn't so hard is it?"

I looked at her wanting to say so many things, but it would be useless, only cause more hard feelings. "Mom do you want a cup of hot chocolate before we go to bed? I would like to get up fairly early so we can have plenty of time." The kids came straggling in about that time, I would wait for a while longer before I blew the horn. It was such a nice quiet evening outside I hated to disturb it.

I would have to say Mom's visit was not a happy one for me. She wouldn't let it be. We took Uncle Tom with us a lot and she didn't bring Frank up as much with Uncle Tom and the kids around except subtle little things like, "What are you moping around for?" or "I wish you would get your mind on something else." I call that sarcasm. I hate that, but it runs in my family. It's just a dirty little way of saying something you shouldn't say.

I loved my mother and I liked to have her around and do things with her, but when she got on something like this, she nearly drove me crazy. I was glad to see her vacation over. I went out to McCall and rented a house before she left so when I took her back home I could get my furniture from her place (in Oregon) and be ready to move out by the time school started.

It was good to see everyone back there in Oregon, but I was so busy trying to visit all my friends and packing and sorting etc. I was worn out. I was beginning to feel the effects of anxiety.

I rushed all the more to get things ready to go. I thought I would feel better when I got back home in that little cabin. Donna and Darrell and Jack and Mary each took a load up for me and I rented a U-Haul trailer. We got it all packed and were ready to go. I hated to leave Mom after having words with her and knowing how she felt. I was ready to say something like I'm sorry Mom for getting upset with you. I don't want you to worry, everything will be fine. She beat me to it when she said, "Now Rose, you know the right thing to do and I want you to promise me you will do it, it is for your own good. Remember that."

"Yes Mom."

I know the story was passed around to the family and close friends. I could feel it by what they didn't say and how they would turn their heads when certain things were brought up. All I wanted to do when I left there was get away from all of them. Go back to the mountains.

Our trip was tiring, slow and hot, everyone was having blowouts. We were all traveling pretty close together and would stop when we found someone in trouble. It was slow. We stopped outside of Burns and slept in the vehicles. The guys threw their sleeping bags down on the ground and thought it was fine but I for one didn't go for that because there were a lot of rattlesnakes there and we were right by a big rock ledge where I felt sure they would be. I slept very uncomfortably sitting up in my car.

We had breakfast from a bag out there under the rock. We stopped at a drive in and got loaded up on coffee and we were on our way.

We got into McCall that evening and it didn't take them long to unload because Jack wanted to go fishing. Donna and Darrell wanted to go back because he had to go to work.

Mary and I stayed in McCall and put away some things and took the trailer to a station to leave it.

Rosana, Janet and Steve were with us, so we went on into Yellow Pine. The guys had all gone to some lake fishing so we had a night to rest and did it feel good. I got up in the morning, made coffee and went out to sit on the porch in my robe drinking coffee. Pretty soon I heard a happy little voice, "Good Morning Rose." Mary was up too and we enjoyed that wonderful peace and quiet. Uncle Tom came strolling over with his cup of coffee and sat and talked to us. It was so good to get back. Thank you God for sending me to this place where I could find peace.

Before the guys got back I had a chance to talk to Mary about Frank. She was so understanding and was so sorry for the way things were. She said she would pray for me.

Jack and Mary spent a few days and left for home, I hated to see them go. Mary and I always had such a good time, she kept me in stitches most of the time, not intentionally but just being Mary.

Mary and I were walking along the East Fork road, waiting for Jack. We passed the time of day with whoever we met. I asked a fisherman if he was getting any fish. He said "No not many."

Mary asked, "Did you know him?"

"Everyone up here is friendly, I just talk to everyone."

"Well, isn't that nice. It is so different up here."

The next fisherman we saw down by the river Mary called to him in a squeaky high-pitched voice, a little unsure of herself, she said, "Are you getting any?" He thought she was flirting with him and he said, "Do you want to come down here and help me?"

Mary looked at me and said, "I said just what you said, why did he say that to me?" This embarrassed her so bad she could have crawled under a rock. We walked back to the car and left. I could hardly contain myself, I laughed until I had a side ache. It was always something like that with Mary. It was so good to spend some time with her. She lightened up my life.

Just after Jack and Mary left my brother Roy drove up in his pickup from Oregon. He had been drinking and I was not too happy to see him that way. We went over to visit Uncle Tom but didn't stay very long as Uncle Tom did not drink anymore. Swede was not having a very good time with me and the kids. He talked a lot but became bored pretty soon.

"Come on, let's go to town. Come on, get your coat let's go."

"I don't want to go up there, you go."

"Oh come on what's the matter with you, do you think you are too good to go with me?"

"Don't be ridiculous, I just don't want to go." He was getting angry. When he drank and got angry it was bad, he embarrassed me so, talking too loud and cursing. I thought I had better go. I didn't want to fuss anymore with him. He did ask me to drive and I was glad of that. He was in no shape to drive.

When we got up town I asked him where he wanted to go. "I want to go see Murf. I haven't seen him for a long time."

We went into Murf's, Roy was disgusting the way he was acting. I tried to wander away, but he wanted me to be right beside him. He found Murf and greeted him, They talked for awhile, there was a group of towns people in the back room sitting by the fireplace visiting. Myrna and Eddie were there. Eddie had his guitar and was singing a few requests. Swede asked me to dance, I felt that I had to as much as I didn't want to. He did pretty well on the dance floor. He is a good dancer and he quit talking when he was dancing. He asked other ladies to dance but every other dance he asked me.

We were dancing and I saw Frank come in the door. He came in the back and sat down by Eddie and Myrna. I spoke very casual to him. He asked Myrna to dance. The next dance he asked me. I got up to dance with him and I could see Swede watching us. We barely talked and when we finished our dance he said, "Well I had a hard day and I'm going home and go to bed." He walked out the door.

Roy watched him and I wondered what was up. "Was that the son of a —— that's after my sister? I'm gonna kill him."

He went out the door, and I was right behind him. He got into the pickup and got a pistol. He took it out of the holster and threw the holster back onto the seat and said, "Which way did he go?" He was looking up and down the street. I was getting very frightened and I began yelling at him "Swede, what is wrong with you. Give me that gun. You are not going to shoot anyone."

"Don't you tell me girl what I am going to do. Now get out of the way, I'm going to kill him."

He was walking down the street in the direction of Frank's cabin, "Where does he live Sis, I want that guy, I will teach him to fool around with my sister. I'll kill him."

I heard a man's voice and he must have heard him too, Frank was saying "Are you looking for me mister, what can I do for you?" Swede went after him. I got in front of him and was trying to get the gun from him. Frank was standing by his car.

I was screaming at Swede, "Don't please don't, give me the gun. You can't shoot anyone." Frank stepped up and took my arm and pulled me away from Swede and said, "You get back, move clear away from here. I can take care of this. Go, now." I looked at him wondering if he knew how crazy my brother was when he got drunk. He looked at me again and said "Go home."

I backed away. Swede went after Frank and Frank grabbed for his hand that held the gun. I saw them wrestling over the gun and I turned and ran up the street. Myrna came after me and took hold of my arm and said "Rose, you come with me into my house, Frank will take care of that, he is a law officer and he has been trained to do this. He doesn't want you anywhere around." I went with her and she took me way back into the back of the house. We sat there for awhile and she said, "I hear your brother's pickup starting. Let's just wait for awhile and I'll walk you home."

"I don't want to go down there if Swede is there. I am afraid of him."

Myrna said "Okay, if we see his pickup there, we will come back."

"But Myrna my kids are there. I really don't think he will hurt them. I always thought he was all bluff but now I don't know. I haven't been around him much lately, never when he was drunk."

"I'll tell you what, if he is or isn't there, would you like for me to come in and spend the night with you, Eddie will be here."

"Yes Myrna would you mind doing that. I would feel so much better. This is terrible, it seems like a bad dream."

"But it isn't Rose, it's real. I'll leave Eddie a note and tell him where I am."

We walked toward the house and didn't see the pickup there. We kept walking closer, no sign of him anywhere. We got into the house and all the kids were in bed asleep and it all looked so good. "Myrna why don't you stay for a while and if he doesn't show up, I would say he went to sleep somewhere in the pickup or he has wrecked his pickup. I can't do anything about that if he did. I had better stay right here. You can go on home though if you want to."

"Are you sure you are all right, you had quite a shock."

"I'm fine. Thank you Myrna, you are such a good friend."

I gave her a big hug and she left. I locked the door behind her and went to bed. I didn't sleep well. I had such a mixture of feelings inside of me. Oh, how terrible what my brother said to the whole town, how can I ever face them again. I felt guilt, I was ashamed, I was afraid, but most of all I was proud of Frank, the way he handled it, and his first concern was for me. No one had ever treated me that way. "Thank you God for Frank."

Chapter 16

"Lonely Again"

1966

The agonizing loneliness I had suffered after the kid's father died, when I seemed to be forever searching to find surcease from my sorrow. In meeting Frank, the vacancy was filled, someone special to think about, and someone who thought about me. Someone I could look forward to seeing. Someone to look special for. Someone with whom I may have a future. It was so good to have these things in my life, I could hardly remember what it was like to not have anyone who cared. With that vacancy filled, there also came some new heartaches and anxieties.

In reflection, I saw a time when Bill was living that I was as lonely as anyone could possibly be. And before that, in the isolated areas of my childhood, the loneliness that I was so aware of every hour of the day.

The only time I had not been lonely were the last two years of Bill's life. I had a satisfying life with someone to love and someone who loved me. So I knew love and then it was gone. I resented Bill for a long time for leaving me. I felt like he hurt me again and it was the last thing he did in his life. If he had lived 100 more years he could not have hurt me any worse than he did then. It took me a long time to work through this and I could not have, had I not known the Lord.

I had a problem accepting love, in my heart I didn't really believe that anyone could love me. Rejection by my father and stepfather, I'm sure had a lot to do with this insecurity. My early life with Bill was a big factor in this problem also. I found that really loving someone was very painful as well as it is beautiful.

What my mother told me was like a knife in my heart bringing back so much pain. In prayer, God enabled me to see that no one can hurt me unless I let them. We can't blame anyone or anything for our lives being what they are. We have a choice. Certainly an influence can mold us one way or the other, but when we give our hearts to the Lord, we give up our rights to our own person. We become what God wants us to be. Usually not willingly but if God can work us through enough trials, we will become what He wants us to be.

Frank was such a gentle person, so tender, so understanding, and so considerate. He accepted my kids and cared deeply for them. He was willing to take my kids as a part of me. He was a good decent man. He was saved, but not living a dedicated Christian life. He knew and lived Christian principals.

After Mom planted the seed of doubt, I was constantly reaffirming our relationship. I was also justifying it. I was so afraid to accept him as he was. What did I have? Was it something from someone's self-seeking sense of judgment or was it a relationship sent from God. There must be a key somewhere to unlock the secret.

Could I ask him to stand up to everyone's expectations?

Even those who didn't know him. He probably reached the mark far beyond their expectations, if they only knew. It wasn't fair, how could anyone do this to another. My very soul was injured, there was always doubt and fear, loving him as I did, I was tortured by it.

The hurt didn't stop when Mom went home. It came just as blunt and torturous as what came from her. Letters that I received were streaked with the stench of censure. He was convicted and sentenced to death by my brother. Only God knew him. Why didn't everyone let God handle it? He had taken care of me thus far. Wouldn't He do it again? It wouldn't have hurt so badly had it come from God. I would have been more inclined to listen to God. Were they making this judgment on hearsay? Yes! They had never met him!

Mom said, "Face the facts! You know that no man will ever marry you with all these kids." Is that what all were basing their opinion on? I desperately rejected that theory. I was not going to put the blame on my kids. I could not bear to think they stood between me and my happiness. They were not to blame! They were my first priority in life; my ministry.

Resentment swelled up in me and I became so defensive. I did not resent Frank, nor the kids, but the unknown. I became careless, and I was falling more in love with Frank every day. I don't consider myself a defiant person, but looking back now I think I was out to prove every one of the critics wrong.

Frank never told me what happened that night. He just said, "Oh there was nothing to it."

Roy left after the night of the gun incident. I felt bad for him, I know he was ashamed. I believe there was an agitator that stirred him up when he wasn't in his right mind. I don't know who it was, and I don't care. It could have left Frank dead and landed Roy in prison for the rest of his life!

We seldom went to town. Frank came to the house frequently bringing his guitar and we sang together. Our favorite song, which was popular then was "Whispering Pines." Our favorite musicals were "Wonderland by Night." and "Baby Elephant Walk."

We took the kids and went on picnics. We went hiking around the country. He took us to a camp site where someone had obviously spent a lot of time; probably many summers by the looks of the camp. The camp was hidden in an enclosed area where no one would ever bother them. It looked like something from a Tarzan movie. He showed us so many things of great interest. We all loved the outdoors and spent a lot of time together.

The kids were very fond of Frank. He joked with them and told them stories. He was so fair with them; he did not choose one above the other. He was supportive and always seemed to be interested in each of them. He liked to look at their report cards and jokingly told them not to be discouraged if they didn't get a real good grade because this is what those scores really meant: "A" was awful, "B" was bad, and so forth until he got to "F" which was FINE. His middle initial was "G." The kids asked what it stood for. He told them Geronimo. They thought that was a good name, the little ones anyway.

Frank was very fond of his mother and wrote to her often. Apparently he told her about me and gave her my address. I received a letter saying she was so happy that Frank found someone to love and who loved him. She told me how he praised me as a good women. It was a very sweet letter. We corresponded for a long time.

Frank wrote poetry. He gave me several of his poems which were very good. Some were very serious, and some were jolly rhymes. He wrote so easily; the words just flowed.

After Mom went home, I just couldn't stop thinking about what Uncle Tom told her. One day I walked over to his house and took my coffee pot just in case he didn't have any made. He was sitting at his table, watching the deer at the salt lick, which was just a few feet from his window. They were so used to him watching them, they didn't pay any attention to him. They were also getting used to us, but not in his window. He made me stand back until they left.

Once when we first came up there, our little dog Smokey saw the deer and ran after them, barking. Uncle Tom came out the door and said, "You had better do something with that dog."

"Yes, Yes, I will Uncle Tom. We can't have him running off the deer." I called Smokey to me and got right down in his face and told him, "If you ever do that again, Uncle Tom will skin you and hang your hide on the fence post. How would you like that? No! No! You can't chase the deer away. Those deer would sure laugh at you hanging on the fence post." He hung his head and his belly was dragging the ground all the way to the house.

Steve said to me "Mom, you hurt his feelings. Would Uncle Tom really do that?"

"No, but Smokey didn't know what I was saying, and don't you tell him." Smokey never chased the deer again. In fact, when he saw a deer he laid down like a sheep dog. He would chase anything else he saw though, unless he was scolded for it.

After the deer left, I scooted my chair up to his table and poured us some coffee.

"Uncle Tom?"

"Y-e-e-e-s-s, what do you want?"

"Who told you about Frank and me going together?" I said, just to open up the subject.

"No one had to tell me, I saw you. Do you think I'm blind and didn't see the two of you coming in here on horses, or him coming to pick you up with that other guy? What was I to think? You didn't say a word to me about anything!"

"Well, that was just before Mom came, and I didn't have the opportunity to talk to you alone. How did you know he was married?"

"Bertha told me he was married," I said.

"Oh, I see. Well Uncle Tom, everyone seems to think he is a bad guy. He isn't, he is a very nice person. Mom thinks that he never has any intentions of marrying me with all my kids. So he is lying when he tells me he is getting a divorce."

"Well maybe he is, how do you know he isn't?"

"Before you call someone a liar you have to know he is lying beyond a shadow of a doubt, until then you have to believe that he is not a liar. Right?"

"Yes I would say you are right. So what was he supposed to have lied to you about."

"Well, I think that they (whoever they are) think he is just taking advantage of me."

"And you don't think he is?"

"No, I don't, I know he is not!"

"Then don't worry about it. Let them say what they want to. You are the only one that matters. It isn't hurting them anyway. What are they trying to do, just get something on you? Are they jealous? They won't say anymore to me about it, I'll tell you that."

"Oh, Uncle Tom, you are wonderful! I was so hurt when I thought you told Mom all this. Thank you, Thank you, for being so understanding. I love you Uncle Tom!"

I got up and put my arms around his neck and hugged him. "Now don't choke me or I'll give you a dutch rub."

I gave him a kiss on top of the head and ran out the door.

Steve discovered some frogs in a swampy bog. He asked permission to wade in there to get them. I said if he didn't get wet, he could. It wasn't very deep so he'd roll up his pant legs. He came home a little later with several frogs. When I saw his feet I couldn't believe it. They were as black as anything I had ever seen! When he saw how shocked I was he became concerned. "Won't it come off Mom?"

"Where was this pond Steve, and what did you wade in?"

"It was down behind the big shop, across the road from the school." He was getting frightened, so I said calmly, "Stand right there and don't move. Let me get the mop bucket and we will wash them." I put some good hot water and laundry soap in it. We went out on the porch and put those black feet to soak in the bucket. We were going to soak them, and I was sure it would come right off. After a half hour they looked the same. I scrubbed them, they looked the same. More hot water and laundry soap, they looked the same. He soaked his feet until bed time but it did not come off. He was on the verge of tears. He didn't want to go to bed with black feet. "We can put some Purex in the water and see if that takes it off. Come back in here and we will try it." I put hot water, soap and Purex in the bucket, he soaked and we waited. After 15 minutes we looked. They were a little lighter. Another half hour, we looked, a little lighter yet. It got to the point that the soak had done as much as it was going to do. He had to go to bed with grey feet. I was concerned he would be burned from all the chemicals and scrubbing, so I put vaseline on in a thick layer all over his feet and legs up to his knees. Then I put socks on him to keep it on. He felt better now. He could go to bed. There was a couple more times that summer that we had to give him the soaks. He had the toughest feet in town. He was so proud when we went to Roosevelt Lake he had to show Jack that he could run on that sharp shale rock and it didn't even hurt.

Frank brought his boys up to stay with him for a week. I knew he was bringing them in, but I was surprised when he brought them down to meet us when they first came to town. They were in high school. They were handsome boys with dark hair and brown eyes.

They were just like Frank: friendly and outgoing. They were a little older than my boys and they all got along well.

Frank was gone a lot of the time that week. There was work that took him out of town. The boys stayed with us. They fit right in, and I was very fond of them by the end of the week. They worshipped their dad. They talked of him often and with great respect. They said one day that they had a lot of clothes that they couldn't wear because they had grown out of them. Would we mind if they gave them to us? They knew some would fit Merrill and Tom. We said sure, we would be glad to have them. Frank brought them back with him when he took the boys home. He said the boys had gone into the house and started cleaning out their bedrooms to get the clothes ready for him, because they knew he had to go right back.

Bonnie and Phyllis asked me if Frank and I would please come to town Saturday night because there was going to be a good band in town. All the ladies in town were coming out to the dance. Well, I said I would ask Frank, or they could. They would probably see him before I did. It was okay with me. (I had this little quickening in my chest when I said I would.)

We went to the dance and I threw all caution to the wind and had a good time. In fact, I was asked to sing. I told them I would only sing Christian songs. They asked for "Supper Time" because someone heard me sing that before. When I began to sing the people became reverent and respectful of a Christian song. If they had drinks they sat them down on the bar and turned around and listened. You could have heard a pin drop. I was so pleased that they showed such respect for the Lord. It was becoming easier for me to go in there. I felt like I could serve a purpose and certainly everyone showed respect. I conducted myself as lady-like as I possibly could. I did not loiter there unless it was with Bonnie and Phyllis and the other local people after business hours. I occasionally went in to talk to Dad. It was a situation that was hard to explain to people on the outside.

In the back of my mind I was asking if my conscience was becoming seared. Was I justifying my actions? I hoped not. I wanted to do the Lord's Will. I wanted to be a good example.

I wasn't sure why I felt uncomfortable, was it because I thought the Lord would disapprove or was it others I was concerned about? I did to the best of my ability, do the Lord's work there or wherever I went.

I had a saying, "It is no struggle to be a Christian in the four walls of your church, but test yourself among the sinners." So often after that, if I came in and if there was live music, I was asked to sing and the response was always the same. Dad asked me to sing "Old Shep." I didn't think the Lord would have any objections to that. They loved it. They didn't have very much entertainment there. This helped me to recover from the personal devastation after the episode with my brother.

Poor soul, I'm sure he wouldn't have done that if he were not drinking. He is a dear, understanding brother to me now. He doesn't drink or smoke anymore, but I have yet to win him for the Lord. I pray for him, and I'm sure it is just a matter of time.

I realized I couldn't alienate myself from these people and have any positive effect on their lives or their souls. They needed Jesus, wherever they were. This may be the only chance for them to hear. I soon learned that it was expected of me to speak to them about the Lord.

Betty was a believer. She came to Church now and then, but she was in the wrong business to live a Christian life. She never objected to me witnessing there. I did not approach just anyone, but it was a common thing for people to draw near to me and want to talk about their problems in relation to the Lord. In some cases they were there for a beer to relieve their anxieties. I wanted them to know I was available to talk to them anytime. They didn't hesitate to come to me. Sometimes they were there to eat and were glad to meet someone who had a church connection.

The church was full every Sunday. More adults seemed to be interested in attending services. People whom I had met at Tom's Place were coming to church. I'm sure they felt the barrier was down and I would accept them. So many times we alienate people not meaning to shun anyone, but by setting ourselves apart, we do. Being a servant of the Lord in a small community such as this, I felt it necessary to make contact with everyone. Some may disagree, but I believe there is a ministry for each of us who will avail ourselves and God puts us where He needs us and where we, as an individual, can be most effective. I was very careful not to compromise my Christian standards, wherever I went.

One afternoon I was working in the church doing some cleaning and I heard someone calling my name. I ran out the door and Betty was running up the street, panic was in her voice as she called, "Come quick Rose, Pat Lewis is dying."

I rushed in the door behind Betty and saw Pat lying in the hall in front of the bathroom. There was blood everywhere. I asked what happened to him and they said he had been vomiting pure blood. He came from the bathroom blood pouring out of his mouth and then vomiting in the hallway. He fell on the floor where he lay. He was not breathing. Laying on his back it was difficult to get to him. I got down and tried to squeeze myself in between Pat and the wall so I could get to his head. He was a very big man and his body filled the narrow hallway. I was trying to turn him over enough so I could check his airway. He was so heavy.

I asked for the men to come down and take his arms and pull him out of the hall. There were three men in there who refused to help. They would not but old Tom Graff, the attorney was saying, "If she brings him back to life, she is an angel. This man is dead, folks."

It was impossible to turn him. I couldn't get a hold of him.

I finally straddled him and laid forward locking my arms under his shoulders. I was able to move him when I rolled right with him. I let go with one hand and reached down his throat and pulled blood clots out. I heard gurgling and a faint, "Mom wait for me." I turned him more and did get his face in a position where the blood could flow out of his mouth and would not stop and clot in his throat. I called for a pillow or something to put under his head, which was laying back because his shoulders were so huge and his neck was so short.

Pat had been a boxer at one time and he did look the part. I kept reaching down his throat to clear it pulling out strings and clots. Finally I saw some red blood running and I knew there was enough room for an airway. All of a sudden he coughed and I was showered in blood laying so close to him. I already was blood from one end to the other. When Tom Graff heard him cough he yelled, "She did it folks, she brought him back, she is an angel for sure."

A jeep pulled up in from of the lodge. It took some six men to carry him out. They sat him in the back seat and asked me to get in there with him. No one else wanted to and I can't say as I blamed them, he looked pretty bad but so did I.

Someone radioed to Cascade and a plane was waiting for us at the airport. We loaded him as a dead weight but his heart was beating. They took him to the McCall Hospital. They began transfusions right away. When he was conscious, the doctor told him he was going to be there for a week. He was very low on blood and they would have to build him up before he could go home. He jerked out the tubes and got up, put his clothes on and came in on the mail stage the next day. He stayed home for some time until he got his strength back. Then he was up town drinking again.

When the plane took off, I turned to walk back to the jeep and Frank was standing there waiting for me with a blanket in his hands. He put the blanket around my shoulders and said "I'll drive you to town. I stopped and asked Phyllis to go down and get you some clean clothes and asked if you could use their shower. Everything will be waiting for you there. You did a good job Babe."

Faye Kissinger was working on the city water. This was his own project that he wanted to do for the community. He had the water source and put in a holding tank. With his backhoe he dug trenches all over town, laid the pipe and connected it to the building and turned on the water. He put water into every house in town. He will long be remembered for his contribution to the community.

A Civil Defense board was organized in the community for the purpose of getting some generators set up for power for the community. The community had to maintain, upkeep and pay for the diesel for the generators. A small charge was levied to each customer to pay that expense.

413

Each homeowner was responsible for the wiring of his house. The poles and wire for running the power lines throughout the community was paid for by Civil Defense.

Don Caward did most of the wiring for the homeowners. He worked around town for most of the summer. He was always such a swell guy to have around, everyone liked him. He gave the people a real cut in cost as most of the people in there were retired or on a limited income. The Stibnite houses were wired previously when Idaho Power came in there. Don had to check it all out and in some cases rewire everything.

Uncle Tom and Dad were so elated that they were finally getting power. It was going to make life so much easier. Now they could have a freezer and refrigerator. Lights they could turn off and on. Everyone was glad to get it but most of the people up town had generators for power.

The dim orange glow in the windows was gone.

I got a tip from Bob Darrow that Carl Woodall might sell his cabin down on Johnson Creek. Bob worked for Carl on the construction of the road down the East Fork. Bob in a way was related to me. I wrote to Carl right away and got a letter back saying he would sell it to me. I was elated to say the least. Carl built that cabin when his construction company was back there. It had been empty for years but some of Carl's family came now and then to stay overnight.

I had seen that cabin for years. Sometimes I walked over there and looked at the beautiful spot where it sat. The cabin was in good condition: stained logs and white shutters on the windows which set it apart from every other cabin in the country. I loved that cabin and always wanted it for my own.

The setting was so tranquil, with the big Yellow Pines all around it and the most beautiful creek in Idaho running by.

The coldest, purest spring water coming out of the hillside down by the creek. I bought the cabin for $50 with the patented mining claims that laid over the flat. I had no intentions of ever mining it, but there were many assessment holes on the flat. Uncle Tom gave me the furniture that was in the cabin where we stayed. We moved in lock, stock, and barrel. We got everything set up so we could go in on weekends to hold church services. The cabin needed some cleaning. We all pitched in and polished all the logs and scrubbed the floors. With one large room, big enough for a kitchen, dining and bedroom with a summer sleeping room on the back porch

Our cabin on Johnson Creek.

enclosed with screen, it didn't take long. When it became colder we put canvas over the screen and it kept out the elements somewhat.

We raked, cleaned the yard, and made a fire pit. We put blocks of wood around the pit to sit on. We cleaned out the trail to the creek so we could get to the spring more easily. We gathered all the broken limbs and stacked them by the fire pit for wood. During the time we lived there, I cooked in the dutch oven over the fire quite often. It was much better cooked that way than inside and it took much less wood. I had a big iron skillet (about an eighteen-inch) with a lid. It baked good corn bread over the fire. We sharpened up a lot of our camping skills while we were there. We enjoyed that place to the fullest.

I missed Uncle Tom's cabin and Uncle Tom, but Ernie Oberbillig was surveying it to be sold off in lots. Uncle Tom came down quite often for dinner or coffee or to visit. Dad came down once in a while. He had an old yellow truck so he would drive down to visit now and then.

The first of August in 1964 we moved to McCall and got settled so the kids could start to school. Soon we could get them registered. We had some school clothes shopping to do. We needed to get the power turned on.

The unpacking was going to be a big job. When we all pitched in to do a job, it didn't take us long. Everyone took care of their own bedrooms after the beds were set up.

We joined forces to organize the kitchen, it wasn't bad. We had it done in no time. Now I needed to go to town and get groceries to stock our shelves and the refrigerator. I was anxious to get back in there to our cabin. I told Frank when to expect us and I wanted to be as punctual as he was. I really appreciated that in him.

We drove in on Thursday afternoon. We met Frank on the East Fork. We stopped and he came over to the car. He gave me a kiss and greeted the kids. He said he had some news for me, but he couldn't take time now. He would stop by the cabin on his way home.

I felt like the news was something I didn't want to hear, my heart began pumping wildly. We drove to the cabin. We opened the shutters and started a fire in the cookstove. I couldn't help but think of the electric range out there and how easy it was to turn on. How easy it would be to wash clothes with a washer and dryer, wash dishes, take a bath, clean house, and, oh yes!, no wood to cut, no water to carry. Now what are the boys going to do. I believe my theory worked out, they did learn responsibility. Now if it only stays with them. That would be up to me to see that it stayed. Oh boy, back to work Mom.

"Oh God, I had taken so much for granted, up here, it was so easy here with the kids. Very little discipline. I guess God, was it because everyone was happy and kept busy. Thank you Lord for every happy hour we had. Thank you for that old cabin we loved so, for Uncle Tom, for the wonderful people that were so good to the kids and made life so great. Thank you Lord for the winter, the spring, and the summer. Most of all I thank you for the church you sent us to help establish. May it continue on until Jesus comes. Oh God it was all so wonderful. You truly gave us treasures. Thank You Lord."

I fixed a light supper that night because we were all tired and just wanted to relax. As we were picking up dishes, Frank drove in. There was enough for another plate so I fixed it for him. He seldom ate with us, but since I had his plate ready, he did sit down. I poured him some coffee. I was anxious to hear the news. I sat down beside him.

"Well, what is the news? I can't wait any longer."

"My transfer came through." He didn't look as happy as he should.

"Where, Frank?"

"Dubois. It is a long way from here. I just about have to take it. Someone has talked to the department and told them that I was seeing someone up here. They frown on that, since I am still married. It is a policy that the officers can't be involved in any kind of gossip. The department said to get my divorce and then they would have no objections. With the divorce not final, I am subject to the same kind of disciplinary action as a married man. It would be good to be up there where no one knows anything about either of us. Then we could get all this cleared up and be free to do what we want."

"Frank, I feel terrible, this is because of me."

"No, No, I had asked for a transfer and this just hurried it up. Think of this in a positive way. She can't fight this any longer. Then we can be free to do as we want. We can get married Sweetheart."

He reached out and squeezed my hand, "And I won't do too well up there without you, so this is going to expedite things."

"Frank who do you think could have done this? Do you think it could have been my family? It surely wasn't yours, she knew about us. There would have been problems before now if it were her."

"Well, I think so, but let's not worry about it. I don't want to blame anyone because it is true. I am still married and I am seeing you. I felt that because the divorce is pending it made a difference, but I guess not. I will have to leave at the end of the month. We will just tell everyone here it is a transfer."

I was more hurt than I wanted him to know. I couldn't imagine being without Frank now, he had made my life so much happier. He gave me a stability that I had never had before.

Now he would be gone. "Oh Lord, You have to be my strength, because mine is all gone," I prayed as I lay in bed in our little cabin waiting for the dawn.

Yellow Pine gave Frank a big going away party with gifts and dinners and cards. So many good wishes. It was so hard for me to hide my feelings during the party. I had to act happy when my heart was breaking.

Frank moved away and a part of me went with him. I knew I had to hold on, this is a long, long trail.

The fall was beautiful in McCall, the aspen trees were absolutely beautiful. I loved seeing their golden reflection on the water. It made me very sad to sit by the water, sending my prayers out over the water for Frank. I always cried before I left, "God my peace seems so short lived, what is there for me now. God I don't feel very strong, please hold my hand."

Janet started school this year, it was hard to see her grow up. She and Steve had been my babies for a long time. She was so happy in school it wasn't long until she was bringing a little schoolmate home with her, Karen Doris. They were two of a kind to be sure. They even looked alike. Oh, how I enjoyed their little plays and their songs and pretending to play the guitar. I laughed at those girls until my sides hurt. Have you ever laughed till you cry and do it discreetly, it's sheer agony. I wouldn't want to embarrass them. Marian Murry lived next door to me and she came over quite often and enjoyed the show in the afternoon also.

I lived for the letters from Frank. There was one in the mailbox everyday. It was full of beautiful words of devotion.

Commitment, future, all the things that a lonely woman wants to hear. I wrote back as soon as I read his letters, when my heart was so full of love for him. He told me about the desert, the antelope, all the different kinds of game in that country. He talked about the lakes and streams, the foliage, trees and parks. He was as lonely as I was, it hurt to know he was hurting.

A very troubling time for me. It was hard to go on to the next day. I felt defeated, like my world was turned wrong side out. What happened? Just a few short weeks ago everything was so beautiful. Now the only thing that gave me hope and peace was when I went over that summit to go to Yellow Pine for Church services. I left all the problems with bills, kids, discipline. I just left life behind. The burden went off my shoulders as I went up that summit with my little brood beside me.

I missed Frank terribly. When I was up there, everything reminded me of him, but spending my time praising the Lord was a good outlet and it gave me hope, hope that if all else was gone I still had the Lord. He was the one constant thing in my life.

The kids were happy with school, they didn't really have the adjustment problems I feared they might have. They made friends easily and became involved in sports which gave them a big boost. Merrill was in Jr. High in Donnelly. He rode the bus to school which picked him up about 6:30 a.m. He got home about 6:30 p.m. or later depending on sports activities. It was a terribly long day but he seemed to tolerate it fine. He still had the energy and the endurance it took to excel in sports.

Tom wasn't a kid anymore, he became very serious. He got into sports; football and wrestling he was especially fond of. Tom needed to work. He wanted more than what I could give him and he soon had a job. When we went into Yellow Pine on weekends he played, he went fishing, sleigh riding and kept busy most all the time at something. I was glad to see that happen. I hated to see him so serious about everything he did.

Bill was a very social person. He had a lot of friends and did things with them, he was also a good person. He led a morally clean life. It seemed that he didn't have the inclinations to be a bad person. There was a time or two when I became alarmed with something he did. It wasn't that the act itself was bad, but what it represented was a red flag for me. I had to nip that in the bud. He and a friend played chicken. I don't know how many games they played but one left a scar. He and his friend held a cigarette between them on their arms. Both holding it there until it burned down and burned into the flesh. They both had bad scars. I don't think he ever completely understood why I fell apart over such a dumb thing.

Another time he shaved his head. That represented rebellion to me, what did he have to rebel against? He had a thing for driving fast. That was about the only daredevil thing he did. He had one wreck before he learned the constant attention fast driving demanded. He crunched up the fender of my car. I was very unhappy to say the least.

Tom was the sensible driver always using good judgment. But he did total three of my cars one year in high school. I was denied insurance unless I kept Tom from driving.

Merrill wasn't as fond of driving as the other boys. He would just as soon ride with someone else. That is what he was doing when the driver ran out of gas. The driver stopped beside another car and with a short hose and a can he was getting gas. The police drove up. The driver dropped everything and ran. Merrill was still in the car with Terry. They were picked up and they couldn't make the police believe they were innocent. I was determined that if Merrill was even involved in the slightest he had to pay the price. He had to learn to be responsible for his own actions.

Yes we had problems, just as any family does and my kids were not perfect even though I expected them to be, they were normal people. They went through the typical rebellious stage where they were finding their identity. With the boys, it became a power struggle wanting their independence. It was hard on all of us and of course I always got panicky with each new crisis, or threat of losing control, praying I wasn't going to lose them before they were old enough to be on their own. When the problems involved money, it literally shattered me and our budget. I had never dreamed how sports could levy such a drain on a budget. The older the kids got, the more I realized how much more it took to manage a household. I would not consider working until Steve was in school, but I knew this would be my last year at home. It was nice when I didn't know that someday it would take more money than we had to live. Had I known I would never have quit worrying.

Frank asked us to come up and see him while the weather was still warm so we could camp out. The kids thought it would be a wonderful idea. We began making plans and deciding what we were going to take. We traveled lightly and bought food up there and mainly took sleeping bags and cooking utensils. Of course Frank had some things we could use. He sent maps and directions of all kinds. We started out going from Landmark through Bear Valley, Stanley and on up. I was surprised that we made it in such good time. We arrived late but Frank had arranged for us to sleep in an old house next to his trailer house. He had it all cleaned. There were two beds in the house so some of the kids had to sleep on the floor.

We took off early the next day exploring some of the most beautiful country. Frank took us all over and I couldn't dream we could cover so much area in one day. We had both cars and we drove until lunch time and stopped to eat. Then took out again, we found a lovely place to camp beside a little stream.

We made supper over a camp fire. The kids fished in the stream, of course Merrill found the fish. The other kids were wandering around a strange country looking it over. We had a beautiful evening. Frank and I spent a lot of time visiting by the campfire. He went into town to spend the night and came out again in the morning before we were up in fact.

Frank told me his divorce was final. We were getting serious about making plans. As we were talking, a fear came creeping into my heart. There were many things I had been forcing to the back of my mind not wanting to think about.

They could be pushed back no longer but I kept silent about it. One was giving up the work in Yellow Pine. Another was my kids having to change schools again. This was such an out-of-the way place, the town was not much of a family town. My heart was aching with doubt.

I think we both had a lot of things on our minds. We were sitting quietly not saying much, just looking at the fire. Frank in deep thought said, "Rose, I love my boys so much, it hurt terribly to leave them. I always want them to know that they are just as important to me as your kids. I pray they never think that I deserted them and took your family instead. Oh Rose if anything ever happened to one of them I wouldn't want to live." I reached my arm around him and held him as he grieved.

A great sorrow came to me then, a sorrow for him and for me, for our families and all that were involved by our relationship. A cloud settled over us, a cloud of fear that something had come between our love for each other. My grief for him was like nothing I had ever experienced before. I understood so well what he was saying because I knew his pain. Would my kids feel that by me marrying Frank, that put them in second place?

We held each other and cried, our pain was unbearable. I got up and walked toward the timber, he came also and we could not talk anymore. We just stood together and cried.

It was agony to leave him, I hurt beyond my consciousness, so deep I didn't know where it began and where it ended. I couldn't stand the hurting. I had hurt before but this was different. I was walking away from the man I loved and I didn't know if I was ever going to see him again. How could I go on living without Frank. How could we ever make it with so many obstacles. Why had God allowed us to meet?

It was a sad trip home for all of us. Even though the kids did not know, they knew something was wrong. I tried to act normal so as not to make them uncomfortable. They felt it and they were sad.

The next weeks and months were some of the most painful I have ever experienced. I wrote to Frank telling him that I couldn't marry him. I loved him dearly and would always love him, but I could not marry him. I could not see him anymore. The tears I shed, writing that letter were wrung from my heart. As soon as he got the letter, he called; he couldn't believe that I had done this.

"Why, why, if you love me like you say you do, how can you do this? Rose we both grieved the other day, but I thought it was something we could work out. I love you more than anything in this world. I love my boys but it is in a different way than I love you." I cried as he spoke pleading with me not to do this.

"Frank, it just won't work. I'm sorry, you know how I love you. I would rather break up loving each other, than hurt one another. It would be so much worse. It can't work, I know."

Every day I would receive a letter, sometimes two. He also called daily, sometimes twice, pleading, begging. He said, "If I move down there will it make a difference?"

"No Frank, nothing will make a difference. I am so sorry, but I just can't do it. I love you." I knew that the financial struggle alone would be enough to drive us apart. I cried for days and days. When I told the kids, they cried and cried, wanting to know, "Why Mom, why are you doing this?"

"I just have to do it, please don't make me explain now, I will tell you later. Please believe it is something I had to do." Frank wrote me the most beautiful poem. I took it to bed with me every night. I read it and cried myself to sleep. I read it several times a day, it helped to work through the pain.

———

This poem I dedicate to you Rose and hope you will cherish reading it, as much as I did writing it.

1964
"God's Love"
Frank Watkins

As I take this pen in hand my dear, to say what's in my heart,
To tell you of my love for you, but I know not where to start.

For it all began so long ago, back through the span of time,
When GOD brought you upon this earth, that someday, to be mine.

He led us through the yesteryears, through tears and happiness,
To build a kingdom bright, strong for the love HE meant for us.

Then from our separate worlds my dear, we met that summer day,
And at that moment, made a vow, our love was here to stay.

But the road of life is rough my dear, with pitfalls all the way,
To test a love that HE had made, To keep, — or take away.

We realize not the precious things, or what our loss can be,
Until we come to a turning tide, like a ship on a stormy sea.

But now my dear I realize, while I write this poem tonight,
As I gaze across the snowy plains, for signs of a guiding light.

The light of which I'm searching for, is the one within your heart,
To guide me home into your arms, and never more to part.

So now I've told you of my heart, of the beauty that I see,
A love for you that will never fade, and what you mean to me.

Soon I shall fold these words of love, my pen I'll lay aside,
But for the world, and you, -unfolds-, a love I cannot hide.

Now as we come to the end of the road, to the parting of the way,
My love will follow you through life, to the end of judgment day.

So now my dear if we must part, our lives we cannot share,
May GOD bless you, and keep you dear, will always be my prayer.

It took so much courage to do this and follow through with it. Many times I was so close to going back and then I thought about the two ministries the Lord had trusted me with and I couldn't do it. God gave me the strength because it was for Him. I had to suffer because I had done wrong to even consider walking away from my obligations. He must have been standing over me holding His "Will" like a staff, before me and would not give up on me. I asked myself time after time "Why, God Why?"

When the pain had lessened, I was able to think. I knew I had compromised my Christian standards. God does not allow us to be "taken away." He sees into the future. Of course I could have ignored His staff and not turned, and He would have let me go and left me to my own destruction. But I was not finished with the work He had for me in Yellow Pine and with my family. I wanted to serve Him, I wanted to be in His will.

Romans 8:26: "And the Holy Spirit helps us in our distress. For we don't even know what we should pray for. But the Holy Spirit prays for us with groanings that cannot be expressed in words." Verse 27 "And the Father who knows all hearts knows what the Spirit is saying, for the Spirit pleads for us believers in harmony with God's own Will."

I would never be satisfied knowing God had turned His face from me, knowing I was not "In His Will." We can sin or make a mistake and repent and receive God's forgiveness, but in a marriage so many lives could be hurt or even destroyed. When you carry as much luggage as I did, there is an even greater possibility of problems and even failure. According to the Bible, being single we can better serve the Lord.

The pain didn't go away as I had hoped it would. Two years later I wrote to him. I told him I had never been able to accept the loss and I still loved him. Could I see him and see how we both felt. So much in my life had changed.

He wrote right back saying, "There is nothing I would like better than to recapture our love for each other. I still feel the same about you, I always will. Think Rose, please think about it. If there is ever a chance of this happening again, I could not live through it. Please unless you know for sure, then let me be. I have started dating a lady here, she is a nice gal and I think I can be content with her. I will give her up in a minute if we really can get back together, but don't ask me to do that unless you are sure."

I never wrote back to him, I didn't want him to give up a chance for happiness. I certainly did not ever want to hurt him again. I opened all the old wounds and myself for another heartache. I suppose I did the same to him.

Now I thank God that He never allowed me to see the love we had for one another die. It has lived on in my heart through all these years as sweet memories. God gave me courage, He saw me through just as I asked Him to. I was blinded by love but He lit my way.

Some years later, I told Mom the whole story, I showed her the poem he wrote. She was reluctant to listen at first, she turned her head and looked away. I continued to talk, until I had told the whole story. I watched as the stiff defiant look was leaving her face, she was beginning to understand, she became involved with my pain and her expression was one of compassion. As the story came to an end, she sat quiet for a long time and my tears profoundly affected her. She said, "Well, Rose it is too bad things did not work out for you and Frank. I can see now that he really loved you and the kids. But it's over now, you will have to carry on with your life."

I was not finished, the Lord invested faith in me when He sent me to the church in Yellow Pine. He was not ready to give that up, there was still a lot of work to be done for Him, and a lot of work to be done with my family. There would have been many left unsaved, but are saved because I stayed, and kept the doors to the church open. Especially those who have passed on and never had another opportunity.

We continued to make the trips into Yellow Pine as long as the roads were passable. We always asked God "To give us a safe journey." He did, when people said we would never make it. We didn't ask about the roads, we just went on blind faith. Sometimes in the midst of a snow storm on Lick Creek when we were traveling in, I asked myself, "Why aren't you afraid? Most people would be." "The Lord is with me. I am not afraid." I would be more afraid on the highway going to Boise than I am here, there is nothing to fear.

My memories of Lick Creek summit in the winter on our trips, the roads had enough traffic to keep them smooth, it was so cold they were not slick but snow pack all the way. The lights from the car reflected on the snow and it looked like millions of diamonds sparkling, draped over the limbs of trees hanging down like a beautiful gown, over the logs, the bushes, the banks along the road. Each corner there was a different scene. It was so beautiful, so peaceful, I wanted it to last forever.

When the weather got real cold, the heat didn't penetrate those frigid mattresses and blankets in the time we had after getting the fire started. We froze one Friday night, no matter how many blankets we piled on the bed. It did no good as there was nothing warm in that bed to get the blankets warm. Our frigid bodies were not going to do it. The older boys brought their sleeping bags back and forth from McCall so they were comfortable.

I went shivering to Elsie and sure enough, she said we could stay there, we were welcome anytime. I brought groceries and there was always plenty for everyone. She was always so good to us, and John too. They were all precious friends.

In McCall the winter was long and so much snow, it piled up around the windows so we had to dig out our light source. The door had about four feet of snow in front of it in the morning. The boys had to shovel it before we could get out the door. There was a tall building between Marion's house and ours. The roof was steep and covered with metal. The snow kept falling off the roof and stacking up until the kids could walk up there and slide down, nearly into our door. Our yard was a very popular place that winter.

In the late fall before the roads closed, we went into Yellow Pine on Thanksgiving weekend. Hunting season was over, most of the hunters were out of the back country. The town was empty except for the locals.

It was so pretty, more snow than usual. I walked down to see Myrna, she closed the cafe and turned out the lights, so she wouldn't have any late comers. We sat down on the stools to visit, facing the window looking out over the street. The moon was shining bright and we could see clearly. We sat until after midnight just talking. No one was in sight. Then we noticed a truck with a box built on the back. It looked like a pretty fancy outfit. The truck was going very slow and quietly. The lights were off. They drove into town and made the loop and went down the back road. We were pondering about what they could be doing especially with their lights off. Were they checking out who was in town, obviously. Why? We could see them drive into an old place on the Circle, they turned their lights on just before they turned into the driveway. There was a garage beside the house. No more activity for an hour or so, I had to go home. We were curious though, Myrna said, "Come down tomorrow night and we'll see if this happens again."

"Okay I'll see you then, good night." I went out the door but I stayed in the shadow of the building just in case someone was walking around checking things out. Before I got up to Elsie's, I had thought of all kinds of things that could be going on. I ran all the way up the hill. I was so glad to get in the house. Everyone was in bed so I just quietly went in and slipped into a nice warm bed.

The rig came through town, just as before and went around the Circle. We then saw several other rigs pull into the same driveway but coming from the other direction. Turning on their headlights just long enough to get through the dark places in the trees. As we watched, we could see small lights, maybe flash lights. It looked like people were walking around and back and forth. They were very busy over there. What could they be doing? Once we saw a jeep with them. We began making plans to see what they were up too. Tomorrow night sounded good to both of us; we would go find out what they were doing. We had to take a route that was under cover of brush all the way. Someone had to know just in case we didn't get back.

We talked to Tom Nicholas, told him what we'd seen and what we were going to do. Tom said, "Girls, if I could talk you out of this, I would but I can see it would do no good. Be careful, I believe there is something going on and it could be dangerous for you."

We made him swear not to tell anyone. "Please look after our kids."

"Come to find me as soon as you get back. I'm going to be worried sick."

We waited until the time when they should be out away from the house. We went out the back and put our warm clothes on and took a flashlight. We circled around to the back of town and behind Dad's house. There was some brush cover there at the crest of the hill. We crossed the road, waiting and looking before we crossed. The brush was thick on the other side and it was wet. We couldn't walk through it, so we crawled, it made less noise too. It took a long time to go such a short distance but we kept going.

When we saw that we were fairly close to the cabin, we circled to the right and came up on the side of the garage that was farthest from the house. We didn't see any trucks parked around the place. We waited to hear any kind of movement but luckily it was quiet. There was always the chance that one of those rigs would come in while we were there. We had to be ready to take off in a hurry and not across an open area.

We walked quietly up to the garage and peeked through the cracks between the boards. We thought we saw something white in there but we couldn't tell what it was. Do we dare use the flashlight? Just a quick flash, be ready, get your eye up to the crack and be looking because we can't leave the light on very long. We got in position and flashed the light. Just a second told us what was going on. We backed off and looked at each other wide eyed and scared. We moved back out of sight where we could not be heard. Then we stopped and faced each other. That was elk. Dozens of elk halves wrapped in game bags. We moved on, every so far we had to stop and talk about it, but we were anxious to get out of there and back home to Tom.

We watched that night late again to see what went on. Same thing and it seemed like more van trucks. We didn't see the jeep again. When we got our wits back we talked about it and reasoned that it had to be a poaching ring. The more we talked the more excited we got. These guys were coming in here and killing dozens of elk. Too many for winter's meat. They must be selling it. We had it, sure enough, that was it.

We went to talk to Tom, we told him what we should do. I went up and told Elsie. Asked her to not say anything to anyone. I would be back as soon as possible. "I will be praying for you Rose." Good, we had the Lord with us. We got into my car and kept the lights out as far as we could and drove as fast as we dared. We spotted some headlights behind us a couple times, we really sped up. We flew over Lick Creek and into McCall. We knew someone was after us. If someone was after us they didn't catch us.

I called the Fish and Game officer in McCall and told him briefly what we had seen. The officer said, "Thank you very much we will get right on it. We'll get some men out there right away."

We didn't find out anything about it for a long time. Several months in fact. It was a poaching ring and they had trucks equipped with radios and had battery-operated freezer boxes on the back. They somehow found out where the game was that particular time of year, going in and slaughtering them by the dozen. The poachers were taking the meat into California and selling it. The Fish and Game tracked them down into California but were not able to catch them.

We were told one of the guys, probably a local connection, lived in Twin Falls. They got a tip on that but the people in the house also got a tip and moved out in the middle of the night. A couple years later I heard they did make one arrest. They got a complete confession from the guy and he told everything.

What really shocked me was that some people in Yellow Pine knew about it but were afraid to say anything. It had been going on for a long time. They were glad someone finally turned them in and it would probably never happen again, so it was worth it all. There were a few people in Yellow Pine who were very angry with me. Until then I wouldn't have thought about a local connection. I ignored the threats and did not treat anyone any different than another.

We seemed to get further behind on our bills every month. By spring I saw no way of catching up unless I moved out of our house. We had the cabin; we could live there. As soon as school was out, we stored our belongings and moved. It didn't take long to catch up when I didn't have to pay rent or utilities. We had a good summer and really enjoyed living in the cabin. The big Yellow Pine flat where the cabin was located was beautiful. That sleepy old Johnson Creek was a place I could sit and watch for hours. It was shallow in the summer and it just gently rolled over the rocks. Deer were abundant in that flat. They walked by our house on a trail that went along the creek. There were several trails back and forth across the flat and I think we explored every one of them.

We put a large horse watering tub down by the creek and filled it in the morning, by late afternoon it was warm enough to bathe in. We had to make sure there were no fishermen along the creek. Sometimes we had another person hold a blanket or big towel in front of us.

There was another cabin just down the road from us that was owned by Pickens. They didn't come in very often. Now and then someone stayed in the cabin and kept their horses there. There was a lot of green grass around the cabin and a beautiful big lilac bush out in front of the old house. I remembered the cabin there when I was just a girl. Someone had put a tin roof on it which naturally preserved it longer.

I remember a story told by the old timers, about that cabin. Seems like they were having a party there, with more than enough moonshine to lay them all out. They were all getting pretty wiped out when one of the fellows, who was laying on the bed, stopped breathing. They noticed it but thought he would be alright after he slept it off.

Later on they tried to wake him, to no avail, he slept on. They were discussing the possibility of him being dead, and how could they tell for sure. Someone suggested sticking him with a pin on the foot—he never moved. Then they put a mirror in front of his mouth, there was no steam. That was a sure sign he was dead. They wanted to do the right thing for the old friend, so they took him out and buried him. Now they could be sure if he wasn't, he would be.

One weekend when I came in from McCall, we arrived in Yellow Pine and drove up to the store to see if I had any mail. Ray Thrall was in there, I hadn't seen him for a long time. We chatted for a while and he said he had driven truck for Shaw on long hauls for a year. He was going to stay in for awhile. About then Phyllis told me that Pickens left a message for me. I said "Do you have the message?"

"Yes, he told me to tell you that if you wanted anything out of that cabin you had better get it out fast because they were going to tear it down. They would take the tin off the roof first."

I said, "Will you give them a message from me, that I will be staying there tonight and I will have my rifle beside my bed and if they come near the cabin it may be a long time before they can leave." (I knew God was always with me.)

Ray stood there with his mouth open. Phyllis said, "But Rose they are drunk and I think they will do it."

I answered, "But I will be there and I won't be drunk and I am a good shot. You can tell them that." I drove up to Elsie's with the kids and asked her if they could stay there because I had to stay at the cabin. I told her a little bit about it but didn't want to frighten her, but that gal believed in prayer.

I went back by the store and was going down to the cabin when Ray came out of the cafe. He walked over where I was standing talking to Phyllis. He said, "If anyone is going to stay at that cabin it will be me. You are not going down there."

I said, "Ray I don't know which would be worse, being shot or having them think that I was afraid of them. They are not going to do anything, they are just trying to scare me. If they think I am afraid of them, then they will have a lot of fun trying to run me off. The Lord will be right there beside me, I have nothing to fear."

"I'll go with you." I shook my head at him and went over and got into the car. He walked over to the car. He bent down and looked in the window and laughed, "You are a stubborn woman. Phyllis, I also have a message for Pickens, 'If they go near Rose or her cabin they will have to deal with me.' You tell them that."

"Okay, Ray I'll tell them that."

"Thanks Ray and thanks Phyllis." I don't have any coffee down there so I will be up pretty early."

I heard hammering and shouting from the Picken's cabin. I went to sleep and didn't hear or see a thing the rest of the night. They must have slept in because it was quiet in the morning. I started my car and drove out. I have never met these people to this day. I understand that they are related to some relation of mine.

We enjoyed our cabin for three years. We spent nearly as much time there as we did in McCall. There was never anything bothered there while we were away. They could have broken in easy enough but no one ever did. The Lord blessed us again.

I got a letter from the B.L.M. They informed me that this piece of ground was claimed as a mining claim by error. This ground was a designated power site. I would have to move the cabin or they would burn it. I went to Boise and tried everything I knew to persuade them to let me keep the cabin there. I had no money to move it. They were relentless about it they wouldn't give an inch.

Mr. David Imel, who had taught school in Yellow Pine one winter, heard about it and offered to buy it. I sold it to him for $500. We still go visit the spot where the cabin was whenever we go in to that country and it brings back so many memories. The kids would love to own the spot. They have never put a power dam there and I don't think they ever will.

Summer was coming to an end and it was time to go back to McCall. We found a house and moved in during late summer. It was closer to town and very convenient. We liked the house. Since I was working and all the kids were in school, a house in town was fine.

I worked at the McCall Hospital in the winter; but I let them know I would not be able to work when the kids were out of school, and I had to have weekends off for church and to be with the kids. They understood and there was no problem with that. I loved hospital work. I did quite well at it. It seemed so natural for me to do that kind of work. I moved up fast as an aide, I worked in any department they needed me. I always had my patient assignment, but was called to help in emergency, X-ray (they called me the tail gunner). I specialized in critical surgery patients. The one thing I could not do was take care of sick children or work in the nursery with newborns.

They unnerved me to where I was not at my best, I was actually frightened for them. I had to ask to be relieved of those duties. They understood. I believe I worked there three years. The paycheck was small but it supplemented enough to get us by.

So much has changed in the hospitals now. At that time, there were few R.N.'s. The rest were aides and we were allowed to do things that only the R.N.'s do now. I often wished I could go to nursing school but until the kids were raised that was out of the question.

After Church in Yellow Pine one Sunday, I was getting ready to go home when the kids came to me and said they had a toboggan and could Bob Gillihan pull them around the Circle with our car. I said, "Yes, but don't go fast, that can be dangerous." They left all excited and in about twenty minutes Tom came running into the cafe. He was pale as a sheet, "Mom, come quick Lee is hurt."

"Where is he?"

"He is on the Circle, he is hurt bad." He took me through the short cut and it didn't take long to get there. When we arrived Lee's parents were already there. His Dad was hysterical, screaming, "He is going to bleed to death. Do something Rose." I walked over to Lee and lifted his pant leg so I could see the injury on his leg. I thought his leg was severed completely. There was so much blood it was hard to tell. Lee was screaming also, "Rose am I going to die?" I squatted down beside him and said, "I can't talk to you while you are screaming. SHUT UP! You were in Church today—do you remember what I talked about? Well I talked about sometimes things get bad for us and when they do, we have to call on God. Then we raise our hand up to Him and He will reach down and take hold of our hand and help us get through our bad time. Will you call on God right now? I will pray with you. Close your eyes Lee. "Jesus, Lee is having one of those bad times and he is reaching his hand up to you. Will You please take his hand and comfort him and help him through this bad time. In Jesus name. Amen." I lifted my hand up with Lee's hand and I said, "Lee do you feel Jesus near, taking your hand." He nodded, "Now you will be fine, don't you worry."

Roy Green, Lee's father, was quiet while we were praying and then he began again with hysterics. I stood up and asked my boys to find a board or something we could use for a stretcher. Then I walked over to Roy. I pushed him up against the car roughly (he was a little guy) to get his attention and said to him, "Roy if you don't shut up, I am going to have someone take you away. The Lord and I are going to save his life but you will kill him by screaming and getting so excited. We have to keep him relaxed and he won't bleed so badly. Shut up or leave." I took my hand from the front of his shirt and he did not say another word.

The guys found a wide board and it just happened to be the right length and width. I don't know where it came from because there was about three feet of snow. I asked Tom, Merrill and Bob to get on each side of Lee and I would stand right by his leg. You pick up his body and I will pick up the leg. I pushed the leg into the stump as much as I could, and putting one hand on each side of the injury, then we lifted. I felt the leg separate and I could very easily have fainted, but I knew that young life depended on me. Lee was on the board. We went to the back of my station wagon and put him in head first. I got snow and packed it around his leg, pushing it up against his leg as tight as I could, then took the pillows that were in my car, and packed them around as tight as possible. I took all the coats from the people standing there and packed them around his leg, to keep it from moving. I was hurting Lee badly, I knew, during all this movement but I had to ignore it and do what I had to do to save his life. I drove slowly over to the store and had them fill my car up.

I asked, "Will one of you men go with me to drive, I may have to take care of Lee. I know there is fresh snow on the hill, the road might be pretty bad." There were several men standing around by now, I looked at each one and no one said anything but dropped their eyes to the ground. Roy and Hoopy asked if they could go and I said, "Yes, but if you say one word you will be standing out in the snow bank." I looked at Tom, my son and said "Tom, can you help me?"

He said, "Yes, Mom I will help."

Betty Nicholas came driving her pickup with a canopy on it. She said, "I have a pain pill here can we give it to him."

I asked what it was, Darvon with Codeine. I said, "Give him half. Someone get some water." I was getting myself ready to ride in a cold car. "We need blankets too. We can't turn the heat on in the car and it will be cold."

Blankets came from everywhere. Betty said she would drive her pickup out and take my kids with her. But she didn't have four wheel drive so she may not make it. "Okay do the best you can. Someone go down to Oberbillig's camp and radio to the hospital. Tell them to send a doctor to meet us."

No one offered to help Betty on the trip. It had snowed that day, there was about four inches of new snow on the road. I pulled out easy, and when the car moved Lee screamed. I went slower to make it easier on him and prayed. When we got down about three miles, he quit screaming and said, "It doesn't hurt anymore Rose."

I said, "Thank the Lord Lee, but don't move. Lay just as still as you can." I said very quietly to Tom, "Tell me what happened." He leaned over as close as he could and whispered.

"There was a barb wire loop sticking out of the snow. We were all sitting on the bobsled with our legs sticking out. Lee's leg hooked in the loop." I nodded and indicated that he didn't need to tell me any more now. We drove on and I picked up a little speed, Lee didn't seem to be hurting. Actually the snow was a soft cushion on the road and it was smooth riding. I drove a steady consistent speed and consistently. I felt like I was driving on eggs.

Thank God for snow, it couldn't be any better. We passed the South Fork, on up the road we started climbing. I wondered how deep the snow would be on Lick Creek. We came to Brown's Camp. I slowly drove into the camp and up to the cookhouse. I stopped very smoothly. I ran in the door and told the lady there, "I have a boy in my car that had his leg severed in an accident. I am going up the hill and I'm worried about the snow, please find someone to drive a four-wheel drive rig and follow us. Hurry as fast as you can, the boy is critical." I didn't give them time to ask any questions, I had told them all that was necessary to get the rig up there. I ran out to the car and drove on in slow motion.

We were still in the grace of the Lord. I prayed all the way, no one was saying much but Lee. I kept trying to reassure Lee to keep him in a positive frame of mind. He seemed fine. The one thing he was worried about was, "If I have to stay in the hospital overnight, will you tell them I don't like peas." I told him I would sure do that for him.

"Are you warm Lee?" (I actually wanted him to be cold.) I said "I'm sorry I can't turn on the heater but you probably have enough blankets to keep you warm."

At Hum Creek area it began to snow or sleet. Without any heat it just froze on the windshield and on the wipers. I had to keep the window down and reach around and be ready to grab the wiper when it came over to that side and snap it to knock off the ice. The higher we got the colder it got and the ice was harder to keep off the wipers. The snow was getting deeper, I was getting a little anxious, so was Roy, he said "Do you have chains Rose?"

"Yes." I didn't tell him they were under Lee in the wheel well, and we didn't dare move him. We kept going slow and steady, I had good snow tires and never needed the chains. I was beginning to feel a little push on the tires from the snow getting deeper and heavy. I thought, I wish that rig from Brown's Camp would come. I looked up in the rear view mirror and they were behind us. At that exact minute there was a turn out. I very smoothly turned out, he went by to get ahead and break the trail. I pulled out again into the road with out a bobble. We kept the ride going smooth on up the hill.

My hand was just about frozen, it was covered with ice. I asked Tom if there was anything in here for my hand. He found a dry glove and emptied a bread wrapper, it worked fine, my hand felt much better. We went on over the hill. The snow didn't get much deeper on the summit. We stayed right behind the four-wheel drive rig. The snowfall was letting up as we got on the other side. We didn't spin a wheel, we maintained the same speed, the snow was smooth and there was not yet a bobble to bother Lee. No one in the car was talking except me to Lee and Lee to me. I was carrying on a chatter with him about anything and everything to keep his mind off himself.

Down on the other side of Lick Creek Summit about 10 miles out of McCall we met Dr. Nokes in a four-wheel drive rig driven by another person. I got out of the car and went around the back to open the tail gate. A cold chill went up my spine as I remembered how much trouble I always had opening the back. I said a quick prayer and took a hold of the handle, lifting it up and the door came open, I praised Him again. The Lord was with us.

Dr. Nokes got out and came to the back of the car. He crawled in with Lee and said lightly, "How are you doing young fellow?" Lee told him "Fine." Dr. Nokes said to me, "Which leg?"

"Right." He pulled back the packing around the leg and said, "Okay, Rose everything is fine, I think I will ride back here with Lee and we won't need to put him in the other rig. You are comfortable here aren't you Lee?"

We drove up to the back of the hospital and backed up to the emergency door. When I stopped the car, I felt for the first time since I went over on the Circle to get Lee, I could breathe. The air went out of my body and I sunk down in a chair.

Someone else was responsible for him now. I was sitting in the hall by the desk and Marion Murry came out of the X-Ray room. She was rushing by me and she said, "Do you know that boy's leg is hanging on by about an inch of flesh? How did you keep him from bleeding to death?"

"The Lord was with us Marion."

Lee was in surgery for about twelve hours. They put his leg back on and connected all of the veins, arteries, muscles, tendons, bones, nerves, flesh and put a cast on it. They left a window in the cast to watch the healing progress.

The family stayed with me until Lee could leave the hospital. He did just fine, he walked again with a limp. That leg didn't grow quite as much as the other. But it did grow and everything on it worked well. What a miracle, Praise God.

Lee was in the hospital for about two months, his parents didn't have any money. I prayed for someone to help us. We were getting down to nothing in the house to eat. A church brought in a big load of groceries. Thank God.

The Lord will see us through anything. There is nothing too big or too small. I have found though that I have to take the first step and then He comes in with His divine assistance. Whatever happens from then on is, you can be sure, the very best for us. Romans 8:28.

Mom, Uncle Tom, and Aunt Clara.

Chapter 17

"We Prayed For Paint"

1967

With the kids in school and doing well, we continued to look forward to our trips into Yellow Pine for church services on weekends. The kids had such good times with their friends, there was no better place in the world to have fun. Any time of year there was something for them to do. Good clean fun, didn't cost anything, and the lessons they were learning from nature and actually being able to live in it, was teaching them what I had dreamed of and prayed for, not only for enjoyment but to benefit them physically, emotionally, mentally and developing their character in a way nothing else could.

God had heard my plight for my children and honored it. I think it could be summed up in Tom's words after he was grown. "Those were the best years of my life, I wouldn't take anything for that experience."

Our church continued to grow as God's word was taught and adhered to. Many souls were saved and ministered to during those years. Several of our congregation, mostly children, fourteen and under were baptized in the Ice Hole on Johnson Creek. (The Ice Hole was named by the old-timers who cut blocks of ice to store in the sawdust all summer.) It was the perfect place for baptism.

We invited an ordained minister to do the services' that day. It was a beautiful ceremony, tears of happiness wet the cheeks of most everyone there. I led a song of dedication for everyone when they came up out of the water, "Jesus I Come," "Shall we Gather at the River," "I Surrender All," "Where He Leads Me I Will Follow," "Is My Name Written There," "Praise God for Whom all Blessings Flow." The Lord gave me a different song pertaining to dedication, for every person when they came up out of the water. The large group of people sang from their hearts and all were Blessed. Mothers were rejoicing for their children. I have been able to follow most of these young people throughout their lives and the majority of them have continued to grow in the Lord and remain faithful to Him. Those who are not among the faithful are still under the blood of Jesus and unless they deliberately denounce Him as Lord, will someday come back. I pray for them.

The adults who gave their lives to the Lord remained faithful and are to this day. Some have passed on but they were faithful until death.

The glory of this work goes to God. He was the one who was in charge of each individual. He caused them to do as they did, and I was an instrument He was able to use. I said, "Yes Lord." I realize this fully and it gives me great joy knowing the Lord did use this poor sinful soul.

Our church building was looking pretty bad. The wood on the outside of the building had weathered, it was dry and unsightly. I doubt that it had ever been painted since it was built. This old building had seen a lot of activity over the years. At one time it was a barber shop, cafe, bar, and a home. It was well built apparently because it was still a good solid structure. I am not sure how old it is but it was there in 1925. The paint did wonders for the church. It made a beautiful little place on the corner for all to see and identify as a church with the cross on the top.

We hired a contractor to come in to do the work. We had saved some money and we all gave a love offering to help pay the contractor. They gave us an estimate of the cost for two coats. After two coats you really couldn't see that it had any new paint. It soaked in as fast as they put it on. We called a meeting to decide what we were going to do. We decided a bake sale could bring in some dollars and it seemed to be a busy weekend. We baked and prayed. We put three stands up in town and put signs at every stand showing that the proceeds were going to the church for paint.

Three coats and four coats still didn't cover the dry wood. We had another meeting, we prayed, and then talked with the painters. We kept praying and baking all day, more cookies, cakes, candies, cinnamon rolls and bread. After about the fourth coat the painters were not charging for their time, only the paint. That little community was busier than I had ever seen it. People were buying up baked things faster than we could get it out. Most of them paid twenty dollars for a little sack of cookies. We finally quit putting prices on anything but just added to the sign, "Proceeds for paint for Church." They could see the church being painted. We earned more than enough money. The church looked beautiful. We were so proud, as was the community. Everyone took part in this fund raising in one way or another. So it truly was something to be proud of.

Jim Cox, Olga's husband came to me one day and asked if I would like to take a horseback trip up to Lookout Mountain to see his daughter Peggy. I was quite fond of her after knowing her for a couple years. Jim said I could take one of the kids, there would be plenty of horses. I asked Danny, he was elated.

Faye Kissinger loaned us his two matched palominos, beautiful big horses, as he well knew a small horse could not be used in the back country climbing those hills. It was sometimes more than a large horse could do. I was thrilled to get to ride them, and I never dreamed he would loan them to anyone. I think I would have been hesitant. The pair was worth a lot of money. Faye loaned the tack and gear also. He had matched saddles, blankets, halters and bridles. He said they looked better all dressed up, and they did. They looked beautiful.

We hauled the horses over to Big Creek early one morning, early like four o'clock. We were ready to leave there before the sun was up. The first stretch was down Big Creek to the mouth of Monumental which was about 14 miles. I had heard that you could travel faster horseback over that road than with a car. It was true. It was such a beautiful ride. I saw things I had never seen before along that road. Danny was so excited to be going on such a trip, as was his mother. The road was no longer open to motorized vehicles, so I saw places I hadn't seen for years. After traveling the first fourteen miles, I was quietly wishing we were there. Danny didn't complain at all. He must have felt as tired as I, but you would never know it.

At the mouth of Crooked Creek we crossed Big Creek on the pack bridge and went up Monumental Creek. What a beautiful ride.

We went past Wilbur Wiles cabin, but it didn't look anything like it did when I was there about 1941. Wilbur wasn't home so we didn't get to stop. Wilbur had been a bachelor all his life. We thought it was because he lived where there were no ladies. Would there ever be a woman who would want to live up here? But low and behold a beautiful woman finally caught up to him and they were married. She lived in Big Creek and of all things he moved out to Big Creek. He kept his cabin back there however. The beautiful woman he married was none other than Katy Thrall, Ray Thrall's mother. We were happy for them, they were a lovely couple. They traveled to Arizona every winter.

We traveled past Monumental Rock, which I had only seen on a post card. It is hard to see, standing down over the bank among some trees that mostly obscure it from view. It seems strange as you look at it that a falling tree or an earthquake or flood washing out the bank or an ice breakup in the spring has never dislodged the huge rock sitting on top of a rock pinnacle. It is a wondrous sight. I would like to have a picture of it.

At one of our breaks along the trail, Jim told us we would be coming to the Murder cabin. I didn't know if I wanted to see this guy or not. We veered off the trail to the left and rode up in front of the cabin. Jim hollered, "Is anyone home?" A lady came out the door exchanging greetings with Jim, apparently knowing him previously. Dan and I kept our horses in back of Jim. We were never acknowledged and I was not sorry. After we had been there a few minutes, a man came to the door and spoke to Jim. This apparently was the murderer, he looked nothing like I had remembered him when he stopped in Yellow Pine on his way over to kill old Slim (Roland Clark) to get his cabin and claims. This man was tall and slim, he acted very nervous when he came to the door. So nervous in fact that his eyes twitched, his ears twitched and his body jerked. It was certainly an involuntary action. I doubted he could even eat by himself, his hands twitched so badly.

My observation of his condition, I couldn't help wonder if he felt like he had ever gained anything. He had jumped Slim's claims, which was legal because Slim had never done his assessment work. It was a law of good conscience, in the back country, that you never jumped a man's claim, especially when his home was on this claim and he had lived there for so many years. He was old and probably not able to do his assessment work. He had been back there so long I doubt that he ever checked into the new laws to find where he stood legally with Burres. When this Burres gave him notice to move off (that he was now the owner of the claims, cabin, garden and the livelihood of an old man). Slim would not budge, he sat right there. Burres gave him several notices but Slim would not respond. Burres told him if he didn't leave, he would be going out of there on a stretcher. Slim told him if he came back, he would have his own gun ready to shoot.

Burres came through Yellow Pine telling everyone what he was going to do. What he didn't tell everyone was that he had several guys with him who stationed themselves in front of Slim's cabin behind bushes and trees.

They came there to take their places in the dark so Slim did not know they all were there. Burres called to him, telling him to come out with his hands up because he had a gun and he would use it unless Slim surrendered.

Slim came out the door with his own rifle, he started firing and all these guys fired at the same time. Slim went down, but he was not dead. Apparently someone in this group had a radio and called the sheriff. They brought in a helicopter to get Slim. The sheriff, Merton Logue, was in the helicopter. Slim told Logue what had happened and that it was Burres that shot him. Slim died a few minutes later.

There was a trial, but Burres was acquitted and got possession of the cabin and claims. I don't think he gained all he thought he was going to. There wasn't a man in the back country that Burres trusted. He felt everyone was out to kill him and I think he may have been right. This man lived in mortal fear for the rest of his life. His wife left him, he only lived there a short time, he didn't gain a thing.

We didn't stay long, we were not invited to get off our horses. It was not a very comfortable place to be and I was glad to be on our way. The way my backside was feeling about then I should have walked for a few miles, but I wasn't sure I could get back on my horse. I wasn't sure I could get off, come to think of it. It was well worth it, the pain wouldn't last forever but the memories would.

We turned off the trail just before we got to Roosevelt Lake at the old McCoy ranch which was about 20 miles up Monumental. There was no sign of a house but we could see an old root cellar. A few items like a coffee pot lid and a broken piece of a fruit jar lay on the ground. I had met some of the McCoy family when I was just a girl. It seemed like there was a bunch of them. They lived back there for more than one generation so I'm not sure who is who. I did know Harriet McCoy and in fact I worked with her. Her husband was a McCoy but he died before I met Harriet. I was well acquainted with Betty McCoy who was an original. She was a gal that I wouldn't want to fool with. She was married to a handsome young guy by the name of Mills. A lady in Cascade was kind of sweet on this young feller and Betty got wind of it. Betty went into the bar, grabbed this gal by the hair and jerked her off the bar stool to the floor, and proceeded to kick the daylights out of her. I think that was the end of that affair. The McCoy family lived up to their name. They were quite a legend in the back country.

Up to this point we traveled on level ground and easy riding country. Dan was beginning to squirm around a little on his saddle. I had to smile, I knew just how he felt, he did not complain though.

We took a break and ate the lunch that Olga had packed for us. I laid down under a tree and straightened out my limbs as best I could. I felt better—but as soon as I got back on the horse I felt all the old hurts. Don't think for a moment that I was hurting so bad I didn't enjoy this. I don't know how bad I would have to hurt to not want to finish a trip. In fact I have told myself that if you ride far enough the pain will go away, it never gets worse. I think Dan believed that, and I am sure there is some credence to it.

We started climbing. We went up Holy Terror Creek and you could see where the name came from. It was the drainage for the mountain and when the snow started melting the water came down the steep draw. This little creek took out everything for hundreds of feet on both sides of it and would dig a little deeper creek bed every spring. It wasn't a very pretty sight with all the rubbish stacked along the creek. This was the best trail going up the mountain however.

The part of the trail I disliked the most was a shale rock slide, it was quite wide. There was not a trail through it, because it slid in whenever anyone or anything stepped on it. The poor horses could hardly keep their feet under them. Sometimes they would start sliding and I didn't think they could stop. There was no way to get their footing. They just slid and scrambled to keep from going down the slide. The trail ended at one side of the slide and on the other side it began again. Man or beast took their life in their hands when they went over a shale slide.

I held my breath all the way across, and I prayed big time. A valley horse could certainly lose his life on a shale slide.

Sometimes I thought my horse was really in trouble but I didn't dare jump off as the rock was as sharp as razors. It could cut you up bad if you fell in it, or you may be under a frantic horse. We all made it across with some very weary horses at the other side. We rested them awhile and went on. I was glad to see that they didn't get their legs cut up. This is one more place where you need a larger horse because the larger the feet, the better the traction.

On up the trail, it was getting more enjoyable as we climbed. The trail leveled off some, we'd ride down in a little swale and up again, over and around, just following a pleasant little path. We didn't have much farther to go on our 45 mile trip.

I thought of the boy at twelve years old who was sent out by his father with nothing but a sling shot and a pocket knife to conquer the wilds. He had traveled this trail also.

His father was a professor at a college back east and he had trained the boy well. The boy came through Yellow Pine and met up with my kids. Merrill brought him to church intending to get him some food, some fishing line, and some hooks. I felt so sorry for that boy but I couldn't help but think that the boy was pulling our leg. We fed him but we were not to tell, because his father told him not to accept food from anyone. He was only to eat what he found. He had a sling shot, hand made. I really couldn't believe this until I checked with the people at Big Creek and some of the other places back there. The boy radioed out to his father and gave a progress report every so often. His destination was the Taylor ranch, which was owned by the U of I. I wondered why the father didn't go on this little trek. The boy made it, but with nothing to spare. He traveled on foot all the way from Yellow Pine to the lookout and visited Peggy on the way (this was 30 years ago so I am sure it is safe to tell.)

Needless to say we were happy to arrive at the lookout. Peggy was glad to see us, she hadn't seen anyone for a month or more. She put some food on the table and I washed up and sat down on a cot to eat. When I finished eating, I couldn't help myself, I stretched out on the cot I was sitting on. I didn't wake up until Danny was shaking me saying, "Mom, get up Jim is ready to go." I couldn't believe it, he was going to go without spending the night. Danny said "We did spend the night, you slept all night."

"Oh, Danny did you sleep?"

"Yes I slept all night too. On the floor right in front of you."

"Oh my goodness what a flake I am. I didn't even get to see anything."

"You saw it all on the way up here."

I turned around and sat up to the table again and ate what was left from breakfast, and got some coffee off the stove. Jim was yelling, he was ready to go. That guy wasn't waiting around for anything. He reminded me of old Kennedy, John's mule. When he had a load to pull he bowed his neck, squatted and stretched and didn't stop until the job was done. He talked about as much as old Kennedy too.

We started down the mountain and Jim took us a different way so we didn't go over the rock slide and we didn't go down Holy Terror Creek. It was like a new trip until we got to Monumental Creek. I could travel Monumental trail every day and love it. It was so pretty, so cool, so peaceful.

We traveled nearly forty-five miles each way on that trip horseback. I was tired for sure but I would do it again at the drop of a hat.

John and Elsie were going to spend the summer at Big Creek at the Neal ranch. John kept his horses there and he needed some fence work done. He hired the boys to help him.

John had about fifty head of horses that he wintered in the valley each year. My three older boys rode in with them on one trip bringing the horses in. They loved the outdoor experience and working with the horses but poor Merrill. He was left with an old nag that was skinny and never walked or ran. She trotted all the way. Merrill couldn't make her do anything else. I guess she had never been ridden much, mostly pulled in a string. They came straight through from Boise to Round Valley, as the bird flies, I guess it isn't that far.

From there they came on over Big Creek summit and down the South Fork. I met them at the Reed Ranch. Merrill was sick from all that bouncing, he didn't say a word, he got off the horse and crawled in the back of the station wagon and wouldn't get out. He didn't want to eat, drink or anything else. He slept off his sickness which took a couple of days. It was a great experience for them and good endurance training.

Herding horses is very exhausting work, it is running all the way. They dart off down an embankment or somewhere they see green grass and of course you have to go after them. However, the cowboys have a special yell that brings the horses up and back with the herd. If you can master that call, you've got it made. You must stay alert and ready to go any direction at a moments notice or you may be going after the whole herd. You must have a good strong, fast horse. Driving horses keeps you alert and on the go constantly. It is fun and it is exciting, but after thirty miles you are ready to go to bed.

In preparation for the horses, Gillihans moved a camp over to the Neal ranch. John pulled in a big trailer, which was a cook trailer and dining hall. It must have been fifty feet long and twelve feet wide. I don't know of anyone else who would try pulling it down Profile summit which is as crooked as a dog's hind leg. He had to back up several times to get around those turns. That was typical of John, he would try anything and usually get the job done.

John had our tent set up, in the jack pines, it was a lovely spot. We put our beds in the tent and found an old cupboard that someone else had used in a tent, and put our groceries in it. We set up a table outside with our camp stove on it and had a place to cook. We were as snug as a bug.

I went over to Yellow Pine every weekend for church. I noticed a drop in attendance. I think it was because we were not there to make contacts. I felt bad about that but, I was so thankful for the opportunity to do this with the kids.

We had a great summer. John and Elsie were in a tent over closer to the kitchen trailer. We fixed our own breakfast and lunch. Then we all had our dinners together in the kitchen trailer. I helped to supply the groceries for the dinner meal. We cooked together and we both cleaned up. Then we usually went for a walk, down that lovely green valley, to the barn and beyond. We checked on the horses. John could take one look and just about every time he could tell you if they were all there. Sometimes he would tell the boys to saddle up the horses in the corral and go out and check on one or two or more of the horses.

The kids had some very interesting experiences and did a lot of work with horses throughout the summer. The Neal ranch was anyone's dream. It was set back off the main road. This lush green valley of about 40 acres was secluded from traffic. In fact we had to ford Big Creek to get over there. There were irrigation ditches all over the ranch to keep feed growing all summer. The water was as cold as ice water. A spring-fed creek came down through the jack pines by our camp.

The kids had such a wonderful time that summer they will never forget it. They didn't make much money from John, but they all had fun. There were a lot of fish in the beaver ponds down behind the barn and they frequented them to bring home beautiful trout for supper.

John leased the ranch for the summer each year for several years for the pasture. From here they took a packstring and went out through the back country to set up their hunting camps.

We all went on one such camp trip. There were my seven kids and myself, John and Elsie and four of their kids. It was an experience of a life time. If you could imagine 14 people in a pack train plus the pack horses. We made quite a sight. If we met anyone on the trail, they took their animals off the trail and stood watching as we went by one by one.

John and Elsie left with nine kids riding from the Neal ranch to Crooked Creak Base Camp near Snowshoe mine which is about 20 miles. Bob packed up 15 horses and mules with the supplies that were needed to set up the camps, ready for the hunters.

We all chose the horses we wanted to ride on these trips. John left the rest up to us. If the horses were not suitable for one reason or another, we had to deal with it. Tom had chosen this beautiful strawberry roan to ride. Bob went on ahead with the packstring and I waited for Tom to get back from a fishing trip. The horse was ready and waiting for him. He was checking the cinch and getting ready to leave. I was on my horse. Tom led his horse through the gate and put his foot in the stirrup and this horse went crazy. Tom jerked him around and tried again, same thing. This went on for at least thirty minutes, those two were dancing all over the field. Neither was going to give up. Tom was getting angry and more rough with the horse each time. I was getting scared because this horse was more angry than Tom. He would snort and squeal every time Tom put any weight in the stirrup. He kicked and bucked and reared, jerking Tom all over the pasture.

My horse was getting excited over this and he began to act up. So we were doing quite a dance. We were going round and round. I had never seen this beautiful black Ranger act up like this. He was big and I didn't know about this. I was getting very nervous over the whole thing.

I was begging Tom not to ride that horse, "Tom, please don't try anymore. Just leave him and go down to the corral and get another horse."

"The only thing they left down there are a couple of old plugs, and I'm not riding them. I'll make it with this horse Mom."

"You can ride my horse, I'll ride one of those plugs."

"No you won't, I'll get this horse wore down in a minute."

Well I would have bet anyone five bucks he would never get on that horse. He was more persistent than the horse.

I began praying. I was so afraid Tom was going to get hurt. It was a long way to the doctor from here. After another fifteen minutes of watching and restraining my horse, Tom tried one more time and put his foot in the stirrup and pulled himself up in the saddle. The horse did some high

446

stepping for a few minutes. Then he was fine for the rest of the trip. He never did that again but if Tom would have let him win, he would have been ruined forever. His horse was a beautiful walking horse, he really stepped out, and covered some ground. My Ranger was a good walker too but I had to keep him going or he would have fallen behind.

I was so proud of Tom, my heart was about to burst. Even though I was afraid for him, I was glad he didn't give up like I wanted him to. I had a great deal of respect for him as a horseman from then on. He had what it takes.

We rode faster than Bob with the packstring so we caught up with him on the other side of Big Creek store. The clouds were rolling and the thunder was clattering when we left Big Creek. We knew we were in for a stormy trip. We had rain gear so we were not too worried. I liked to ride in the rain.

We rode down Big Creek road until we came to the bridge crossing Big Creek going up over Miners hill. We took the trail, a short cut, and followed Big Creek. The trail along the creek was chiseled out of the rock bluff. The bluff overhung in several places, at times the horses were walking on solid rock. We were traveling behind Bob's packstring.

The storm was raging, thunder, lightning, pouring down rain and pitch black. The only time we saw anything was by lightning that illuminated everything before us. It was a beautiful sight and one I will never forget. It's as fresh in my memory as if it were yesterday.

We rode along in silence on down Big Creek. We could hear the horses feet in the rocks and hear the leather squeaking as the horses walked. Occasionally we heard the thunder and the crack of lightning. It was still raining. It didn't seem to bother the horses anymore than it did us. They just plodded along.

After a couple hours, we took another shortcut off the road. It was somewhere down around Big Ramey. I really couldn't tell where it was, it was so dark. The trail was high above the water, very narrow, and curved around the mountain. I could hear the creek way down below us, the trail was muddy and slick and often the horses hooves would give way and slide and then recover and go on. I have never liked high places, this was just about too much. I was praying all the way, I had to close my eyes, not that I could see anything anyway but it made me feel a little safer. I continued to pray. The Lord did give me courage to go on, because mine was almost gone. I was so relieved when we got on the road again.

When we turned off Big Creek and started up Crooked Creek Road, we had to stop and open a gate. Just when we got to the gate we heard some wire buzzing. One of the horses had stepped on or in some wire and pulled it with his foot. All the horses instantly got nervous and spooky, their heads were all high and their ears were pointed just waiting for one horse to bolt and the bunch was ready to go. Bob yelled at me to come up and hold the packstring so he could get off and open the gate and for Tom to stay back to control the horses back there.

I rode up the string talking to them all the way trying to calm them. I got up front and took the rope. Bob said, "Now be careful when I open the gate. There may be a wire pull somewhere and that would set them off."

I took the string and he very carefully opened the gate, the horses began to mill and I started cooing to them again. He said the gate was open and take them through very easy and slow. I kept talking because that seemed to quiet them more than anything. I moved my horse and the rope tightened on the first pack horse. He jerked. Several were coming through the gate at once, I kept moving and talking, I didn't dare stop because they would circle my horse and get me in a terrible mess. I talked and cooed those horses up the trail and got them straightened out again, I didn't stop and wait for Bob because I was afraid of what might happen. When Bob started closing the gate, I could hear a squeak and then Tom's voice back there talking the horses down. We were not just about to stop until we got to camp, we had to keep the horses moving. We made it without a wreck but just barely. Bob came walking in and Tom came in holding the ropes of some side-stepping horses, which had their back ends in front of their heads.

John had gone on up Crooked Creek to set up tents for the next night's stay. They had left the base camp on Crooked Creek early but they stoked the stove up good and it was still warm. The coffee was still warm sitting on the back of the old cook range. Elsie had baked a salmon and wrapped it in foil and put it in the warming oven. I have never been too much of a fish eater but that was wonderful. There was also some beans on the back of the stove. What a homecoming. We were starved and ate until we couldn't eat another bite. This was Tom's birthday dinner on the 16th day of August.

There was one cot in the cook tent and guess who got it. I laid down and pulled the covers over myself and went sound to sleep. Quite a day.

The following day when we went up to the next camp to meet the rest of the group was the 17th day of August, my birthday.

We got up early and left. It wasn't very far so we were there about noon. The weather turned out pretty nice. We kind of lulled around camp that day and John and Bob did what they had to, to make it ready for the hunters that would be coming in about two weeks.

We all went to bed early so we could get an early start in the morning. I heard it raining on the tent during the night but it didn't rain long. The kids and I were tucked into our beds as warm as could be. The fire was going and it was so cozy.

The next morning John got up and stepped out of their tent and let out a war hoop that brought every head out the tent door, to see what was the matter, but they didn't go much farther. There was about a foot of snow. Oh! it was beautiful. The kids were thrilled to death. The snow was hanging heavy on all the trees and bushes. John decided we had better stay there that day because it would be too cold for the kids to ride in the snow.

The next day the sun was shining and it was warm. The snow was all gone. We all had to wear coats but it was nice to be out. Elsie and I fixed lunches to take with each day. Anything you eat like that is the best thing you have ever eaten. When we all sat around in a circle to eat, it was quite a sight. There were thirteen of us all laughing and talking and enjoying every bite. It seemed to be a delight for everyone, John didn't mind the extra work to take us all along. I think he enjoyed it. Of course the kids helped him and I helped Elsie. We all worked and helped with everything.

Elsie was not a horse woman, in fact she didn't like horses. She said she would rather walk but John wouldn't let her. He teased her saying that if she would ride like she was supposed to, the horse would know someone was on his back and wouldn't be wandering off and eating and so forth. Elsie would laugh. Once we were riding on a trail that had a wash in the middle leaving a ditch about a foot deep and that wide. We all kept our horses out of the ditch and walking beside it, but for some reason Elsie's horse walked in the ditch. She called John and had him take the horse out of the ditch. Then he did razz her.

Not long after that her horse dropped down to his knees, she yelled at John again. John said, "Jerk his head up and make him get up." She did so and he did get up. John shook his head, "See I told you that horse doesn't know you are on his back. You set like a stump up there. A horse never rolls when he is being ridden by anyone but you." Elsie laughed, and of course we all laughed. The whole trip went like that.

Kristy and Janet rode Beepo. He was the strangest looking horse. He had very short legs. The kids only had to throw their leg over him. He had a good stout body and a very big head. He was so gentle they could do anything with him. Rosana and the girls stuck pretty close together so they could sing, they would giggle, and they had more fun. I stayed behind the kids so I got to see all this. Dan and Steve rode together. The others all had their own horses. John and Elsie rode in front and Bob with them.

We went over some pretty steep trail but for the most part it was pleasant riding. I was seeing some new country up around Frog Springs where we put up one camp. There were about five camps in all.

We were getting toward the end of our trip. We went down a steep narrow trail with big rocks and tree roots that the horses had to step over or go around. The girls were afraid, Janet was calling to me, "Mom I'm afraid to go down this trail, I'm afraid the horse will fall."

"No Janet, Beepo won't fall, you've got the best horse in the outfit to go down places like this. He is so sure footed, just pray and keep praying until we get to the bottom, you too Kristy and Rosana." To tell the truth I was also a bit nervous. The trail was too steep and narrow for me to go down to get the girls or do anything for them. The only thing I could do was what I did. To reassure them. John didn't think about anyone being afraid, he just rode on. He was way ahead but we could hear him scolding Elsie now and then, so she must have been complaining.

I noticed the horses were pricking up their ears and snorting and acting up like they were bothered about something, but everyone kept moving not saying anything. I thought there may be a bear around. I kept praying. It was some tense moments for all of us but no one said a word, not even the girls. We finally got to the bottom of the hill. Janet rang out, at the top of her lungs with, "Praise the Lord" loud and clear. We all laughed like she was the only one who was afraid. I certainly wasn't going to say I was afraid. When we all got down off the hill and safe, John went back through the horses and found the fishing line on "you know who's" pole, Merrill's, was caught on a bush or tree and was unwinding all the way down the hill. It was singing and the horses could hear it.

He said "This is what was the matter with the horses coming down the hill. I knew what it was but I couldn't go back there on that hill, I just prayed that the horses wouldn't blow up before we got down. That would have been a mess." I thought I was the only one who noticed the horses being nervous. Come to find out we all felt the same way coming down the hill.

The summer went well over at the Neal Ranch. We all kept busy. I changed a lot of water on the upper part of the ranch. I was busy taking care of a colt someone brought over that had run his foot through the bottom of the trailer when they were hauling it in. I took over the doctoring of the foot and leg. I soaked it twice a day and cleaned out the infection, then sprayed it with Blue Vitrol and wrapped it. The man didn't think the colt would ever walk but it did and walked without a limp. They didn't have the courtesy to say thank you. Oh well, I did it for the colt.

The kids swam that summer in Big Creek. As cold as it was, that is where they took most of their baths. Steve still remembers me taking him down there. He and Janet were too young to swim, but I took them down and washed their hair. Steve said that was so cold he could hardly stand it. The others didn't seem to mind swimming in it so I wasn't too concerned. He still complains about that and he is a tough guy.

John had a mule he called Kennedy. That mule was so big he stood head and shoulders above other horses. In the back of John's truck, Kennedy was so tall his head and shoulders were above the rack. You could barely see the ears of the others.

The truck was stuck in a bog of mud out in the field. They tried everything to get it out but it couldn't be done. John got Kennedy harnessed up and hooked him up to the front of the truck. John told Tom to get in the truck and start it up so it wouldn't be so hard on Kennedy. Before Tom could get the truck started, Old Kennedy knew what he was there for and he stretched out and began to pull. That truck came out of there and he trotted off across the field pulling the truck. I have never seen anything like it.

The summer was great for all of us. Elsie and I had a lot of time to read the scriptures and praise the Lord.

One day, some friends camped on the other side of Big Creek and I walked over to see them. I had been there a couple hours when Elsie had Milton drive her over through the creek to get me.

"Rose, there is one of John's best horses bleeding to death over there. He had a wart on his neck over the jugular vein and he scratched it off I guess. The blood is just pumping out of him." I jumped in their car and drove it over through the creek.

Elsie had Milton bring the horse up by our camp. He certainly was bleeding. I looked it over and decided I needed to try to stop the bleeding. I really didn't think I could keep the blood from spurting out.

"Elsie will you get the flour, tell the kids where they can find some gunny sacks. I'll need a couple of boards and some rope. Please hurry." In the meantime, I walked the horse where his back legs were in the ditch and his head was high. I took the outer skin and squeezed it closed as much as possible to try to stop the bleeding. It was no use. Elsie came with the flour, I reached in with my hand and got a large handful of flour and packed it on his neck. It bled right off. I just kept doing that and had the biggest lump of bloody flour you ever saw. When I got that built up, I asked for a gunny sack. I couldn't move my hand from the flour clot. I asked Elsie to wad up the sack and give it to me. I moved it onto the clot, and pushed, it was slowing up, I asked for another, I pressed it on. As long as I stood there holding it, the bleeding let up; but if I took my hand off, it would begin to bleed and push everything off the hole. I held it until my arms were shaking. I got the two boards and crossed them over the sacks and kept the pressure on. I had the boys put ropes on the ends of the boards and stretch them behind the horse and pull, keep them tight and pull these boards. All through this the horse never moved. He knew he was in danger and welcomed the help. It's strange but they will let you do anything when they think they are going to die. I kept the pressure on and had them keep pulling until the front stayed when I let go. It finally did. I lowered my arms and watched, it did not bleed.

Oh what a relief! My arms were shaking so bad I couldn't hold a cup of water. I backed off and looked at the horse. He looked so funny with all that stuff tied on him. I laughed and laughed. Elsie said, "That's all right if he does look funny, I think you have saved his life. John will not be laughing when he gets home. He will be mighty happy he still has the horse."

"Elsie I don't know if this is going to work. It seems to be slowing it now, but we can't keep him in that contraption too long. He is going to want to move, then what will happen. He should have a drink now, but I would be afraid to give him one yet, just that movement on his neck of swallowing could start it all over."

"Milton, Merrill, Tom, You boys get over here and see that horse doesn't move, if he starts to move you stop him." Elsie couldn't touch the horse, she was so afraid. Poor thing. She told me so many times how thankful she was that I was there that day.

The boys stayed there all day and watched, I was close by. In the evening we decided to check, I pushed on the boards while they were untying the ropes. When the pressure was off, it did not bleed. Very carefully I removed the sacks, They were so saturated I was afraid to move them, but oh so gradual, I loosened them. I asked Elsie if she had any old sheets or something to put over this now. When she brought them out, I finished taking the sacks off. It was oozing just a little. So I knew I would have to put something else on it. I cleaned it up the best I could and put more flour on it, then some pads of sheets. We tore some sheets into strips and wound them around his front legs and crossed them and over his back and back in front over the pads and back around. I watched for sometime to see if the oozing stopped and it did. We got some water and held it up for him to drink, he emptied the bucket. He was still okay. Little by little I led him around and he seemed to wait on me to make the next move. He was still unsure, so was I. You know I fell in love with that horse that day, and he fell in love with me. He followed me around and when he went by, if I was close and spoke to him, he would always stop and come over to me.

We kept him around the camp for several days, took him out in the pasture to feed and then bring him back. He followed me wherever I went.

I have noticed over the years with animals, when you feel something special for them, they sense that through your touch, and they return the devotion to you. It is also true of the opposite, they sense if someone does not like them, they will act out in some contrary way. They know by instinct how you feel about them. I think it is also true of wild animals to a certain degree. But they have been chased and shot at too much to trust many people.

Uncle Tom's lots were being sold and developed. Houses were being moved in from Stibnite, and some houses were being built. I think it made Uncle Tom feel pretty good, that this was something that came from his planning. He had lived such a quiet and secluded life that he really didn't leave much of a mark on this earth, except for those of us who dearly loved him. He never had any children so his name was not carried on. The rest of the Hagens were girls.

Uncle Tom told me that summer he had cancer of the bladder. They found these little tumors and had taken them out, so there was no immediate danger. He seemed to be taking it well and was not upset by this news. I had to hide my feelings and not respond to the news any differently than he did. That was hard for me. They kept it under control by removing the tumors for a couple years. It was growing too fast, they started chemotherapy. That really took a toll on him. He was never the same after that. I think he was afraid for one thing. Mom talked to him about the Lord and he said "Oh ya, ya, I remember Mama talking about that. What good is that going to do me now?" Mom couldn't make him listen. Nor could I. He wanted some other kind of help. He got so bad he couldn't go into Yellow Pine any longer. He left everything the way it was. He locked the doors knowing he would never be back. He went to Emmett and lived with John and Elsie. Elsie talked to him about the Lord. He listened but there was no response.

When the final days came, it was agony for all of us. We could hardly stay in his room. He would plead for us to do something for him, he was dying, "Help me. Help me."

Ed and Lois sent for their minister to talk with him. When he came out he said, "Uncle Tom was saved, he accepted the Lord, and now he has gone to be with Him. We all praised the Lord and thanked Him over and over. I missed him so much. I felt like I had lost my best friend. This loss was hard, it was a bad time in my life, I couldn't cope with it or accept it. I was traveling from Emmett to Boise and working 10 hours a day. My thoughts went to Uncle Tom. When I was alone in the car, I cried my heart out, I couldn't give him up. After, what seemed like forever, the tears dried, but my heart still aches when I think of him, a very special memory of my life. I am so glad I had that time with him to renew our relationship. It had taken some bad turns, with his saucy tongue and my sensitive and stubborn nature.

Dad (Fred) was in the hospital at the time Uncle Tom died. We went up and told him and he was really shocked and hurt. I was quite surprised to see his response. I thought "Oh you guys, try to act like you don't care, now look at you. What about the years when you wouldn't speak to one another. I am so glad that was all resolved before now. What a heartache that would be.

Dad didn't live very long after that, he had congestive heart failure. His heart just wore out, he had such bad lungs, it took his heart. He was suffering a lack of oxygen to the brain and when he slipped away, he was not conscious of what was happening. It was really hard to lose them so close together. I was happy for the time I had with him so we could put aside old grudges and hurts. It is so much easier to forgive than to carry hurts around forever. About the only thing he ever revealed about himself was that his mother was a very staunch Christian, so I have always hoped he was saved through her.

Clarence and Kenny Pond organized a sledding party up on Lick Creek. The summit was closed so there was no danger of traffic. They took a trailer to haul up the sleds. I took my car and we had another couple cars there to bring up the kids. The men drove up as far as it was safe to ride sleds down. They let the kids off and down the hill they went loving every minute. We had a big fire at the bottom of the hill for the kids to warm up and plenty of hot chocolate. While this group was warming up, they took up a different load. They would rotate. The younger kids took their sleds down the hill from where the fire was but they were bummed because no one drove them back up the hill. Steve recalls with laughter, when the twins were on one sled they came racing down the hill and ran right through the fire. The fire went every which way but they were going so fast they didn't even get burned. They were sure frightened.

We stayed up there until it was nearly dark. It got too cold and we had to come home. The kids would like to have stayed up there all night.

It was getting more difficult all the time to find a place to stay in Yellow Pine, especially since Elsie had to take the kids out in the fall to go to high school. I had John move a trailer house in there for me. It worked out fine. It was convenient and modern, so we had to live like uptown folk. We loved the camp type living until it got cold, then we couldn't handle it.

Pat and Georgia had a house party one fall evening. I had no idea who was coming but they invited me. We were all just visiting and having a good time when the door opened and Louie Rebillet and one of his cougar hunters came in. I was surprised to see Louie. I hadn't seen him for a long time. He usually stayed pretty close to home because they had hunting up in Big Creek country in the fall and down at the ranch on the South Fork later in the fall. They had stock and a ranch to take care of all winter. They didn't socialize much any time of year. The family lived there and worked the ranch. His parents, his sister and himself.

It was good to see him. He was always such a nice clean-cut guy. Friendly, talkative, in fact a real storyteller. Everyone was interested in the stories he had to tell. He could draw a crowd anytime.

They were introduced around and then he came over and sat beside me on the couch. He told me he had almost froze that afternoon. I was curious and asked what happened. He began to explain, "We went out cougar hunting this morning and took the dogs. They picked up a scent and went after it. One dog got so excited he was not following the others and went across the river. I had to go after him. I crossed the river to find him and of course was wet. I ran with the dog up to the bridge which was several miles, this other fellow was bringing the truck up there. We got the old heater in the pickup cranked up and finally got warm and somewhat dry. I'm still wet, but I'm not cold now. I could have killed that darn dog for going across the river, I had plans of coming up here but not wet."

I was amazed at what he was telling me, no one could cross that river. I said, "Louie you didn't swim the river did you?"

"Yes I had to or I'd never get my dog back. He would stay over there and starve to death. A hound is smart in one way and that is hunting and he is as dumb as a stump in every other way."

We talked for quite awhile and he was telling one story after the other. Stories that were hard to believe. What did this guy take me for? But he told everything so matter of fact, like he thought anyone else would do that if there was a need. I was amazed at this man. No wonder he was known as a great storyteller. I said, "Well I have to go. My kids are over at the hotel so I had better get over there."

"Oh can I walk you over?"

"Sure if you won't freeze. It's cold out there."

We walked like it was a summer evening. He was in his shirt sleeves and they were rolled up above his elbows.

We went into the lobby and sat down on a couch. The only light that was on was in the hallway. After we had sat for awhile, he stretched back and put his arm over the top of the couch, then it slid down to touch my shoulder, and finally across my shoulders with his hand resting on my arm. That was as far as that approach went. When he left, he said he would be getting back to see me very soon. "That will be fine. Good night Louie."

"Good night Rose."

After church one Sunday afternoon, Gail Green came to see me there, she was crying. I walked over to her putting my arms around her. I had always liked Gail, she was a sweet girl. She was always so friendly and wore a smile for everyone.

Gail was Lee Green's sister, the boy in the sledding accident. She was trying to get control of herself so she could talk. "I am pregnant, and my Dad has kicked me out. Can you tell me where to go for help."

"Yes, of course Gail, when do you have to leave home?"

"Right now, he won't let me come back, he says he isn't going to pay for the baby. What can I do, where can I go?"

"Go get your clothes and you can come home with me, I will find some help for you."

Gail lived with us until the baby was born. We all loved Gail, she was so sweet to everyone. She did her share of the work, she wasn't a bit lazy, she got up on time and was willing and ready to help anyone with anything.

You couldn't find a sweeter girl. I made arrangements with the county for her to go into the county hospital in Cascade and have her baby and they took care of all the costs.

I was hoping for her to stay with us indefinitely. I could use her help, and it would be the perfect answer for me to go to work. I hadn't asked her about it, I wanted to wait for the baby to be born.

She had not heard from her family and she didn't write to them. I thought it rather strange but I was not to judge. The baby was born in the spring just after the roads opened into Yellow Pine. Her parents were there, and I was not welcome to be there with Gail when they were there. I thought it would be better for them to bury their differences and I would step aside.

They wanted to take her back to Yellow Pine right then but the doctor would not release her to go. She came back to our house and stayed for a couple of weeks.

We all fell in love with the baby, the kids fought over who was going to feed her. They rushed home from school to get first chance. It was good. Her folks came and took her and little Trisha back. It broke our hearts to lose them.

She wasn't home long when she was kicked out again. The formula for the baby was expensive and they couldn't afford it. Gail came back to see me and ask where she could get help until she could go to work. I was not so anxious this time to help, as I found out Gail was dating someone I wouldn't approve of.

I did help her get on welfare. She got a cabin to live in and fixed it up as cute as could be. We went to see her often and kept track of her until she moved to Boise. I didn't see her much after that. Gail and little Trisha left some wonderful loving memories at our home.

Things were different at Yellow Pine. New people were coming in. Betty and Tom sold "Tom's Place" to Jensens from over around Fruitland. They had been farmers but wanted a small business to retire with. They had a teenage son, Phil, who became a life-long friend of my boys. They were a very nice family.

Their son Garth bought the store from the Ponds. He and his wife and little daughter were also new residents. While we were happy to have this new family, we missed the Ponds and Betty and Tom. However, Tom kept his home there, so they came in quite often.

In the late summer of 1968, Mrs. Jensen became very ill and was taken out to the hospital. They discovered she had meningitis. She would not be able to come back or to work for a long time. They asked me to work for them in the cafe. They were going to sell but in order to sell, the business had to be running. I told them I would do that for a while, but I had to get back out to be with my kids who were in high school. My mother was living with us, we were living in the trailer house which was parked close in. I took on the job of running the restaurant. It was exhausting for me. Early breakfast hours until ten at night. Seven days a week. Mom was not able to help. Janet was a great deal of help. I couldn't believe what a waitress she was, just like she had been doing this forever. Danny was a lot of help too, he cleaned the floors and bathrooms, and Steve helped him.

Bill got married that spring of '67 to Shara Dee Adair, a sweet girl whom I loved like my own. They were married young just out of high school. Bill started his long career in truck driving. He has driven for Morgan for 30 years. He is an outstanding driver and is Morgan's top driver at this time. I have two grandchildren from this marriage and five great grandchildren. Bill made me a grandmother at 37. I never held it against him.

Rosana was starting her freshman year in high school. I arranged for her to go to Emmett to live with John and Elsie until I could get out there. Tom and Merrill were living in a cabin at the Northwest Mountain Mission, as they did not want to change high schools now. This was all very unsatisfactory with me. I did not like the kids split up like this, and here I was and couldn't get away. There were never any buyers for the cafe to my knowledge. I didn't know what their plans were. I only knew that I had given my word and I couldn't walk off and leave the place. They had hired another lady to take care of the bar. I was getting minimum wage, but I spent far more than I made feeding my kids. On weekends I bought the groceries to make chili or spaghetti so I could feed my kids when they came in for the weekend.

It was nearly impossible to have Sunday School. I would try to get up there for at least an hour every Sunday but it seemed that everything was going wrong. If I didn't get out of there soon, I may not be able to get out. The roads could close anytime.

Surely any time they would have some buyers. I was in a quandary as to know what to do. Then finally one day some new buyers did come in to look at the place. But they couldn't move for a month or so as he worked for the police department and his contract would be up at that time. The people bought the place but Jensens sold me with it. They told them I would stay until they could come in. I was not asked about this—I was told. I became uncooperative at this point. I was sorry for Mrs. Jensen but this was too much.

Dan, Janet and Steve were in school in Yellow Pine. After school, they came up and helped me. Mom was getting very put out about all this and she was wanting me to do something about it. Her nagging became unbearable. I was getting very short and curt with her and that offended her terribly. The stress I was under at that time was too much for me.

On a busy Saturday, when hunters were standing in line to get something to eat before they went over Profile, Olga came to the door and said, "Rose come out here for a minute I have to talk to you." I rushed out the door and stood with one foot holding the screen door open. I had hamburgers on the grill.

Olga looked terrible, "Rose you have to help me. Jim is going to kill me."

"What? Why Olga, have you done something or is he drunk?"

"He is mad because when he was over the hill hunting, I did come down here and sit and talk to Ray. You know Ray, he would never do anything wrong. I certainly didn't do anything wrong. He is jealous of Ray. Rose I did have a couple of beers, but you know I can't drink. I shouldn't have done that. Jim came in when I was sitting by Ray drinking a beer. He took me home and he is crazy Rose. He beat the heck out of me and he says he is going to kill me."

"Olga what can I do, do you want me to take you out now to get away from him? I'll get you some help. I will. I'll just load up my family and Mom and go right now."

"Oh no, he would kill you too. You don't know him Rose."

"I don't need to know him. If you will go, I'll take you."

"I have to get back before he wakes up. He is so drunk. I will get back to you, and maybe I can get away from him and we can get out of here." I put my arms around her and held her for a moment, "The Lord is with you Olga."

As she was leaving I said to her, "Olga pray, I will pray for you. I love you."

"I love you too, and I will pray. God is with me isn't He?"

"Yes, Olga, yes He is." She was off up the street, I watched her go and prayed that God would be with her. Oh, what could I do? I was worried sick, I had seen Jim in some foul moods, and I didn't know what he would do in a circumstance like this. All I could do was wait and pray. I couldn't get her off my mind all day. As busy as I was, my mind was on her continuously. Janet was cooking hamburgers and serving like a pro when I got back in there. We finished out that shift.

Through the next week work went on as usual. There was a lot of people coming in and out now during hunting season, and they all wanted to eat. I was so anxious about Olga, I didn't dare tell anyone what she told me. If it got back to Jim, he would be more angry with her. I watched every day for her to come out, but no one saw her. I couldn't help wonder if she was alive or dead.

Jim came to town everyday and went to the store to buy some whiskey. He walked back to the house carrying that familiar bottle in a paper bag. He didn't look either way or speak to anyone. He returned to his house.

One night after we had all been in bed asleep for several hours, there was a pounding on the door and Jim was calling. "Rose, Rose come quickly,

Mama is dead. Rose, do you hear me, Mama is dead." Mom came out of her bedroom the same time I did and we stood frozen with fear in the middle of the room. Mom said, "Rose do you think he did this?"

"I don't know, but I don't want to go up there with him."

"Go by and get Ray. He will go up there and I will go too, so there are plenty of witnesses."

She began pulling on some clothes and I went back in the bedroom to grab my clothes. Thinking I should answer Jim, he was still standing out there calling me, "Okay Jim I will be right there, I'm getting dressed."

Mom and I went to the door together. Jim grabbed me and started to cry. "Mama is dead, I woke up and went into the front room and she was laying there dead. What will I ever do without her?"

"I'm so sorry, what did she die of?"

"I don't know. She is just dead."

"Okay Jim, I want to stop and get Ray on the way up to your house."

"Okay, Okay."

We all started walking down the road, no one saying a word. We were walking slowly, dreading what we would have to face. When we got to Ray's cabin, Jim stood back and I pounded on the door. He answered right away. I told him what happened, just as Jim told me. He put his clothes on and came outside. He went to embrace Jim, no one saying anything and Ray put his arm around Jim and one around me. Jim put his arm around Mom and we walked up the road that way. Jim opened the door and went in first. Ray stepped back so Mom and I could go in, then he came in. Olga was laying on the couch, like she had been laid out. There was not a sign of anything, in fact it looked too perfect to me. There were no glasses or bottles sitting around. There was nothing out of order. Everything was clean. Jim was talking and leading us around from one room to the other. Her bed in the bedroom had clean sheets and the sheet and blanket was turned back about six inches. No one had slept in that bed since it was made. Jim's bed was crumpled up and looked like it had been slept in. We didn't touch anything, except I went over and kissed Olga on the cheek. She was cold.

Ray said, "Well I think we had better go out and inform the sheriff so they can come in and pick up the body."

Jim said, "Yes, yes, Rose will you come with me?"

Ray offered to go and drive, as the roads were not too good. Mom said she would go back with the kids. We took off as soon as Ray got his pickup started. We drove out without ten words being spoken. We went to the funeral home and talked to the mortician. I stood back wanting Jim to take care of this. He told him he wanted her sent to California. He answered questions as the man asked.

"Well, I'll call the sheriff to go in with me. It won't take us very long, so you can go on in and meet us at your house."

Our trip in was as silent as the trip out. We were all in shock I think. All this time I was thinking about Olga coming to the cafe. I was thinking of a murderer sitting beside me. I wondered if the coroner and sheriff would search the house good for evidence.

I was glad to get back to Yellow Pine. Ray drove me up to the house and Mom came out to meet us. I told her the coroner and sheriff were coming in to pick up the body.

Mom had told the kids and they were wondering what had happened to her. "I don't know. They will find out later when they come after her." I had to hurry and get to work.

Jim didn't say anything except that he thought she bled to death.

He asked me to go with him to Boise to get the body shipped off to California. I only agreed to go if I could take someone else with me. I made arrangements for the cafe to be taken care of while I was gone.

Shari, my new daughter-in-law, went along and I was so glad she did, as we only had one room with two beds. Shari and I in one and Jim in the other. He said, "I hope you don't mind, but I can't be alone."

I could understand that. We were there most of the day. Jim got the plane tickets and made arrangements. He then took us back, dropped Shari off in McCall, and I rode in with him to Yellow Pine. There was hardly any conversation between us. I couldn't talk to him. There was nothing I had to say to him. I was feeling a lot of guilt for allowing Olga to die. What could I have done? I wondered if he did it. I was repulsed by being near him after what Olga told me. I was afraid of him. I was grieving for her. Was I being hypocritical for being with him, making these arrangements? It was the last thing I could ever do for Olga.

I went in later to talk to the coroner and asked if he found anything unusual on Olga's body. He said she had terrible bruises all over her body, her neck, her head, she had been hit with fists all over. I had to tell someone what Olga had told me so I told him. He said, "Well, if she drank whiskey it could sure have caused this hemorrhage from her liver. She may have wanted to die because she couldn't take any more abuse. In any case, there would be no way to prove it."

I left feeling thankful that Olga had gone to be with the Lord and would never have to suffer again. God looks out for His own.

Jim came back in after the funeral with Peggy, his daughter.

He wanted Peggy to take care of some of her things. It was very difficult for her to do this, she was grieving terribly. She came down to my house to talk to me. I was shocked when she expressed the same fears I had. She said, "What do you think she died of Rose?"

"Peggy, I only know what the coroner told me."

"We all knew how abusive he was to her. Rose I am so afraid of him. I feel like he is coming up behind me with a knife or a gun. I can't turn my back on him."

"Peggy after we have been through a shocking experience like this, we can associate a person with the horrors we feel about the death. I think when we become so saturated with grief, our mind plays tricks on us and this strange association takes place. Maybe it is to blame someone for their death. Subconsciously we think it will make us feel better. I have experienced this very thing. I know how it makes you feel."

She talked more trying to convince me that he had done something wrong. "Peggy if you feel so strongly about this why don't you go out and talk to the sheriff."

Epilogue

1968

There were so many questions about Olga's death but also so many possible answers. There are some things we are better off not knowing.

I can't forget Olga coming to me for help. Why didn't I do something for her? I will always wish I had.

Jim Cox was in my trailer house one day when I came home. He was tearing things out of it. I walked in on him and asked, "What in the world are you doing?"

He said, "It belongs to me now. You have not kept up the payments on it so I bought it from the guy you owe money."

I said, "Jim! stop right now. I am going out to get the sheriff." He sheepishly walked off toward his house.

I made a trip out. The sheriff contacted the previous owner and found out that I was not in default. Shortly after, the trailer house caught on fire. The wiring was burned and I could no longer stay in there. We went up to Gillihan's house to stay. Danny, Janet and Steve were with me. I took Mom out and Donna came to McCall to take her back to Oregon. This was just too much for her, which ultimately made it too much for me.

John came out of the back country, his hunts were over for the year. When he came to his house and found our things there, he walked down to the cafe to see what was wrong. After I explained everything, he said "Just hang in there for a while longer, I will go out to Emmett and unload my outfitting stuff and come back for you."

Jim had a series of accidents after that and he became so frightened and paranoid. He was working getting some old lumber from a building in Stibnite, when a jagged board flew up and hit him in the eye. There was no one there and he had to drive out alone, 25 miles to Yellow Pine. I guess it was a nightmare for him as the eye was laying out on his cheek. He was blinded from that accident and wore a black patch for the rest of his life.

Another incident nearly scared him to death. He was driving down the East Fork, which was a washboard road so bumpy you could hardly stay on the road, and he nearly went into the river when his wheel fell off. He thought someone had loosened his lug bolts, and he told people around town, "Rose is responsible for this, I know she is doing these things, to try to kill me." I was living in Emmett at the time.

From what I heard he was in a constant state of fear of what I was going to do. His paranoia got the best of him, he had to leave Yellow Pine. He later moved back to California. He died of a heart attack a couple years later. The poor man. If he did something wrong, he couldn't live with it.

I wanted to get out of Yellow Pine in the worst way. It was like an evil spirit had taken control, I was very uncomfortable.

I felt obligated to keep the cafe open, I had given my word. My belongings were in there and no way to move them out, and without a house to move into, what could I do.

Tom was working and planned to go to college mid-term. Merrill wanted to graduate in McCall. Rosana was staying with Elsie in Emmett going to high school until I could get out. I hated not being out there with them.

It was late in the season and one night of heavy snow could keep me there all winter. I had made a foolish decision, but I had no idea it would be this long. I felt they had taken advantage of me and I was not very happy about it.

The new owners finally came in to take over the business. It turned out that I never did get any wages for all that time and inconvenience to my family.

What had happened to this place wasn't hard to figure out. The Christian people had all moved away, the church doors were closed. When we were gone, the church would be left unattended. The thought of closing the doors for good was not what I wanted, but I knew I couldn't come back if I lived in the valley and worked full-time.

I had a lot of time to think and meditate in the next two weeks. I prayed until wee hours every night. I knew without a doubt that the Lord had spoken to me. In the stillness of the night His words were clear, "Your ministry is over here. The ones you were to minister to have gone on. Now it is time for you to go. Your kids need you."

It was a sad day for me facing this big change in my life and not being in the church anymore, giving up what I loved so much.

We contacted the Coles since Rufus and Ann had shown interest in the back country ministry. We sent a letter to them that we were leaving and gave them permission to pastor the church. There were many denominations interested in the work there when they found out I was leaving, but we still felt strongly that our work continue as it had started, without denominational affiliation.

Everything that I had known here that was so precious to me was gone now. So many have died, so many have moved away. It will never be the same without Uncle Tom and Dad. The Gillihans, the Ponds, the Hathaways, the Nicholas', the Brownings, the Kissingers, the Raneys' and many other individuals and families. My ministry here was needed for a time, but God is reminding me now of my first ministry to my children.

Yes, my work was finished. The ones who were so very special to God, the ones He gave me the call to work with, to bring them into His fold, are safely in His care now. I felt like I had accomplished what the Lord had sent me here to do. It was sad to see it all end.

Seven years later I was called to sing at Ray Thrall's funeral. He died suddenly after seeing a great flash of light. He was on a trail over by Thunder Mountain with several men who were contemplating buying a mine.

His funeral was in Yellow Pine. Someone had made an arrangement of lilacs into the shape of a violin. It was hung so the water dripped from the flowers onto the casket. As I sang, I watched those tears fall expressing my emotions. The effect brought sadness from deep within my soul and I cried. I had lost a true friend, but somehow I knew that all my prayers for him were answered and he was with the Lord.

1997

Those seven kids who were surely going to be the end of me in about June 1959, are the greatest blessing to me any mother has ever had. They are still filling my life with blessings. In fact there are forty-five in all, counting spouses, children, grand-children and great grand-children. Had it not been for them my life would have been nothing. As it is, I am the richest woman in the world.

I am proud to tell the world that they are all happily married and doing well in successful careers. Three are college graduates, one with two plus years of college and the others have security in their employment. I'm sure that most of their success is due to the fact that they were chosen by God and were blessed, and they learned to enjoy the out-of-doors and can work off their stress. Which is also an incentive to stay in shape to be able to climb those mountains. None would want the other to be in better shape than he. Tom just recently sent me a postcard from France where his work had taken him for a two-week business trip. He said, "Leaving France tomorrow and heading for the South Fork to go hunting." They are equally blessed in that way. I thank God when I hear them talk about their hunting trips, high-mountain lake fishing trips and other outdoor adventures. I know God must have arranged all that. It thrills me beyond words.

I praise God for what He has done in their lives and for what he has done for me. For giving me that insurmountable task 38 years ago. The Bible says, God will be a father to the fatherless.

When I left McCall and moved to Emmett, it was quite a transition. Life was so different down here, no place to run away to, no church to plan for every weekend. No more trips into the back country. I now had to concentrate on my own career and supporting my family, and seeing them get their education.

I so wanted to get some education. There was no way I could plan on four years of college, that was out of the question with four kids still at home and two others still in college. I wanted to help them, not that they expected it, they made their own way. They worked very hard to get where they are today. I am very proud of them all. We have continued to love the Lord and serve Him through the years.

I first got my high school diploma, then a couple years of business school. I took other college courses when I could work it in. I took advantage of every opportunity through my work for college credits. I received additional training from many educational courses, and every training opportunity and schooling available, to update my skills which qualified me to work in the positions requiring a college degree. I have had a very satisfying work career. I am retired now and enjoy my family, especially these grandchildren.

The nice-looking young man whom I met at the Hathaway's house party played a major role in our lives for eleven years. A life that is unequaled in excitement and adventure. That is another story. I thanked God, and told Him my life could not have been complete without the years I spent with Louie, on the trail and in hunting camps, just being a companion to the best cowboy, the greatest outdoors man ever in the country and the one and only man who was qualified to top off the boys' hunting and outdoor skills. The boys said he was the best.

The End

Post Script

I received a call from Peggy Cox, Jim and Olga's daughter.

I was surprised and delighted, but best of all she gave me some information about Jim that blessed me. She said Jim remarried a Christian woman. She led Jim to the Lord and he was saved before he died. A seed was sown and God gave the increase.

Praise the LORD. R.R.

To order copies of *HE Gave Me a Song*, contact:

Rose Marie Rebillet
3753 Manchester St.
Boise, ID 83704
208-387-1277